RELOCATING to NEW YORK CITY and SURROUNDING AREAS

RELOCATING to NEW YORK CITY and SURROUNDING AREAS

Revised and Updated 2nd Edition

By Ellen R. Shapiro

THREE RIVERS PRESS
NEW YORK

Although all prices, opening times, addresses and other details in this book are based on information supplied to us at press time, changes occur all the time in New York, and Three Rivers Press cannot accept responsibility for facts that become outdated or for inadvertant errors or omissions. So always confirm information when it matters.

Published in the United States by Three Rivers Press, an imprint of the Crown Publishing Group, a division of Random House, Inc., New York.
www.crownpublishing.com

Three Rivers Press and the Tugboat design are registered trademarks of Random House, Inc.

This is a revised edition of a work originally published by Prima Publishing, Roseville, California, a division of Random House, Inc., New York, in 2000.

Library of Congress Cataloging-in-Publication Data
Shapiro, Ellen R. (Ellen Renée)
Relocating to New York City and surrounding areas / Ellen R. Shapiro.—
rev. and updated 2nd ed.
1. New York (N.Y.)—Guidebooks. 2. New York Region—Guidebooks.
3. Moving, Household—New York Region—Handbooks, manuals, etc. I. Title.
F128.18.S426 2007
917.47'10444—dc22 2007035487

ISBN 978-0-307-39409-5

Printed in the United States of America

Design by Maria Elias
Maps by Nathaniel Levine
Charts by Dave Scantland

10 9 8 7 6 5 4 3 2

Second Edition

For my father

ACKNOWLEDGMENTS

New Yorkers can be the most generous people in the world, and I was the grateful beneficiary of that generosity when I researched and wrote this book. I'd like to thank all the people who were so giving of their time, expertise, and support.

Thanks as well to my agent, Michael Psaltis, and my editors, Lindsay Orman and Brandi Bowles; to my mother-in-law, Penny, who provided hours of babysitting when I was down to the wire, and to my mother, who jumped in for babysitting over the phone. Thanks also to Wayne and Julie Shovelin for the use of their beach house as a writer's retreat.

Dave Scantland's skillfully designed charts have helped to bring many dry statistics to life, and Nathaniel Levine—who also did the maps for the first edition—has once again made the city comprehensible through his great cartography. Robin Slutzky did a bang-up job with copyediting and fact-checking. I'm indebted to all of them, as well as to Ben Dominitz, the original publisher, who took a leap of faith by contracting me to write the first edition of this book—which was my first book—as well as the others that followed.

My son, PJ, and my bulldog, Momo, provided indispensable companionship and ample distraction throughout the writing and editorial process. And finally, thanks to my husband and unofficial editorial assistant, Steven Shaw.

ACKNOWLEDGMENTS

CONTENTS

RELOCATING to NEW YORK CITY and SURROUNDING AREAS

INTRODUCTION

If you want to become a real New Yorker, there's only one rule: You have to believe New York is, has been, and always will be the greatest city on earth. The center of the universe. The Big Apple. Every native New Yorker absorbs this knowledge in the womb, and every successful transplant acquires it upon arrival. This is a key part of the City's strength and attitude.

Whatever your dream, you can realize it in New York City. There's nothing the City doesn't offer—if you want it badly enough. For those willing to clear the hurdles and beat the odds, New York City is the last true bastion of the American dream. In this town, opportunity is limited only by imagination.

New York is that rarest of things: a real city. People work, live, and play in the same physical space, bringing the City alive at all hours of the day and night. There are no cloistered neighborhoods or gated communities. Supermodels strut the streets like common folk, and big stars take their kids to the neighborhood playgrounds and schools just like you, me, and the nanny up the block. Many of them came to New York with nothing more than empty pockets and overflowing ambition. Look at the lives (and lifestyles) they created for themselves in the City.

Opportunity is knocking. Now it's time to answer the door.

THE GREATEST SHOW ON EARTH

The events of 9-11 struck the City and its citizens hard—right in the heart. But New Yorkers are a tough bunch and rather than being brought to our knees, we pulled together, strengthened by the outpouring of support and love of people around the country and the world. As a result, New York City is now stronger, better, and still growing, despite the tragedy that befell us all.

In four centuries, there has never been a better time to live in New York. Tourism continues to grow and thrive despite the events of 9-11, and crime rates are the lowest they've been in over four decades. Unemployment is shrinking; industry is booming; construction is growing (up, of course); and every nook and cranny of the City is blossoming on account of it all.

- A revitalized Grand Central Station has exceeded the expectations of even the most optimistic New Yorkers: It has even become a favorite dining destination (with the views it offers from restaurants like Charlie Palmer's Métrazur and Michael Jordan's The Steak House N.Y.C., how could it not?). Combined with other standout projects—like the building of the Time Warner Center (opened in 2004), Chelsea Piers (opened in 1995 and still growing in 2007), the Hearst Magazine Building (an Art Deco skyscraper whose construction was interrupted and finished to only six stories due to the Great Depression, and has now been completed with a grand tower of 596 feet), and the groundbreaking One Bryant Park building, which houses the Bank of America (it's the world's most environmentally responsible high-rise, made primarily from recycled and recyclable materials)—the City is enjoying an unprecedented rate of renewal, expansion, and growth.
- Most of the action in New York City happens on a tiny island, Manhattan, which occupies only 22.7 square miles of space—probably smaller than your hometown. The total area of all five boroughs of New York City (Manhattan, Brooklyn, Queens, the Bronx, and Staten Island) is just 301 square miles. Yet the City has 6,374.6 miles of streets, and annually hosts around 40 million tourists from every nation on earth. They spend more than $23 billion here each year.

• With 714 miles of track, 469 stations, and 6,089 subway cars, NYC's subway system is the largest in the world. The subways run 24 hours a day and carry 1.2 billion passengers a year, while the City's public bus system consists of 300 routes and carries 600 million people a year (by far the most in the nation) on 4,200 buses.

• With immigrants continuing to pour in, the City boasts more than 100 ethnic newspapers, including 25 catering to the Russian community alone. And the public schools are microcosms of the world's population, with truly multiracial, multilingual student bodies. The languages spoken in the hallways range from Spanish, Arabic, Urdu, and Korean to Chinese, Hindi, Hebrew, and Russian.

• A major boost to the City's image, and celebrity status, the film industry also plays a major role in the New York economy. There are 60 to 90 productions filmed here daily, with a total of 34,718 aggregate shooting days per year. Just walk around the City any day of the week and you're bound to bump into a film crew, walk onto a set, or spy a star. If you aren't willing to leave it up to chance, simply plan a trip to Long Island City (which is actually located in Queens) and visit one of the City's television and film studios.

• Culturally speaking, you can't do better than more than 150 museums, 38 Broadway playhouses, scores of Off-Broadway and Off-Off-Broadway productions, more galleries even than museums, hundreds of dance clubs, music clubs, poetry readings, and bookstores—and that's just the tip of the mainstream iceberg.

GREAT CITIES DON'T GROW ON TREES

Since its inception, New York has been a key locale for commerce and trade, primarily on account of its strategic location.

• The area we now call the City was first inhabited by Native Americans and later discovered by Giovanni da Verrazano, in 1524.

In 1609, when Englishman Henry Hudson (employed by the Dutch East India Company) reported back on the beauty of Manhattan and its ample natural treasures (furs, birds, fruits), news spread and all of Europe began to make significant investments in the new land.

- The first industry on the island was the Dutch fur trade, back when the town was known as New Amsterdam (the name was changed in 1664). Legend has it that the Dutch settlers purchased Manhattan from its original Native American inhabitants for approximately $24 in beads and trinkets. Later, under British rule, Manhattan's economy blossomed on account of the shipping opportunities—with its perfect natural harbor, extensive riverfront, and easy ocean access, it was the perfect port for trade, and the perfect place to settle if you were getting into business.
- In 1783 the British surrendered to the revolutionary colonists. New York City was the nation's capital from 1789 to 1790.
- Already a melting pot in the 1700s, New York attracted, and continues to attract, immigrants from other cultures and countries all around the world. Ellis Island first started registering immigrants on Friday, January 1, 1892. Famous immigrants to pass through its doors include Bob Hope, Marcus Garvey, Irving Berlin, and the von Trapp family.
- It wasn't until 1898 that the five boroughs—Manhattan, the Bronx, Queens, Brooklyn, and Staten Island—were incorporated into the entity of Greater New York.
- Babe Ruth hit his first home run in Yankee Stadium in the first game he ever played there.
- Although it had been scheduled to dock in New York at the end of its maiden voyage, the *Titanic*'s tragedy prevented it from ever reaching the City. Of the 2,200 passengers aboard the oceanliner, 675 were rescued by a Cunard liner, which ironically delivered the passengers to the very same dock at which the *Titanic* was supposed to arrive.

LOOKING AHEAD

The City that Never Sleeps is also the city that never rests on its laurels. Never still or silent, New York is always changing and evolving, and looking ahead with grand ambition. From expanding and updating the classic draws, like the Museum of Modern Art and Radio City Music Hall, to revitalizing long-neglected neighborhoods like Harlem, the City's growth and booming economy promise to preserve New York's position as a world leader among cities.

- The Freedom Tower, the first building to be built on the former World Trade Center site, is slated for completion in 2011. When finished, the building will be the world's tallest and will incorporate the latest in modern technology, safety, and aesthetics, emblematic of the City's forward progress.
- Harlem, a thriving cultural center during the 1920s and 1930s, began a steady decline for many decades thereafter. Now it is experiencing a renaissance to rival its heyday. Even former President Bill Clinton keeps his office smack dab in the middle of Harlem, on 125th Street. New construction of shopping centers and suburban-size grocery stores is also under way, along with face-lifts for famous locales like the Apollo Theater, Minton's Playhouse, the Art Deco Lenox Lounge, and the Renaissance Ballroom. Countless beautiful, aging brownstones that had fallen into disrepair have been refurbished by longtime residents and newcomers, and new construction has been booming in an effort to keep up with the recent demand.
- A $750 million project is under way to convert 350,000 square feet of the majestic Farley Post Office Building (the twin of the original Penn Station, which was torn down in 1963, despite the protests of conservationists) into a Penn Station annex, to be called the Moynihan Station (for the late senator Daniel Patrick Moynihan). The

station is slated to open to passengers in 2010 and the results promise to be spectacular.

• Times Square, no longer the seedy area it was only fifteen years ago, will keep getting brighter, cleaner, and safer with each passing year. Recent developments in the area include: fresh hotels like the Doubletree and the Westin New York (with almost 450 and 850 rooms respectively); the Forest City Ratner entertainment complex (which includes 25 movie screens, shops, and Madame Tussauds wax museum), B. B. King's 550-seat Blues Club & Grill music club and restaurant; the corporate headquarters of companies including Viacom, MTV, VH-1, ABC-TV's *Good Morning America,* Condé Nast Publications, and Reuters; the ESPN Zone dining and entertainment complex; and the $25-million 8-story NASDAQ sign—the world's largest video screen to date.

• Ground has been broken for the new Yankee Stadium, slated to open in 2009. The new stadium will replace the current Yankee Stadium, and will stand just a stone's throw away from the original.

• Not to be outdone by their rivals, the Mets will have a new stadium, Citi Field, in Willets Point, Queens, slated for completion by opening day, 2009.

• Plans are well under way for a Second Avenue subway line. The two-track line will run from 125th Street to the Financial District and will greatly improve transportation for residents on the East Side of Manhattan.

THE TOOLS TO MAKE IT HAPPEN

Now that you're ready to take the next steps, this book will give you the tools you need to take them like a local.

I wish somebody had written this book (and given it to me!)

when I first moved to New York City. Lucky for you, though, I've spent years making every conceivable mistake (or listening to friends who did), so you don't have to.

- Part One, "Getting to Know the Neighborhoods," includes detailed information on neighborhoods in and around Manhattan, as well as brief descriptions of the major suburbs and areas beyond. There's also a wealth of statistical data. This section answers a newcomer's most commonly asked questions: Where should I live? What can I afford? Are the neighborhoods within NYC really that different from one another?
- Part Two, "Finding a Home," is the essential guide to locating, buying, and renting a home, and contains comprehensive listings of real estate agents and other resources. You'll find tips from locals, advice from experts, and answers to key questions like: Should I use a real estate agent? How do I find a roommate? Where do I live while I'm looking for an apartment? What the heck is rent control anyway?
- Part Three, "Moving," offers information on moving and critical details for getting yourself established once you've signed the lease (or mortgage).
- Part Four, "Getting to Know New York," is about what to see and do when you get here, and how to capitalize on the best (often free) events and activities the City has to offer. There's also a calendar of events (don't miss the July 4th fireworks), and details on the essentials: navigating the City via public transportation, hospitals, and more.
- Part Five, "Schools, Jobs, and Volunteering," covers schools at all levels (from preschool for your kids to advanced studies for yourself), gives you the resources you need to look for a job (whether you've been employed before or are starting out fresh), and tells you where and how to get involved in the City's many volunteer programs.

Now let's get going. You've got a lot of work to do!

NEW YORK WEATHER

January temperature average
Low 26°F High 38°F

April temperature average
Low 44°F High 61°F

July temperature average
Low 68°F High 85°F

October temperature average
Low 50°F High 66°F

Average rainfall

January	3.11 inches
July	3.67 inches

Average snowfall

January	7 inches
July	0 inches

PART ONE

GETTING TO KNOW THE NEIGHBORHOODS

CHAPTER ONE

ABOUT NEW YORK'S NEIGHBORHOODS

Apart from the actual decision to relocate, perhaps the most significant and challenging decision you'll have to make when you relocate to New York is deciding where you'll live. New York itself is geographically small, but your day-to-day life will center around two even smaller areas: the neighborhood where you live and the one where you work.

Many aspects of your life (the restaurants you frequent, your gym, the services you utilize, and to some extent the friends you make—especially if you have kids) will flow from your choice of neighborhood, and even from your choice of block (New Yorkers often say "block" instead of "street") and building. Still, all is not what it seems on the surface, and your ultimate choice of neighborhood may be very different from what your first instinct might lead you to believe.

In an ideal New York City, you'd be able to get a large, airy, sunny apartment in your neighborhood of choice for exactly the amount of money you're willing and able to spend. But in the real New York City, even multimillionaires have to make some compromises—and the rest of us have to compromise a whole lot more. The delicate balance between the need for a space in which you'll be happy and the need for a few dollars left over to cover other essentials (like food) is an elusive target for most every New Yorker.

When considering a neighborhood, you'll want to weigh the following primary factors:

- Your personality and the personality of the neighborhood
- Cost of housing
- Availability of desirable housing
- Safety
- Proximity to work

Consider these factors against the backdrop of three very important distinguishing factors about the neighborhoods in New York City (as opposed to neighborhoods almost everywhere else):

First, although the human brain uses generalizations to make sense of the world, the neighborhoods of New York City are mind-boggling in their diversity, and they defy generalization. Although it's possible to characterize neighborhoods based on the characteristics of the majority of their residents, the simple truth is that every kind of person lives in just about every neighborhood of New York. Sure, some neighborhoods have greater percentages of families or hipsters or gay men or specific ethnic groups, but without question you'll find everyone living everywhere.

For example, Chelsea is known as a gay neighborhood, but plenty of young, upwardly mobile, heterosexual thirty-something couples with kids choose to live there, perhaps because they work downtown and found a good apartment in the London Terrace complex, because they love the boutiques and cafés that that neighborhood boasts, or perhaps because they just like their neighbors. The stereotype of the Upper East Side is that it's stodgy and wealthy, but some young artists choose to live there rather than in SoHo because, ironically, there are now more housing bargains to be found on the Upper East Side.

Not every building can be on Fifth Avenue facing Central Park—the side streets are full of deals—plus, though the galleries may be downtown, the museums are uptown. You'll find plenty of corporate lawyer- and investment-banker-types too, some of them living in the working-class neighborhoods of Carroll Gardens in Brooklyn, or Astoria in Queens, because there's more space for the money and the commute to Wall Street is more convenient than from many neighborhoods within Manhattan. And Staten Island is not just for the big-haired crowd anymore (like Melanie Griffith and Joan Cusack in *Working Girl*)—there are plenty of young professionals who choose to live in the apartments near the Staten Island ferry because they work downtown, the view is great, the rent is lower, and all they have to do is walk off the boat and one block to the office—an easy and interesting commute by all accounts.

"Statistically, New York City is now safer than most other cities in America, but you still have to be careful. In particular, always be aware of your surroundings, know exactly where you are, keep a close eye on your property at all times, and, if you feel you're being followed or harassed, step into a shop or restaurant, hop in a taxi, or call the police. When walking alone at night, walk briskly and with confidence. Have your keys ready when entering your building—never stand around fumbling for your keys in the vestibule."

—Jonathan Shapiro, criminal prosecutor

Even within a specific building, it's hard to generalize. Almost every brownstone in New York has one highly desirable ground-floor garden apartment with a backyard—and a nearly identical apartment (with no yard) on the fifth floor, which can be reached only by climbing five flights of stairs. These two apartments may be in the same building, with the same internal square footage, same exposure, and same address—yet one may cost three times as much as the other! While the garden apartment may be occupied by a lawyer and a doctor, their newborn baby, and a golden retriever, the fifth-floor walk-up may be shared by three aspiring actors or models.

Second—and this always takes newcomers a while to grasp—neighborhoods in New York change dramatically in just a few feet. For example, in the case of East 96th Street, one of the most genteel neighborhoods in America (Carnegie Hill) ends on the south side of the street, and one of the formerly most rough-and-tumble (East Harlem) begins on the north. Until a couple of years ago "El Barrio," or "Spanish Harlem," as it was known, used to be one of the most run-down and dangerous neighborhoods in Manhattan, but now, East Harlem is changing, and young professionals, artists, and tree huggers are moving into the neighborhood.

Most of the Upper West Side was a slum in 1970. Now it's perhaps the most desirable (judging by popularity and cost) neighborhood in town. TriBeCa, a former manufacturing district, has gone residential, as have the areas of Williamsburg and Dumbo (an acronym for Down Under the Manhattan Bridge Overpass). Only a decade or

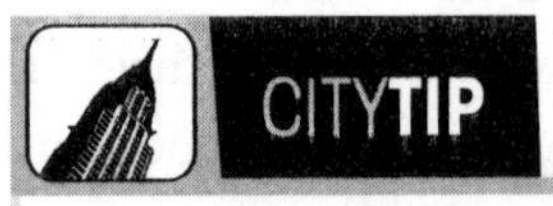

"One of most effective ways to learn all about New York is to spend a ton of time walking around the City. Treat it as a formal course of study—make a schedule and say, 'Today I'm going to explore SoHo; next weekend, TriBeCa!' In addition to providing unlimited free entertainment, the act of exploring by foot makes you more of a New Yorker with every step you take."

—Andrea Hendler, Global Volunteer Programs Officer

two ago, it would have been almost unthinkable for a newcomer to live in the neighborhood now known as Clinton, which used to be called Hell's Kitchen. Now it abounds with hipsters, families, wannabes, and longtime residents, which translates to more restaurants, coffee shops and cafés, and, of course, higher rents.

It's hard to believe it until you've seen it yourself, and even then it takes time for this reality to sink in. There are subtle and not-so-subtle dividing lines all over New York, and it takes a practiced eye to see them—the neighborhoods are always evolving, like living things. Apartments in New York can be bigger or smaller, more or less desirable, cheaper or more expensive, all based on these subtle dividing lines.

You can't expect to know where you want to live right away, and for the majority of people who choose to relocate to New York (young folks with no kids), that's not a problem. The thing to do is find yourself a space with which you'll be reasonably happy for the money you're paying and then spend the next year (the length of your lease, probably) exploring the town. Take this time to decide if the neighborhood you live in feels like home and, if it doesn't, by the end of your lease you should know the city well enough to find a place to call your own.

BASIC NEW YORK CITY GEOGRAPHY

New York City is made up of five boroughs: Manhattan, Queens, the Bronx, Staten Island, and Brooklyn. There is also an emerging "sixth borough," which consists of the nearby New Jersey cities of Hoboken and Jersey City (discussed later in Chapter 4, "The Suburbs").

That said, when most people think of "the City" they're visualizing Manhattan, and Manhattan was, in the past, the most likely destination for the overwhelming majority of newcomers (most newcomers figure, "Why move to the City if you're not going to live in the City¿"). But in recent years, with the dramatic rise in real estate costs, there has been a trend for locals and newcomers alike to consider the "outer boroughs" (all boroughs other than Manhattan) and the "sixth borough" of Hoboken and Jersey City as equally valid options.

The primary focus of this section is on the major neighborhoods within Manhattan and the most popular and commutable communities within the other four boroughs. There are many other lovely neighborhoods within those boroughs, but they're simply not as convenient or close to Manhattan. Also, this section contains an overview of neighborhoods and suburbs in northern New Jersey, Long Island, Westchester/Rockland, and southern Connecticut (the "tristate area") and beyond, which are mostly of interest to families with children (who want a house with a yard). The areas covered in this section are:

NEW YORK CITY

Manhattan

- Financial District and TriBeCa
- Greenwich Village and SoHo
- East Village, Lower East Side, and Chinatown
- Chelsea and Clinton (Midtown West)
- Gramercy, Murray Hill, Turtle Bay (Midtown East), Stuyvesant Town, and Peter Cooper Village
- Upper East Side
- Upper West Side
- Morningside Heights and Hamilton Heights
- Central Harlem
- East Harlem
- Washington Heights and Inwood

OUTER BOROUGHS

Brooklyn

- Brooklyn Heights, Downtown Brooklyn, Dumbo, and Fort Greene
- Cobble Hill, Carroll Gardens, Park Slope, Red Hook
- Williamsburg, Greenpoint

Queens

- Astoria and Long Island City
- Jackson Heights

Staten Island

- Northern Staten Island

The Bronx

- The South Bronx (SoBro)
- Riverdale and Fieldston

Suburbs

- Westchester/Rockland
- Long Island
- Northern New Jersey
- Southern Connecticut

Outside the Area

- Upstate New York
- Central and Southern New Jersey
- Western and Upstate Connecticut
- The East End of Long Island

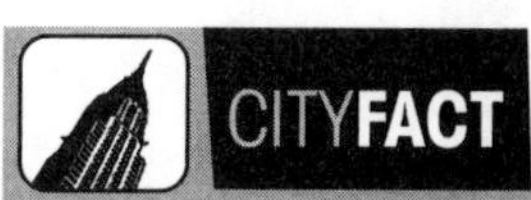

New Yorkers have a language all their own. "The City" means Manhattan—even to residents of the other four boroughs. Although Manhattan is an island, "the Island" always means Long Island. Real New Yorkers stand "on line," not "in line." Visitors and commuters from New Jersey and Long Island are the "B&T" (bridge and tunnel) crowd. And in New York it never hurts to know a little Yiddish, especially when ordering a bagel with a "schmear" (a little cream cheese).

2 miles
2 kms
N
Westchester
87
95
Long Island Sound
BRONX
678
Eastchester Bay
NEW JERSEY
278
295
Hudson River
Nassau
East River
Little Neck Bay
MANHATTAN
LaGuardia Airport
QUEENS
25A
495

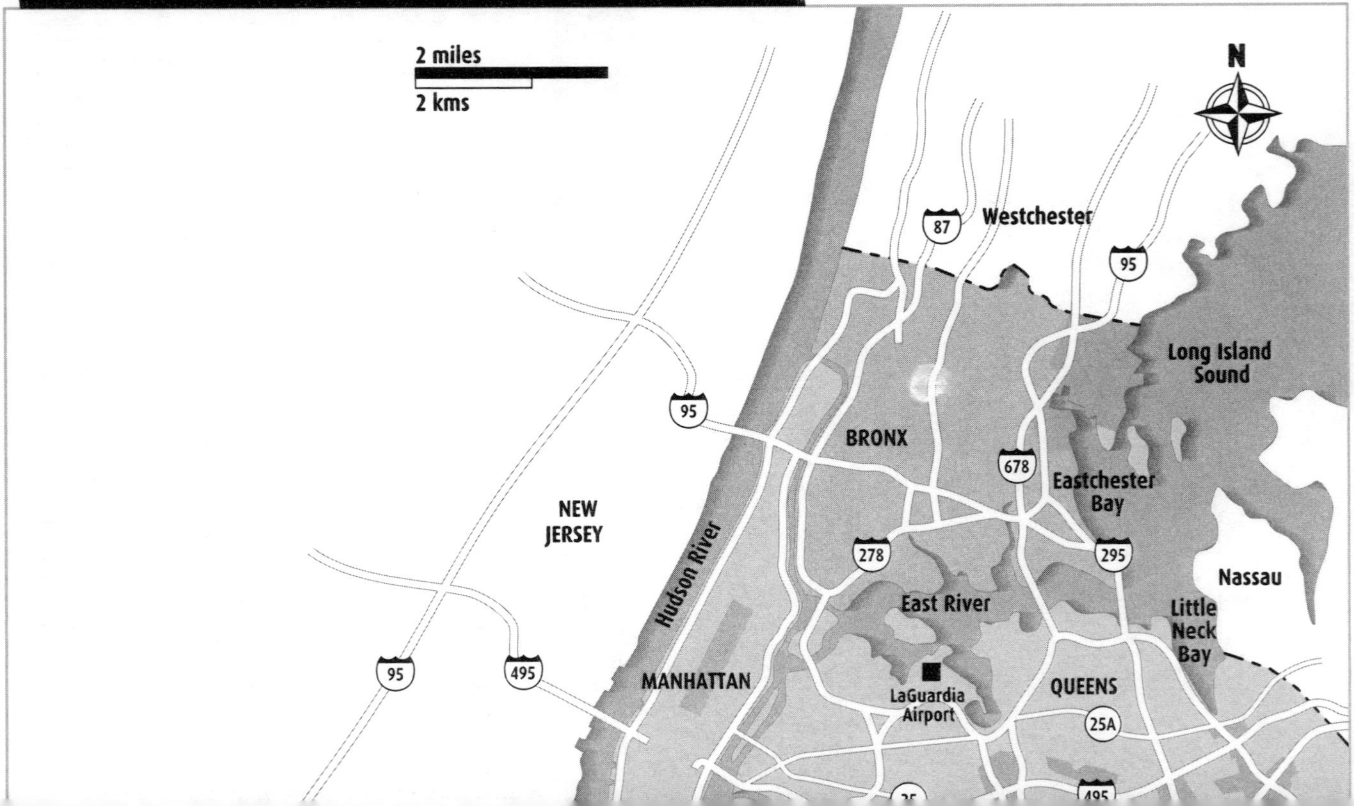

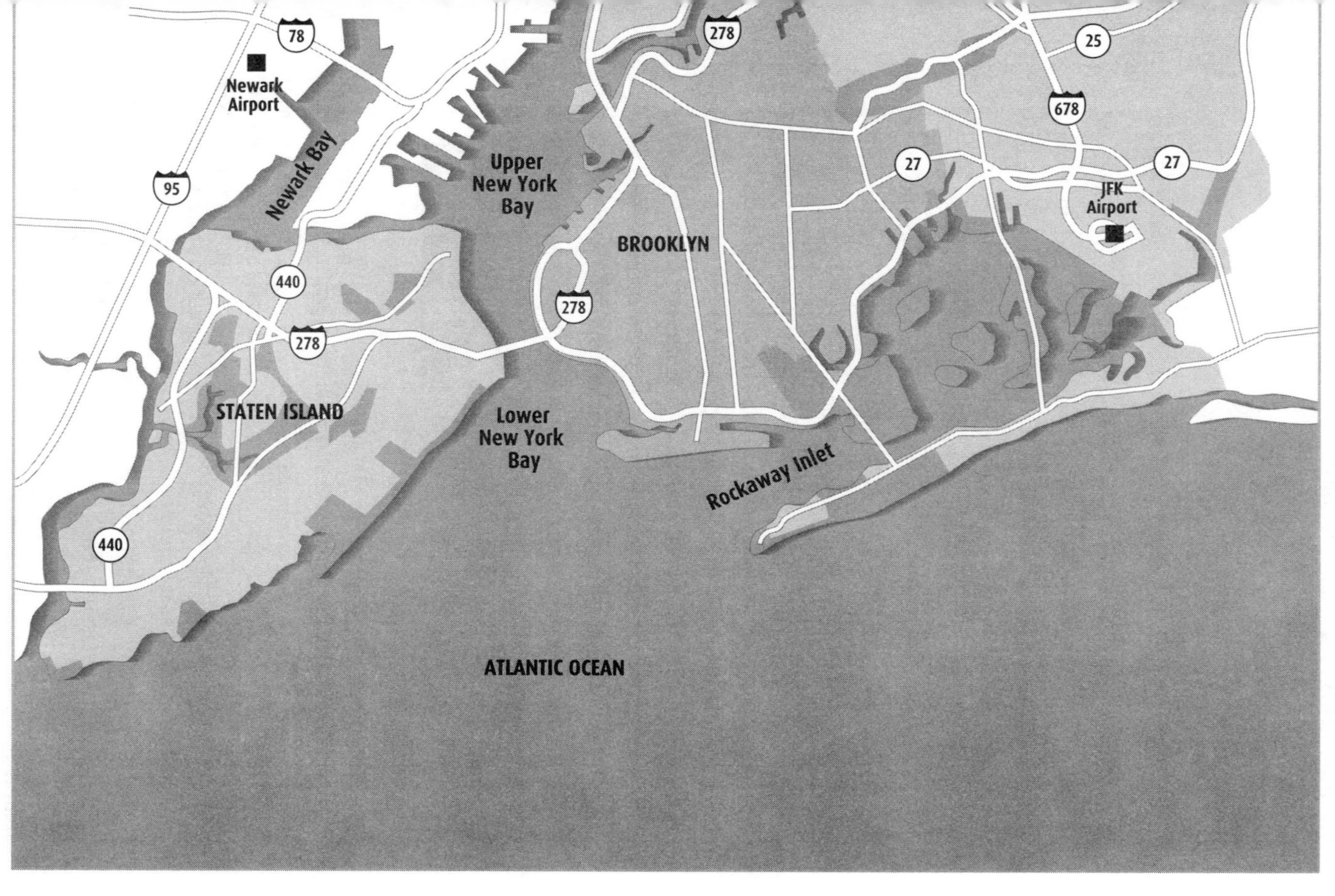

78
Newark Airport
Newark Bay
95
Upper New York Bay
278
25
678
27
27
JFK Airport
BROOKLYN
440
278
278
STATEN ISLAND
Lower New York Bay
Rockaway Inlet
440
ATLANTIC OCEAN

CRIME IN NEW YORK CITY

By now it's hardly news that safety in New York City has improved by leaps and bounds over the past two decades, and that trend shows no signs of abating. It is now safer to live in New York City than in any other large city in America.

Crime in New York has been dropping steadily since 1991, and the City now has the lowest crime rate of the ten largest cities in the United States. Murders in 2005 were at their lowest since 1963, and there has been a 75 percent overall drop in crime since 1991. New York City now has a rate of 2,802 crimes per 100,000 people, a far lower number per 100,000 than in the other large cities: 8,960 in Dallas; 7,904 in Detroit; 7,402 in Phoenix; 7,347 in San Antonio; 7,195 in Houston; 5,471 in Philadelphia; 4,376 in Los Angeles; and 4,103 in San Diego.

Major recent crime-fighting initiatives in the areas of statistics gathering, DNA testing, school safety, domestic violence, aggressive driving, and criminal justice reform promise to continue improving New York's reputation as a safe, livable city. Plus, it's important to remember that the bulk of New York City's violent crimes occur in neighborhoods that won't be under consideration in this book. In a safe neighborhood like Carnegie Hill, where my husband and I have lived for almost two decades, any incident of violent crime (and there are very few) is major news in the community, just as it would be in any small town anywhere in America.

Some crime is unavoidable, but most can be prevented through a combination of vigilance and common sense.

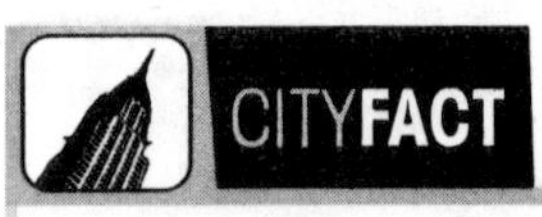

The Empire State Building, which is the tallest building in New York, has its own zip code and 11 dedicated mail carriers. In July 1945, a B-25 army cargo plane crashed into the building between the 79th and 80th floors, killing 14 people and sending one elevator plummeting to the bottom of its shaft. The structure at the top of the building was designed as a mooring mast for dirigibles, although it was only ever used once.

Don't let yourself be a statistic. Be aware of your surroundings, don't get into situations or confrontations that you can't handle, and don't be afraid to call for help. Keep your doors locked and your eyes open. Plan for safety, and your safety is much more likely to be assured.

Also, safety is often in the eye of the beholder. Some neighborhoods, like Mott Haven in the Bronx, may be perfectly safe for groups of young males sharing an apartment, but not as comfortable for families with young children or women living alone (although that neighborhood is improving so rapidly that, by next year, it will likely be far more desirable). Up-and-coming, formerly unsafe (but not totally safe yet) neighborhoods are favorite destinations for young people who, in exchange for a bigger apartment with a smaller rent, are often willing to forgo conveniences (like twenty-four-hour markets) and dodge the sketchy characters who might be loitering around the area. Obviously, not everyone would make this choice.

NOTEWORTHY IN THE NEIGHBORHOOD

Were I writing this book about any other city, I'd tell you where in each neighborhood you could find a dry cleaner, a supermarket, and a health club. But any well-populated neighborhood, especially in Manhattan, is likely to have at least 150 dry cleaners, thirty supermarkets (not to mention a couple of hundred smaller markets), and a dozen health clubs—as well as scores of hair salons, nail salons, acupuncturists, acupressurists, chiropractors, and palm readers. Just about every service

More than 200 major studio films are shot on location in New York City each year—and that only accounts for a quarter of the filming done on the city streets. Combined with television shows and commercials, the City grants permits for more than 35,000 "production days" of filming per year.

imaginable is going to lie within a few blocks of your front door if you live in Manhattan—and the rest you can get delivered.

So, instead of listing basic services, I've tried to include just a few significant landmarks and points of interest for each neighborhood. These are the sites that I think typify and characterize each neighborhood—to the extent that that's possible. Think of this as a tool to help you get started thinking about each neighborhood.

Other services and attractions: For information about restaurants, arts, entertainment, events, and transportation in and around the City, see the listings in Chapter 10. For essential services, such as how to locate your nearest hospital, see Chapter 11. And for schools, please consult the listings in Chapter 12.

UNDERSTANDING THE NEIGHBORHOOD STATISTICS

Averages can be deceiving, especially in a city of extremes, where you're unlikely to meet an average person or have an average day. Thus, when talking about New York City, statistics can never tell the whole story—and, worse, they can be misleading.

The smallest geographic unit in New York City for which comprehensive statistics are tracked is the community district. For the most part, the community districts (which are, essentially, the smallest units of local governance) correspond to established neighborhoods. But community districts can easily contain as many as two, four, or six *distinct* neighborhoods (for example, one affluent and one working-class, one extremely safe and one questionable), and even within a specific neighborhood there are pockets of poverty and wealth, crime and safety. Moreover, some individual apartment complexes (Lincoln Towers, Battery Park City, Stuyvesant Town) are so large (with tens of thousands of residents) that they nearly constitute their own neighborhoods.

As with everything in New York City, there is no substitute for close-up examination of the specific neighborhood you're considering.

The demographic statistics in the coming chapters (population, ethnicity, age, gender) come from New York's Department of City Planning and New York University's Furman Center for Real Estate and Urban Policy. They are based on the most recent census updates, which occurred in 2005. While some of the demographic statistics listed here will have changed to a certain extent, they are still largely accurate.

The official city statistics regarding average rents and apartment purchase prices, however, are all but irrelevant to the newcomer. For example, you'll be surprised to learn that the average monthly rent for an apartment in Manhattan is $1,150. But don't get your hopes up. Unless you moved into an apartment forty years ago and are protected by rent-control laws (as many New Yorkers are), or you live in city-owned low-income housing, this $1,150 apartment for all intents and purposes does not exist.

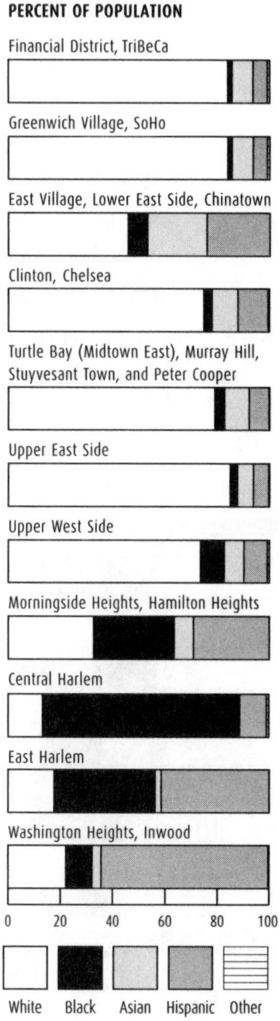

For real estate purchase and rental price statistics that are more relevant to real-world buyers and renters, it's best to ask an agent. If, for example, you ask Douglas Elliman, one of New York City's largest real estate firms, what the average rent is on actual, available apartments, you'll learn that $1,600 per month is pretty much the lower limit for a clean, safe, small studio apartment in a good building—and that a similar two-bedroom will

PERCENT OF POPULATION

Financial District, TriBeCa
Greenwich Village, SoHo
East Village, Lower East Side, Chinatown
Clinton, Chelsea
Turtle Bay (Midtown East), Murray Hill, Stuyvesant Town, and Peter Cooper
Upper East Side
Upper West Side
Morningside Heights, Hamilton Heights
Central Harlem
East Harlem
Washington Heights, Inwood

0 20 40 60 80 100

White Black Asian Hispanic Other

run you $2,500 to $4,000 or more. The government's housing purchase price statistics are somewhat more reliable, but they can also be deceptive.

I list the government data as a reference point, however I've also gathered data from dozens of brokers to arrive at much more realistic averages for each neighborhood. You may find those numbers discouraging—New York can be expensive. *Again, however, these are just averages.* A two-bedroom apartment on Fifth Avenue with a view of Central Park could easily cost three or four times as much to rent or buy as the same-size apartment on the top floor of a walk-up brownstone on a nearby side street.

The most important numbers for determining averages in each neighborhood are the prices per square foot. Thus, for each neighborhood, I list an average price per square foot for purchased property, and an average monthly rent per square foot for rentals. I then translate those figures into average prices for different types of apartments. For purchased apartments, I assume 600 square feet for a studio, 800 square feet for a one-bedroom, 1,000 square feet for a two-bedroom, 1,200 square feet for a three-bedroom, and 1,500 square feet for a palatial four-plus bedroom apartment. Rentals are often a hair smaller, and there are not a lot of large rentals available, so for rentals the assumption is 500 square feet for a studio, 700 square feet for a one-bedroom, and 900 square feet for a two-bedroom. Sound small? Yes, in Manhattan living space comes at a premium, but again, we're only talking about averages.

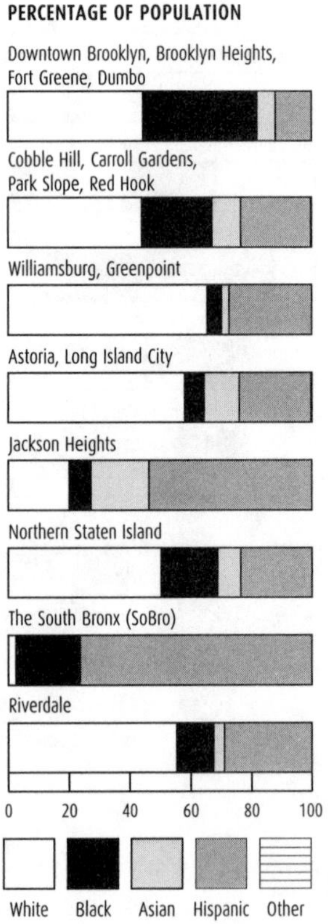

Thus, in a neighborhood where property costs an average of $1,000 per square foot to buy and $4.50 per square foot per month to rent, the figures would be:

PERCENTAGE OF POPULATION

Downtown Brooklyn, Brooklyn Heights, Fort Greene, Dumbo

Cobble Hill, Carroll Gardens, Park Slope, Red Hook

Williamsburg, Greenpoint

Astoria, Long Island City

Jackson Heights

Northern Staten Island

The South Bronx (SoBro)

Riverdale

0 20 40 60 80 100

White Black Asian Hispanic Other

PURCHASE AND RENTAL STATISTICS FROM BROKERS

Buying	
Average price per square foot	$1,000
Studio	$600,000
1 bedroom	$800,000
2 bedroom	$1,000,000
3 bedroom	$1,200,000
4+ bedroom	$1,500,000

Renting	
Average monthly rent per square foot	$4.50
Studio	$2,250
1 bedroom	$3,150
2 bedroom	$4,050

Now for the bad news: $1,000 per square foot is really about average for desirable New York City neighborhoods. But the good news is that there are neighborhoods where the numbers are lower, and even in a neighborhood with a $1,000-per-square-foot average there can be apartments that cost half that, or rent for closer to $3 per square foot per month. Part of the reason the averages are high is that they're held up by new construction of luxury buildings, which represent a large percentage of new sales and rentals in many neighborhoods. These buildings, with many staff and services, and with large construction loans to pay off, are expensive to get into.

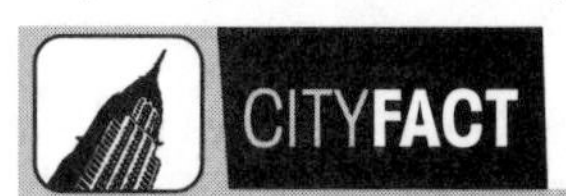

New York's unusual and massive underground steam delivery system, built by Consolidated Edison in the 1890s, is by far the largest in the world. In winter, the system carries more than 10 million pounds of 400-degree steam per hour to heat thousands of large office and apartment buildings.

CITYWIDE STATISTICAL COMPARISON

	NYC Overall	*Manhattan*
Population	8,213,839	1,606,275
Median Household Income	$40,000	$50,000
Median Monthly Rent*	$900	$1,150
Median Price/Unit in a multiple dwelling*	$238,500	$412,500
Number of Housing Units	3,260,856	815,265
Percent of Rental Units that Are Rent-Regulated	52.20%	61.80%
Homeownership Rate	33.30%	23.60%
Percent Immigrant Households	38.30%	23.80%
Percent Asian Households	9.50%	8.20%
Percent Black Households	23.00%	13.20%
Percent Hispanic Households	23.00%	18.10%
Percent White (non-Hispanic) Households	44.20%	60.20%
Percent Other Race Households	0.30%	0.40%

*Government statistics based on all homes. Costs for apartments currently on the market will be higher.

Crime statistics in New York are likewise very complex (and political). Rather than bury you in raw data, I've chosen simply to give a summary of the safety picture for each neighborhood (which, ultimately, given all the conflicting data, represents my judgment as a New Yorker combined with the judgment of several experts with whom I spoke). With regard to income, I have done the same, painting neighborhoods with broad brushstrokes as "affluent," "middle-class," or "working-class." Commuting times are mostly for mass transit (which is, typically, how New Yorkers commute). They are based on discussions with neighborhood residents and on actual tests by me. These

Brooklyn	*Queens*	*Staten Island*	*The Bronx*
2,511,408	2,256,576	475,014	1,364,566
$35,000	$45,000	$60,000	$27,500
$850	$950	$825	$775
$236,000	$262,500	$250,000	$196,667
944,731	828,001	173,850	499,029
45.20%	47.60%	15.90%	60.10%
29.20%	46.40%	67.70%	22.10%
44.10%	51.20%	20.20%	32.00%
7.30%	18.10%	5.60%	2.80%
32.40%	19.60%	7.60%	31.40%
16.60%	22.40%	14.20%	46.80%
42.40%	39.70%	72.50%	18.70%
0.20%	0.20%	0.00%	0.20%

times also assume good weather and apply only if you live and work within a short walk of mass transit on each end of your trip.

NEIGHBORHOODS IN NEW YORK CITY

Just to give you an overall feel for New York City, and to set a benchmark for comparison when evaluating neighborhood statistics, the chart above is a portrait of the population for all five of New York's boroughs.

CHAPTER TWO

MANHATTAN NEIGHBORHOODS

This is it—the City. As far as the average citizen of Earth is concerned, New York and Manhattan are synonymous. (Although, because of films like *Saturday Night Fever,* Brooklyn does enter into some people's consideration, and those who have immigrant relatives from, say, Greece might then be familiar with places like Astoria, Queens.)

As a newcomer, absent extraordinary circumstances, you'll likely choose Manhattan or a nearby neighborhood in one of the boroughs as the site of your first apartment. Thus, most of this chapter is devoted to a discussion of these neighborhoods.

MANHATTAN GEOGRAPHY CHEAT SHEET

Though it has a few twists and turns, once you understand the basics Manhattan is one of the easiest places in the world to navigate.

Manhattan is an island, and it points north to south (technically it's on a bit of an east-leaning angle—but we ignore that for the purpose of orientation and navigation). Thus, up is north (Uptown), down is south (Downtown), left is west, and right is east. Central Park lies almost dead center on this island, and that big street running north–south along the east (right) side of Central Park is Fifth Avenue, the dividing line between the East Side and the West Side.

If you started at the Hudson River (on the west side of the island) and walked along, say, 50th Street, you'd start by seeing buildings with high numbers: 401 West 50th Street and the like (by the way, odd numbers are always on the north side of the street; even numbers on the south). As you walked east, you'd see those numbers decline until, as you approached Fifth Avenue, the numbers would reach 1 West 50th. Then, on crossing Fifth Avenue, you'd encounter 1 East 50th Street, and the numbers would begin counting up until you reached the extreme east end of the island, otherwise known as the East River.

The highway-like road along the East River is the FDR Drive; the one along the Hudson River is called the Henry Hudson Parkway, West Side Highway, or West Street, depending on exactly which portion you're on. Over the Hudson River to the west, that's New Jersey. Over the East River, to the east, you've got Brooklyn and Queens. And of course you know the Bronx is up and the Battery (the southern tip of Manhattan) is down. And south of that, across the water, is Staten Island.

Most of Manhattan (aside from the historic Downtown areas) is organized on an eminently sensible grid: All avenues run north or south, while streets run east or west. Street numbers climb as you go north. So if you are on the corner of 59th Street and you turn south, the next street number will be 58th. Likewise, if you were to turn north (or uptown) the next street would be 60th Street. Because the island is not a perfect square, and because it developed over many years and under several regimes (Dutch, English, American, Giuliani), the avenues, which for the most part, run the length of Manhattan, do occasionally end or change their names. For instance, Eighth Avenue becomes Central Park West at 59th Street (where Central Park begins).

As a rough guide (we'll get more specific as we examine each neighborhood), Midtown is the area between 34th and 59th Streets. North of that is what we call Uptown. South of Midtown is what we call . . . Downtown. In New Yorkese, though, uptown and downtown (lowercase) are also used as directions, so 92nd Street is downtown from 93rd Street even though both streets are technically Uptown—you'll get the hang of it.

Although it may sound confusing on paper, the bulk of Manhattan is easy to grasp. However, navigation-wise, all bets are off once you reach Greenwich Village, below 14th Street. These meandering streets (which follow all sorts of natural and political boundaries) date back to the seventeenth and eighteenth centuries, before the grid was established. Some streets are even older—

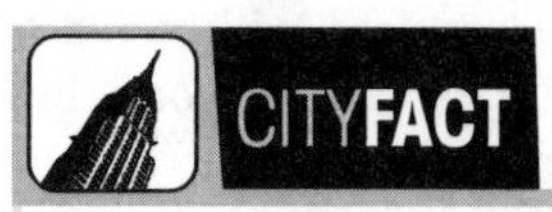

The Dakota, completed in 1884 on the corner of Central Park West and 72nd Street, was New York's first luxury apartment building. It has been featured prominently in literature (Jack Finney's *Time and Again*) and film *(Rosemary's Baby)* and has been home to many celebrities (such as Leonard Bernstein, Lauren Bacall, and Judy Garland). Perhaps the Dakota's most famous occupant, John Lennon, was murdered in front of the building in the early morning hours of December 8, 1980.

Broadway, for example, follows a trail created by Native Americans. You'll need a map or a very good memory to get around Downtown. Farther downtown, below Houston Street (please—it's pronounced "how-ston," not "hew-ston"), streets have names and not numbers.

Any questions?

A WORD ON UPTOWN VERSUS DOWNTOWN

There still remains the stereotype among some New Yorkers that there are "Uptown people" and "Downtown people." Those terms are also used to describe people: "Uptown" meaning snooty, ritzy, or unattainable (as in the Billy Joel song "Uptown Girl") and "Downtown" meaning hip, countercultural, and artist types (like the MTV veejay—yes, I'm dating myself—"Downtown" Julie Brown). I certainly still know some hipster and artist types who won't go above 14th Street if they can help it, except in the case of a dire emergency (and maybe not even then). For years, the Downtown crowd thought the Uptown crowd was stuffy, snobbish, and shallow. The Uptown crowd thought the Downtown crowd was self-consciously hip, artsy, and slacker/pseudointellectual.

These days, neighborhood stereotypes have been so eroded and crossover populations so common that it's hard to maintain this hard-line distinction between Uptown and Downtown. Plus, you now have a fair number of people living in the middle—in newly developed neighborhoods that are culturally affiliated with neither extreme. There's still an artsy attribute to Downtown Manhattan, and there's still a clean-cut conformism about the Uptown neighborhoods—but don't be fooled into thinking that these are hard-and-fast rules. As a newcomer, you should cast all prejudices aside,

MANHATTAN

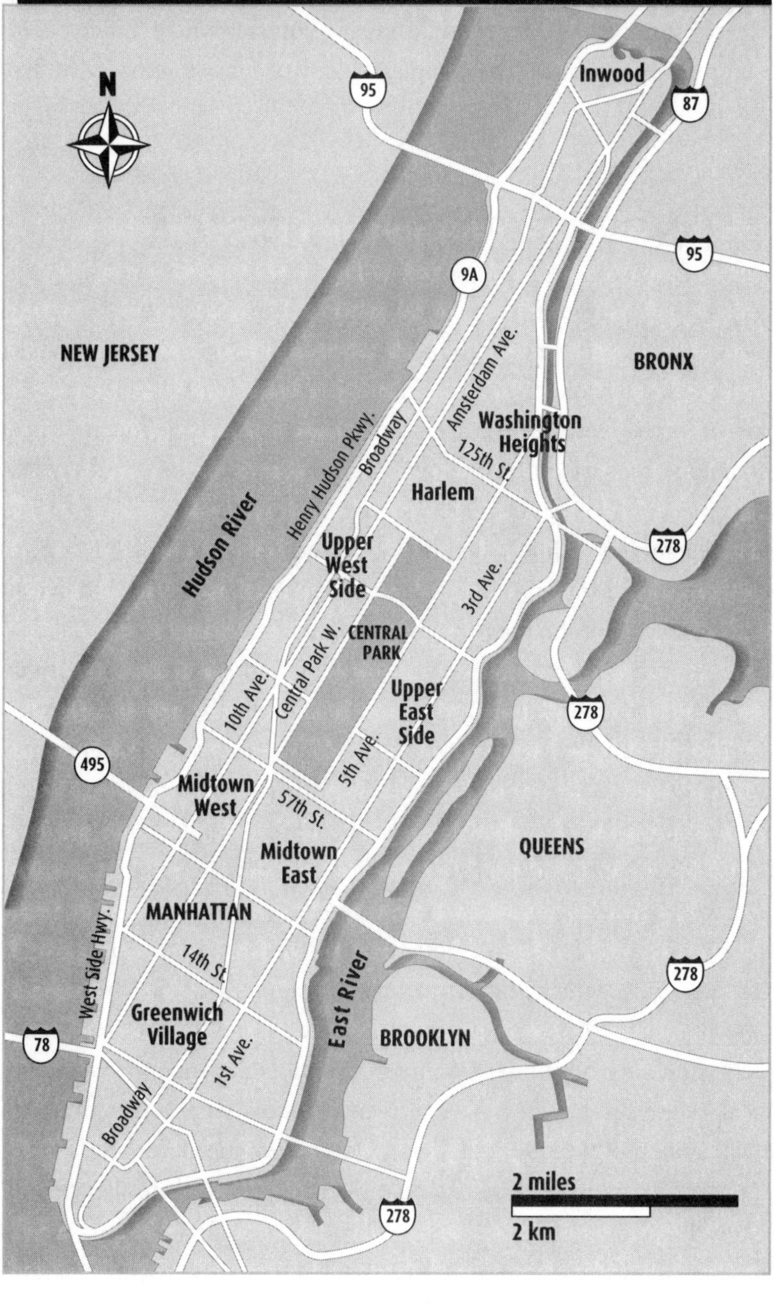

N
95
Inwood
87
95
9A
NEW JERSEY
BRONX
Amsterdam Ave.
Washington Heights
125th St.
Henry Hudson Pkwy.
Broadway
Harlem
Hudson River
Upper West Side
278
3rd Ave.
CENTRAL PARK
Central Park W.
10th Ave.
Upper East Side
278
5th Ave.
495
Midtown West
57th St.
Midtown East
QUEENS
West Side Hwy.
MANHATTAN
14th St.
East River
278
Greenwich Village
1st Ave.
BROOKLYN
78
Broadway
2 miles
2 km
278

keep your options open, and decide for yourself where to live based upon where you will be happiest—and of course, what you can afford.

FINANCIAL DISTRICT AND TRIBECA

A lot has changed in New York City since and on account of 9-11, and Downtown neighborhoods were affected most of all. While 9-11 was a terrible tragedy and something residents of this city will never forget, New Yorkers are a resilient and optimistic bunch. When someone tries to knock us down, not only do we come out on our feet, we come out in better shape than we were before.

There was a time when nobody used to live in lower Manhattan, except for traders and investment bankers who seemed to live at their offices. For the longest time, this was strictly a commercial district. But, during the few years preceding September 11, 2001, the dominos had started to fall, first in TriBeCa, then with the construction of Battery Park City, and, finally, with new development right near Wall Street, in the heart of the Financial District. And since 9-11, while things certainly slowed there for a couple of years, all of these neighborhoods are back in action and growing faster than ever before.

Whereas before 9-11, you would have to walk to Chinatown or the South Street Seaport to find a restaurant open past 6:00 in the Financial District, now there are dozens to choose from. Battery Park City now boasts some of the most appealing Downtown real estate for families. The residents of this city don't cower in fear, and the evolution of these Downtown neighborhoods over the past years is a prime example of that New York resilience and attitude.

TriBeCa (an acronym for Triangle Below Canal Street), with its large-windowed cast-iron buildings, now looks more like SoHo than the industrial neighborhood it once was. The warehouses and small factories are being reborn as residential apartments—expensive ones. The restaurant situation is excellent, spurred by low rents in the 1980s and now sustained by a desirable clientele. Not as artsy as SoHo, TriBeCa nonetheless has an exceptionally active nightlife, an attractive park (Duane Park), a bike path along the Hudson, a fair number of clothing and design shops, and some galleries.

Battery Park City, a ninety-two-acre area adjacent to the site of the World Trade Center complexes and the World Financial Center, is an easy walk from the downtown business district. It is a carefully planned development of apartment complexes, with private security, bronze sculptures, an esplanade, Hudson River breezes, and a beautiful marina. Shops and restaurants are not as plentiful as compared with the rest of the City, but residents find them sufficient given the neighborhood's other benefits (some apartments have incredible views of the harbor) and it's a short walk to nearby TriBeCa, where the City's favorite restaurants continue to thrive.

The changes around the Financial District are most dramatic. New apartment complexes (some in renovated former office buildings) are springing up all around and the investment bankers and traders are moving in. Unlike some emerging neighborhoods, this area is not characterized by low prices. Expect to pay top dollar for newly renovated apartments in full-service buildings. Neighborhood services are still not on par with other more established Manhattan neighborhoods, but restaurants, twenty-four-hour markets, and dry cleaners are gaining a foothold.

NEIGHBORHOOD STATISTICAL PROFILE

Population		34,420
	White	(84.0%)
	Black	(1.6%)
	Asian	(8.1%)
	Hispanic	(5.4%)
	Other	(0.9%)
Median Monthly Rent (government statistics)		$1,630
Median Price/Unit in a condominium (government statistics)		$751,863
Median Household Income		$75,000
Percent of Rental Units that Are Rent-Regulated		54.6%
Homeownership Rate		30.3%
Age of Householder:		
	15 to 24 years	6.1%
	25 to 44 years	53.0%
	45 to 64 years	29.5%
	65 years and over	11.4%

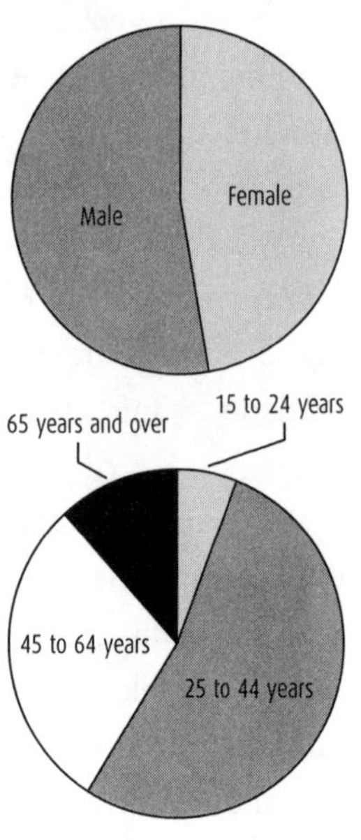

PURCHASE AND RENTAL STATISTICS FROM BROKERS

Buying

Average price per square foot	$954
Studio	$572,400
1 bedroom	$763,200
2 bedroom	$954,000
3 bedroom	$1,144,800
4+ bedroom	$1,431,000

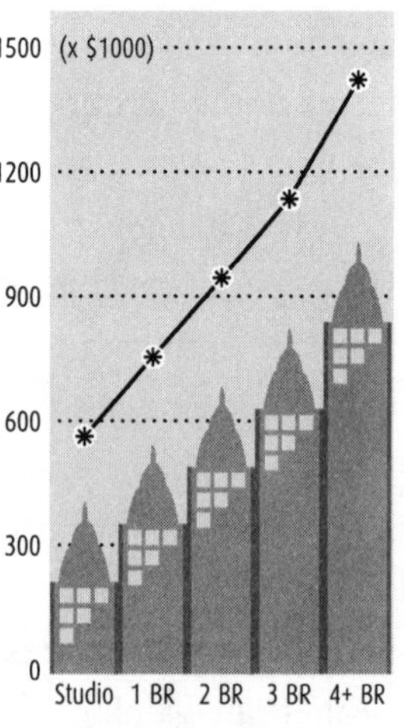

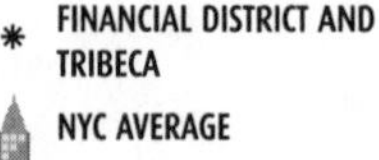

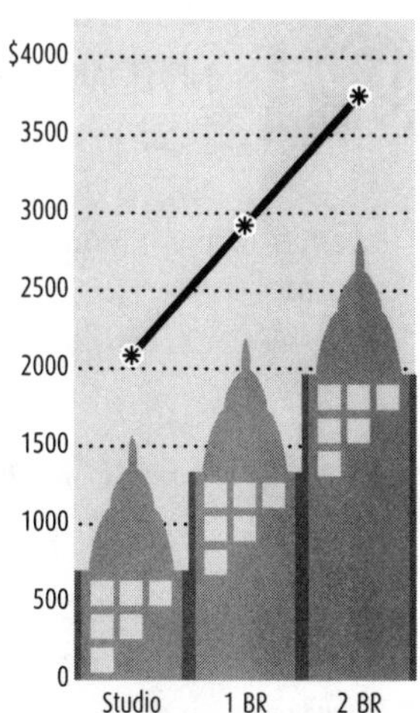

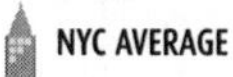

Renting

Average monthly rent per square foot	$4.17
Studio	$2,085
1 bedroom	$2,919
2 bedroom	$3,753

CRIME PICTURE

This is considered a safe area, although somewhat deserted at night.

INCOME PICTURE

This is an upwardly mobile area, with some pockets of lower income.

SUBWAYS

So many people commute to Downtown Manhattan by subway that residents of the area benefit greatly: the same trains that bring people to the neighborhood can be used by residents to get almost anywhere in town. On the east side of the neighborhood, TriBeCa is served primarily by the 1, 2, 3, E, A, and C trains. Farther downtown and west, in the Wall Street area, those lines are joined by the 4, 5, J, Z, M, R, and W trains.

Commuting Times

Midtown East	30–40 minutes
Midtown West	25–35 minutes
Wall Street	5–10 minutes

NOTEWORTHY **IN THE NEIGHBORHOOD**

Center of the nation's financial markets (New York Stock Exchange, World Financial Center)

World Trade Center Memorial (and future new World Trade Center)

Site of many historic landmarks (Brooklyn Bridge, Trinity Church, Woolworth Building)

Headquarters of government (City Hall, Municipal Building, Federal Building) **and courts** (state and federal)

Departure point for ferries to Staten Island and the Statue of Liberty and Ellis Island

Fraunces Tavern (where Washington said farewell to his officers), 54 Pearl Street (at Broad Street)

South Street Seaport and Pier 17 (shopping, dining, concerts, and outdoor cultural events)

Many artsy and cultural attractions in TriBeCa, dining, and independent one-of-a-kind stores

GREENWICH VILLAGE AND SOHO

The areas of Greenwich Village (pronounced "greh-nitch") and SoHo (an acronym for South of Houston Street) are two of the most-sought-after neighborhoods in the City. For the past several decades they were known as alternative, bohemian neighborhoods. But in recent years, the artists have given way to the more well-to-do and professional types (and some got rich selling their art), so that it's now more expensive to live in Greenwich Village or SoHo than almost anywhere else in New York.

By Greenwich Village I mean what some people now call the Central or West Village. The center of the neighborhood, physically and spiritually, is New York University. The residential streets in the center of the Village are elegant and full of attractive old brick town-houses, plus a few apartment buildings. If you're thinking funky and unusual, you've got the wrong image—many of the streets in the Village are as quiet and dignified as they come. The students and alternative types have been pushed farther and farther east and west, where funkiness—and affordability—is still more of a possibility.

SoHo, home to a large concentration of galleries in New York City, is another artists' neighborhood that has undergone extensive gentrification. Price-wise, SoHo is downright prohibitive, and the artists have been pushed south, first into TriBeCa, then into the boroughs. SoHo is still a lively and fun area, though, with incredible restaurants and a bustling nightlife.

The gentrification of SoHo has, as is often the case, caused an outward growth in the areas immediately surrounding it. Now, the nearby areas of NoHo (North of Houston), Little Italy (which no longer houses many Italians), and NoLIta (a new-ish designation, meaning North of Little Italy) are very desirable residential areas as well—and each has gained its own clout and the price tag to prove it.

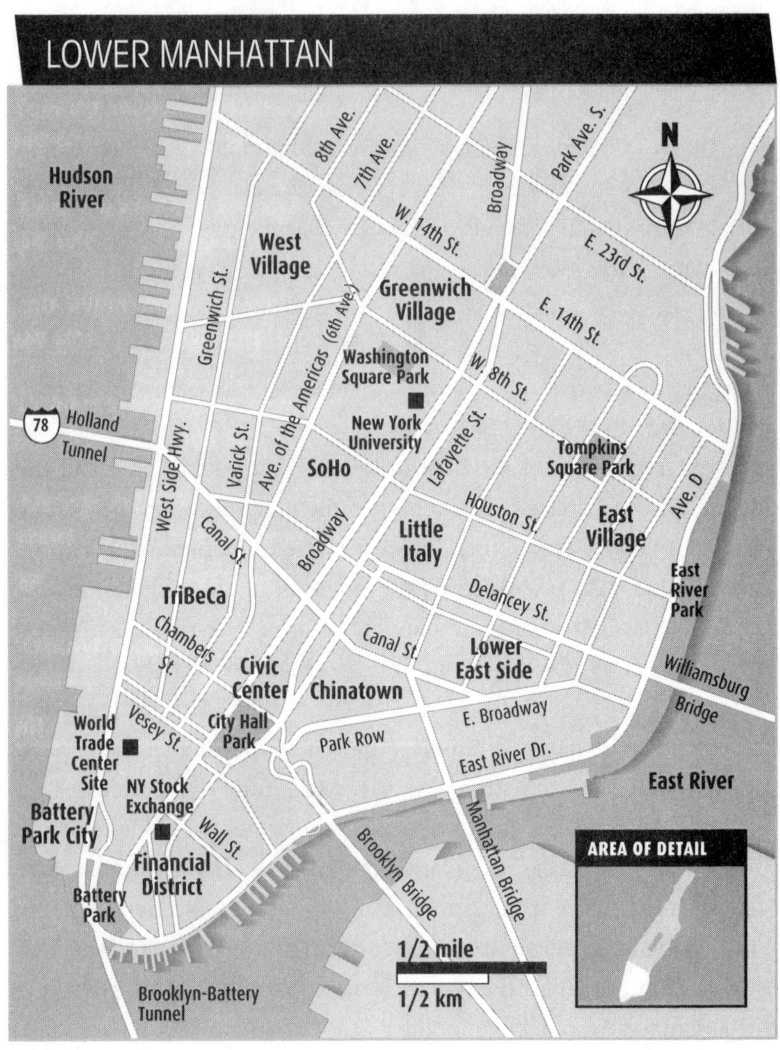
LOWER MANHATTAN
Hudson River
8th Ave.
7th Ave.
Broadway
Park Ave. S.
N
West Village
W. 14th St.
E. 23rd St.
Greenwich St.
Greenwich Village
E. 14th St.
Ave. of the Americas (6th Ave.)
Washington Square Park
W. 8th St.
78
Holland Tunnel
West Side Hwy.
Varick St.
New York University
Lafayette St.
Tompkins Square Park
SoHo
Houston St.
East Village
Ave. D
Canal St.
Broadway
Little Italy
East River Park
TriBeCa
Delancey St.
Chambers St.
Civic Center
Canal St.
Lower East Side
Williamsburg Bridge
Chinatown
World Trade Center Site
Vesey St.
City Hall Park
E. Broadway
Park Row
East River Dr.
East River
NY Stock Exchange
Battery Park City
Wall St.
Brooklyn Bridge
Manhattan Bridge
AREA OF DETAIL
Financial District
Battery Park
1/2 mile
1/2 km
Brooklyn-Battery Tunnel

NEIGHBORHOOD STATISTICAL PROFILE

Population		93,119
	White	(84.0%)
	Black	(1.6%)
	Asian	(8.1%)
	Hispanic	(5.4%)
	Other	(0.9%)
Median Monthly Rent (government statistics)		$1,630
Median Price/Unit in a condominium (government statistics)		$1,619,463
Median Household Income		$75,000
Percent of Rental Units that Are Rent-Regulated		54.6%
Homeownership Rate		30.3%
Age of Householder:		
	15 to 24 years	5.6%
	25 to 44 years	50.0%
	45 to 64 years	28.9%
	65 years and over	15.5%

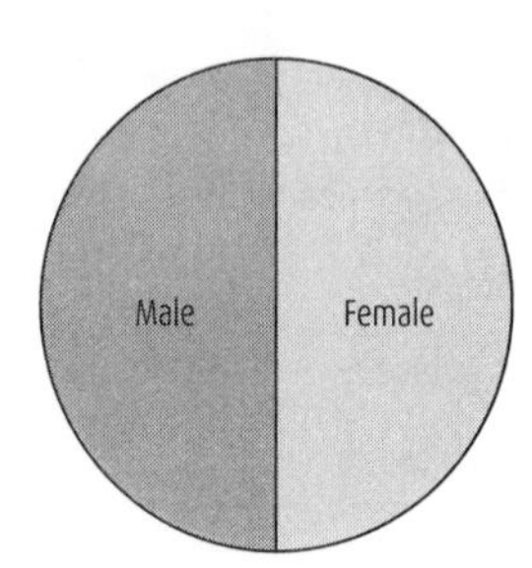

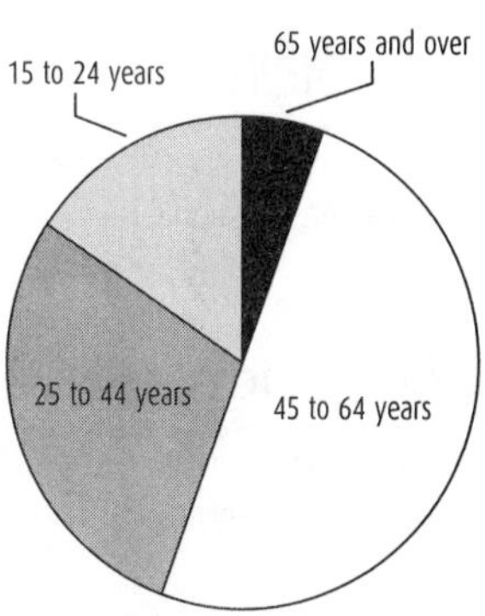

PURCHASE AND RENTAL STATISTICS FROM BROKERS

Buying

Average price per square foot	$1,177
Studio	$706,200
1 bedroom	$941,600
2 bedroom	$1,177,000
3 bedroom	$1,412,400
4+ bedroom	$1,765,500

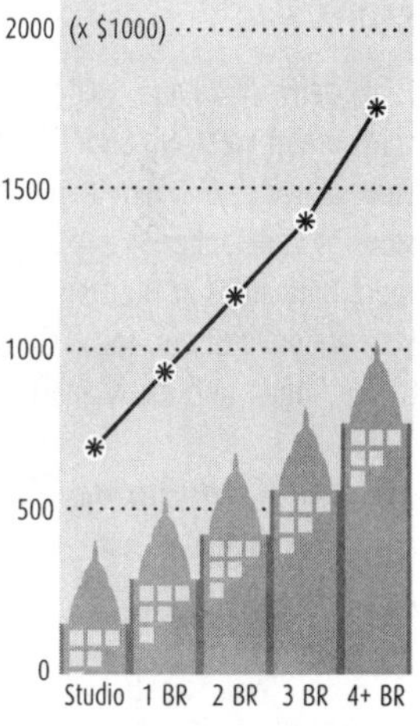

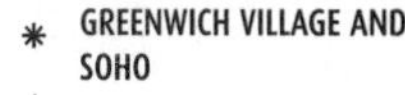

Renting

Average monthly rent per square foot	$4.75
Studio	$2,375
1 bedroom	$3,325
2 bedroom	$4,275

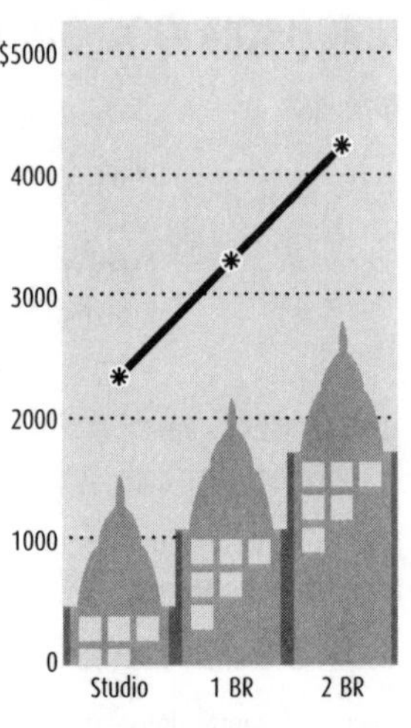

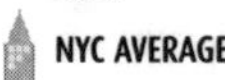

CRIME PICTURE

This is considered a very safe area, although the fringe can be questionable.

INCOME PICTURE

At its core, this is an affluent area, although there are pockets of lower income.

SUBWAYS

For Greenwich Village residents, several subway lines converge at West 4th Street near Washington Square Park: the A, C, E, F, and V. In addition, the 1 train stops at Christopher Street/Sheridan Square. In SoHo, the 1 train stops at Houston Street, the C and E trains stop at Spring Street, the 6 stops farther east also on Spring Street, and the N and R stop at Prince Street.

Commuting Times

Midtown East	25–35 minutes
Midtown West	15–25 minutes
Wall Street	20–30 minutes

NOTEWORTHY **IN THE NEIGHBORHOOD**

Numerous playhouses, music venues, galleries, designer showrooms, and high-end boutiques

Washington Square Park (largest public space downtown, the focal point being the large Memorial Arch)

New York University (major institution of higher learning and a defining voice in the neighborhood), from West 3rd Street to Waverly Place and Mercer Street to La Guardia Place

Film Forum (New York's premier art house movie theater), 209 West Houston Street (Sixth Avenue and Varick Street)

EAST VILLAGE, LOWER EAST SIDE, AND CHINATOWN

Fifteen years ago, I wouldn't have included these neighborhoods in this book, save perhaps for the East Village as a place for nonconformists. But today these are some of the trendiest neighborhoods on the Downtown scene.

The designation "East Village" was created by real estate brokers to bestow some legitimacy on this formerly run-down part of the Lower East Side. And it worked. The neighborhood has evolved and changed so much that hardly a tattoo parlor, a shaven head, or a twenty-something with body piercings can be found. Even the dreaded

"Alphabet City" (the area jutting out into the river, where the extra avenues that appear nowhere else in Manhattan are designated by letters) has been cleaned up dramatically by both a police presence and the hipsters, artists, and other urban pioneers who moved into the neighborhood when other bordering neighborhoods became too expensive. As you might have guessed, the area is especially popular with the young, antiestablishment crowd, but in this neighborhood, as with all others, you'll find all kinds living here—and more and more varieties of people are moving in every day.

The Lower East Side has changed so dramatically in the last fifteen years that it boggles the mind. This used to be a neighborhood that was more than borderline: prostitutes, drug dealers, and graffiti were the norm and sometimes more than one body was found on the streets at dawn. Now the streets are lined with trendy one-of-a-kind boutiques, funky cafés, and restaurants, and with high-end hotels. At night the streets are chock-full of music lovers and young hipsters there for the trendy dive bars, dance clubs, and burgeoning indie music scene. Traditionally the landing point for new immigrants to the City, the Lower East Side still has more ethnic character than most neighborhoods. But the latest immigrants are more likely to be American-born than foreign-born.

Likewise, many non-Chinese people are finding good housing in Chinatown. While the physical borders of Chinatown remain the same, the neighborhood and population of Chinatown keep pushing outward farther and farther. As for authenticity, you'll still find slippery fish guts on the sidewalks along Canal and Mulberry Streets and have the pick of the season with fresh produce sold by street vendors at busy intersections; and Chinese is still the dominant language on the streets. But more "outsiders" are moving into the neighborhood because there is great character, vivacity, and true New York City (and Chinese) flavor.

NEIGHBORHOOD STATISTICAL PROFILE

Population		164,407
	White	(46.0%)
	Black	(7.4%)
	Asian	(22.8%)
	Hispanic	(23.9%)
Median Monthly Rent (government statistics)		$1,000
Median Price/Unit in a multiple dwelling (government statistics)		$177,114
Median Household Income		$33,000
Percent of Rental Units that Are Rent-Regulated		45.9%
Homeownership Rate		17.4%
Age of Householder:		
	15 to 24 years	5.3%
	25 to 44 years	42.7%
	45 to 64 years	29.8%
	65 years and over	22.1%

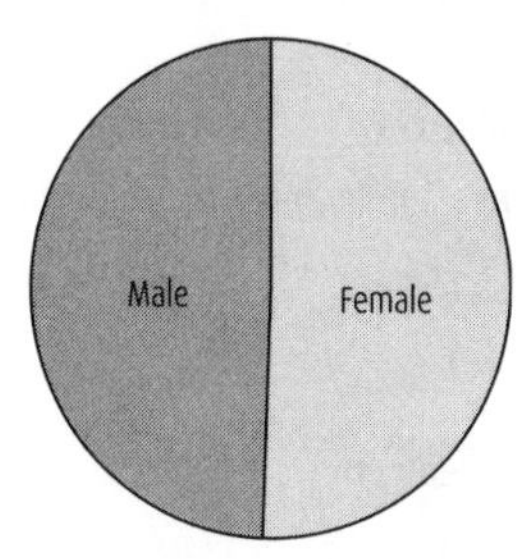

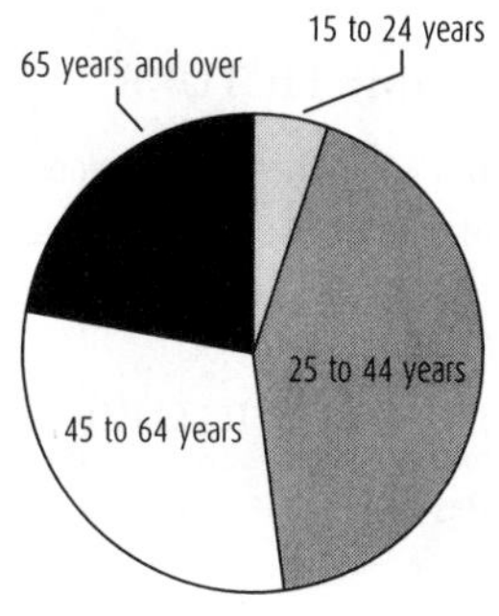

PURCHASE AND RENTAL STATISTICS FROM BROKERS

Buying

Average price per square foot	$887
Studio	$532,200
1 bedroom	$709,600
2 bedroom	$887,000
3 bedroom	$1,064,400
4+ bedroom	$1,330,500

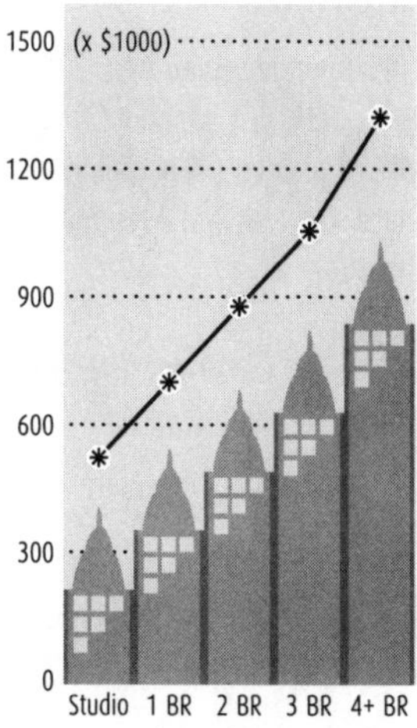

✱ **EAST VILLAGE, LOWER EAST SIDE, AND CHINATOWN**

 **NYC AVERAGE**

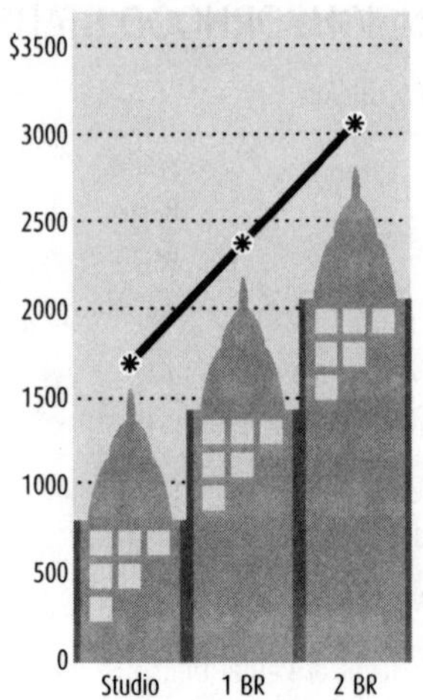

Renting

Average monthly rent per square foot	$3.42
Studio	$1,710
1 bedroom	$2,394
2 bedroom	$3,078

CRIME PICTURE

This is considered a developing area; caution is still recommended although there are many safe sections.

INCOME PICTURE

This is a middle- and working-class area.

SUBWAYS

Chinatown is served by the D at Grand Street and the N, R, Q, W, 6, J, M, and Z trains at Canal Street. East Village residents rely mainly on the 6 train at Astor Place, the F at 2nd Avenue, and the N and R trains at 8th Street.

Commuting Times

Midtown East	15–25 minutes
Midtown West	25–35 minutes
Wall Street	15–25 minutes

NOTEWORTHY **IN THE NEIGHBORHOOD**

Major center of alternative culture, including music, body art, and boutiques

St. Mark's Place (the most visible representation of East Village culture, boasting countless independent boutiques, retail stands, bars, and restaurants), from Avenue A to Third Avenue

Cooper Union (a famous private college renowned for its art program, in the oldest steel-beam building in America), 7 East 7th Street (Fourth Avenue)

Orchard Street (center of the old Jewish Lower East Side, now a pedestrian mall on weekends), from Delancey Street to Houston Street

Mott and Canal Streets, the gateway to Chinatown, a destination that virtually every tourist to New York visits

CHELSEA AND CLINTON (MIDTOWN WEST)

Chelsea is not unlike many other young, affluent areas of New York. You'll see attractive couples out for the evening or just walking hand in hand down the street. But in Chelsea, the couples are often men.

New York has a substantial gay population, and the City is historically very tolerant. And, while Chelsea is probably the most visibly gay neighborhood in New York right now, it is also home to many happily coexisting people of all stripes and preferences.

MIDTOWN EAST AND WEST

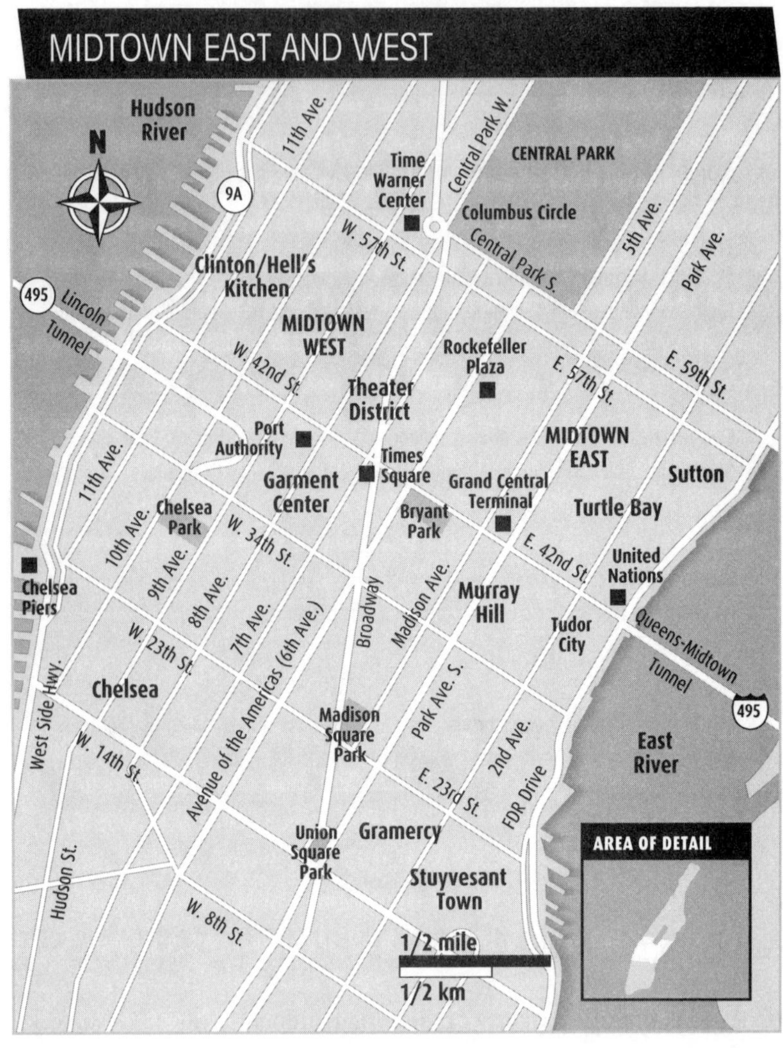

Chelsea is near the Garment Center and encompasses what is called the Flower District. The streets feel open, as there are few high-rise buildings there (except for a few large complexes like the Chelsea Towers). There are many attractive walk-up buildings and brownstones, plus a few loft buildings. An array of stores, big (Old Navy, The Container Store, BuyBuyBaby) and little (boutiques and the like), have opened along Sixth Avenue in recent years, restaurants and shops now line Seventh and Eighth Avenues, and the western part of Chelsea contains many art galleries. The Chelsea Piers athletic and recreation complex, a facility unlike any other in the world, provides the neighborhood's final touch. This area isn't big on housing bargains, but if this sounds like heaven to you, give it a shot—it's always worth a try.

North of Chelsea is what is now called Clinton, and used to be called Hell's Kitchen. In the early 1990s, a few prestigious corporations and law firms, tired of paying Midtown rents, struck out into Midtown West and relocated their corporate headquarters into this neighborhood, which was formerly made up of porn shops, slums, and a few artists' residences (mostly actors and dancers). The presence of these large companies spurred housing growth and these days this neighborhood has really turned the corner. Although still "edgy" (translation: not as reliably safe as the Upper West Side or Chelsea), it is a fine neighborhood for young people and continues to improve each year. There has been some high-rise condo construction in recent years, but most of the housing is in smaller prewar buildings and lofts.

NEIGHBORHOOD STATISTICAL PROFILE

Population		87,479
	White	(75.0%)
	Black	(3.1%)
	Asian	(9.8%)
	Hispanic	(11.5%)
	Other	(0.5%)
Median Monthly Rent (government statistics)		$1,400
Median Price/Unit in a condominium (government statistics)		$675,000
Median Household Income		$54,752
Percent of Rental Units that Are Rent-Regulated		61.5%
Homeownership Rate		24.4%
Age of Householder:		
	15 to 24 years	4.5%
	25 to 44 years	51.0%
	45 to 64 years	28.8%
	65 years and over	15.8%

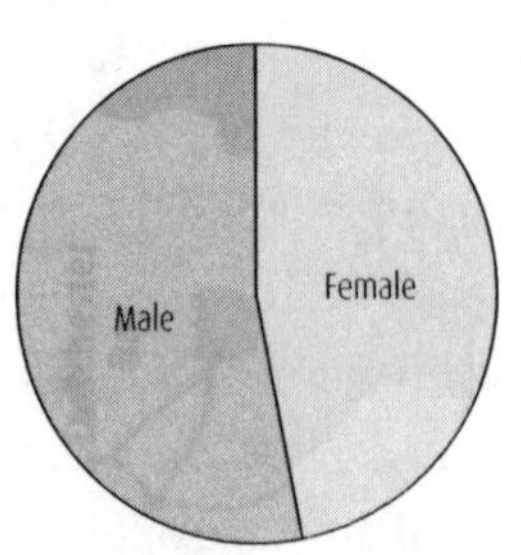

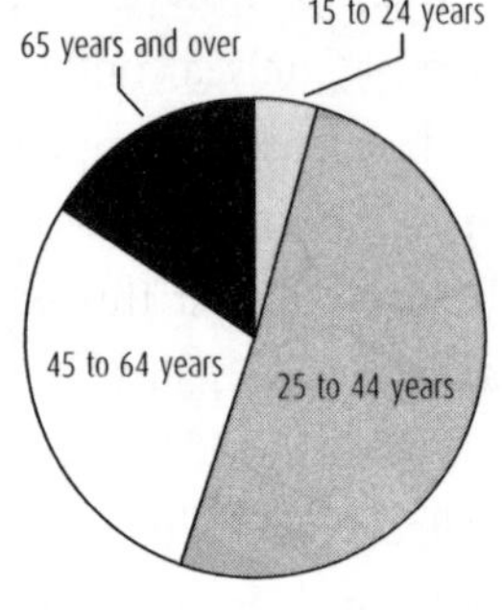

PURCHASE AND RENTAL STATISTICS FROM BROKERS

Buying

Average price per square foot	$1,054
Studio	$632,400
1 bedroom	$843,200
2 bedroom	$1,054,000
3 bedroom	$1,264,800
4+ bedroom	$1,581,000

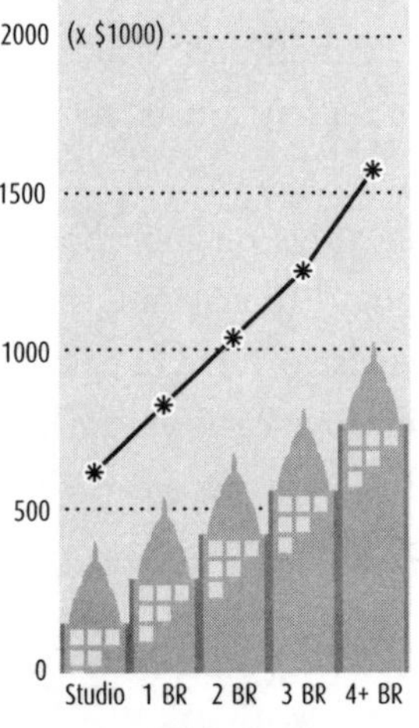

Renting

Average monthly rent per square foot	$4.66
Studio	$2,330
1 bedroom	$3,262
2 bedroom	$4,194

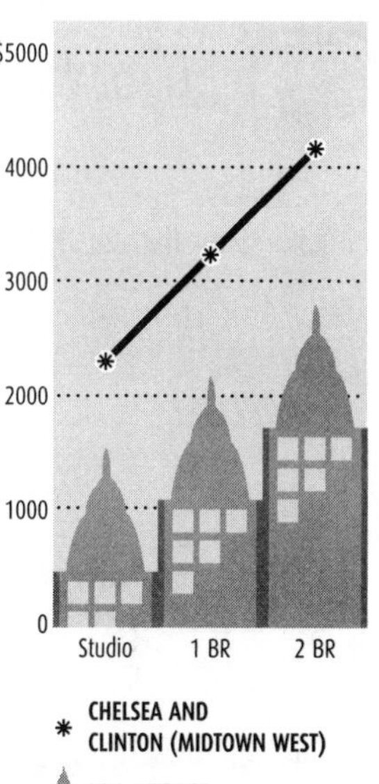

CRIME PICTURE

Traditionally a marginal area, this is now a safe (and improving daily) area, although there are some still-developing segments around the fringes.

INCOME PICTURE

This area ranges from affluent to working-class, depending on specific location.

SUBWAYS

Chelsea and Clinton are primarily served by the A, C, and E trains along Eighth Avenue. In addition, some parts of Clinton are an easy walk to the N, R, and W at 49th Street and the 1 at 50th Street. People toward the eastern part of Chelsea also have access to the 1, 2, and 3 trains, and those who live near the south end of Chelsea are near the L train, one of the few Manhattan subway lines that runs east to west—it gives great access to many other subway lines.

Commuting Times

Midtown East	15–25 minutes
Midtown West	5–15 minutes
Wall Street	30–40 minutes

NOTEWORTHY **IN THE NEIGHBORHOOD**

Broadway theater district (most of the major theaters are here)

Flower District (wholesale and retail), Sixth Avenue from 27th to 30th Streets

Antiques (this is a major center of antiques in New York City), Ninth Avenue from 20th to 22nd Streets

Chelsea Piers (gigantic sports and recreation complex), West Street from 17th to 23rd Streets

Javits Center (New York's largest convention center), 655 West 34th Street (Eleventh and Twelfth Avenues)

Port Authority (the main bus terminal for New York), Eighth and Ninth Avenues from 40th to 42nd Streets

Penn Station (train station for Long Island Rail Road, New Jersey Transit, and Amtrak), Seventh and Eighth Avenues from 31st to 33rd Streets

Intrepid Sea, Air & Space Museum (beautifully preserved World War II aircraft carrier), 46th Street and Twelfth Avenue

Galleries line the side streets, especially 20th through 26th Streets, and you'll find a smattering along Tenth and Eleventh Avenues in the same area.

GRAMERCY, MURRAY HILL, AND TURTLE BAY (MIDTOWN EAST)

To the east and south of Midtown Manhattan you'll find a mixed bag of neighborhoods, each with its own personality. Turtle Bay, Murray Hill, and Gramercy are the most well-defined of these, although there are also several large apartment complexes, like Tudor City (from 40th to 43rd Streets between First and Second Avenues), Peter Cooper Village (from 20th to 23rd Streets between First Avenue and the East River), and Stuyvesant Town (from 14th to 20th Streets between First Avenue and the East River), that are neighborhoods in their own right (they are, individually, larger than many towns).

Gramercy is centered around the beautiful Gramercy Park, the only private park in the City, open only to residents of buildings in the neighborhood. It's a quiet neighborhood because the park cuts up the streets and prevents most through-traffic. The park is surrounded by nineteenth-century townhouses, and there are many attractive small buildings nearby. Prices are highest closest to the park.

Murray Hill, sandwiched between Gramercy Park and Turtle Bay, is centrally located and provides good access to most areas of Manhattan. Many people choose to live here so they can walk to work; therefore the neighborhood is rife with professionals (although not necessarily young ones). There are townhouses near Park Avenue and high-rises near First Avenue, and Third Avenue is an emerging restaurant and entertainment venue.

Turtle Bay is a small area north of the United Nations with a fiercely de-

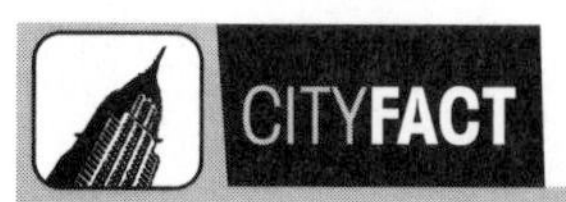

The Great Fire of 1835 lasted three days and destroyed most of lower Manhattan. The blaze engulfed 17 city blocks and ruined 700 buildings, including many important commercial buildings (such as the original Merchants' Exchange) and beautiful churches from the Dutch period.

voted populace (it even has its own newspaper). Smack in the middle of Midtown action, the farther east you get the more noticeably peaceful it becomes. Despite the office buildings that tower over the neighborhood, it is home to many interesting restaurants and people. While the most notable landmark in the neighborhood is obviously the United Nations, there are many consulates nearby, and proximity to Midtown offices is extraordinary. Also near Turtle Bay are the areas of Sutton Place and Beekman Place, which are genteel and affluent.

NEIGHBORHOOD STATISTICAL PROFILE

Population		136,152
	White	(79.2%)
	Black	(3.6%)
	Asian	(9.4%)
	Hispanic	(7.6%)
	Other	(0.2%)
Median Monthly Rent (government statistics)		$1,469
Median Price/Unit in a condominium (government statistics)		$740,000
Median Household Income		$76,010
Percent of Rental Units that Are Rent-Regulated		60.6%
Homeownership Rate		29.8%
Age of Householder:		
	15 to 24 years	4.7%
	25 to 44 years	47.1%
	45 to 64 years	30.3%
	65 years and over	17.9%

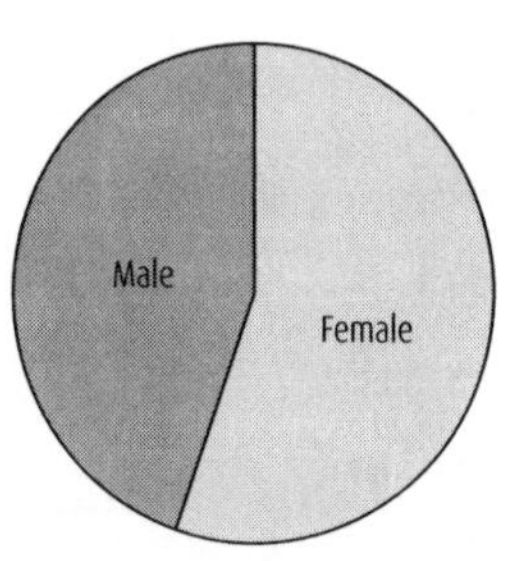

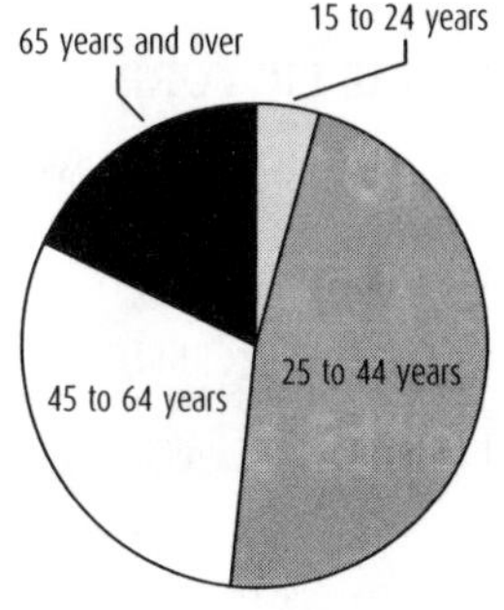

PURCHASE AND RENTAL STATISTICS FROM BROKERS

Buying

Average price per square foot	$1,187
Studio	$712,200
1 bedroom	$949,600
2 bedroom	$1,187,000
3 bedroom	$1,424,400
4+ bedroom	$1,780,500

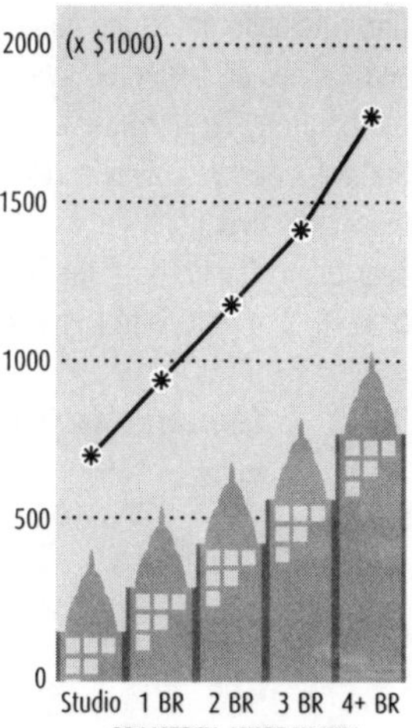

Renting

Average monthly rent per square foot	$4.58
Studio	$2,290
1 bedroom	$3,206
2 bedroom	$4,122

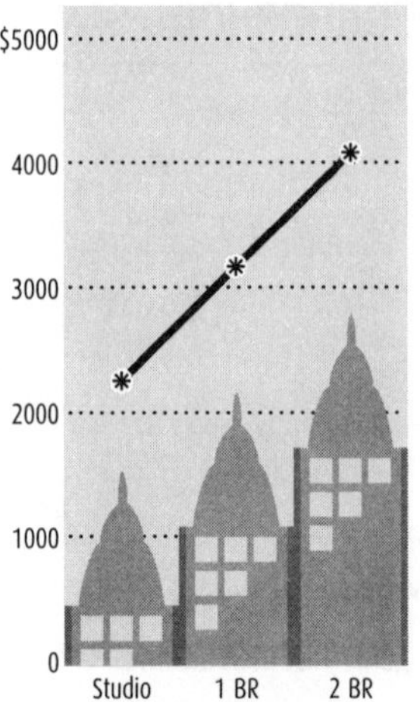

CRIME PICTURE

This is considered a very safe area.

INCOME PICTURE

This is an affluent area.

SUBWAYS

These neighborhoods are mainly served by the 4, 5, and 6 trains on Lexington Avenue. The subway stops can be pretty far from the easternmost avenues, and the lack of easy subway access is a main complaint of those who live along the East River. Those who live near Union Square have the best options, with the Q, W, N, R, 4, 5, 6, and L lines converging there.

Commuting Times

Midtown East	5–15 minutes
Midtown West	15–25 minutes
Wall Street	25–35 minutes

NOTEWORTHY **IN THE NEIGHBORHOOD**

Union Square Park (including the Union Square Greenmarket), from 14th to 17th Streets bounded by Union Square East and Union Square West

Theodore Roosevelt Birthplace (one of New York's most charming attractions), 28 East 20th Street

Flatiron Building (called "flatiron" for its shape), 175 Fifth Avenue (22nd and 23rd Streets)

Gramercy Park (from 20th to 21st Streets and Park Avenue South to Third Avenue)

"Curry Hill" (where Murray Hill ends and Gramercy begins, home to a thriving row of Indian restaurants)

Morgan Library & Museum (America's finest collection of medieval and Renaissance manuscripts, and then some), 29 East 36th Street (Park & Madison Avenues)

The United Nations (from 42nd to 48th Streets on First Avenue)

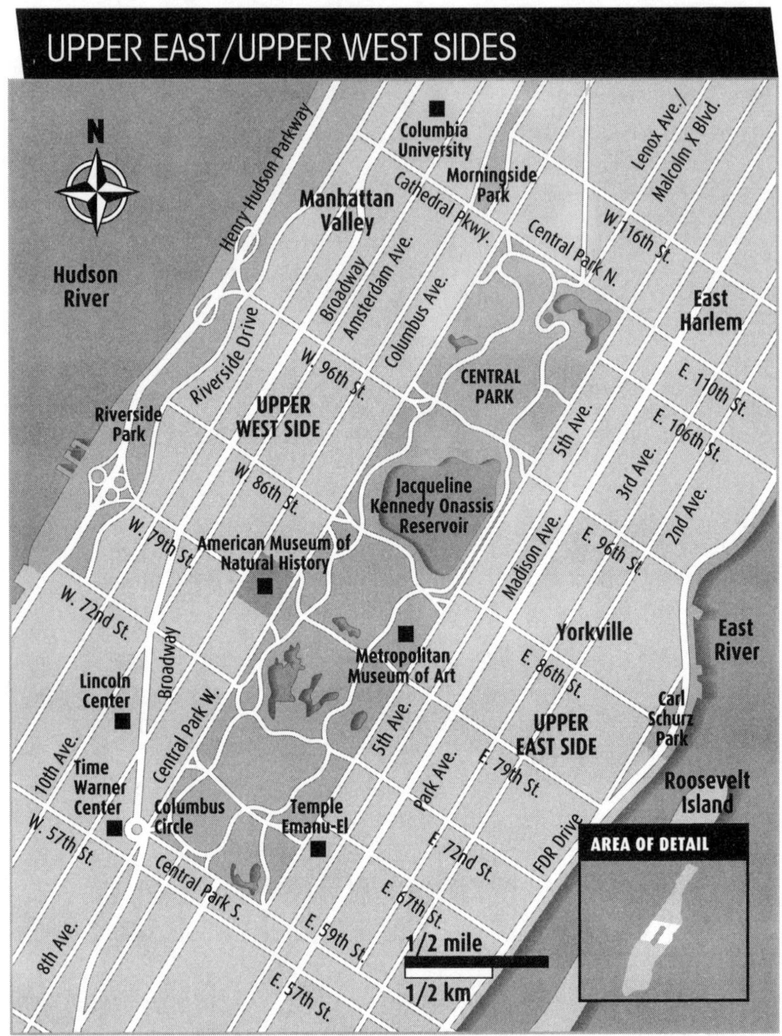

UPPER EAST SIDE

New Yorkers are fiercely loyal to their neighborhoods, and I must admit I'm partial to the Upper East Side because this is where I live. And here we have lesson number one: Every neighborhood contains numerous subdivisions, and subdivisions of subdivisions. You see, I don't *really* live on the Upper East Side. Sure, as a strict matter of geography, I live there. But when people ask, I generally tell them I live in Carnegie Hill, a small slice of the Upper East Side that runs from 86th to 96th Streets, and from Fifth to Lexington Avenues. To be exact, within Carnegie Hill, I live near Madison Avenue in the 90s—a very specific area within Carnegie Hill that is characterized by small neighborhood restaurants and cafés, upscale boutiques, a family atmosphere (you'll see my neighbors Paul Newman and Joanne Woodward, as well as Ralph Lauren, Phoebe Cates and Kevin Kline, and Michael J. Fox strolling the neighborhood along with everyone else), countless private schools, and proximity to Central Park.

Other folks who live in Carnegie Hill might live on Park Avenue or Fifth Avenue (those are the rich people, for the most part), but they're not really my neighbors. Even within my block, I live in a sub-community: I live in one of Ken's buildings. Ken is my landlord, and he owns a number of buildings (mostly old townhouses that, like many of the beautiful landmark townhouses in Carnegie Hill, have been divided into "walk-up" apartments) in the neighborhood. Though we New Yorkers live in a gigantic metropolis, we tend to define ourselves in precise terms that create communities. So, if you live in one of Ken's buildings, and you meet someone who lives in another of Ken's buildings, you're already seven-tenths of the way toward being friends.

The rest of the Upper East Side (if I must talk about it) is also quite nice and houses some of the wealthiest people in America (regretfully I don't count myself among them). Moving east from Carnegie Hill, there's Yorkville, which used to be a German neighborhood (you'll still find a few German shops along First Avenue near 86th Street but they are fast disappearing) but is now home to numerous high-rise apartment buildings that serve as homes to a growing number of young professionals.

South of 86th Street lies the genuine Upper East Side, where you'll find many of New York's best co-ops and condos along Park Avenue, Fifth Avenue, and East End Avenue. These are some of the most expensive properties not only in New York, but in the world. The Upper East Side is very safe and is therefore perfect for families. It has interesting shops and boutiques, many of the best private and public schools, easy access to Central Park, and most of New York's major museums. Some people say the Upper East Side is too predictable or too staid, but residents value it for just that reason.

Still, despite the Upper East Side's reputation as a wealthy area (the East 60s and 70s are, statistically speaking, one of the two or three wealthiest communities in America), I and many others like me (writers, younger people starting out in their careers, and even some artists) live here, and I assure you we're not rich. As with all neighborhoods, there are housing bargains to be had on the Upper East Side—and in fact they're easier to find here than in many other areas, because this neighborhood has yet to become as popular as the Upper West Side or Downtown.

Finally, as a matter of political organization (if not cultural similarity), the unusual area of Roosevelt Island is technically part of this district. An island in the middle of the East River, Roosevelt Island holds a series of middle-class apartment complexes, some of which provide excellent views of Manhattan. Roosevelt Island feels like its own city, and is unlike anything in Manhattan or the boroughs. There is little automobile traffic, and everything (including the shops) is centrally planned. The famous Roosevelt Island Tramway (a cable car running from Manhattan to Roosevelt Island) is still in use, although the construction of a subway station on the island has made it largely outdated. The only bridge connection from the island to the mainland is to Queens—there is no bridge to Manhattan from Roosevelt Island.

NEIGHBORHOOD STATISTICAL PROFILE

Population		217,063
	White	(85.0%)
	Black	(2.7%)
	Asian	(6.2%)
	Hispanic	(5.8%)
	Other	(0.3%)
Median Monthly Rent (government statistics)		$1,600
Median Price/Unit in a condominium (government statistics)		$783,000
Median Household Income		$74,700
Percent of Rental Units that Are Rent-Regulated		58.4%
Homeownership Rate		34.9%
Age of Householder:		
	15 to 24 years	4.7%
	25 to 44 years	47.1%
	45 to 64 years	30.3%
	65 years and over	17.9%

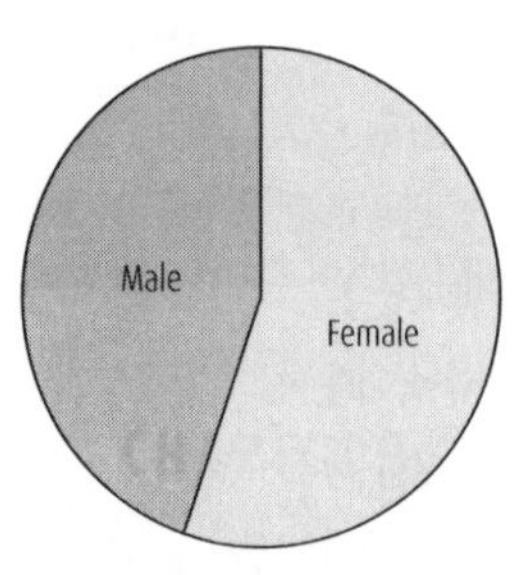

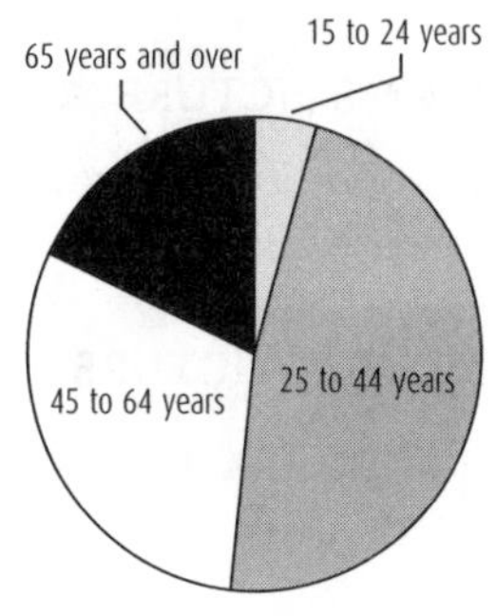

PURCHASE AND RENTAL STATISTICS FROM BROKERS

Buying

Average price per square foot	$1,349
Studio	$809,400
1 bedroom	$1,079,200
2 bedroom	$1,349,000
3 bedroom	$1,618,800
4+ bedroom	$2,023,500

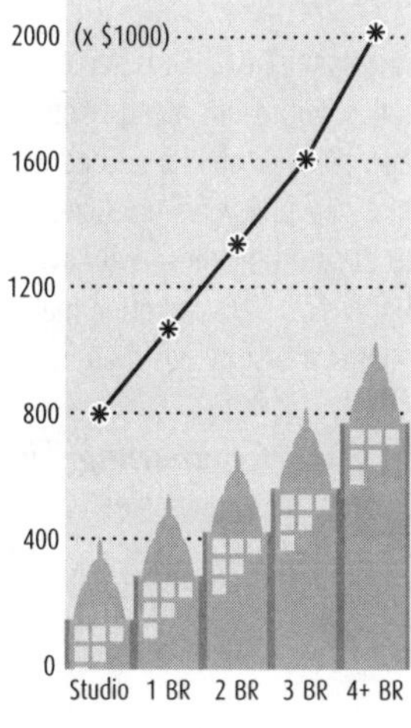

✱ UPPER EAST SIDE

 NYC AVERAGE

Renting

Average monthly rent per square foot	$4.50
Studio	$2,250
1 bedroom	$3,150
2 bedroom	$4,050

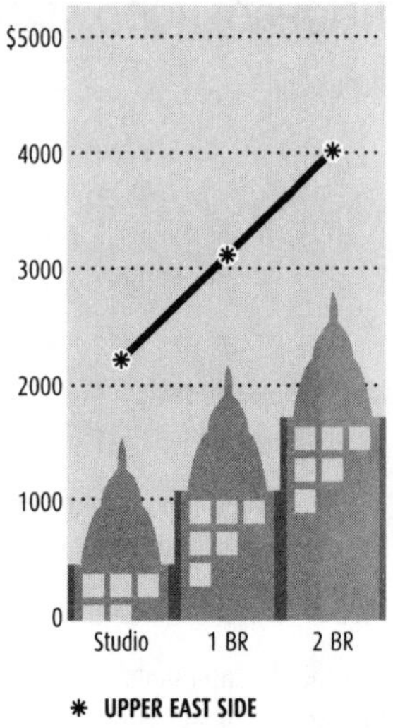

CRIME PICTURE

This is considered an extremely safe area.

INCOME PICTURE

This is one of the most affluent neighborhoods in the world.

SUBWAYS

The Upper East Side is served by the 4, 5, and 6 trains, with stops along Lexington Avenue. There are also plans to build a Second Avenue subway line, but that's several years off. Given the distance of the walk to the subway, those who live all the way east on the Upper East Side can often make better time to Midtown East by bus than by subway.

Commuting Times

Midtown East	10–20 minutes
Midtown West	25–35 minutes
Wall Street	30–40 minutes

NOTEWORTHY **IN THE NEIGHBORHOOD**

Madison Avenue shopping district (Barneys, Polo, numerous high-end baby-clothing boutiques, and high-end designer boutiques running the length of the entire neighborhood)

Central Park (Conservatory Garden, Reservoir, Zoo)

Museum Mile (Metropolitan Museum of Art, Guggenheim Museum, Cooper-Hewitt National Design Museum, Jewish Museum, and others)

Gracie Mansion (mayor's residence)

Numerous distinguished private clubs (Harmonie Club, Metropolitan Club, Lotos Club)

Temple Emanu-El (largest—bigger than St. Patrick's Cathedral—and oldest Reform Jewish congregation), 1 East 65th Street (Fifth Avenue)

Asia Society (art collection assembled by John D. Rockefeller), 725 Park Avenue (70th Street)

Frank E. Campbell Funeral Chapel (most prestigious in world; boasts James Cagney, John Lennon, Mae West, and Tennessee Williams as previous "clients"), 1076 Madison Avenue (81st Street)

NOTEWORTHY **IN THE NEIGHBORHOOD**

92nd Street Y (major Jewish cultural and community center), 1395 Lexington Avenue (92nd Street)

Synod of Bishops of the Russian Orthodox Church Outside Russia (dramatic 1917 Georgian mansion, now a cathedral), 75 East 93rd Street (Park and Madison Avenues)

Islamic Center of New York (New York's first major mosque, designed by Skidmore, Owings & Merrill), 1711 Third Avenue (96th Street)

UPPER WEST SIDE

If you stood at the corner of 68th Street and Columbus Avenue (near where my husband grew up) in 1970 and then traveled via time machine to the same corner in the year 2010, you'd assume your time machine had taken you to the wrong place. What was basically a slum in 1970 is now the site of one of New York's most luxurious apartment buildings (which also houses the exclusive Reebok Club and a Sony IMAX theater). The transformation of the Upper West Side, triggered by the construction of Lincoln Center in the 1960s and bolstered by frantic luxury high-rise construction in the 1980s and '90s, has made this neighborhood one of the world's great urban reclamation stories.

The Lincoln Square area (the complex of high-rise buildings surrounding Lincoln Center) is the southernmost part of the Upper West Side, and has most of the newest buildings. The more traditional residential area, from the high 60s to the 90s, has some new construction along the avenues but also many glorious old buildings along Central Park West (most notably the Dakota, where Yoko Ono lives and in front of which John Lennon was shot) and Riverside Drive (with great views of the river and proximity to Riverside Park), with many attractive brownstones in the middle. Also of interest here is the gigantic Lincoln Towers apartment complex in the West 60s and 70s, which offers some of the more reasonably priced apartments for sale in the area (though all is relative—the Upper West Side is one of the most expensive neighborhoods in Manhattan). The northernmost part of the neighborhood, according to the City's designation, ends at 110th Street (called Central Park North where it borders on Central Park), but in reality City residents think of the Upper West Side as the area running right up to and around Columbia University (which is at 116th Street). Until not long ago, the blocks between 96th and just shy of Columbia were somewhat of a "no-man's-land" and great bargains were still to be found. Things have improved in recent years and the bargains, along with many City residents, are now moving northward.

The traditional residents of the Upper West Side are quite diverse, ranging from professors at Columbia University and Fordham Law School to wealthy residents on Central Park West, a smattering of current and former students, and an eclectic group of older tenants left over from the days when the neighborhood was inexpensive and not entirely safe. Today, good private schools, access to Central Park and Riverside Park, a wealth of restaurants and shops, and proximity to cultural attractions make the Upper West Side the choice of many young professionals. The neighborhood is also home to many young Modern Orthodox Jews who come to live near the Lincoln Square Synagogue, the relatively new Jewish Community Center (new by NYC standards—it opened in 2002, as compared with the 92nd Street Y on the Upper East Side, which was founded in 1874) and an abundance of kosher restaurants in the 70s, 80s, and 90s, and, of course, the presence of many other members of their faith. There has always been a strong Jewish influence in this neighborhood (New York's oldest congregation is here), and the phrase "Upper West Side intellectual" was traditionally code for "Jewish intellectual." Indeed, it is often said that the major difference between the Upper West Side and the Upper East Side is that the Upper West is more Jewish and the Upper East is more WASP-y. But in reality, there are plenty of representatives of each group on either side of the park.

If there is a downside to the dramatic improvement of the Upper West Side, it is that the neighborhood is crowded. Parking is next to impossible (really!) and restaurants are always packed. Old-timers in the neighborhood bemoan the loss of space and light, but few would go back to the way things were.

NEIGHBORHOOD STATISTICAL PROFILE

Population		207,699
	White	(73.8%)
	Black	(9.0%)
	Asian	(7.5%)
	Hispanic	(8.9%)
	Other	(0.8%)
Median Monthly Rent (government statistics)		$1,200
Median Price/Unit in a condominium (government statistics)		$844,000
Median Household Income		$70,000
Percent of Rental Units that Are Rent-Regulated		68.7%
Homeownership Rate		32.0%
Age of Householder:		
	15 to 24 years	3.5%
	25 to 44 years	46.1%
	45 to 64 years	32.4%
	65 years and over	18.0%

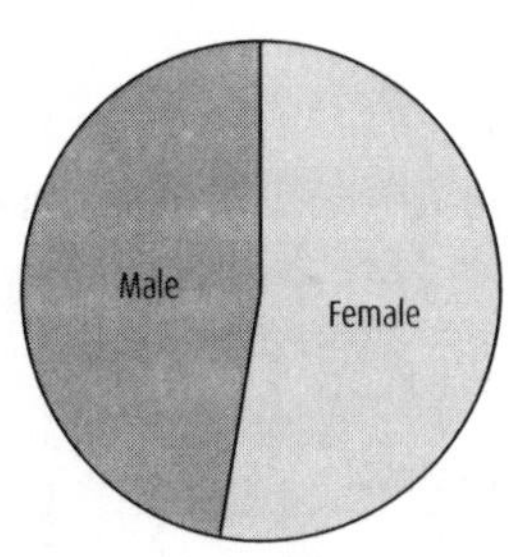

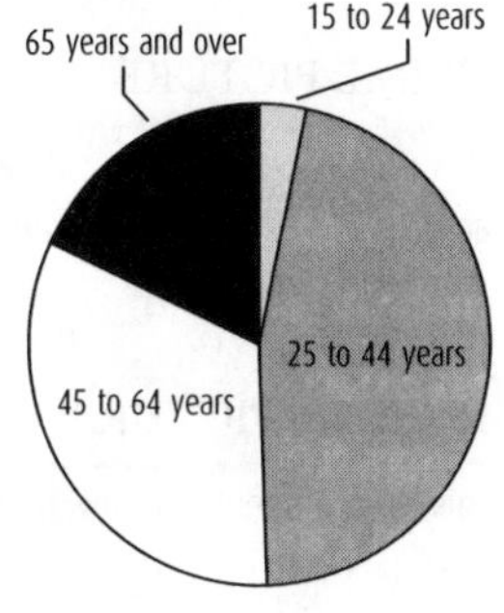

PURCHASE AND RENTAL STATISTICS FROM BROKERS

Buying

Average price per square foot	$992
Studio	$595,200
1 bedroom	$793,600
2 bedroom	$992,000
3 bedroom	$1,190,400
4+ bedroom	$1,488,000

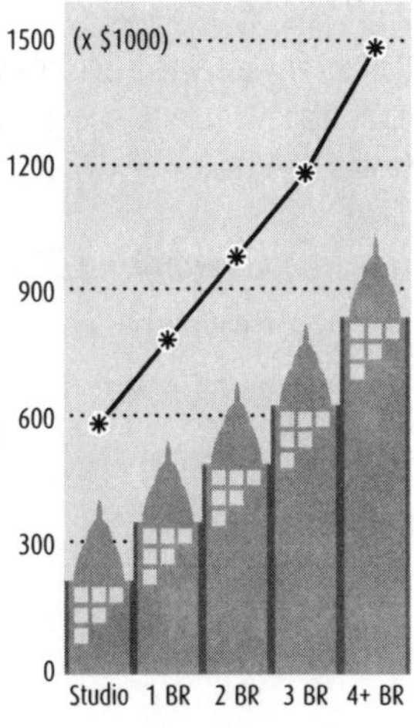

Renting

Average monthly rent per square foot	$4.75
Studio	$2,375
1 bedroom	$3,325
2 bedroom	$4,275

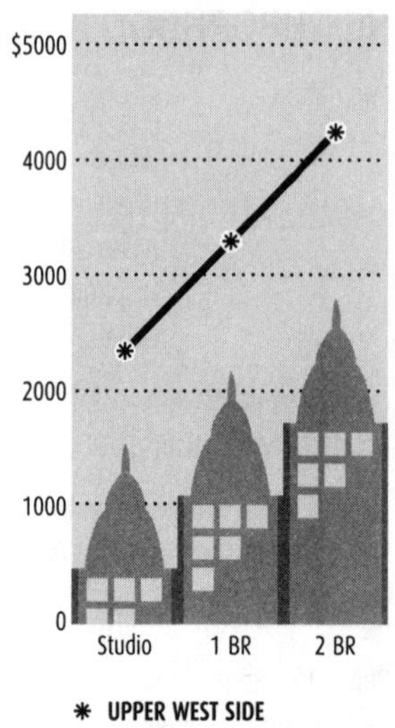

CRIME PICTURE

This is considered a very safe area, although the north and south ends of the area are still developing.

INCOME PICTURE

This is an affluent and upwardly mobile neighborhood.

SUBWAYS

The Upper West Side is served by the 1, 2, and 3 trains along Broadway, and the B and C trains on Central Park West.

Commuting Times

Midtown East	25–35 minutes
Midtown West	10–20 minutes
Wall Street	35–45 minutes

NOTEWORTHY **IN THE NEIGHBORHOOD**

Central Park (Reservoir, The Lake, Strawberry Fields, Sheep Meadow, Tavern on the Green)

Lincoln Center (New York's major center of the performing arts, including the Metropolitan Opera House, Avery Fisher Hall, and New York State Theater), West 62nd through West 66th Streets, between Columbus and Amsterdam Avenues

Christ and St. Stephen's Church (uncharacteristically rural church in the middle of a developed city block), 120 West 69th Street (Columbus Avenue and Broadway)

Lincoln Square Synagogue (1970 Hausman & Rosenberg building, now a leader of the Modern Orthodox movement), 200 Amsterdam Avenue (69th Street)

Beacon Theater (gorgeous old 2,700-seat theater used for a variety of performances), 2124 Broadway (75th Street)

New-York Historical Society (spelled with a hyphen, it's one of the best American collections around), 170 Central Park West (76th and 77th Streets)

American Museum of Natural History (the premier natural-history museum and research institute, now with a dramatic new planetarium), Central Park West at 79th Street

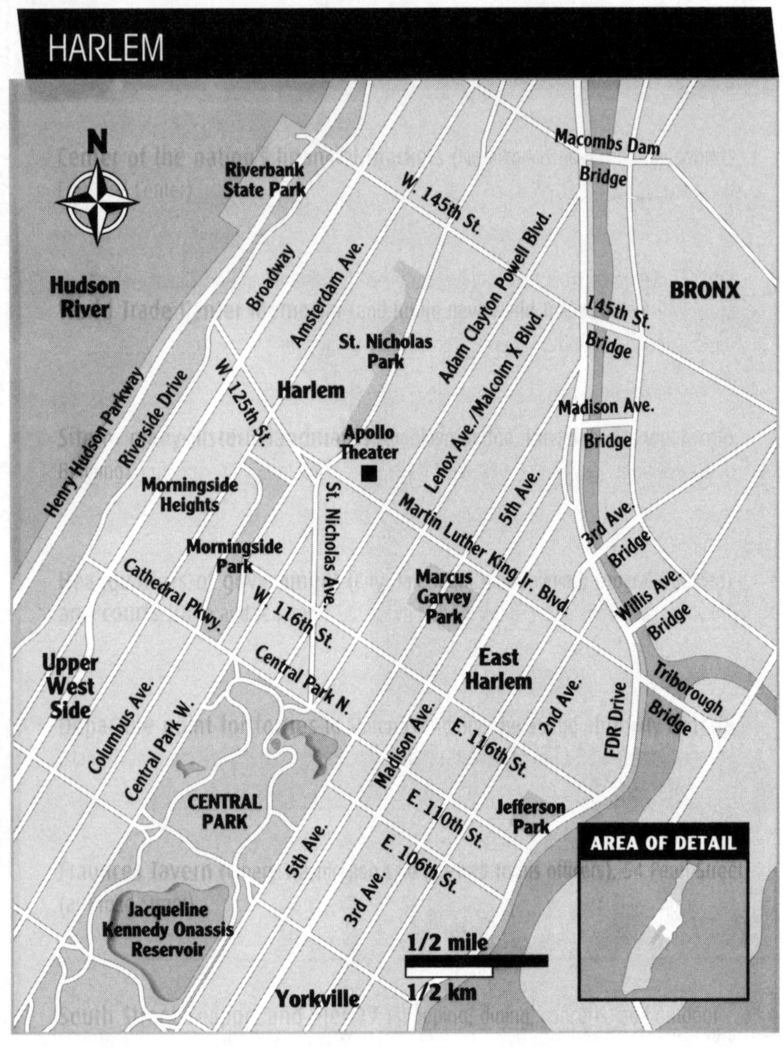
HARLEM
N
Hudson River
Riverbank State Park
Broadway
Amsterdam Ave.
W. 145th St.
Adam Clayton Powell Blvd.
Macombs Dam Bridge
145th St. Bridge
BRONX
St. Nicholas Park
Harlem
Lenox Ave./Malcolm X Blvd.
Madison Ave. Bridge
Henry Hudson Parkway
Riverside Drive
W. 125th St.
Apollo Theater
Morningside Heights
St. Nicholas Ave.
5th Ave.
Martin Luther King Jr. Blvd.
3rd Ave. Bridge
Morningside Park
Cathedral Pkwy.
W. 116th St.
Marcus Garvey Park
Willis Ave. Bridge
Upper West Side
Central Park N.
East Harlem
Triborough Bridge
Columbus Ave.
Central Park W.
Madison Ave.
E. 116th St.
2nd Ave.
FDR Drive
CENTRAL PARK
E. 110th St.
Jefferson Park
5th Ave.
E. 106th St.
3rd Ave.
AREA OF DETAIL
Jacqueline Kennedy Onassis Reservoir
1/2 mile
1/2 km
Yorkville

MORNINGSIDE HEIGHTS, HAMILTON HEIGHTS AND SUGAR HILL (WEST HARLEM)

Morningside Heights is a neighborhood bustling with college students (Columbia and Barnard contribute greatly to the makeup of the population), families, professors, and pretty much anyone else who was looking to get a little more space for their money. Unfortunately, prices here have gotten pretty steep in the last few years too, so the bargain hunters have moved farther north still, to Hamilton Heights.

Even so, there are apartments to be had here, and some areas (east of Broadway, for example) are likely to be more affordable than others. Prices in Morningside Heights are surely less daunting than south of 96th Street, and the neighborhood has a wonderful, vibrant feel. Every mother of infant- and toddler-aged children I meet, it seems, lives in or near Morningside Heights. But, singles, don't be deterred—between the college crowd, the graduate students, and the holdovers ten years past graduation, this neighborhood is welcoming to all.

Just north of Morningside Heights (in what is also known as West Harlem) is Hamilton Heights (and within this neighborhood is Sugar Hill). If you want to be on the West Side, this is currently the place to get the best value for your hard-earned dollars. Realtors mark the gentrification by the number of Starbucks in the neighborhood and thankfully for some (for more reasons than

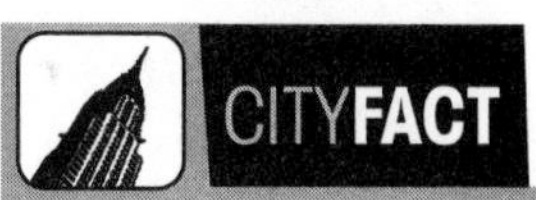

Central Park was designed by Frederick Law Olmsted and Calvert Vaux in 1858. The entire 843-acre park was carefully landscaped; very few of the original topographic features remain. Five million trees were planted and ten million cartloads of dirt and rocks were moved by thousands of workers. The park took twenty years to complete.

coffee), there is more than one—but they have not yet assumed complete neighborhood domination.

This neighborhood is full of history, and Sugar Hill (named for the "sweet life" that affluent African Americans enjoyed in the neighborhood during the 1920s and 1930s) is of particular interest to African Americans. Many historically important and famous African Americans passed through the doors of some of these buildings (most notably, Thurgood Marshall, Count Basie, and W.E.B. DuBois, who all lived on Edgecombe Avenue) and the designation by the Landmarks Preservation Commission to preserve the architecture here shows promise for the neighborhood's complete revitalization.

NEIGHBORHOOD STATISTICAL PROFILE

Population		111,724
	White	(32.8%)
	Black	(30.8%)
	Asian	(7.5%)
	Hispanic	(28.9%)
Median Monthly Rent (government statistics)		$884
Median Price/Unit in a multiple dwelling (government statistics)		$125,611
Median Household Income		$32,918
Percent of Rental Units that Are Rent-Regulated		64.9%
Homeownership Rate		12.5%
Age of Householder:		
	15 to 24 years	5.4%
	25 to 44 years	43.8%
	45 to 64 years	31.4%
	65 years and over	19.4%

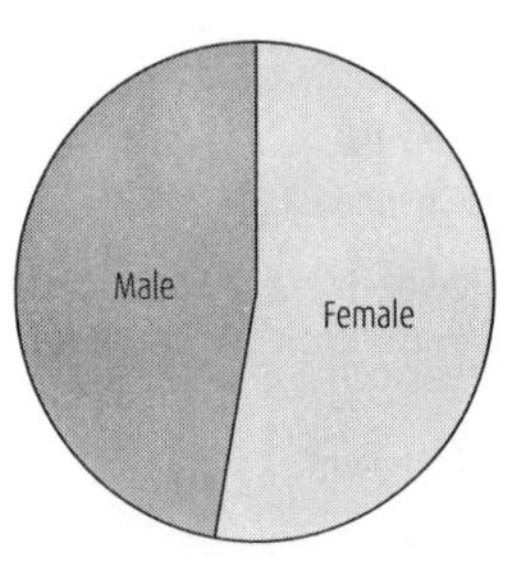

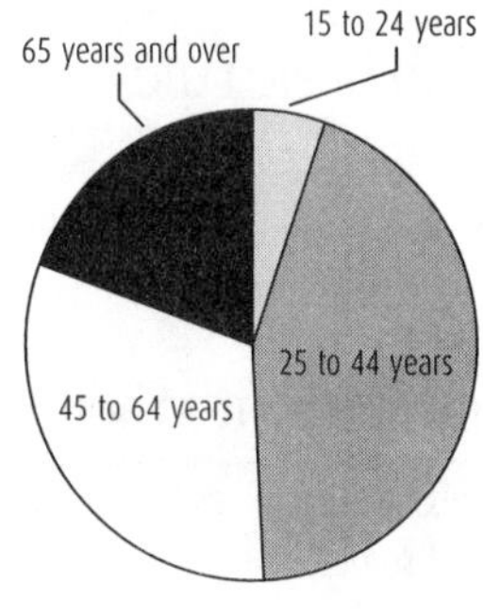

PURCHASE AND RENTAL STATISTICS FROM BROKERS

Buying

Average price per square foot	$369
Studio	$221,400
1 bedroom	$295,200
2 bedroom	$369,000
3 bedroom	$442,800
4+ bedroom	$553,500

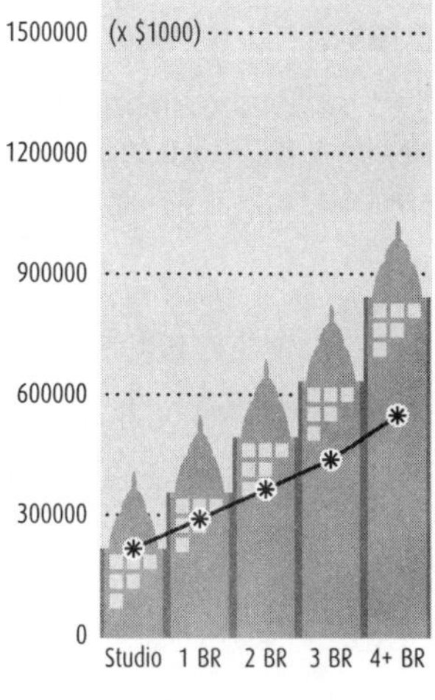

Renting

Average monthly rent per square foot	$2.50
Studio	$1,250
1 bedroom	$1,750
2 bedroom	$2,250

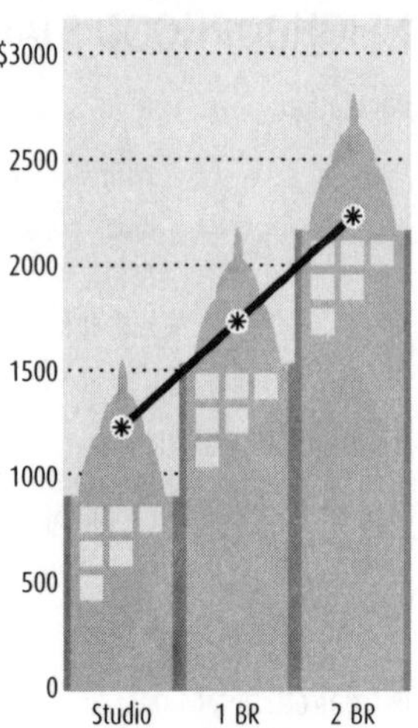

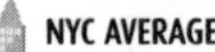

CRIME PICTURE

This is considered a still-improving area, with good overall safety and some still-rough sections.

INCOME PICTURE

This area combines working-class, upwardly mobile, and some affluent residents.

SUBWAYS

The 1 train stops locally along Broadway, and there are also A, B, C, and D train stops on St. Nicholas Avenue.

Commuting Times

Midtown East	30–40 minutes
Midtown West	15–25 minutes
Wall Street	40–50 minutes

NOTEWORTHY **IN THE NEIGHBORHOOD**

Columbia University, 2960 Broadway (main entrance at 116th and Broadway)

Barnard College, 3009 Broadway (main gate is at 117th Street)

The Cathedral Church of St. John the Divine (the world's largest Gothic cathedral, hosting artistic events and religious services), 1047 Amsterdam Ave. (at 112th Street)

Fairway Market, 2328 12th Avenue (at 132nd Street)

Jewish Theological Seminary (JTS), 3080 Broadway (at 122nd Street)

Grant's Tomb, 701 West 122nd Street

CENTRAL HARLEM

When people say "Harlem," they're usually talking about Central Harlem. While, in recent history, Harlem was a neighborhood to be avoided, it has undergone such a remarkable transformation over the last decade or more that former President Clinton has chosen to have his office smack dab in the middle of it, and tour buses now crowd the busy streets and avenues.

Harlem is one of the most interesting neighborhoods in Manhattan and its history is rich with famous African American musicians (Ella Fitzgerald, Billie Holiday, Stevie Wonder, Marvin Gaye, and James Brown—who, after his death in 2007, was laid out at none other than the Apollo Theater for several days), writers (Langston Hughes and Maya Angelou), and political citizens (Malcolm X and Martin Luther King Jr.) who have passed through the many majestic brownstones that line the side streets.

Things are a bit different now from the days of the original Harlem Renaissance, but Central Harlem is undergoing its own kind of a new renaissance now and, based upon the cost of real estate along 125th Street (among the most expensive commercial real estate in the City), it's all good. But unless you're planning to open up a store on 125th, don't be scared away by the cost of real estate here. There are still apartments that are of good value both for renters and buyers, and the neighborhood has a lot to offer.

NEIGHBORHOOD STATISTICAL PROFILE

Population		107,109
	White	(13.2%)
	Black	(75.1%)
	Asian	(0.4%)
	Hispanic	(10.3%)
	Other	(0.9%)
Median Monthly Rent (government statistics)		$600
Median Price/Unit in a multiple dwelling (government statistics)		$91,138
Median Household Income		$26,000
Percent of Rental Units that Are Rent-Regulated		70.0%
Homeownership Rate		13.8%
Age of Householder:		
	15 to 24 years	4.1%
	25 to 44 years	43.0%
	45 to 64 years	31.6%
	65 years and over	21.3%

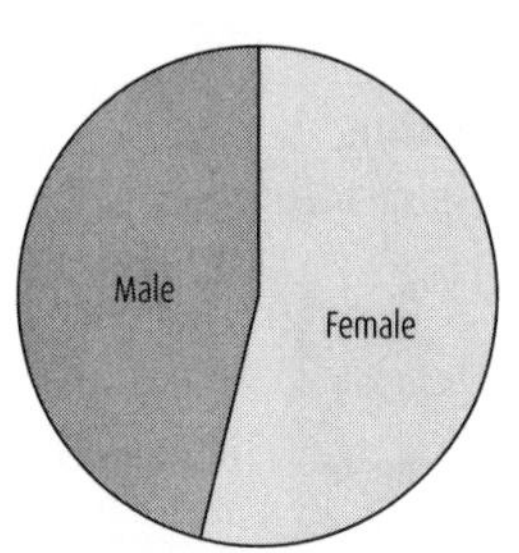

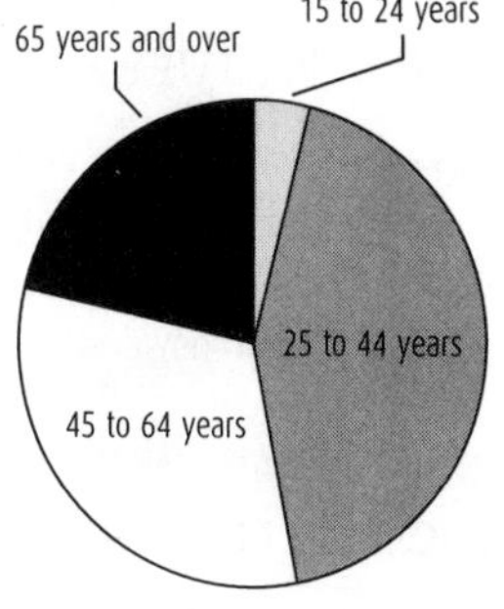

PURCHASE AND RENTAL STATISTICS FROM BROKERS

Buying

Average price per square foot	$377
Studio	$226,200
1 bedroom	$301,600
2 bedroom	$377,000
3 bedroom	$452,400
4+ bedroom	$565,500

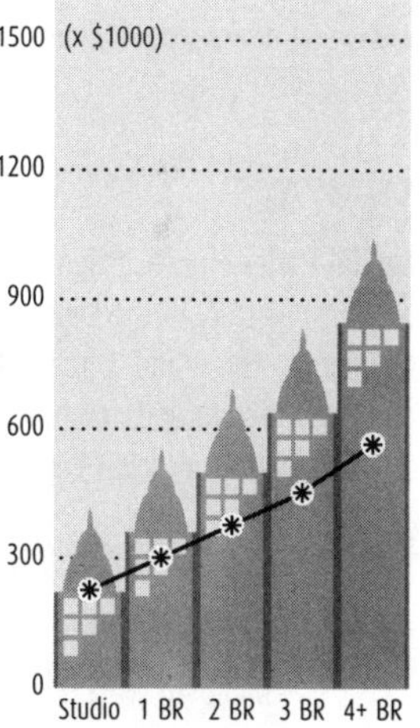

Renting

Average monthly rent per square foot	$2.58
Studio	$1,290
1 bedroom	$1,806
2 bedroom	$2,322

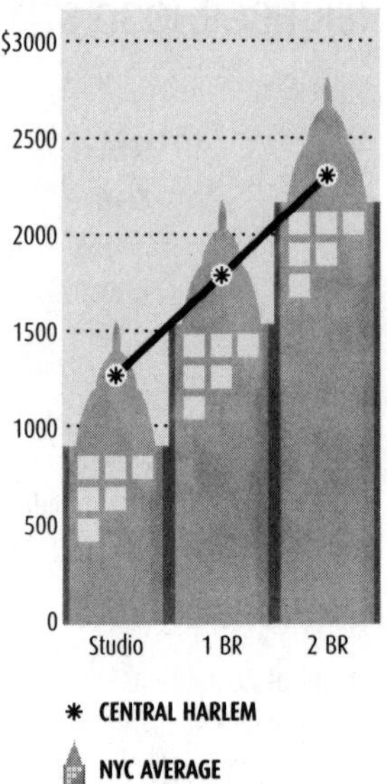

CRIME PICTURE

This area is considered to be rapidly improving, and has witnessed a dramatic drop in crime over the past decade. There are still side streets that should be avoided at night, however.

INCOME PICTURE

This is a working-class neighborhood, though it is also now attracting upwardly mobile residents, especially to several new luxury buildings.

SUBWAYS

Central Harlem has excellent transportation connections to both the East and West Sides of Manhattan. The 2 and 3 trains stop on Lenox Avenue and head over to and down the West Side, and the 4, 5, and 6 trains run down Lexington Avenue.

Commuting Times

Midtown East	20–30 minutes
Midtown West	15–25 minutes
Wall Street	40–50 minutes

NOTEWORTHY **IN THE NEIGHBORHOOD**

The Apollo Theater, 253 West 125th Street

The Studio Museum in Harlem (a museum specializing in African American artists and artists of African descent), 144 West 125th Street

Schomburg Center for Research in Black Culture, 515 Malcolm X Boulevard

Minton's Playhouse (closed since the 1970s, this famed Harlem jazz club that featured musical giants such as Duke Ellington and Count Basie recently reopened its doors) 206–210 West 118th Street (between Seventh Avenue and St. Nicholas Avenue)

Sylvia's Restaurant of Harlem (established in 1962), 328 Lenox Avenue

EAST HARLEM

I have been watching East Harlem change and evolve for the past decade or more, and have been continuously impressed and delighted. Here, as with Central Harlem, the change has been slow and steady, but over time the difference is dramatic.

Housing values can still be had here, and the neighborhood showcases what New York City evolution is all about. Longtime East Harlem residents live alongside transplants from other parts of the city and new high-rises (six- and eight-story buildings that are pleasantly small in comparison with other parts of the City) are populated with a mixture of old-timers and newcomers alike. The beauty of East Harlem is that it is a melting pot. Central Harlem has a large population of African Americans, whereas East Harlem has traditionally been dominated by a more Latino population (hence its nickname, "El Barrio"). You are far more likely to hear Spanish spoken on the street here than English—but mixed in are people of all other ethnicities, making for a real New York story.

There are a number of streets with major commerce, and they mostly correspond to the main east to west crosstown transverses—106th Street (this is an exception to the transverse rule, because it is blocked by Central Park), 116th Street, and 125th Street. There are numerous options for shoppers, churchgoers, and entertainment-seekers throughout the neighborhood. There is a large Pathmark grocery store on 125th Street (at Lexington Avenue) as well as other big stores, with the promise of more to come. And in addition to being at one of the greatest transportation hubs in Manhattan (the 4, 5, and 6 trains stop at 125th and Lexington Avenue; the 2 train stops at 125th and Lenox; Metro North has a station at Park Avenue and 125th; and a huge selection of buses runs on the avenues), you're close to Patsy's, what many would argue is New York City's best pizza parlor. There are also long-term plans to build a Second Avenue subway. It may take a decade or more for it to reach up into this neighborhood, but those who live along the route may find their property values skyrocketing once a subway line comes to the far eastern part of the neighborhood.

NEIGHBORHOOD STATISTICAL PROFILE

Population		117,743
	White	(17.7%)
	Black	(38.8%)
	Asian	(2.3%)
	Hispanic	(41.3%)
Median Monthly Rent (government statistics)		$900
Median Price/Unit in a multiple dwelling (government statistics)		$126,563
Median Household Income		$23,000
Percent of Rental Units that Are Rent-Regulated		34.3%
Homeownership Rate		8.6%
Age of Householder:		
	15 to 24 years	4.4%
	25 to 44 years	40.7%
	45 to 64 years	32.8%
	65 years and over	22.1%

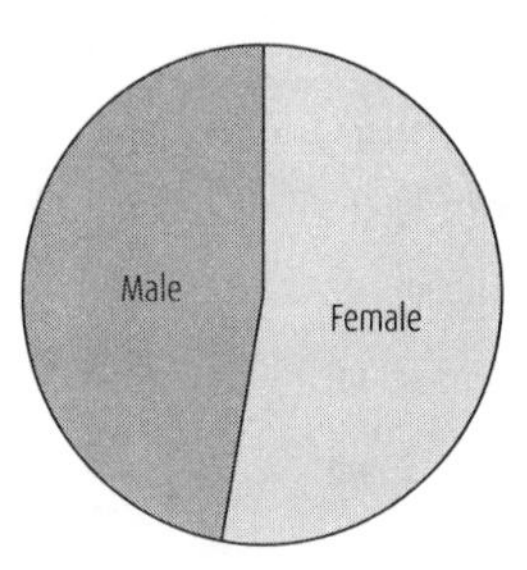

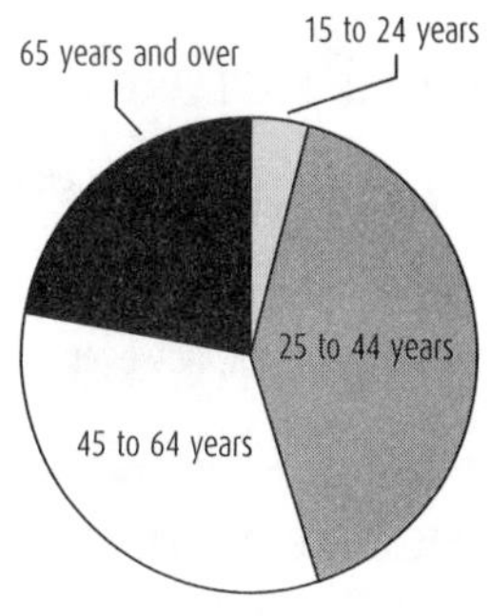

PURCHASE AND RENTAL STATISTICS FROM BROKERS

Buying

Average price per square foot	$423
Studio	$253,800
1 bedroom	$338,400
2 bedroom	$423,000
3 bedroom	$507,600
4+ bedroom	$634,500

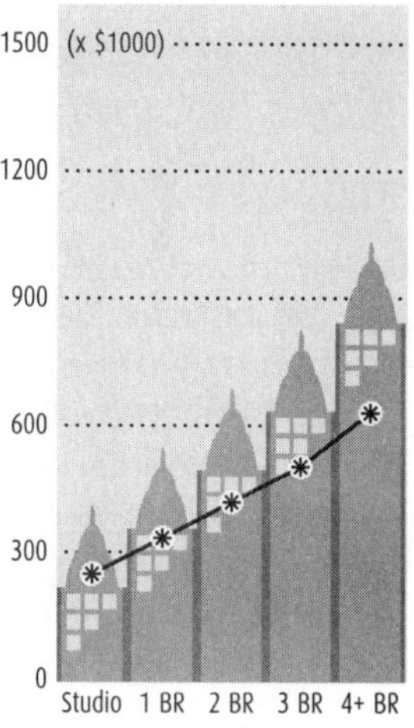

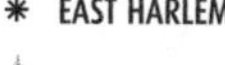

Renting

Average monthly rent per square foot	$2.65
Studio	$1,325
1 bedroom	$1,855
2 bedroom	$2,385

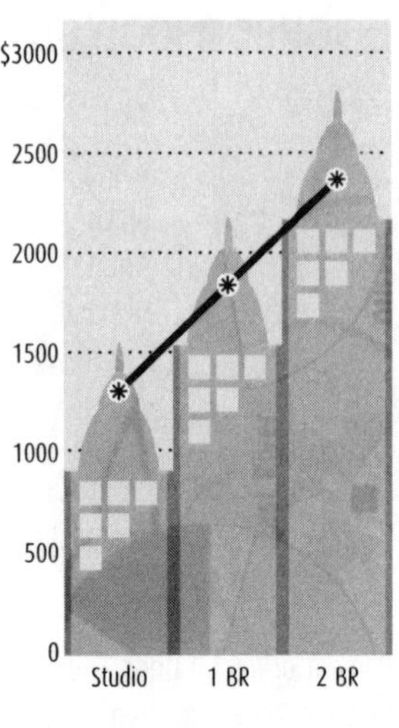

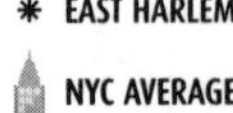

CRIME PICTURE

This area is considered to be rapidly improving, and has witnessed a dramatic drop in crime over the past decade. There are still side streets that should be avoided at night, however.

INCOME PICTURE

This is a working-class neighborhood, though it is also now attracting upwardly mobile residents, especially to several new luxury buildings.

SUBWAYS

East Harlem is served by the 4, 5, and 6 trains, with stops along Lexington Avenue. There are also plans to build a Second Avenue subway line, but that's several years off. Given the distance of the walk to the subway, those who live all the way east in East Harlem can often make better time to Midtown East by bus than by subway.

Commuting Times

Midtown East	15–20 minutes
Midtown West	20–25 minutes
Wall Street	40–50 minutes

NOTEWORTHY **IN THE NEIGHBORHOOD**

Marcus Garvey Park (from 120th to 124th Streets and from Madison Avenue to Mount Morris Park West) and **Pelham Fritz Recreation Center** (with a children's playroom, performance spaces, weight-lifting room, game room, computer center, and reading room)

El Museo del Barrio, 1230 Fifth Avenue (at 104th Street)

Patsy's Pizza, since 1932—this is the original! 2287 First Avenue (between 117th and 118th Streets)

The National Museum of Catholic Art and History, 443 East 115th Street

Museum of the City of New York, 1220 Fifth Avenue (at 103rd Street)

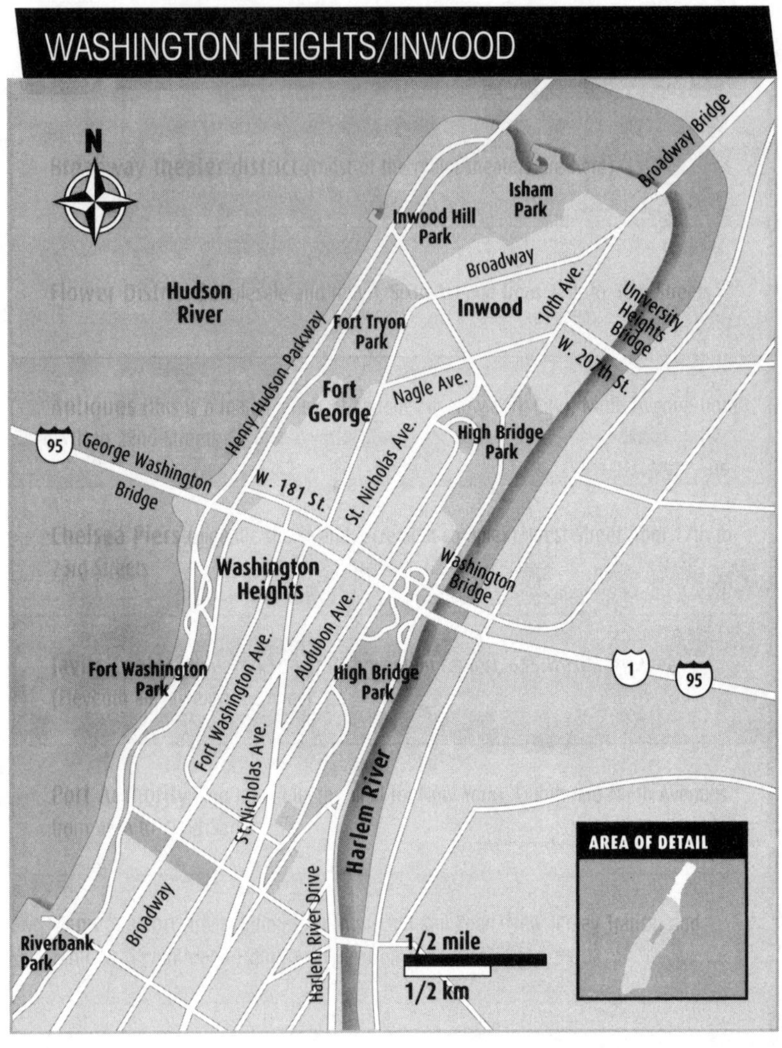
WASHINGTON HEIGHTS/INWOOD
N
Isham Park
Broadway Bridge
Inwood Hill Park
Broadway
Hudson River
Inwood
10th Ave.
University Heights Bridge
Fort Tryon Park
Henry Hudson Parkway
W. 207th St.
Fort George
Nagle Ave.
St. Nicholas Ave.
High Bridge Park
95
George Washington Bridge
W. 181 St.
Washington Heights
Washington Bridge
Audubon Ave.
Fort Washington Ave.
Fort Washington Park
High Bridge Park
1
95
St.Nicholas Ave.
Harlem River
Harlem River Drive
AREA OF DETAIL
Broadway
Riverbank Park
1/2 mile
1/2 km

WASHINGTON HEIGHTS AND INWOOD

At the northern tip of Manhattan, on the island's highest ground, are two peaceful, mostly working-class neighborhoods that offer some very attractive housing values for those interested in getting out of the hustle and bustle and moving north. Many people outside of the City don't imagine there's anything north of Harlem, but there you will find the rising neighborhoods of Washington Heights and Inwood.

For one, they are visually stunning, with the George Washington Bridge and the major Manhattan waterways framing the area. Housing is good, with a few new buildings and many buildings newly renovated. These areas are ideal bastions for artists, musicians, and actors—as well as professionals—who want to escape the City's urban core and save money, but don't actually want to go suburban.

Inwood is traditionally considered safer and more desirable than Washington Heights, but each is a collection of better and worse areas. These neighborhoods only stand to improve, and with good transportation (express A train, the 1 and 9 trains, and express buses to lower Manhattan), many young people and families are opting for these neighborhoods over the boroughs.

NEIGHBORHOOD STATISTICAL PROFILE

Population		208,414
	White	(22.2%)
	Black	(10.1%)
	Asian	(3.5%)
	Hispanic	(63.9%)
	Other	(0.3%)
Median Monthly Rent (government statistics)		$763
Median Price/Unit in a multiple dwelling (government statistics)		$84,357
Median Household Income		$30,000
Percent of Rental Units that Are Rent-Regulated		89%
Homeownership Rate		9.5%
Age of Householder:		
	15 to 24 years	4.5%
	25 to 44 years	43.0%
	45 to 64 years	34.0%
	65 years and over	18.5%

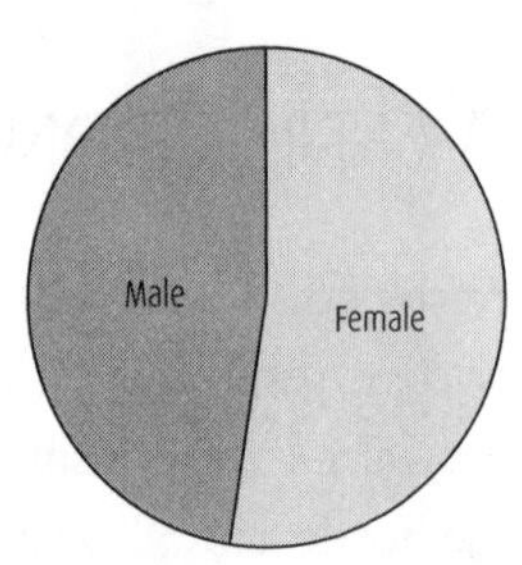

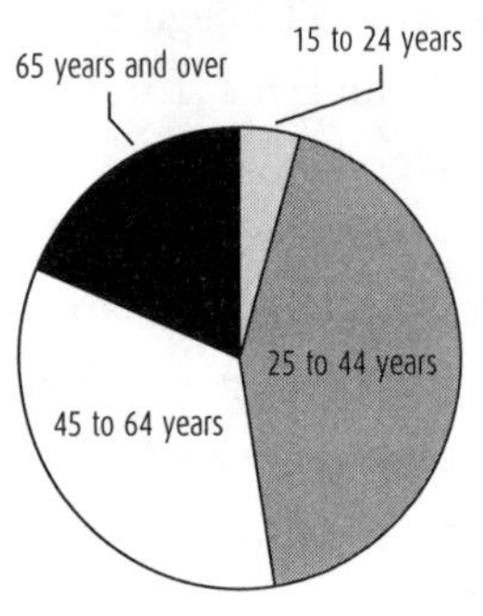

PURCHASE AND RENTAL STATISTICS FROM BROKERS

Buying

Average price per square foot	$370
Studio	$222,000
1 bedroom	$296,000
2 bedroom	$370,000
3 bedroom	$444,000
4+ bedroom	$555,000

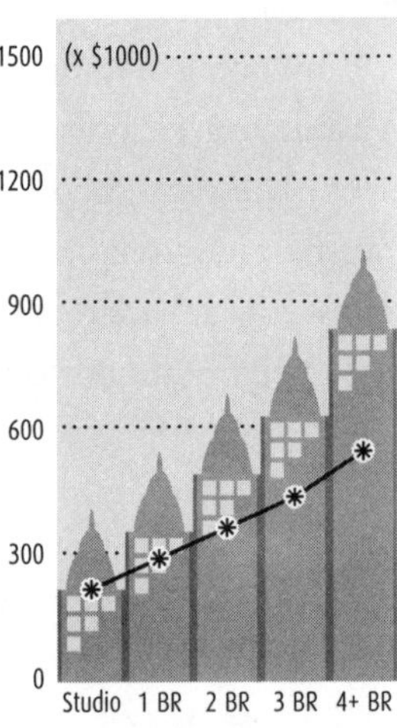

Renting

Average monthly rent per square foot	$2.00
Studio	$1,000
1 bedroom	$1,400
2 bedroom	$1,800

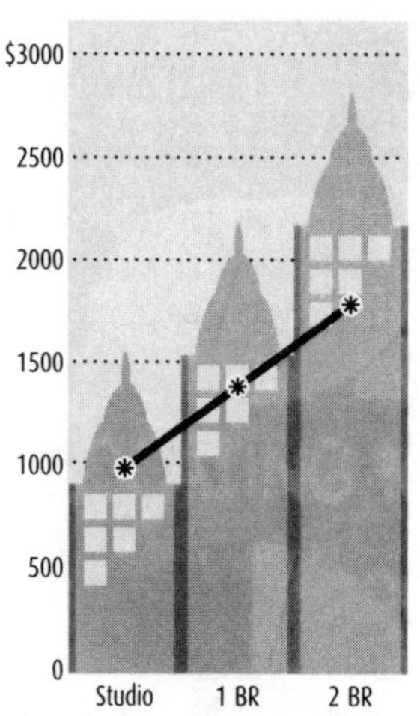

CRIME PICTURE

This is a mixed area but there are some very safe sections; you have to choose your block and building carefully.

INCOME PICTURE

This is a working-class area.

SUBWAYS

The 1, A, and C trains serve this area; however, only the A express train is speedy. Residents of Washington Heights and Inwood also make heavy use of express buses to Midtown.

Commuting Times

Midtown East	40–50 minutes
Midtown West	35–45 minutes
Wall Street	50–60 minutes

NOTEWORTHY **IN THE NEIGHBORHOOD**

Fort Tryon Park (includes the Cloisters, which houses the medieval collection of the Metropolitan Museum of Art), from 192nd to Dyckman Streets and Broadway to Riverside Drive

Yeshiva University (major center of Jewish learning), 186th Street and Amsterdam Avenue

Baker Field (Columbia University's football stadium—the only one in Manhattan), 218th Street between Broadway and Seaman Avenue

George Washington Bridge (the visual focal point of the neighborhood, carrying traffic to New Jersey), at 178th Street

The Little Red Lighthouse (a lighthouse built in 1921 in Fort Washington Park), under the George Washington Bridge

Inwood Hill Park (196 acres) and adjoining **Isham Park** (20 acres)

CHAPTER THREE

OUTER BOROUGH NEIGHBORHOODS

Though most out-of-towners assume that New York City equals Manhattan, the reality is that most New Yorkers don't live in Manhattan, but in the surrounding boroughs of Brooklyn, Queens, the Bronx, and Staten Island. If you're on a budget, you may very well wind up living in these places too. That's good news, because there are a lot of advantages to the non-Manhattan boroughs: not only are they cheaper, but they tend also to be quieter and less densely populated. You may even be able to live in a house with basement storage, a washer and dryer, and your own parking space.

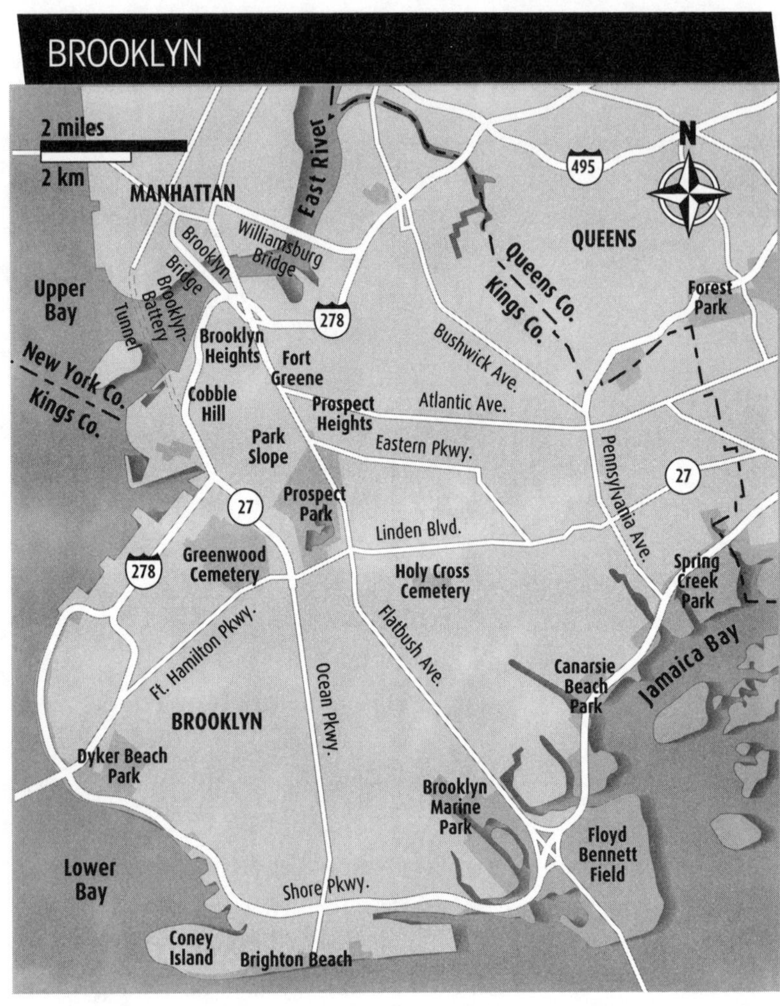
BROOKLYN
2 miles
2 km
MANHATTAN
East River
495
N
QUEENS
Williamsburg Bridge
Brooklyn Bridge
Brooklyn-Battery Tunnel
Upper Bay
278
Queens Co.
Kings Co.
Forest Park
New York Co.
Kings Co.
Brooklyn Heights
Fort Greene
Bushwick Ave.
Cobble Hill
Prospect Heights
Atlantic Ave.
Park Slope
Eastern Pkwy.
Pennsylvania Ave.
27
Prospect Park
Linden Blvd.
Greenwood Cemetery
Holy Cross Cemetery
Spring Creek Park
Flatbush Ave.
Ft. Hamilton Pkwy.
Ocean Pkwy.
Canarsie Beach Park
Jamaica Bay
BROOKLYN
Dyker Beach Park
Brooklyn Marine Park
Floyd Bennett Field
Lower Bay
Shore Pkwy.
Coney Island
Brighton Beach

BROOKLYN

If Brooklyn broke from New York and became its own city, as it once was, it would still be one of the largest in the country. It dwarfs Manhattan in terms of both population and physical space. The parts of Brooklyn that lie closest to Manhattan are very popular because of their proximity to Manhattan, the neighborly neighborhoods, and the promise of more space for the money.

BROOKLYN HEIGHTS, DOWNTOWN BROOKLYN, DUMBO, AND FORT GREENE

Brooklyn Heights, the area directly over the Brooklyn Bridge and north of Atlantic Avenue, has become so popular with Wall Street professionals that many residents don't acknowledge the Heights as part of the "real Brooklyn" anymore. And, walking around Brooklyn Heights, one would be forgiven for agreeing—it looks a lot like a residential neighborhood in Manhattan, although it's impossible to get views of the City this good from within the City itself.

The Brooklyn Heights Esplanade, a magnificent walkway above the Brooklyn-Queens Expressway, affords incomparable vistas of Downtown Manhattan, Governors Island, and the Statue of Liberty to the south, and the Manhattan Bridge, Brooklyn Bridge, the Chrysler Building, and the Empire State Building to the north. In 1965 Brooklyn Heights was declared the City's first historic district (there are now many others), and Civil War–era architecture dominates. Montague Street is the main commercial street in the Heights, and is rife with shops and restaurants (and, these days, unfortunately, traffic). When the weather is nice, Heights residents walk (or bike) to Manhattan via the Brooklyn Bridge pedestrian walkway.

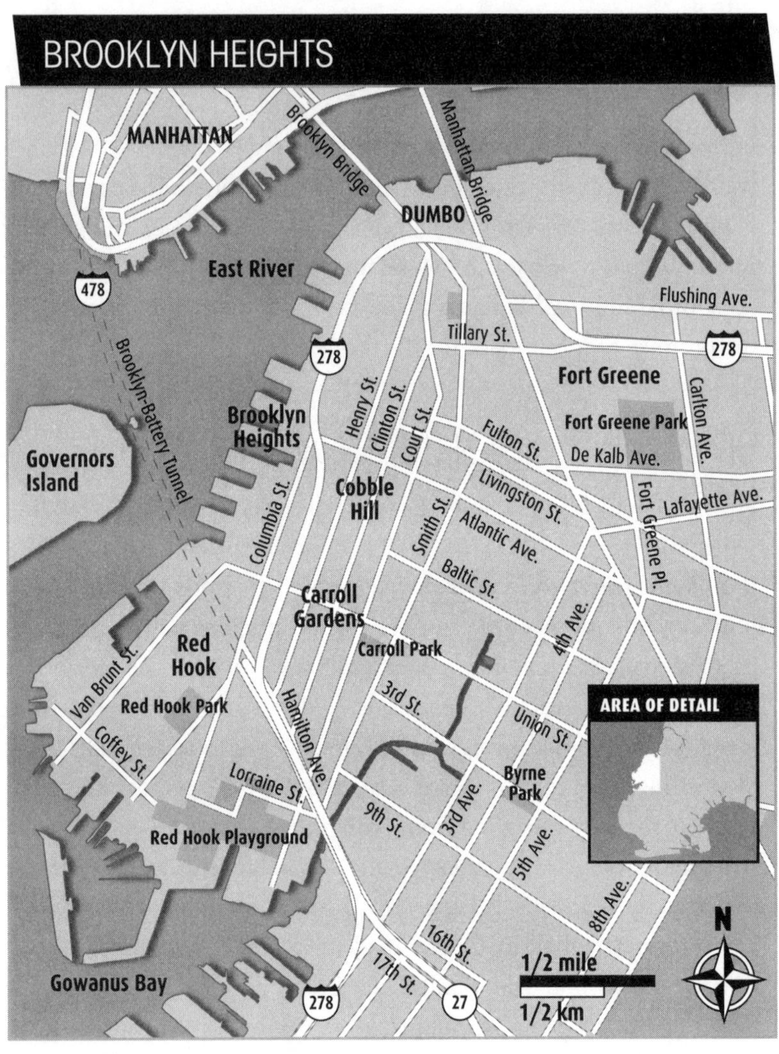

It's a quicker commute from Brooklyn Heights to Wall Street than from almost any residential neighborhood in Manhattan, but don't expect to find any housing bargains here anymore: prices are on par with many Manhattan neighborhoods.

Downtown Brooklyn (which gets its name from back when

Brooklyn was its own city, independent of Manhattan, and this was its downtown), is growing (up) by leaps and bounds. Wherever you walk, it seems, high-rise co-ops and condos are going up. In recent years, this area was more commercial than residential, but recent demand and rezoning has allowed for a building boom and that translates, according to a 2007 article in the *New York Times,* to more than 7,000 new units in the neighborhood.

People love acronyms, and New Yorkers (especially New York Realtors) are no exception to this rule. Dumbo is an acronym for Down Under the Manhattan Bridge Overpass, and is the name of a neighborhood that, like many others in New York City, has seen its fair share of change and growth in recent years. It was once a warehouse district, but Manhattan artists settled here when prices elsewhere became out of reach. Now the area is full of loft apartments and popular eateries (Grimaldi's Pizzeria, the Brooklyn Ice Cream Factory, and Jacques Torres Chocolate) abound. An added bonus: you can commute to Manhattan by ferry.

Fort Greene is what some people refer to as an "edgy" neighborhood, and it has seen its fair share of hard knocks, suffering from the economic downturn that many New York City neighborhoods felt in the 1970s and 1980s due to drugs and crime. It was in the late 1980s that many African American professionals (including Spike Lee) worked in earnest to reclaim and preserve the neighborhood. The socioeconomically diverse community there hosts an incredible blend of ethnic groups, and the neighborhood is ripe with promising housing options, plenty of cultural activities—Brooklyn Academy of Music (BAM) and the Museum of Contemporary African Diasporan Arts (MoCADA), to name two—and good public transportation.

NEIGHBORHOOD STATISTICAL PROFILE

Population		98,620
	White	(44.7%)
	Black	(37.5%)
	Asian	(6.0%)
	Hispanic	(11.8%)
Median Monthly Rent (government statistics)		$950
Median Price/Unit in a multiple dwelling (government statistics)		$446,667
Median Household Income		$42,500
Percent of Rental Units that Are Rent-Regulated		41%
Homeownership Rate		29.2%
Age of Householder:		
	15 to 24 years	5.4%
	25 to 44 years	48.8%
	45 to 64 years	30.5%
	65 years and over	15.3%

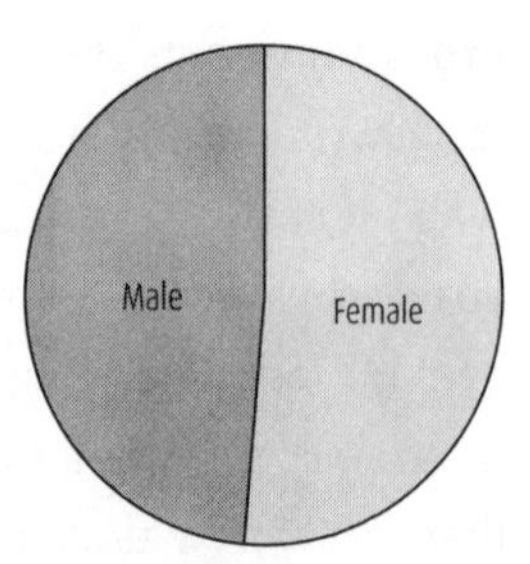

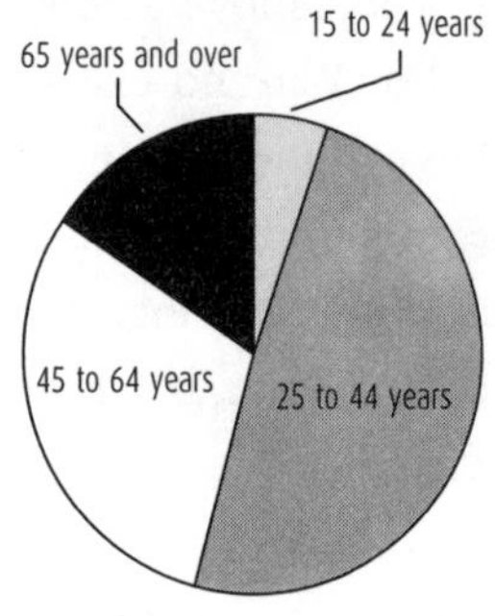

PURCHASE AND RENTAL STATISTICS FROM BROKERS

Buying

Average price per square foot	$984
Studio	$590,400
1 bedroom	$787,200
2 bedroom	$984,000
3 bedroom	$1,180,800
4+ bedroom	$1,476,000

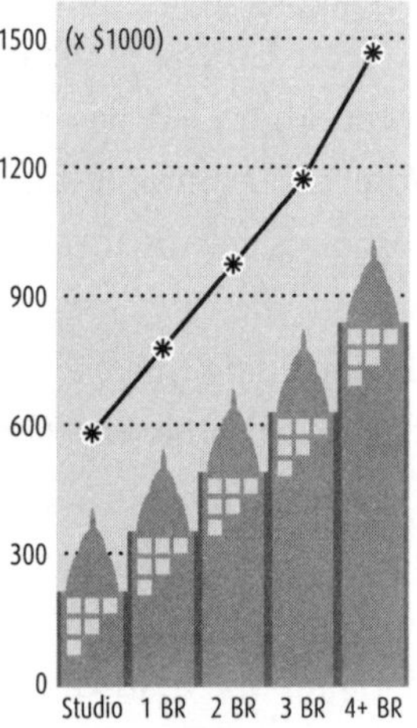

DOWNTOWN BROOKLYN, BROOKLYN HEIGHTS, FORT GREENE, AND DUMBO

NYC AVERAGE

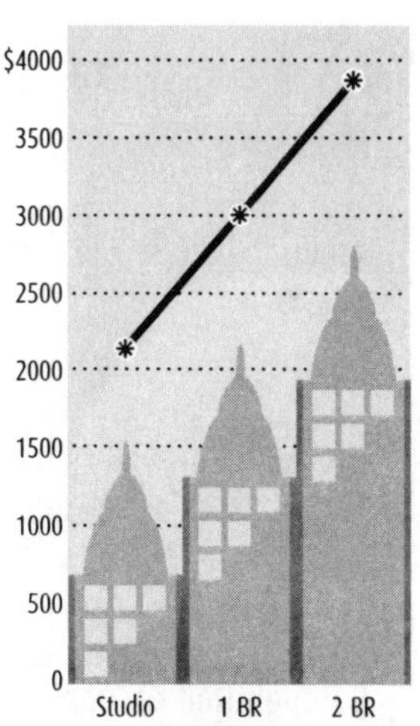

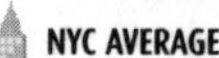

Renting

Average monthly rent per square foot	$4.33
Studio	$2,165
1 bedroom	$3,031
2 bedroom	$3,897

CRIME PICTURE

This is considered a safe area, with a couple of still-developing pockets.

INCOME PICTURE

This is a middle-class area, with some affluent residents.

SUBWAYS

Virtually all the city subway lines that run from Manhattan to Brooklyn stop somewhere near Downtown Brooklyn, Brooklyn Heights, and Fort Greene before fanning out to cover the rest of the borough. For example, the stops around Borough Hall offer the M, N, R, W, 2, 3, 4, 5, A, C, and F trains. Dumbo is served by the A, C, and F trains.

Commuting Times

Midtown East	30–40 minutes
Midtown West	35–45 minutes
Wall Street	10–20 minutes

NOTEWORTHY **IN THE NEIGHBORHOOD**

Atlantic Avenue (great restaurants and the center of Middle Eastern culture in New York)

Brooklyn Borough Hall (similar to City Hall in Manhattan) and **Borough Hall Park** (10 acres of park space), 209 Joralemon Street

Borough Hall Greenmarket (three days a week), Court and Remsen Streets

Brooklyn Academy of Music (known by locals as BAM), 30 Lafayette Avenue (St. Felix Street and Ashland Place)

COBBLE HILL, CARROLL GARDENS, PARK SLOPE, AND RED HOOK

Cobble Hill is much like Brooklyn Heights (it too is a historic district and has similar architecture), but is on the south side of Atlantic Avenue and not quite as close to the City proper. Those who live in Cobble Hill, however, consider it a more neighborly and less apartment-oriented area. Truly an oasis, Cobble Hill has one of the lowest crime rates in the city, and boasts many trees and the attractive Cobble Hill Park. Transportation to Manhattan is excellent, with four subway lines making stops in the neighborhood.

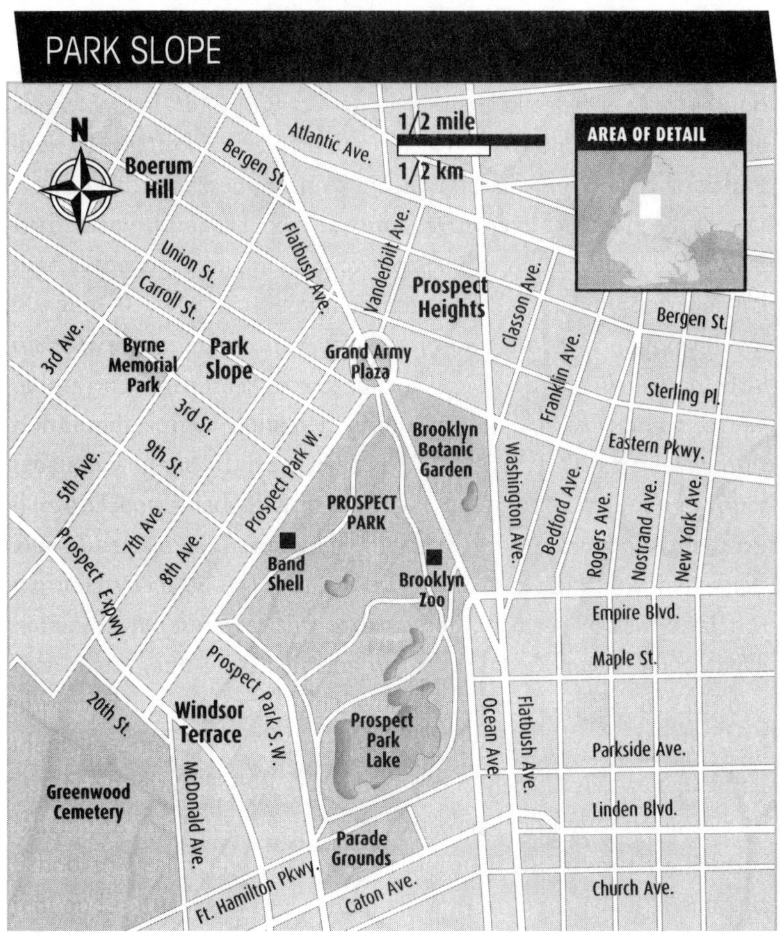

Carroll Gardens, to the south of Cobble Hill, only recently burst on the scene as an emerging commuter neighborhood, and now has scores of good restaurants and plenty of activity along its avenues.

To the east of Cobble Hill and Carroll Gardens, a little farther from Manhattan (but still quite close by subway), is Park Slope. Those who live here are unusually loyal to the neighborhood (even for New Yorkers). The salient landmark, Prospect Park, is reminiscent of Central Park (same designers), albeit not as large (nor as crowded). Park Slope has many interesting churches and brownstone row houses, plus diverse shopping along Seventh and Fifth Avenues and a growing number of eclectic restaurants and boutiques. Neo-Renaissance and neo-Classical architecture are dominant, and this is one of the most architecturally attractive neighborhoods in the City. Park Slope is a good neighborhood for families, as it's safe and low-key, but it also boasts a happening nightlife.

Bearing in mind that no one could ever say real estate in New York City is "cheap," it's all about value—and there are good values to be found in Red Hook. Previously a blue-collar neighborhood through and through, Red Hook has been shifting gears over the past few years, and the tradewinds are shifting. Much of the space you'll get there is larger than what you'll find elsewhere. Set on a peninsula that extends into the East River, the location is to be envied, though on account of its seclusion it is a hike to the nearest subway stop. There is, however, a commuter ferry service and some of the large commercial additions to the neighborhood (IKEA) are working to improve bus transportation. A tremendous addition to the neighborhood, Fairway Market opened an outpost here (I wish they'd open one in *my* neighborhood!), and Carnival Cruise Lines opened its terminal in 2006.

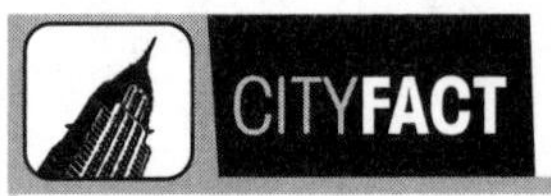

The five boroughs of New York—Brooklyn, Queens, Staten Island, the Bronx, and Manhattan—were separate cities and counties until 1898, when they were consolidated into one municipal entity. In 1993, in a show of voter anger at the municipal government, the residents of Staten Island voted two to one to secede from the City, but the referendum was never approved by the state legislature.

NEIGHBORHOOD STATISTICAL PROFILE

Population		102,228
	White	(44.2%)
	Black	(23.0%)
	Asian	(9.5%)
	Hispanic	(23.0%)
	Other	(0.3%)
Median Monthly Rent (government statistics)		$1,090
Median Price/Unit in a multiple dwelling (government statistics)		$450,000
Median Household Income		$50,000
Percent of Rental Units that Are Rent-Regulated		30%
Homeownership Rate		29.5%
Age of Householder:		
	15 to 24 years	4.8%
	25 to 44 years	53.1%
	45 to 64 years	28.9%
	65 years and over	13.2%

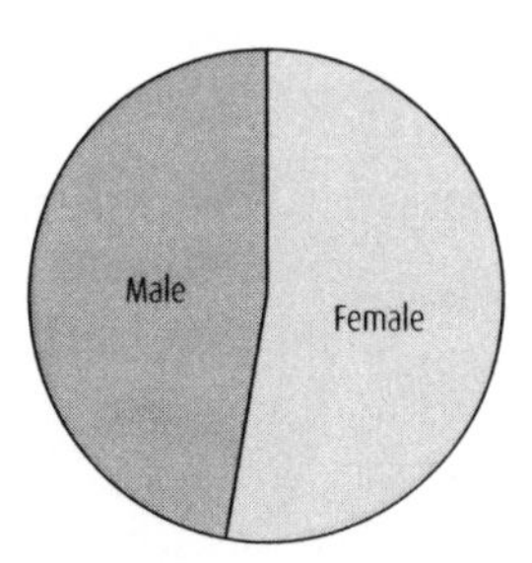

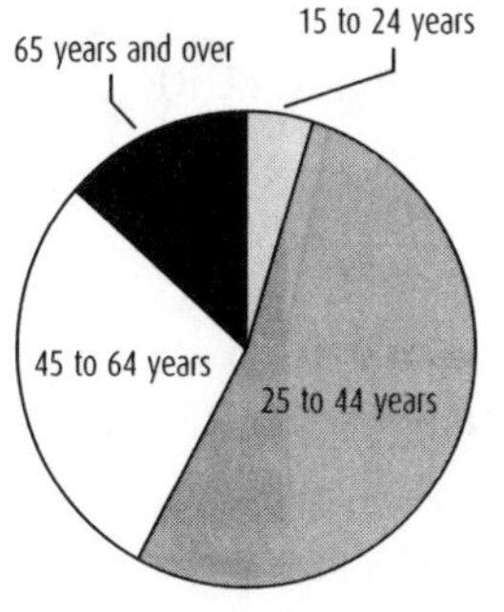

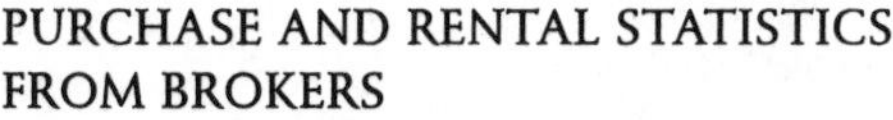

PURCHASE AND RENTAL STATISTICS FROM BROKERS

Buying

Average price per square foot	$661
Studio	$396,600
1 bedroom	$528,800
2 bedroom	$661,000
3 bedroom	$793,200
4+ bedroom	$991,500

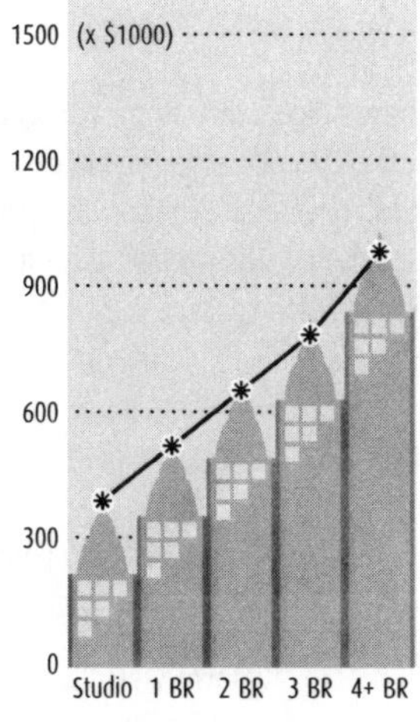

Renting

Average monthly rent per square foot	$2.70
Studio	$1,350
1 bedroom	$1,890
2 bedroom	$2,430

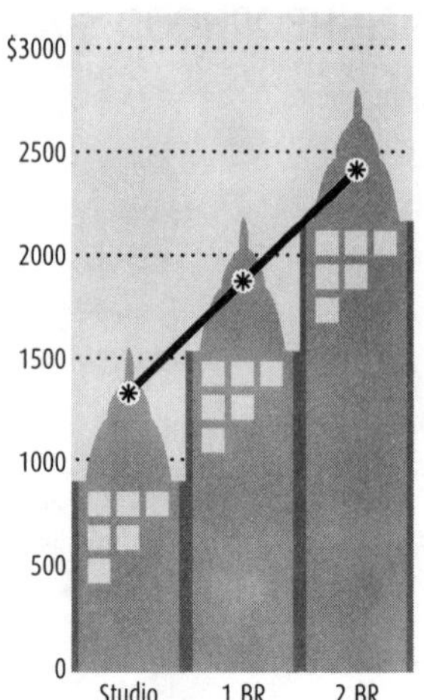

CRIME PICTURE

This is considered a safe area, with some sections being safer than others.

INCOME PICTURE

This is a middle- and working-class area, with some affluent residents.

SUBWAYS

These neighborhoods are well covered by subway service. Particularly if you live near Atlantic Avenue, you'll have many choices. For example, the subway stops at Atlantic Avenue and Pacific Streets are served by the M, N, Q, R, W, 2, 3, 4, and 5 trains. Some parts of the neighborhood may have only one subway connection, but wherever you are in the area you'll likely be close to a station.

Commuting Times

Midtown East	30–40 minutes
Midtown West	35–45 minutes
Wall Street	10–20 minutes

NOTEWORTHY **IN THE NEIGHBORHOOD**

Prospect Park (designed by Olmsted and Vaux, of Central Park fame)

Grand Army Plaza (leading up to Prospect Park, with several interesting monuments)

Brooklyn Museum (one of New York's best collections), 200 Eastern Parkway (Washington Avenue)

IKEA, on Beard Street at Richards Street

Fairway Market, 480–500 Van Brunt Street

Full view of the Statue of Liberty—Red Hook is the only place in New York City that has a head-on view of the statue from land.

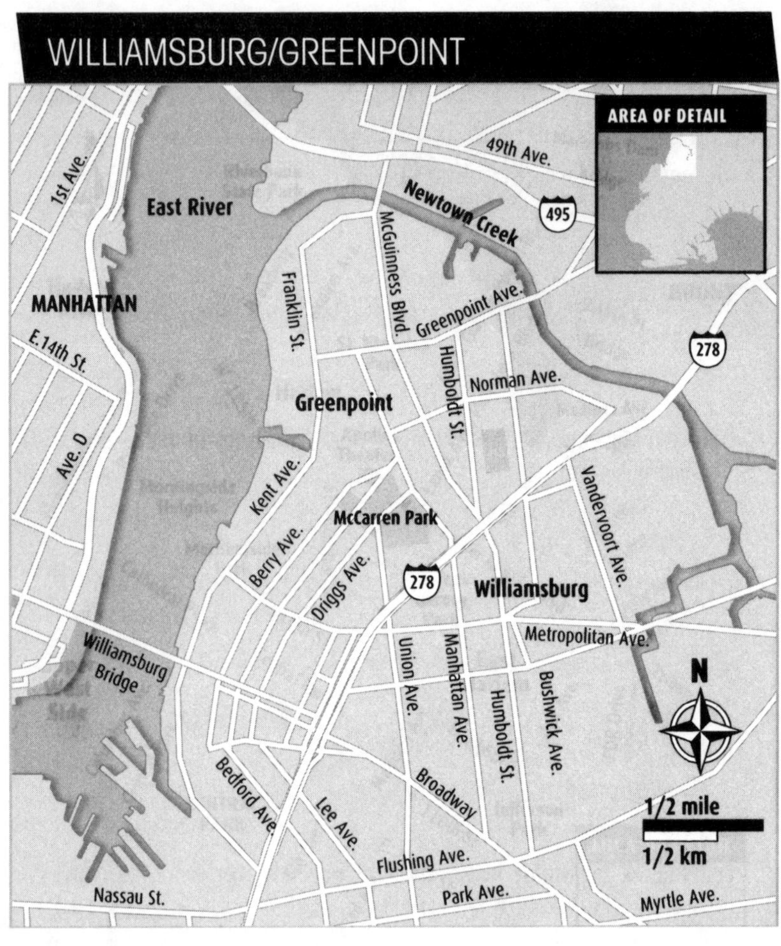
WILLIAMSBURG/GREENPOINT
AREA OF DETAIL
49th Ave.
495
Newtown Creek
1st Ave.
East River
McGuinness Blvd.
Franklin St.
Greenpoint Ave.
MANHATTAN
E.14th St.
Humboldt St.
278
Norman Ave.
Greenpoint
Ave. D
Kent Ave.
Vandervoort Ave.
McCarren Park
Berry Ave.
Driggs Ave.
278
Williamsburg
Metropolitan Ave.
Williamsburg Bridge
Union Ave.
Manhattan Ave.
Humboldt St.
Bushwick Ave.
N
Bedford Ave.
Lee Ave.
Broadway
1/2 mile
1/2 km
Flushing Ave.
Nassau St.
Park Ave.
Myrtle Ave.

WILLIAMSBURG AND GREENPOINT

Williamsburg is now so hip that the hipsters who live here are somewhat self-conscious about it and often claim to live in the bordering neighborhood of Greenpoint or neighboring Bushwick because they're "edgier." To some, that may seem counterintuitive: "Hey, wait, isn't the goal to live in the *nicer* neighborhood?" Here's a lesson about New York City: if you have to ask *that* question, you don't belong in either of these two neighborhoods. Unless of course you're moving to Greenpoint for the very reason that many other residents have come to settle here in the first place: more space, less money.

Williamsburg is just over the Williamsburg Bridge, with the Lower East Side directly at the other end. The multiple subways running to this neighborhood make it an easy commute to Manhattan. Bedford Avenue is where "it's happening," and is lined with plenty of coffee shops, art galleries, and boutiques, though there is plenty going on all over the neighborhood. Whether you're renting or buying, Williamsburg is expensive and prices have been increasing steadily (and dramatically) for years. There is an amazing music scene, which some claim has eclipsed that of Manhattan, and the artists who are still in the neighborhood must be doing something right or they wouldn't be able to afford it.

Located adjacent to Williamsburg, Greenpoint is a promising alternative, at least for the time being. In 2005, the New York City Council passed a large-scale rezoning for the Greenpoint waterfront. What this means is that the neighborhood will continue to become more gentrified, as the waterfront was approved for "high density" residential use. If the current building trend is any indication, you'll want to get in while the rents are still manageable: new buildings are going up and old buildings are being renovated to accommodate the current demand.

NEIGHBORHOOD STATISTICAL PROFILE

Population		160,338
	White	(65.6%)
	Black	(4.7%)
	Asian	(2.5%)
	Hispanic	(27.2%)
Median Monthly Rent (government statistics)		$900
Median Price/Unit in a multiple dwelling (government statistics)		$270,000
Median Household Income		$35,000
Percent of Rental Units that Are Rent-Regulated		54.6%
Homeownership Rate		16.8%
Age of Householder:		
	15 to 24 years	7.3%
	25 to 44 years	42.8%
	45 to 64 years	30.6%
	65 years and over	19.3%

Male
Female

65 years and over
15 to 24 years
25 to 44 years
45 to 64 years

PURCHASE AND RENTAL STATISTICS FROM BROKERS

Buying

Average price per square foot	$338
Studio	$202,800
1 bedroom	$270,400
2 bedroom	$338,000
3 bedroom	$405,600
4+ bedroom	$507,000

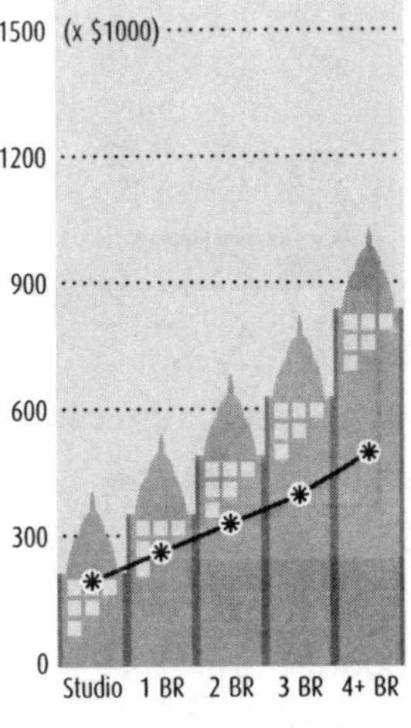

✱ **WILLIAMSBURG, GREENPOINT**

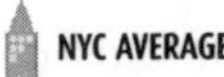

Renting

Average monthly rent per square foot	$2.33
Studio	$1,165
1 bedroom	$1,631
2 bedroom	$2,097

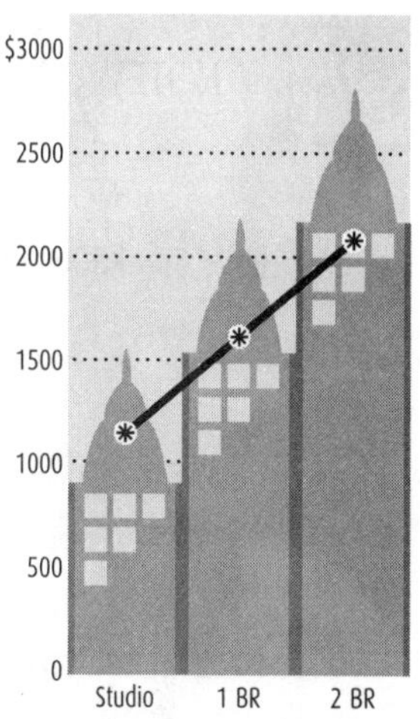

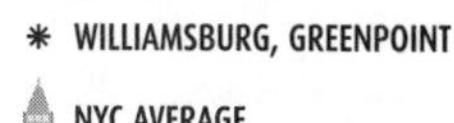

CRIME PICTURE

This is considered a safe area, with some sections being safer than others.

INCOME PICTURE

This is a middle- and working-class area, with some affluent residents.

SUBWAYS

Williamsburg is served by the J, M, and Z trains.

Commuting Times

Midtown East	30–40 minutes
Midtown West	35–45 minutes
Wall Street	10–20 minutes

NOTEWORTHY **IN THE NEIGHBORHOOD**

Peter Luger Steakhouse (established in 1887), 178 Broadway

New York Water Taxi to Financial District in downtown Manhattan

Our Lady of Mount Carmel Church, Havemeyer and North 8th Streets (don't miss the Feast of St. Paulinus)

Countless hip clubs showcasing up-and-coming indie rock bands

Art abounds: hunt for a piece that speaks to you, or take some classes and make something yourself at one of several local studios or schools

QUEENS

Queens is geographically the City's largest borough, and right now it may very well be the most ethnically diverse place in the world (many of the residents of the old ethnic neighborhoods of Manhattan, or their children, now live in Queens). The borough presents a dizzying array of housing options, most of which are solidly working-class (it is often said that every cabdriver lives in Queens), but one neighbor-

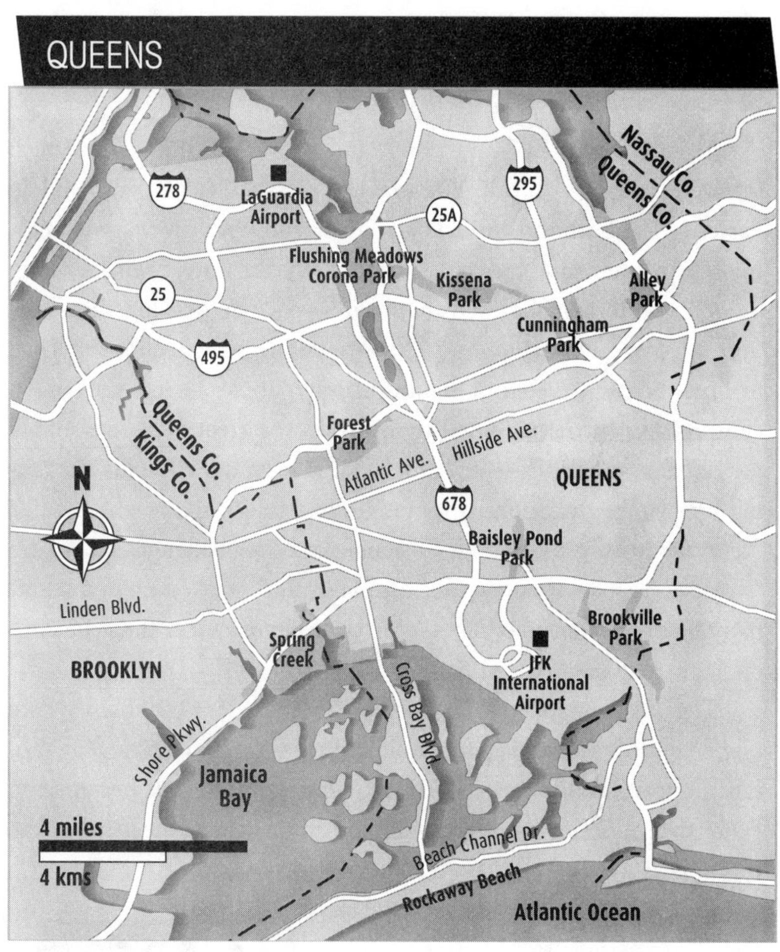

hood in particular—Astoria—has fast gained popularity with professionals who work in Manhattan. Astoria's neighbor, Long Island City, is also popular with artists and hipsters and the usual crowd of City dwellers just looking for more space. A little farther out, Jackson Heights provides some of the best housing values for a neighborhood that is still convenient to Manhattan.

ASTORIA AND LONG ISLAND CITY

Formerly a center of filmmaking, and now (depending on which street you cross) a Greek, Yugoslavian, Russian, Asian, and Middle Eastern neighborhood, Astoria is a quick subway commute to Midtown Manhattan and has, for a number of years now, been attracting a young professional crowd that values space and savings. It's safe, you can live in an actual house (many young people choose to live in apartments carved out of multifamily houses), and the ethnic composition of the neighborhood makes for great (and reasonably priced) dining options—at more than 200 restaurants—plus a dizzying array of nightlife and shopping along major thoroughfares like Steinway Street. Navigating Queens can be a challenge—there are "streets," "roads," "boulevards," and "avenues" stacked up in a seemingly incomprehensible manner—but residents swear there's a simple logic to it all.

The adjacent area of Long Island City (debates rage about where one neighborhood ends and the other begins) is also developing rapidly. Long a haven of artists when other neighborhoods became too expensive, LIC has been growing and improving, especially in the recent past.

Old factories and warehouses are being converted to apartments but, more notably, there is a lot of *new* construction going up around the neighborhood. I know plenty of people who swear that LIC is "the place to live" (and it doesn't hurt that it's still affordable), but as with many developing neighborhoods you have to have somewhat of a

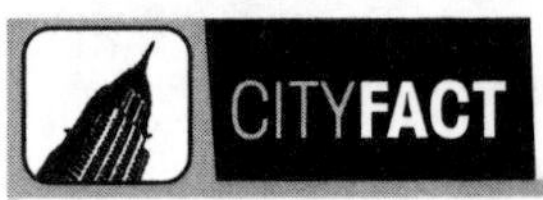

New York City boasts more than 100 ethnic newspapers, including 25 catering to the Russian community alone. A typical neighborhood newsstand in Queens stocks newspapers in a dozen languages.

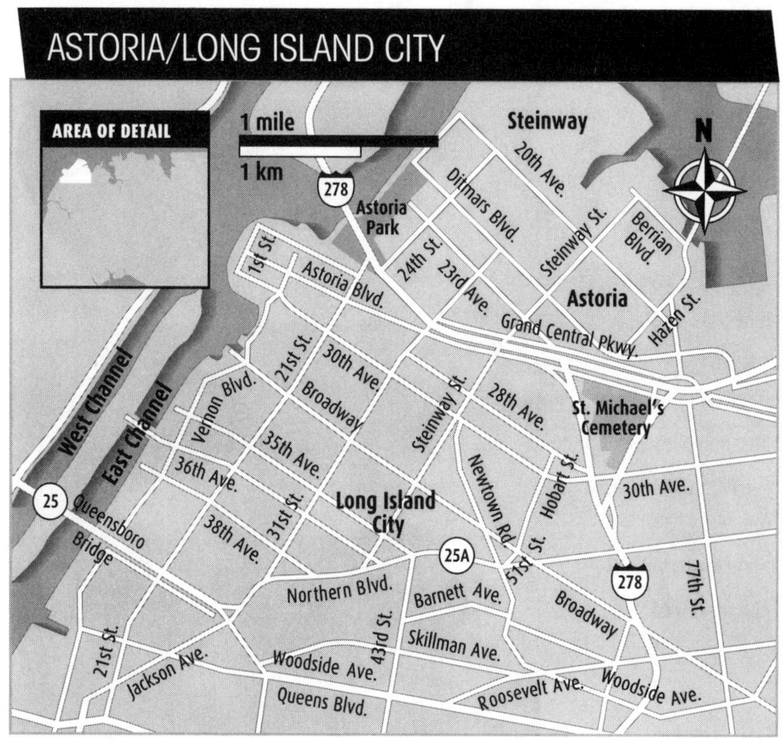

frontier personality to appreciate living here. There are parts of LIC that have the services you'll want and need (restaurants, shops, grocery stores, dry cleaners, etc.), but there are other patches where you'll be hard pressed to find a good meal. At the same time, the neighborhood is growing quickly, and, as these things go, an influx of new residents creates the demand that some wise entrepreneur will surely aim to meet. Another plus about LIC is that transportation options to Manhattan include subway, New York Water Taxi, and buses (plus multiple bridges for cars).

NEIGHBORHOOD STATISTICAL PROFILE

Population		211,220
	White	(58.3%)
	Black	(6.3%)
	Asian	(11.6%)
	Hispanic	(23.6%)
	Other	(0.3%)
Median Monthly Rent (government statistics)		$950
Median Price/Unit in a multiple dwelling (government statistics)		$297,500
Median Household Income		$38,300
Percent of Rental Units that Are Rent-Regulated		52.4%
Homeownership Rate		18.1%
Age of Householder:		
	15 to 24 years	5.6%
	25 to 44 years	46.3%
	45 to 64 years	28.4%
	65 years and over	19.7%

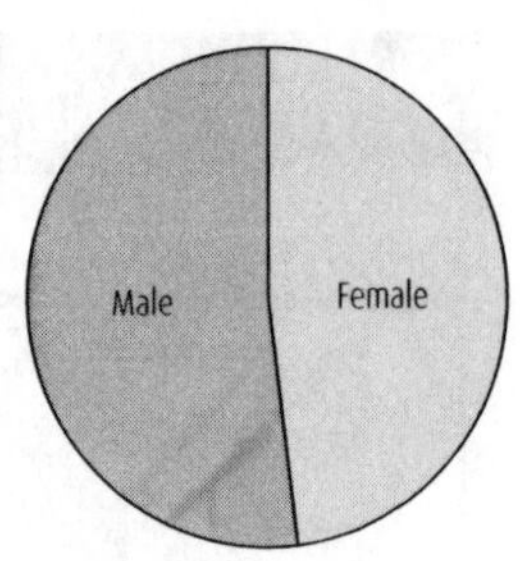

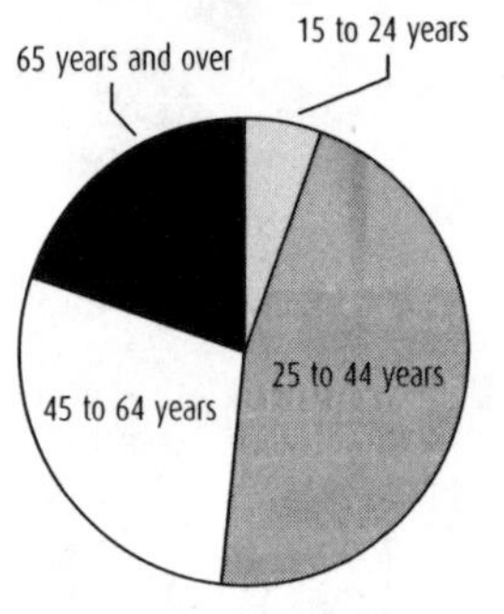

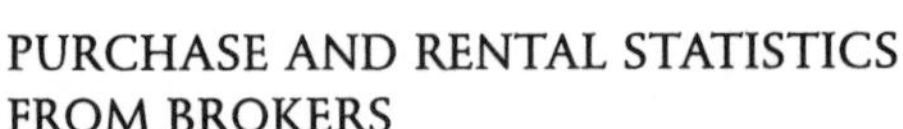

PURCHASE AND RENTAL STATISTICS FROM BROKERS

Buying

Average price per square foot	$634
Studio	$380,400
1 bedroom	$507,200
2 bedroom	$634,000
3 bedroom	$760,800
4+ bedroom	$951,000

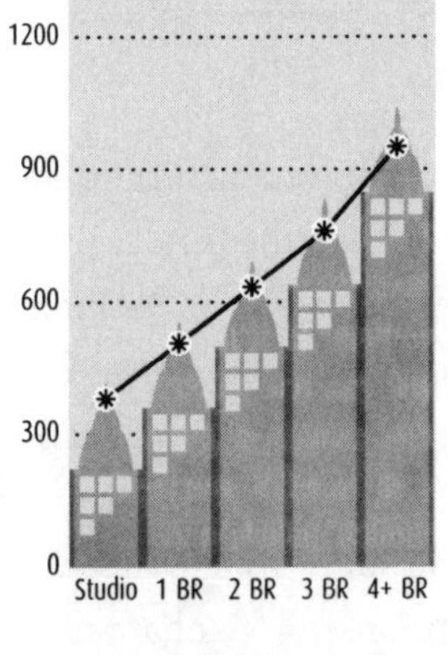

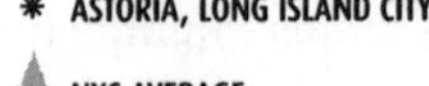

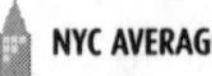

Renting

Average monthly rent per square foot	$2.41
Studio	$1,205
1 bedroom	$1,687
2 bedroom	$2,169

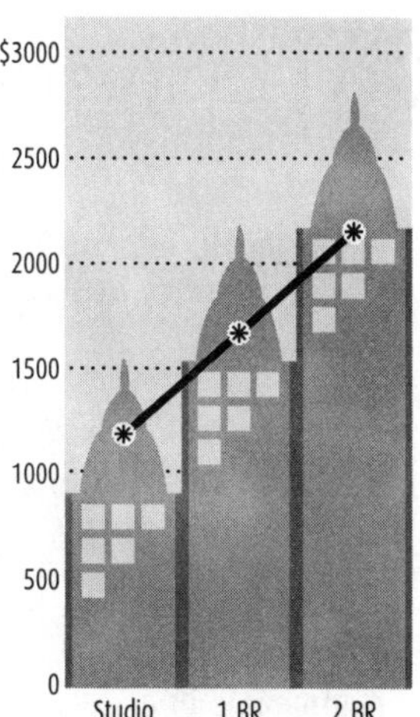

CRIME PICTURE

This is considered a safe area, but you must choose your location carefully.

INCOME PICTURE

This is a working-class area.

SUBWAYS

Astoria is served by the N and W trains. Long Island City is rather large, and depending on your exact location you might be served by the N and W, the 7, or the E, F, G, R, and V lines.

Commuting Times

Midtown East	20–30 minutes
Midtown West	30–40 minutes
Wall Street	40–50 minutes

NOTEWORTHY **IN THE NEIGHBORHOOD**

American Museum of the Moving Image (incredible collection of pop culture), 36-01 35th Avenue (36th Street)

Silvercup Studios (the largest independent television and film production company in New York City, which was once home to *The Sopranos* and *Sex and the City)*, Main Lot 42-22 22nd Street

Kaufman Astoria Studios, 34-12 36th Street (34th Avenue)

Steinway Mansion (as in the pianos—the factory is still in Astoria), 18-33 41st Street (Berrian Boulevard)

Isamu Noguchi Garden Museum (housing more than 250 works by this renowned sculptor), 32-37 Vernon Boulevard

JACKSON HEIGHTS

If you want the true experience of living in the multicultural city that is New York—and you want a little extra space—Jackson Heights may just be the neighborhood for you. This area boasts a population composed of more than 50 percent immigrants, the majority of whom are from India and other South Asian countries or from Colombia and

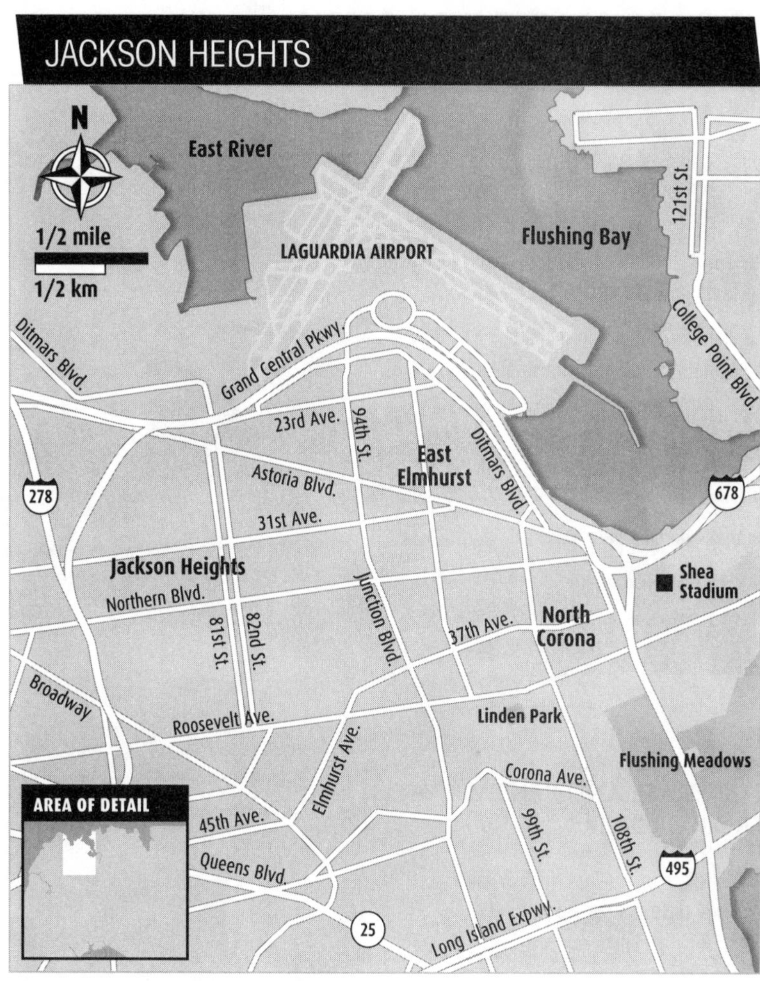

other Latin American countries. It is one of the most diverse neighborhoods in the country—and the world.

You will eat well in this neighborhood (Jackson Heights has its own Little India and a host of Latin American restaurants too) and find it difficult not to get caught up in the spirit with your neighbors when "football" (soccer, to us Americans) season arrives.

NEIGHBORHOOD STATISTICAL PROFILE

Population		169,083
	White	(20.2%)
	Black	(6.9%)
	Asian	(19.4%)
	Hispanic	(53.5%)
Median Monthly Rent (government statistics)		$960
Median Price/Unit in a multiple dwelling (government statistics)		$285,000
Median Household Income		$35,600
Percent of Rental Units that Are Rent-Regulated		40.4%
Homeownership Rate		34%
Age of Householder:		
	15 to 24 years	4.1%
	25 to 44 years	43.1%
	45 to 64 years	33.6%
	65 years and over	19.2%

Male
Female

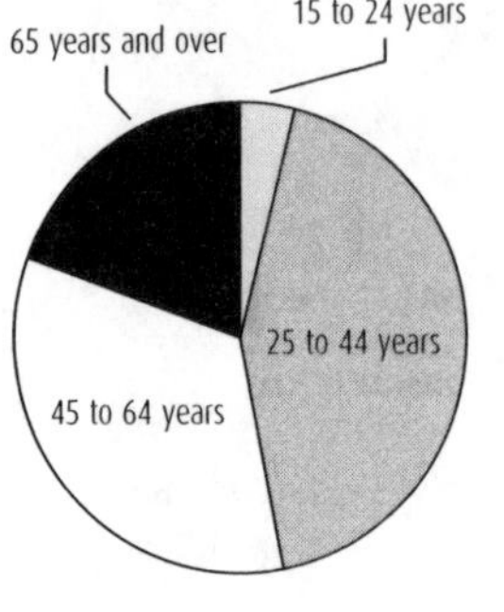

PURCHASE AND RENTAL STATISTICS FROM BROKERS

Buying

Average price per square foot	$514
Studio	$308,400
1 bedroom	$411,200
2 bedroom	$514,000
3 bedroom	$616,800
4+ bedroom	$771,000

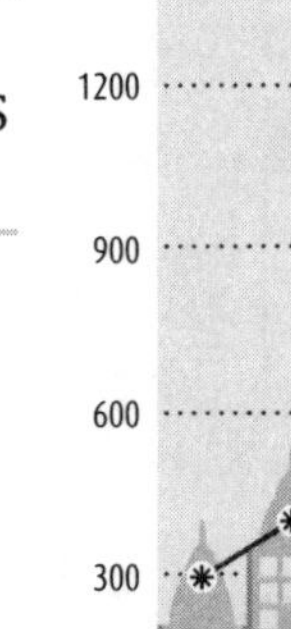

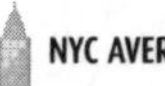

Renting

Average monthly rent per square foot	$2.12
Studio	$1,060
1 bedroom	$1,484
2 bedroom	$1,908

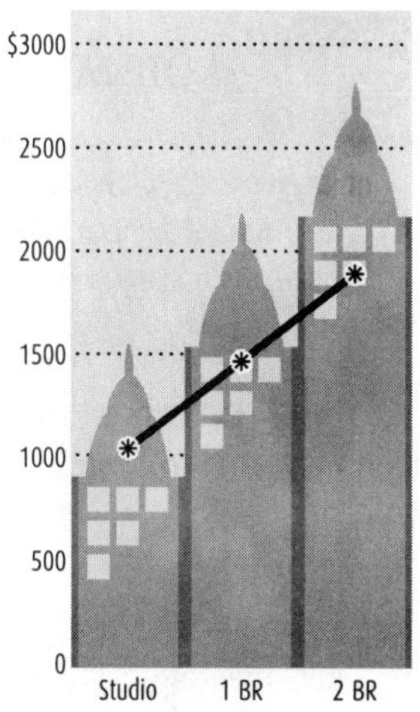

CRIME PICTURE

This is considered a safe area, but you must choose your location carefully.

INCOME PICTURE

This is a working-class area.

SUBWAYS

The Jackson Avenue/Roosevelt Avenue subway stop is an excellent transit hub, with five subway lines converging that will get you to most Midtown and Downtown Manhattan locations in a straight shot: the 7, E, F, G, R, and V.

Commuting Times

Midtown East	25–35 minutes
Midtown West	35–45 minutes
Wall Street	45–55 minutes

NOTEWORTHY **IN THE NEIGHBORHOOD**

Little India (restaurants, sari shops, and storefronts blaring Bollywood videos abound), 74th Street between Roosevelt Avenue and 37th Avenue

Travers Park (the only public park in Jackson Heights, the site of spring and summer concerts and a Sunday morning farmers' market), 34th Avenue between 77th and 78th Streets

Eagle Theater (for Bollywood films on the big screen), 73-07 37th Road

Jackson Heights library, 35-51 81st Street

STATEN ISLAND

Staten Island is one of the least examined (and the least populous) of the boroughs, and residents like it that way. One of my friends, who grew up on Staten Island, says that if you tell people elsewhere in America that you "come from Staten Island," they have no idea what you're talking about—but they assume you're tough because of the syncopated sound of "STA-ten IS-land." Even resident New Yorkers are often in the dark; they know it only as "that place the Staten Island ferry goes to."

But Staten Island, for the most part, is anything but tough. It's the most suburban and spacious part of the City by far, and many residents can't imagine living anywhere else. Staten Island is so

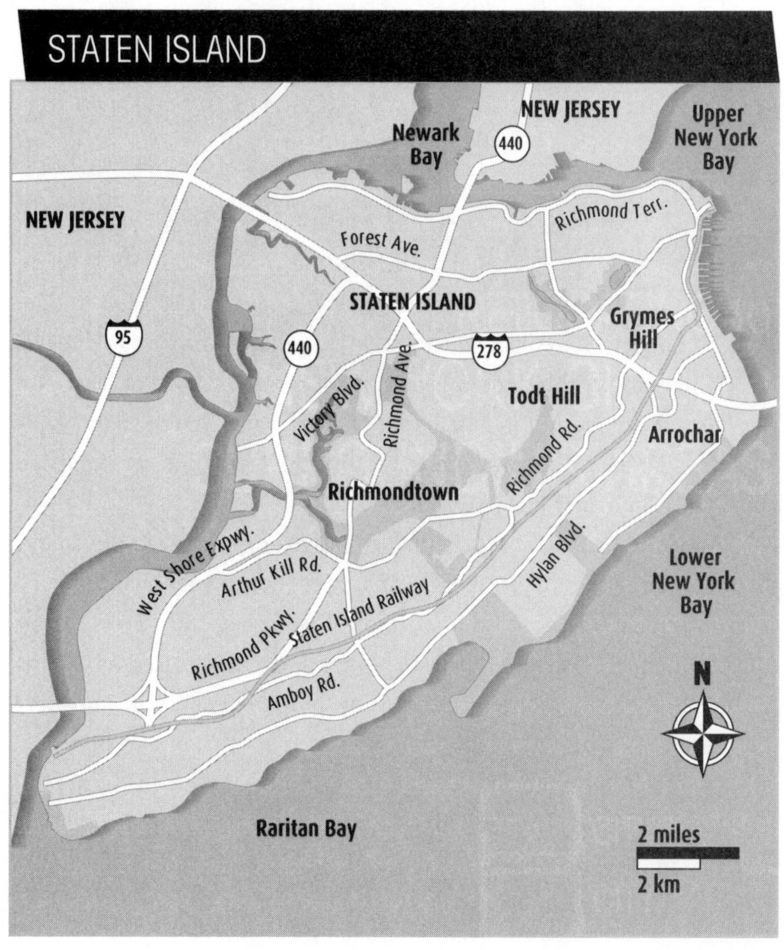
STATEN ISLAND
NEW JERSEY
Newark Bay
440
NEW JERSEY
Upper New York Bay
Richmond Terr.
Forest Ave.
STATEN ISLAND
95
440
278
Grymes Hill
Victory Blvd.
Richmond Ave.
Todt Hill
Richmond Rd.
Arrochar
Richmondtown
West Shore Expwy.
Arthur Kill Rd.
Hylan Blvd.
Lower New York Bay
Staten Island Railway
Richmond Pkwy.
Amboy Rd.
N
Raritan Bay
2 miles
2 km

unlike the rest of the City that it occasionally threatens to secede from the larger political whole—an attempt that is not likely to succeed anytime soon. It also boasts the nation's largest Sri Lankan population, with enough Sri Lankan restaurants and grocery stores to back it up.

You can get to and from Staten Island by ferry from lower Manhattan (for free), or via several bridges (the most noteworthy being the Verrazano-Narrows Bridge, the world's longest suspension bridge, which connects Staten Island to Brooklyn). There is no bridge directly to Manhattan. Within Staten Island, most residents have at least one car (almost unheard of in Manhattan). There's also Staten Island Railway (similar to the subways in the rest of the City), and an extensive local and commuter bus network.

Almost exclusively residential, this sixty-one-square-mile island has everything to offer, from large apartment complexes near the ferry terminal (ideal for those who work on Wall Street) to a diverse array of apartments in converted private homes and townhouses, as well as single family homes, and large mansions with extensive grounds farther south. Nearest to Manhattan are a series of dramatic hills and slopes stretching from St. George to Richmondtown. In Todt Hill, Emerson Hill, and Grymes Hill, you can live in a multimillion-dollar home with a view of Manhattan or Brooklyn—or both. The local paper is the *Staten Island Advance,* which contains the most relevant housing ads.

NEIGHBORHOOD STATISTICAL PROFILE

Population		162,609
	White	(50.5%)
	Black	(18.5%)
	Asian	(7.7%)
	Hispanic	(23.4%)
Median Monthly Rent (government statistics)		$890
Median Price/Unit in a multiple dwelling (government statistics)		$350,000
Median Household Income		$52,500
Percent of Rental Units that Are Rent-Regulated		23.3%
Homeownership Rate		58.1%
Age of Householder:		
	15 to 24 years	3.5%
	25 to 44 years	43.4%
	45 to 64 years	34.1%
	65 years and over	19.0%

Male

Female

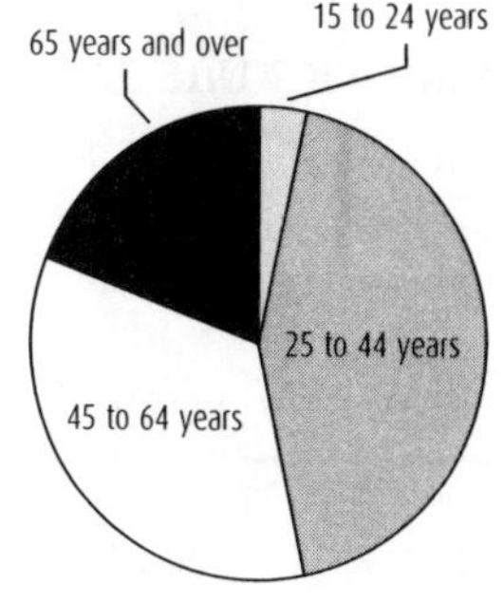

PURCHASE AND RENTAL STATISTICS FROM BROKERS

Buying

Average price per square foot	$260
Studio	$156,000
1 bedroom	$208,000
2 bedroom	$260,000
3 bedroom	$312,000
4+ bedroom	$390,000

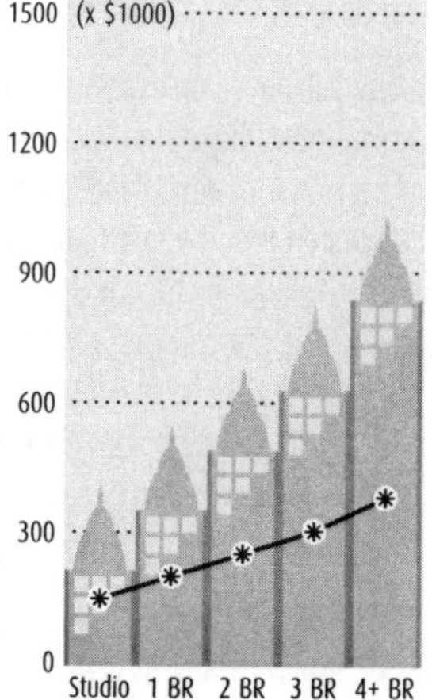

✱ **NORTHERN STATEN ISLAND**

 **NYC AVERAGE**

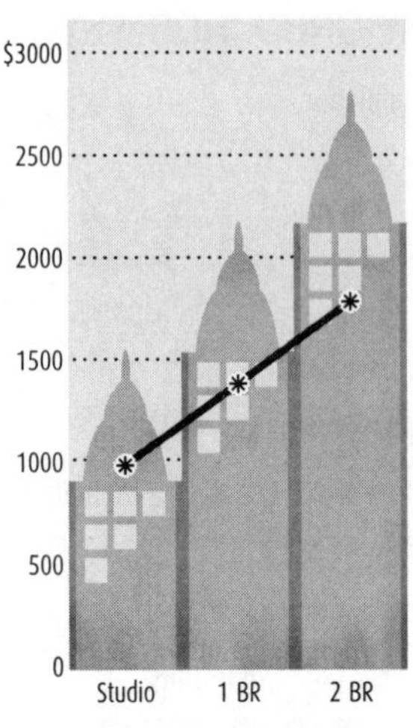

Renting

Average monthly rent per square foot	$2.00
Studio	$1,000
1 bedroom	$1,400
2 bedroom	$1,800

CRIME PICTURE

This is considered a very safe area, with some variation depending on specific regions.

INCOME PICTURE

This is a mostly middle-class area, with pockets of affluence and some poverty.

SUBWAYS

The city subways don't cross the river to Staten Island; however, from the Staten Island Ferry commuters can connect to the Staten Island Railway (it was formerly called Staten Island Rapid Transit, and most people still refer to it as such), which functions much the same way as the subway.

Commuting Times

Midtown East	45–55 minutes
Midtown West	45–55 minutes
Wall Street	25–35 minutes (assuming you live within 5 to 10 minutes of the ferry; longer otherwise)

NOTEWORTHY **IN THE NEIGHBORHOOD**

Snug Harbor Cultural Center (83-acre visual and performing arts center), 1000 Richmond Terrace (Tysen Street)

Verrazano-Narrows Bridge (the world's longest suspension bridge—longer than the Golden Gate—and the starting point of the NYC Marathon)

Historic Richmond Town (twenty-nine buildings dating from the seventeenth to nineteenth centuries), 441 Clarke Avenue (Richmond and Arthur Kill Roads)

Alice Austen House (named for the *Life* magazine photographer), 2 Hylan Boulevard (Bay Street)

Fresh Kills (New York's notorious—and huge—garbage dump)

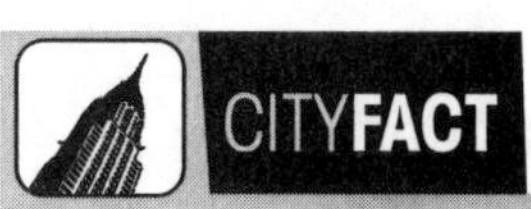

More than 16 million immigrants passed through the Ellis Island immigration station in New York Harbor between 1892 and 1924.

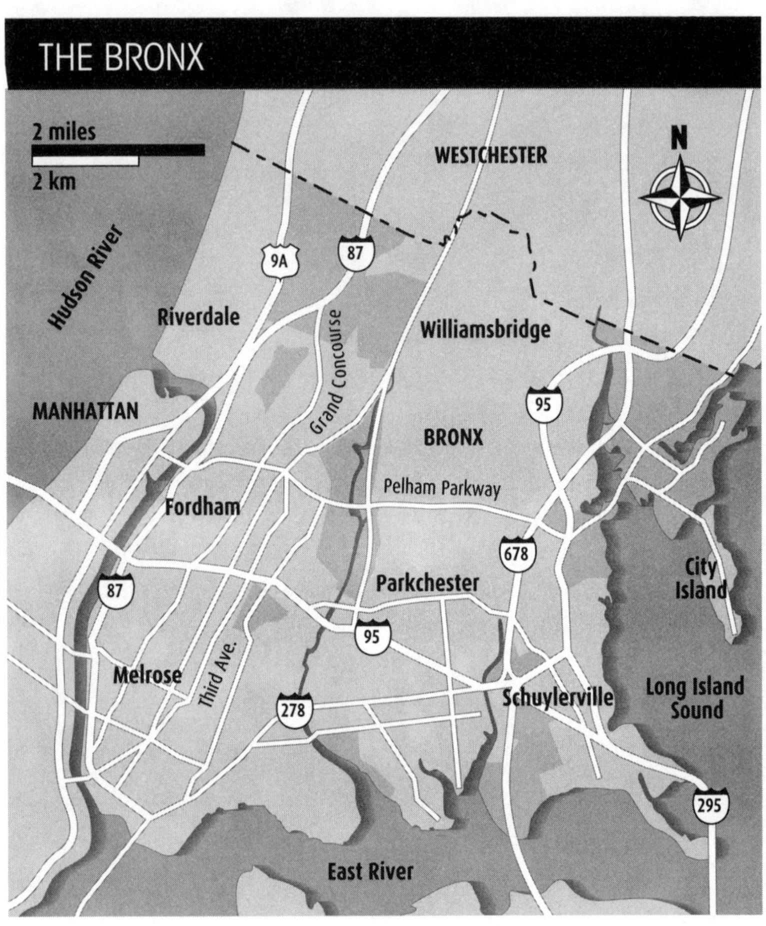

THE BRONX

As a whole, the Bronx has historically been the roughest of the five boroughs (ever seen the movie *Fort Apache, the Bronx*?), but in the past decade there has been a great renaissance and the Bronx has seen dramatic improvement.

THE SOUTH BRONX: MOTT HAVEN AND MELROSE

Mott Haven, to the south of the Major Deegan Expressway (I-87), has improved dramatically in recent years (to the north, not so much). Long known as one of the poorest neighborhoods in the City—and the country—Mott Haven has more recently become the home to many artists and professionals, who have settled into reclaimed and refurbished warehouses and brownstones in parts of the area. If you're after "edgy" and economical, this neighborhood still has it. As more and more residents move in, the South Bronx is changing for the better (a little more slowly than Manhattan and other boroughs, but it is changing), and Mott Haven is proof positive of that change.

You might hear the neighborhood referred to as SoBro, which mostly amuses local residents (who wouldn't be caught dead calling it SoBro), and in reality this seems to be a rebranding effort by the brokers and real estate magnates working in the neighborhood. A burgeoning antiques trade has sprung up along Bruckner Boulevard and restaurants are starting to pop up too, to meet the demand of new incoming residents.

There is a great revitalization and reclamation effort under way in the Melrose section of the Bronx. New two- and three-family homes have been built for "moderate" and "middle-income" families, as well as condo complexes, which are centered around private courtyards. St. Mary's Park, a focal point of the neighborhood, is

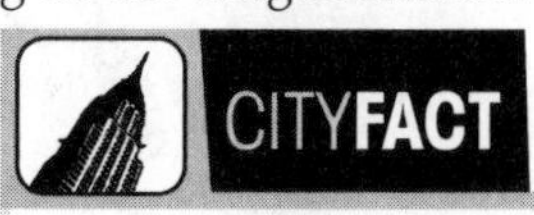

The neighborhood of Marble Hill used to sit at the northernmost point in Manhattan. In 1895, in order to accommodate large ships, the City channeled the Harlem River to run south of Marble Hill and filled in the canal that had formerly separated Marble Hill from the Bronx. Today, Marble Hill is geographically in the Bronx—but politically it remains part of the borough of Manhattan.

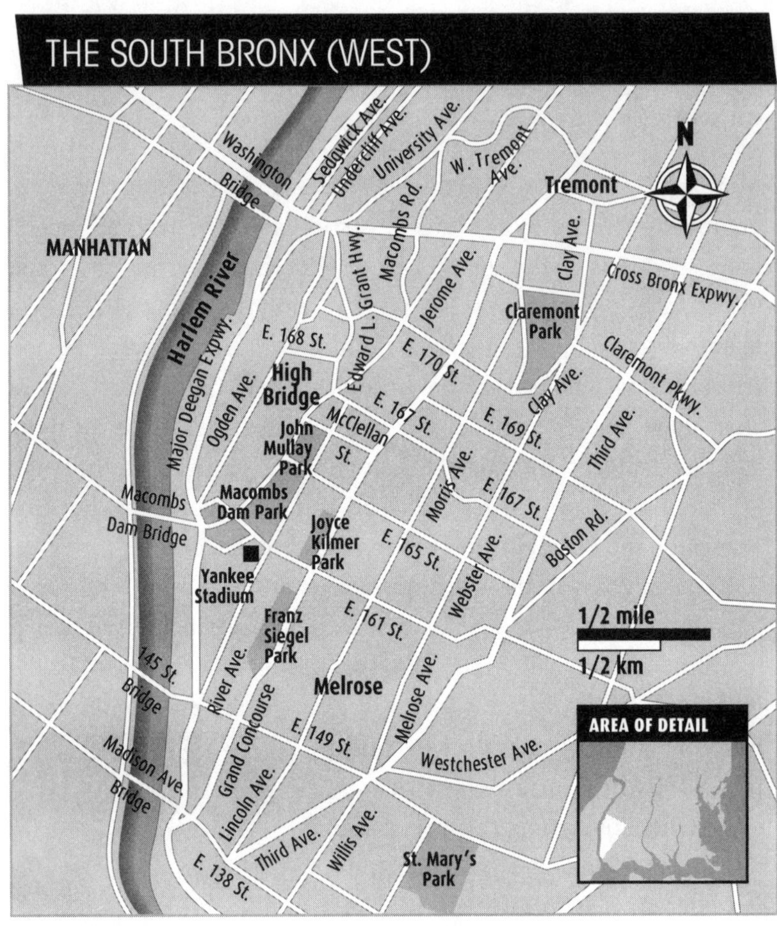

more than 35 acres and has ball fields, basketball courts, picnic and barbecue areas, and a swimming pool. The main drag in this neighborhood is 149th Street. You won't find the tranquillity of Park Avenue here, but all signs indicate that this neighborhood is still in a transitional stage, so the bargains abound, and public transportation here is great.

THE SOUTH BRONX (EAST)

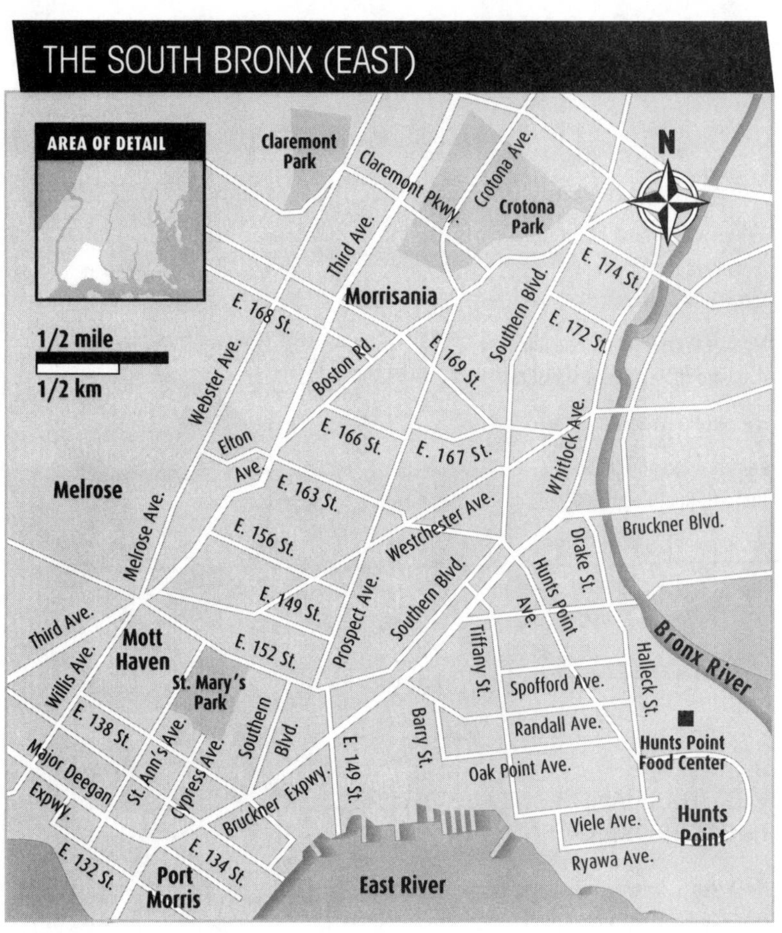

NEIGHBORHOOD STATISTICAL PROFILE

Population		82,159
	White	(2.5%)
	Black	(21.1%)
	Asian	(0.0%)
	Hispanic	(76.4%)
Median Monthly Rent (government statistics)		$650
Median Price/Unit in a multiple dwelling (government statistics)		$149,000
Median Household Income		$15,544
Percent of Rental Units that Are Rent-Regulated		42.4%
Homeownership Rate		6.1%
Age of Householder:		
	15 to 24 years	5.1%
	25 to 44 years	42.3%
	45 to 64 years	34.9%
	65 years and over	17.6%

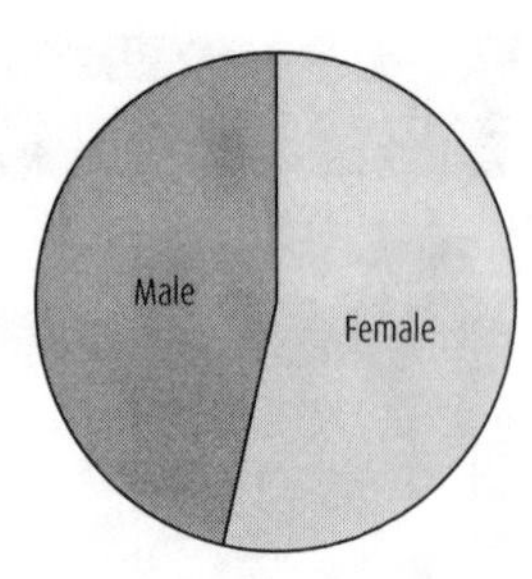

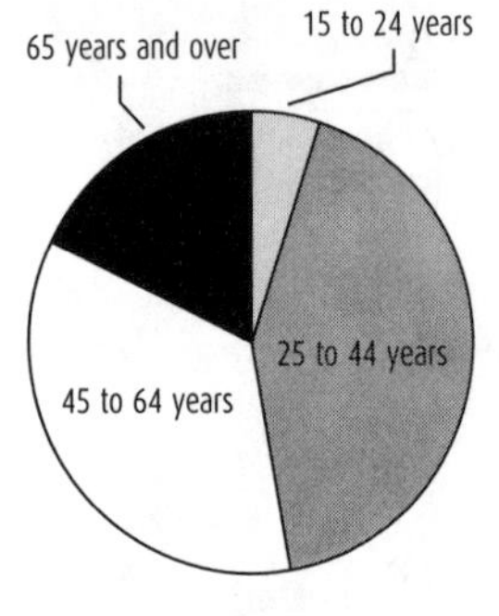

PURCHASE AND RENTAL STATISTICS FROM BROKERS

Buying

Average price per square foot	$144
Studio	$86,400
1 bedroom	$115,200
2 bedroom	$144,000
3 bedroom	$172,800
4+ bedroom	$216,000

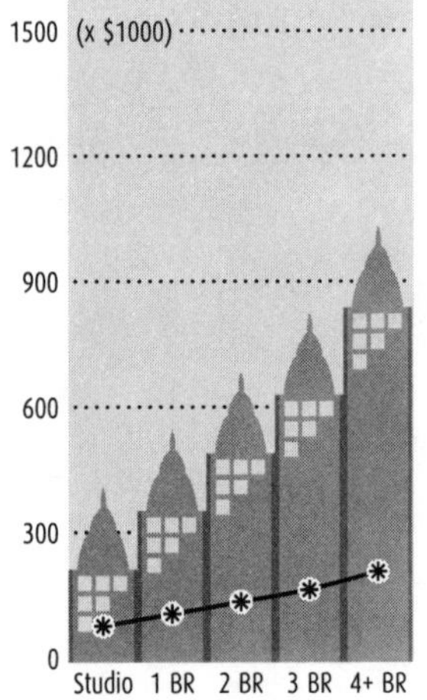

✱ THE SOUTH BRONX (SOBRO)

 NYC AVERAGE

Renting

Average monthly rent per square foot	$1.58
Studio	$790
1 bedroom	$1,106
2 bedroom	$1,422

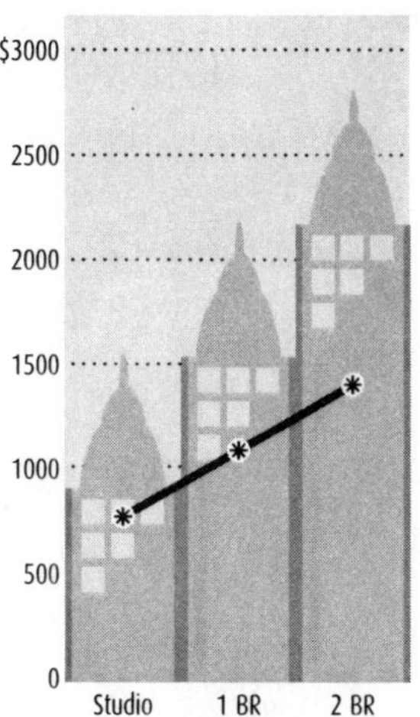

CRIME PICTURE

This is considered a borderline area, with some pockets of safety and many areas to avoid, especially around the big public housing projects.

INCOME PICTURE

This is a mostly working-class area, with pockets of artists and professionals as well as areas of poverty.

SUBWAYS

One of the major benefits of the South Bronx is that it is so well served by the subway. Depending on where exactly you live, you may be served by the 4, 5, 6, 2, B, or D trains, and possibly several of them.

Commuting Times

Midtown East	30–40 minutes
Midtown West	30–40 minutes
Wall Street	40–50 minutes

NOTEWORTHY **IN THE NEIGHBORHOOD**

St. Mary's Park, Jackson Avenue and East 147th Street

Yankee Stadium, 161st Street and River Avenue

RIVERDALE AND FIELDSTON

The Bronx (the smallest borough and the only one beginning with a definite article) is not the first choice of most New York City residents when it comes to choosing a borough. But Riverdale (which also includes the neighborhoods of Spuyten Duyvil and the high-end Fieldston, one of the most exclusive neighborhoods in New York City), is the exception to that rule. One of the most beautiful places to live in New York City, Riverdale is more like a suburb than a neighborhood of the Bronx (many people, even New Yorkers, assume it is part of Westchester and not part of the City). It offers both houses and apartments in a spacious, mostly low-rise setting near the water. The narrow streets of Fieldston meander over rocky bluffs, past nineteenth-century landmark mansions overlooking Manhattan and the Palisades (a series of cliffs across the Hudson River, in New Jersey).

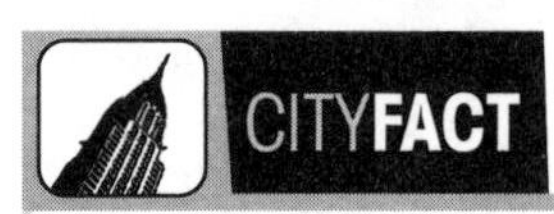

The Bronx is the only borough of New York City that is part of the North American mainland. All of the other boroughs are on islands (Manhattan and Staten Island are their own islands, while both Brooklyn and Queens are geographically part of Long Island).

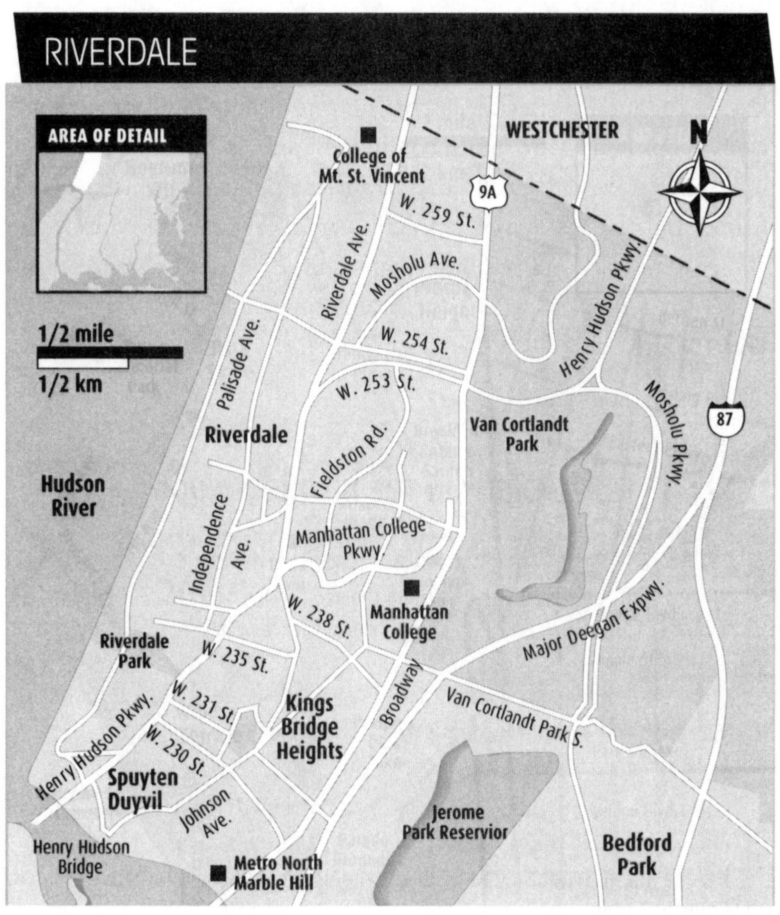

There are apartment complexes built in the 1950s and 1960s, and recently there has been a building boom and a number of new apartment buildings have gone up. The new construction has been mostly condominiums but rentals are available too.

Because of the open spaces available in the Bronx, there are several prestigious high school campuses nearby (Fieldston, Horace Mann, Riverdale Country Day, Bronx Science), as well as immense parks and even golf courses. There is a strong Jewish community, with three excellent Jewish schools and numerous synagogues and kosher restaurants. Residents commute to Manhattan primarily by express bus and Metro North commuter train.

Spuyten Duyvil (a collection of apartment buildings facing Manhattan and the Harlem River) and Marble Hill also provide some attractive housing options. Elsewhere in the Bronx, City Island seems more like a New England fishing community than like part of New York (or any city).

NOTEWORTHY **IN THE NEIGHBORHOOD**

Wave Hill (twenty-eight-acre nineteenth-century mansion with beautiful gardens and greenhouses), 675 East 252nd Street (Independence Avenue)

Van Cortlandt House Museum (restored Georgian-Colonial mansion), Broadway at West 246th Street

Horace Mann School, Ethical Culture Fieldston School, Riverdale Country School

NEIGHBORHOOD STATISTICAL PROFILE

Population		101,332
	White	(55.6%)
	Black	(12.0%)
	Asian	(3.6%)
	Hispanic	(28.8%)
Median Monthly Rent (government statistics)		$863
Median Price/Unit in a multiple dwelling (government statistics)		$725,000
Median Household Income		$44,000
Percent of Rental Units that Are Rent-Regulated		78.2%
Homeownership Rate		33.1%
Age of Householder:		
	15 to 24 years	3.4%
	25 to 44 years	38.3%
	45 to 64 years	32.8%
	65 years and over	25.5%

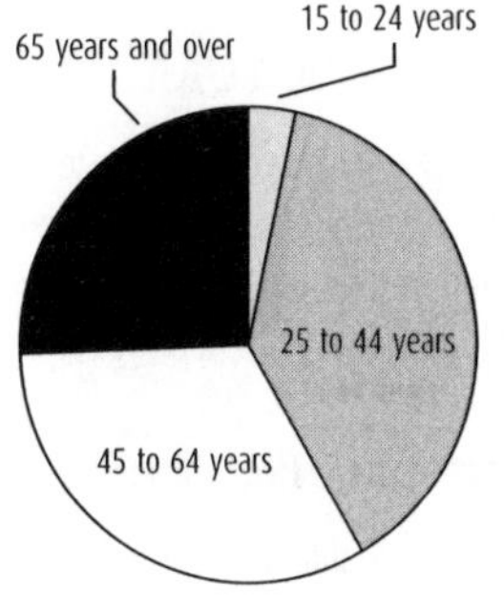

PURCHASE AND RENTAL STATISTICS FROM BROKERS

Buying

Average price per square foot	$537
Studio	$322,200
1 bedroom	$429,600
2 bedroom	$537,000
3 bedroom	$644,400
4+ bedroom	$805,500

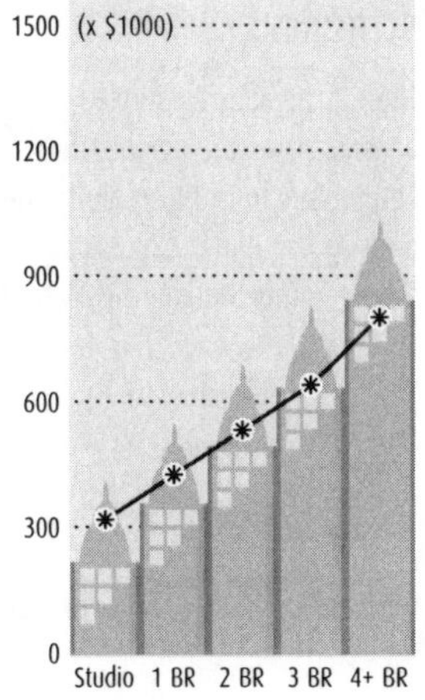

Renting

Average monthly rent per square foot	$1.90
Studio	$950
1 bedroom	$1,330
2 bedroom	$1,710

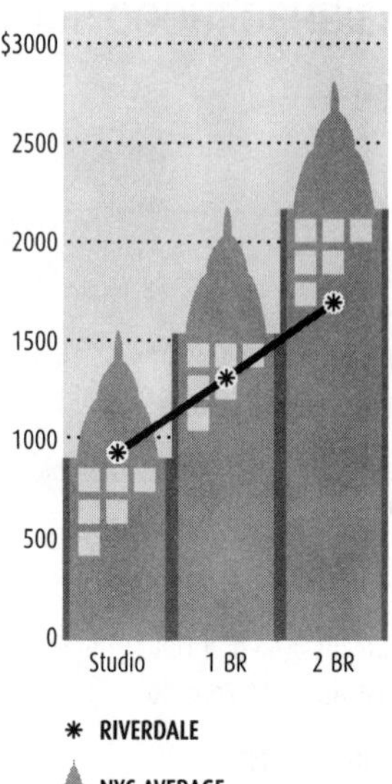

CRIME PICTURE

This is considered a very safe area, but it is an enclave within the Bronx, so be aware if you are thinking of living in one of the boundary areas.

INCOME PICTURE

This is an affluent area.

SUBWAYS

There is no subway service to Riverdale, which is part of what gives the neighborhood its suburban feel. Commuters from Riverdale to the Manhattan business districts use either express buses or, if they work near Grand Central Station, the Metro North commuter train.

Commuting Times

Midtown East	40–50 minutes
Midtown West	40–50 minutes
Wall Street	55–65 minutes

CHAPTER FOUR

THE SUBURBS AND BEYOND

Living outside of the city, especially if you are new to the area, may add challenges to your life that you won't especially relish. It is important to try to keep your search focused on areas that will keep your commute time to a minimum. If you expect to work twelve-hour days, a ninety-minute commute (one hour and fifteen minutes on the train, then fifteen minutes within the City) will extend that day to fifteen hours or more.

That said, the suburbs in the tristate area do include some lovely towns that, in other parts of the country, would be considered major cities. Some of these, like Yonkers and Jersey City, which rank in the top 100 largest U.S. cities (numbers 94 and 71 respectively), would be the largest city in an entire state. Others, like White Plains and Stamford, are home to powerhouse companies like IBM and GE. Deciding to live in one of these towns is a good start, but you'll still have to narrow your scope, because within each, there are many neighborhoods to choose from, each with distinct personalities. You still need to do your homework and enlist the help of a local, experienced real estate broker (ask for someone who's a specialist on relocating), who can be a real asset in helping you make a good choice.

The desirability of commuter suburbs in the tristate area is primarily determined by one thing, and that's public transportation. You will find pockets of commuters in a town that has a train or bus line, and (especially in New Jersey) virtually no commuters living in the town next door if that town does not offer its residents quick, easy transportation into the City. This one factor also makes a big difference in real estate prices.

PROS AND CONS OF LIVING IN THE SUBURBS

If you are considering living in the suburbs (with the exception of New Jersey towns like Hoboken and Jersey City, which are just on the other side of the river), I will assume, for purposes of clarity, two things about you (forgive me): (1) You already have a job in the City, and (2) you have a family.

Hundreds of thousands of people commute thirty minutes to two hours into Manhattan from the outlying suburbs every day. The primary reason for this is a lifestyle choice: these commuters want to live with their families in a house with a yard. People have other reasons for living outside of the City, but when you get down to the heart of the matter, the ability to live in a house with a yard supersedes all. Are you willing to commute up to two hours for that kind of space? If so, the suburbs may be right for you.

It is a generally held assumption that the schools are better here and the children will be safer, but you should note that in recent years the City has gotten much safer and some of the suburbs have even slipped a little. It is no longer true that suburban neighborhoods are free of drugs and dealers, and that all of the neighborhood schools provide top-notch education. I don't mean to scare you into thinking that the suburbs are dangerous or detrimental to your child's development—plenty of children play out in their yards, attend the public schools, and graduate on to great success—it just isn't universal anymore, anywhere.

Clearly, by opting to live outside of the City, you will have far more space, inside and out (the closets alone make me green with envy), and you will have mega–grocery stores, shopping malls, and discount shopping for added convenience. If you select your neighborhood with the school system in mind, chances are good that your child will attend the local public school for free. Getting your child to Little League on Saturday mornings won't be a struggle, and having a pet is a whole lot easier (particularly as no one is telling you whether or not you can).

But don't forget that if you're working in the City, you will have to face that commute every day, twice a day. You'll have to drive yourself and your children everywhere and you will pay a premium for proximity to something (Manhattan) that you may not take advantage of on a regular basis. If you have a child who is gifted in music or art, that child has fewer options in the suburbs than in the City. Also, in living there, you probably won't be as exposed to the dozens of different cultures, ethnicities, and lifestyles that you get in the City, and your children won't either.

Living outside of the city, especially if you are working and commuting, is a major lifestyle choice. Sure, you can still go to the opera, museums, and Broadway shows; you can still have dim sum in Chinatown or take a walk over the Brooklyn Bridge. But, realistically, you'll do it less often and it will take more out of you than if it was right around the corner. So before you decide, lay out your list of pros and cons and figure out what lifestyle suits you and your family best.

Pros of Living in the Suburbs

- More space for your money
- Property, a yard for children to play in, a place for a garden
- Shopping conveniences like bigger grocery stores, malls, and discount stores
- If you select a neighborhood with a strong school system, you'll be more likely to send your children to public school

Cons of Living in the Suburbs

- Commute time: you will see your family less
- Paying for proximity to something (Manhattan) that you don't have immediate access to
- Car dependency: you will have to drive everywhere
- You are more likely to live in a sheltered and homogeneous community

WHERE TO LIVE: REGIONS AND NEIGHBORHOODS

Where you decide to live outside of the City is a matter of taste and priorities. The general rule is that the farther away from the City you live, the more house and land you get for your money. You also want to factor in which communities have the best school systems, the most valued attractions, and easy access to train and bus lines. In deciding on each of those factors, you are also adding or subtracting dollars from the price of your house. Because, just like all over the country and the world, you're not just buying a house, you're buying in to a community, and that's something that you pay for no matter where you choose to live.

There are many regions outside of New York City and within the tristate area from which you can choose to live. They consist primarily of:

Westchester/Rockland (New York)
Long Island (New York)
Northern New Jersey
Southern Connecticut

Long Island includes the North Shore, South Shore, and East End. The North Shore of Long Island, made up of communities like Roslyn and Great Neck, is more affluent and expensive. The South Shore is generally made up of working-class communities. Schools on the North Shore are widely thought to be better than those on the South (if this is a point of interest for you, check the local schools before you buy). The East End of Long Island is, for anyone but the most ambitious (or masochistic), too far for easy commuting, and is made up of communities like the trendy, and very costly, Hamptons.

The state of New Jersey is made up of a multiplicity of cities and towns. There are the nearby urban communities like Hoboken and Jersey City, which are made up of young, single, twenty- and thirty-somethings who've

Opened in 1854, the Astor Library was the first privately endowed, independent, free public reference library in the United States.

moved there for more space and lower rents (and great views of the City).

North and west of the George Washington Bridge (GWB) are the so-called bedroom communities, like Teaneck and Fair Lawn, which are as close as some commutes from within the City (a convenience for which you will pay dearly, I'm afraid). The far-reaching suburbs, like Parsippany and Whippany, which are northwest of the City, are very suburban, but no farther away than many commutes from Long Island. And the Northeast Corridor, from (but not including) Newark down to (but not including) Trenton, is where you can own, and be surrounded by, a lot of land because the region is still used for agricultural production. In general, you will get more house for your money in New Jersey than in any other state in the region.

Westchester and southern Connecticut are the areas where especially affluent people live. The coastal strip from Larchmont to Westport could be likened to a Gold Coast. A few towns, like New Rochelle and Rye, along with the more affluent neighborhoods, have many of the problems common to urban areas. On the west side of the Hudson River in New York lies Rockland County, and this area tends to be more working-class. This isn't to say that there aren't millionaires living in Rockland County too, but Westchester is considered the more desirable address.

THINGS TO CONSIDER WHEN CHOOSING A SUBURB

As I hope I've made clear, there are many extremely livable communities outside of New York City, and deciding which one is right for you will take into account a number of different things. Do as much research on your own as you can, and also talk to a real estate broker. A good broker should be able to answer most of your questions satisfactorily (and you can also test the extent of that person's knowledge by seeing if the answers mesh with what you learned on your own). The rest of the pros and cons, like commute and budget, only you can decide.

The two most important factors to consider are the distance to your workplace and the mode of transportation you will use to get back and forth. Driving is largely impractical and expensive, unless you will be traveling at off hours (avoiding 8:00 to 9:30 coming into the city and 4:15 to 7:30 leaving) or carpooling, and parking your car in a very convenient garage (which will cost you upward of $400 per month). If your community is on a train line, there will be a schedule that is commuter-friendly, as long as you are traveling at peak hours. If you expect to work odd or long hours, find out about the train schedule outside of rush hours so that you don't find yourself stuck planning your life around the train (which, to some extent, everyone outside of the City must do). If you are commuting from Long Island (on Long Island Rail Road) or New Jersey (on New Jersey Transit or the PATH train), your train will come into Penn Station (34th Street and Seventh Avenue). Is that convenient to where you'll be working? How far is your commute from the station to your office? If you live in Connecticut and Westchester, you'll be coming into Grand Central Station (42nd Street between Lexington and Vanderbilt Avenues) on Metro North trains. Can you walk to your office from there? It's worthwhile to do some research on your commute to determine both the actual commute time from the City to your prospective home and the add-on time from the station to the office. Although you shouldn't buy a house exclusively based on where you are planning to work (because you're likely to switch jobs before you switch houses), arriving into Penn Station versus Grand Central could make a big difference in your commute time.

Some areas, like Rockland County and parts of northwestern New Jersey such as Teaneck and Englewood, aren't serviced by trains. In these regions, there are commuter buses, which some people actually prefer. One of the benefits of the bus lines is that rather than pulling directly into Port Authority (New York's bus station), they make stops and drops within the New York City street grid, which gets you closer to your office and removes an extra step from your commute.

Choosing the Right Suburb

- What is my budget?
- How far am I willing to commute each day?
- What are my commuting options?
- Is there a train line accessible to my town? How frequent is the service?
- Is there a commuter bus? Which buses have routes near my home? Can I walk to the bus stop?
- Where does the bus let me off in relation to my office?
- How are the schools in the community?
- Are there sidewalks?
- Are there children living in the neighborhood?
- Is the neighborhood safe?
- Do I want a big yard (how important is the *amount* of property)?
- How far away are the closest conveniences—grocery store, dry cleaner, video rental?

SUBURBAN COMMUNITIES

The following are condensed portraits of a few communities that represent the major suburban regions in all their diversity. This summary cannot, owing to the sheer overwhelming number and variety of suburbs, be a comprehensive list, but it is a good starting point to get you thinking about these areas. Likewise, I have not provided extensive statistical portraits for the suburbs—that would require a whole separate book. Once you start narrowing your choices and regions, you'll want to move on to local sources, experts, and brokers.

WESTCHESTER/ROCKLAND

BRONXVILLE (WESTCHESTER)

Many adults, having grown up in Bronxville, return there after settling down with families of their own. Very similar to Riverdale, though a bit more ritzy and suburban, Bronxville is only 2½ miles north of the New York City boundary. Renowned for its excellent public school system (100 percent of recent graduating high school seniors went on to higher education) and ideal physical location, Bronxville is a community where the housing doesn't come cheap. The commute is thirty minutes to Midtown via Metro North.

CHAPPAQUA (WESTCHESTER)

Chappaqua, located just nine miles north of White Plains, is in the Town of New Castle, which is the fastest-growing community in Westchester County. Chappaqua prides itself on its public education system, and its schools continuously rate among the nation's best. A country atmosphere prevails, even though the town is less than an hour from Manhattan. Real estate prices and property taxes (to pay for those excellent schools) are high. Commuting time on Metro North is approximately fifty minutes to Grand Central Station.

Lincoln Center for the Performing Arts is the largest performing arts complex in the United States. The center consists of Avery Fisher Hall, the New York State Theater (home to the New York City Ballet and New York City Opera), the Metropolitan Opera House, the Juilliard School, Alice Tully Hall, and the Vivian Beaumont and Mitzi E. Newhouse Theaters.

MAMARONECK (WESTCHESTER)

A waterfront town, Mamaroneck boasts diversity in population, restaurants, housing options, and schools. Children attend schools in one of two districts, depending on where they reside. Both districts have good programs: The Mamaroneck school system counts about 90 percent of its graduating high school seniors going on to higher education, and the Rye Neck District counts approximately 85 percent. The commute to Grand Central is forty minutes on Metro North.

THE NYACKS (ROCKLAND)

Diversity is the salient feature of the Nyacks, a community made up of Nyack, South Nyack, West Nyack, and Upper Nyack. The downtown of Nyack is a bustling village that attracts a host of tourists, too. Because it is only twenty-five miles from Midtown, many City transplants have chosen Nyack as their home, which might in part explain the variety. Students in all the Nyacks, except for West Nyack, go to school in the Nyack School District. Students in West Nyack go to school in the Clarkstown Central School District. Both systems boast 95 percent of graduating high school seniors continuing their education. The Nyacks are approximately eighty minutes to Midtown on a combination of the Red & Tan bus line and the subway to Manhattan.

LONG ISLAND

DIX HILLS (SUFFOLK COUNTY)

A wealthy neighborhood centrally located between the two major east to west thoroughfares on Long Island (the Long Island Expressway, or LIE, and the Northern State Parkway), Dix Hills

Central Park, in the middle of Manhattan, covers a larger area than the principality of Monaco.

is also regarded for its excellent schools, especially those in the Half Hollow Hills School District. Dix Hills is now home to many young families and puts a strong emphasis on family and community. Real estate is expensive; many homes sit on large lots because of local zoning laws, which in some areas require lots to be one acre or larger.

GARDEN CITY (NASSAU COUNTY)

From its inception in 1869, Garden City has been one of the most sought-after addresses in Nassau County. Boasting an excellent school district and easy access to Long Island Rail Road (LIRR) train service, this town continues to be a community in which people aspire to live. Garden City is forty-five minutes from Penn Station on the LIRR.

GLEN COVE (NASSAU COUNTY)

One of the great elements about this community is its ethnic diversity. A melting pot unto itself, Glen Cove welcomed immigrants arriving from Europe starting in the 1860s and now arriving from Puerto Rico, Africa, and elsewhere. One of only two actual cities on Long Island, Glen Cove has many affordable homes. The schools are solid, and nearly 60 percent of students continue on to four-year colleges. Glen Cove offers views of Long Island Sound and Hempstead Harbor, three public beaches, and an easy one-hour commute to the City on the LIRR.

GREAT NECK ESTATES (NASSAU COUNTY)

Once home to F. Scott Fitzgerald and his wife, Zelda, Great Neck Estates is an affluent community that has a very highly regarded school system (often sending 95 percent or more of its high school graduates on to higher education) and well-regulated appearance (no tree may be cut down without a permit).

OYSTER BAY (NASSAU COUNTY)

Public slips (for docking your boat) at the marina (for town residents only) are only one example of what sets Oyster Bay apart from its neighbors. Somewhat off the beaten path of traffic, this town is a real community, and its downtown, populated by mom-and-pop businesses, local hardware stores, and cafés, really drives that point home. By LIRR alone, the commute can be lengthy, but by driving to the Syosset station ten minutes away, you can cut the train ride by thirty minutes.

WEST ISLIP (SUFFOLK COUNTY)

It's not unusual for second-generation West Islipers to settle back into the community with their own families. This area is quite neighborly and cozy. A bit far from the city for those keeping long hours in the office, West Islip has good schools (boasting 90 percent and upward of graduating high school students continuing on to some form of higher education), varied property, and extra-friendly people.

NORTHERN NEW JERSEY

HOBOKEN AND JERSEY CITY (HUDSON COUNTY)

These two satellite cities, which would be considered a major urban axis in any other region of the country, are collectively known as the "sixth borough," and for good reason. Like the Brooklyn and Queens neighborhoods to the east, Hoboken and Jersey City have emerged as extremely desirable residential options for New Yorkers (that's right; though they live in Jersey, many residents of these cities consider themselves New Yorkers—and for all intents and purposes they are).

Rents, at this point, are comparable to rents in less expensive parts of the City, but you get more space for the same money and you're right across the river—closer than you'd be in most of the boroughs. Superb and efficient public transportation via PATH train (the New Jersey Transit equivalent of the New York City subway system) gets you into the City in just a few minutes, and there are extensive bus and ferry options as well. Directly across from the World Financial Center and Downtown Manhattan, Jersey City and Hoboken offer superior commutes for those who work in the Financial District.

Housing is diverse, ranging from large, new apartment complexes with New York skyline views to apartments in subdivided former private homes—and there are still large loft spaces available. Continued waterfront development promises that these areas will continue to improve. Despite easy access to Manhattan, Jersey City and especially Hoboken have developed thriving restaurant and entertainment industries of their own. The local newspapers, the *Hoboken Reporter* and the *Jersey Journal,* are the best sources for housing advertisements.

FORT LEE (BERGEN COUNTY)

Only six miles from Midtown, the town of Fort Lee is as centrally located outside of the city as you can get. Sitting in the shadow of the picturesque George Washington Bridge (GWB), Fort Lee offers residents several options from co-ops and condos to single-family homes. Most of the town's households are without children (mainly because the children have grown up and the parents have relocated to Fort Lee for the convenience), as is indicated by the less than 10 percent of the population in the school system. The commute to Midtown is thirty minutes via New Jersey Transit bus.

MORRISTOWN (MORRIS COUNTY)

Whereas less than ten years ago Morristown had vacant storefronts and a shrinking downtown; now the town that is historically known as Washington's headquarters (twice) during the Revolutionary War is a booming example of an astonishing rebound. With a strong public school system (more than 85 percent of graduating high school seniors continue on to higher education) and several Fortune 500 companies, the community is now very diverse, with as many as 50 percent of residents renting and the rest owning their homes.

MOUNTAINSIDE (UNION COUNTY)

A true suburban community without the strip malls, Mountainside is a peaceful, family town on the rise. Here you will find no apartments for rent, no condos or co-ops. The preponderance of the homes in Mountainside are single-family homes, and most of those that are now going on the market (just shy of 40 percent) are being sold off by the large percentage of residents who are over sixty-five. Attracted by vast parkland, a community pool in the summertime, free concerts, and boating on Echo Lake, the majority of people moving here are young couples in their late twenties to early forties with children in tow or on the way. The public schools are highly desirable, with 95 percent of all high school graduates attending institutions of higher education. The commute is about an hour by commuter bus to Midtown.

SCOTCH PLAINS (UNION COUNTY)

There is a real feeling of community in this town, originally settled in 1684 by Scottish immigrants, and it is evidenced by the small but thriving downtown, the influx of new young residents, and the increase in property values. Schools are solid, with 90 percent of graduating high school seniors going on to higher education.

SOUTHERN CONNECTICUT

NORTH STAMFORD (FAIRFIELD COUNTY)

Slightly removed from the hustle and bustle of Stamford proper, North Stamford is its antithesis: quiet streets and peaceful neighborhoods predominate. Previously a summer retreat for worn-out New Yorkers, North Stamford is now a community unto itself with a highly regarded public school system (over 85 percent of graduating high school seniors go on to higher education), as well as a preparatory school, a parochial school, and other education options. The town is approximately 65 minutes from Grand Central via Metro North.

GREENWICH (FAIRFIELD COUNTY)

Long known as a very white, very exclusive area, Greenwich has slowly been diversifying and has become a more accepting, tolerant community as a result. The highly regarded public school system (close to 90 percent of graduating high school seniors go on to higher education) offers not only the usual range of classes in foreign languages and the sciences, but also team sports including fencing, rugby, and water polo. There are also nine private schools in the community in the event that the public schools don't fit the bill. Beaches, ice skating, golf courses, and playing fields are among the facilities open to community members. The commute is approximately one hour to the City via Metro North.

ROWAYTON (FAIRFIELD COUNTY)

This traditional New England community, once home to farmers and oystermen, maintains the atmosphere of a village despite its proximity to Norwalk. The small town offers strong schools (with almost 85 percent of graduating high school seniors going on to higher education), which are very diverse and border on artsy, and a strong community spirit. New York is approximately a seventy-minute commute via Metro North.

OUTSIDE THE AREA

If your career has forced you to move to the New York area but you absolutely, positively can't abide the urban or hard-core suburban lifestyle, you still have some options. Likewise, special circumstances may require you to commute from farther than you might choose in the best of all possible worlds.

I've known people who commuted to Manhattan from as far north as Vermont, as far south as Virginia, and as far west as Pittsburgh. Where there's a will there's a way, and with modern transportation and enough money you can work in New York and live just about anywhere in the northeastern or Middle Atlantic states.

Here I've assembled brief sketches of the most convenient areas outside the traditional urban and suburban corridor. As with the suburbs (but even more so here), we'll rely on representative examples to characterize each region.

UPSTATE NEW YORK

Stretching north and west from Westchester and Rockland is the vast expanse of New York State, one of the largest in America. Once you leave the urban, southern portion of New York, you're in an area that looks a lot more like New England. For example, in Dutchess County, just a couple of hours' drive from Manhattan on the Taconic State Parkway, are the rural towns of Red Hook and Rhinebeck, where farming is still a way of life. Red Hook and Rhinebeck are approximately forty-five minutes north of Poughkeepsie (home of Vassar College), and they offer small-town country living within reasonable grasp of the Big City. This region of upstate New York is

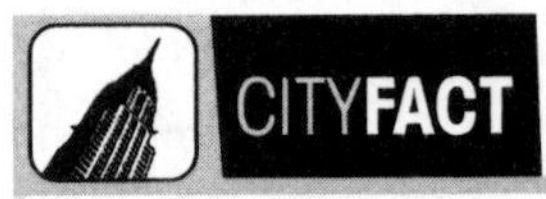

The first children's gardening program ever established at a botanic garden was begun at the Brooklyn Botanic Garden in 1914.

becoming somewhat popular as a weekend and summer destination for Manhattanites, and a few have fallen in love with the area and taken up year-round residence. Noteworthy in Rhinebeck is the Omega Institute, a meditation center. Nearby Bard College is a small school especially known for liberal arts and artistic studies. Public schools in these communities are very respectable and offer honors classes for children who are gifted in particular subject areas. Rhinecliff, approximately a ten- to fifteen-minute drive from Rhinebeck and Red Hook, has train service that takes two hours into Midtown.

CENTRAL AND SOUTHERN NEW JERSEY

As you head south past the major commuter suburbs of New Jersey, you come to Princeton. It doesn't get much more collegiate than this, and the Ivy League town lives up to the Ivy League school's reputation. Public schools here are likened to prep schools in other communities, and though just under 90 percent of graduating high school seniors go on to higher education, class averages of SAT scores are often nearly 175 points above the national average. What's more, at least 70 percent of teachers at Princeton (public) High School hold advanced degrees. On New Jersey Transit, the commute is approximately seventy-five minutes, but if time is of the essence, you can take the Amtrak train to Penn Station (though it'll cost you) and shave about thirty minutes off your time. Beyond Princeton and Trenton is the large mass of coastal land that constitutes southern New Jersey and the Jersey shore. Atlantic City is the most notorious town in this area, but all along the shore (and inland) sit interesting towns with a lot of history.

WESTERN AND UPSTATE CONNECTICUT

Those who don't like the affluent Westchester-like atmosphere of the southern Connecticut suburbs might do well to explore an area like Litchfield County. The picture of New England tranquillity and small-town quaintness is what you'll find in this region that is approximately two hours from New York City. Towns like Washington, Washington Depot, Litchfield, and Bethlehem are among the upstate towns that typify the area. Old homes and farms dating back to the 1900s (and before) dot the area. For grocery shopping and shopping malls, you'll have to travel, because these towns guard their community images like a dog guarding sheep. The schools are solid, and there are also many prestigious boarding and day schools nearby, such as the Canterbury School, Hotchkiss, and Choate Rosemary Hall, where many children from Manhattan enroll as boarders upon reaching high school age. There is no train service, and though you could drive thirty or more minutes to the New Milford train depot, the most efficient way to get to NYC is by car.

THE EAST END OF LONG ISLAND

Long a favorite weekend and summer resort for the beautiful people of Manhattan, the Hamptons, which lie on the South Fork of eastern Long Island, have exploded in popularity in the past two decades. This commute isn't for the faint of heart—the drive takes you through the worst areas of traffic congestion in Long Island and Queens (unless you can afford to commute by helicopter). Residents suffer the indignity of the commute in order to live in what is one of America's most beautiful coastal regions—it is evocative of Normandy, albeit with better weather, and there are numerous vineyards in the area (mostly on the nearby North Fork). Plus, on account of all the affluent Manhattanites staying or vacationing in the area at any given time, the dining and nightlife in the Hamptons is simply fabulous (you can't talk about the Hamptons without using the word "fabulous" at least once!). The North Fork is less settled and less of a scene, but as Hamptons prices have become astronomical, overflow to the North Fork has been inevitable. Train and bus service is available, but it's slow.

PART TWO
FINDING A HOME

CHAPTER FIVE
RENTING

New York is one of the few cities in the world where it is a common and accepted practice to rent for life. Over the years, renting in New York City has evolved, both culturally and legally, into a form of quasi-ownership wherein the apartment you rent can truly be called a home. Although now, given the current state of the housing market—very tight for renters, very brisk for buyers and sellers—more and more people, including young singles, are buying. Even if you're planning to buy an apartment, however, don't skip ahead—this chapter is full of useful information for buyers and renters alike.

New Yorkers can enjoy a truly excellent lifestyle by renting for an extended period of time. I've been living in the same rental apartment for the past sixteen years—longer than the average family stays in a purchased home—and have raised a dog, child, and husband here. Moreover, unlike in most towns, the quality of housing available to renters and buyers in New York City is essentially the same.

Renting allows the occupant more freedom than buying does. If you want to move, you can do so easily. If you want to save your money for something other than a mortgage, you can do that as well. Renting is also a very quick and relatively simple process. When you see the apartment of your dreams, you put your money down (generally first and last month's rent, plus a security deposit equal to a month's rent) immediately, process the necessary paperwork, and move in—perhaps just a couple of days later. There's no mortgage to secure, no attorneys to hire, and no closing dates to set, postpone, and postpone again.

In most towns, the word "rent" is synonymous with "apartment," and the concept of ownership is synonymous with buying a house. But in New York, for all intents and purposes, there are no houses. Other than a very small handful of luxury townhouse dwellings (which are only of concern to the superrich) and multifamily homes in the boroughs, everybody in Manhattan lives in a multiple-dwelling apartment building. So, whether you buy or rent in New York City, you're going to be living in an apartment of some sort.

When you rent an apartment in New York, it's called a "rental" or just an "apartment." When you buy, it's called a "condo" or a "co-op" (see Chapter 6 for more details on condos and co-ops), but technically it's still an apartment. You can get a rental in one brownstone

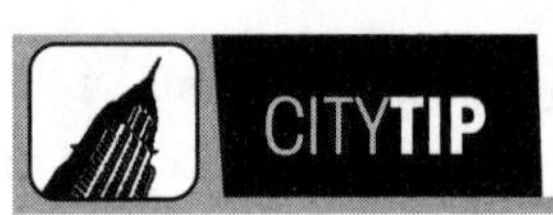

"If you have a limited budget, be flexible about where you're willing to live. Chances are, you'll do a lot better than if you limit yourself to one specific neighborhood, especially a trendy one."

—Irene Keating,
Director of Relocation Services,
Douglas Elliman

or buy a condo or co-op in an identical brownstone up the block. You can rent in a high-rise or buy in a high-rise. The physical options are mostly the same, although they vary from building to building. Some buildings only have rentals and others only have purchase options, but throughout any neighborhood—and even mixed within some buildings—you will have the option to rent or buy.

Even the services in rental apartment buildings rival those of nice co-ops and condos: dry-cleaning pickup and delivery, newspaper delivery to your apartment door, rooftop sun deck, common storage areas, laundry rooms—you can have all those things. Still, when you get into the category of the superlarge and superluxurious (apartments valued in the millions), it becomes more and more likely that the apartments you're looking at will be for sale only. And the more you spend—and the higher up the food chain you move in purchase price—the more exclusive the buildings become. The apartments get larger, there are fewer apartments per building, and there are more extensive services offered (squash courts, swimming pools, elevator operators, etc.). In this city that never sleeps and has everything to offer at the snap of a finger, often it is those extra services that distinguish you from the multimillionaire in the building next door. As a renter, you can still live in the neighborhood, but perhaps not in the building.

If at all possible, newcomers to the City should start with rentals. Unless you're especially familiar with the neighborhoods and the culture of New York City, you want to be in a specific neighborhood for the school district, or you're committed to living near your office or mother-in-law, you're taking a rather large risk in buying an apartment in a neighborhood that you don't know and may not like. And there's always the risk of a drop in the market imprisoning you in a particular home. Even if you have kids and you've selected a specific neighborhood based on the public schools, if you rent in that neighborhood, your kids are entitled to attend the same schools. One exception to this rule would be if you have pets, in which case rental buildings can be more restrictive than co-ops and condos (although this is not always the case—you have to ask). Otherwise, I'd advise you to get to know the city first and, possibly, buy later.

When New Yorkers hunt for apartments, they generally select an apartment based on the following factors:

- Space or size
- Cost
- Neighborhood
- Safety
- Conveniences
- Location (proximity to work or schools)
- Transportation (proximity to subway and buses)

Different people have different priorities, but the most common balance to strike is among cost, size, and neighborhood. The considerations of safety, location, transportation, and conveniences tend to be secondary.

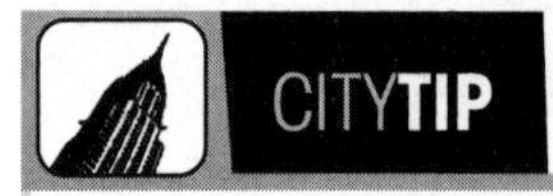

"Treat each apartment viewing as if it might be The One. Make your appointments for early in the morning—so you're the first person to see the apartment—and bring a deposit so you can put money down on the spot. If you don't, someone else will."

—John Munson, photographer

REALTORS AND RESOURCES

Most of the resources you'll use for renting and buying apartments are the same: the same Realtors, the same websites, the same newspapers. All those resources are gathered in Chapter 7, "Realtors and Resources."

RENTING VERSUS BUYING

Pros of Renting

- Get to know the city before you buy
- More options
- More freedom
- More financial freedom
- Better for temporary residence
- More money going into your pocket every month
- Good option for young people
- Less restrictive—condo and co-op buildings have lots of rules
- It's quicker and easier to rent

Cons of Renting

- Rent money goes to landlord, not toward the purchase of your home
- No tax benefits
- Most of the nicest and most exclusive apartments are condos and co-ops
- More and better services in high-end condo and co-op buildings
- A limited number of large (three-bedroom and bigger) apartments for rent
- Limits on renovations—you're making improvements on someone else's property
- More restrictive on pets

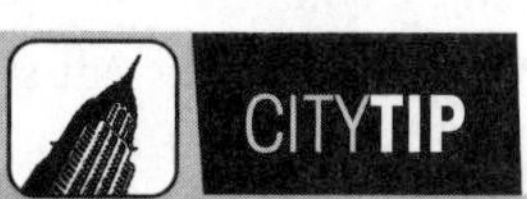

"To avoid a broker's fee, try renting an apartment in one of the no-fee buildings. There are several books that include listings of all the buildings in a given neighborhood—that's how I found my apartment."

—Daphne Matalene, advertising sales representative

RENTAL JARGON

You don't have to be in New York long before you start hearing the phrases "rent controlled" and "rent stabilized" tossed around. In fact, it is a favorite joke of New Yorkers that there are only three topics of conversation at New York cocktail parties: (1) co-ops versus condos; (2) someone who knows someone who has a rent-controlled apartment ("Can you believe what they're paying¿"), and, in true Woody Allen fashion, (3) who's seeing which therapist. A slight exaggeration (slight), but housing is such an important factor in every New Yorker's life that we've all caught ourselves (natives and transplants alike) saying these sorts of things—or at least thinking them. While it's important to understand these terms, it's also important not to obsess about them. Wherever you rent in New York City, the laws are extremely favorable to tenants. It's just that some sets of laws are more favorable than others.

RENT STABILIZATION

Rent stabilization is a body of regulations that apply to any rental building with multiple apartments built between February 1947 and January 1974. The rent-stabilization guidelines limit the percentage that a landlord can raise the rent with each lease renewal. The percentage varies from year to year and is decided by the Rent Guidelines Board. The landlord is also entitled to increase the rent by a certain percentage when a tenant vacates an apartment and when renovations and improvements are made. Tenants in rent-stabilized apartments must be offered either a one- or two-year lease and have an automatic right to renew their leases indefinitely.

An apartment is legally allowed to be destabilized (exempted from the rent-stabilization guidelines) when it is vacated and reaches a rent of $2,000. Most rental apartments built after January 1974, all rental apartments in co-op and condo buildings, and buildings with five or fewer apartments are exempt from the rent-stabilization laws.

If you're lucky enough to find a rent-stabilized apartment, grab it. I've heard many a sad tale of newcomers who lost great apartments because they didn't comprehend the absurd urgency with which a renter must put money down in order to secure an apartment.

RENT CONTROL

This much-misused term (people often say "rent control" when they really mean "rent stabilization") has a very specific legal meaning. Rent control was started during the early 1940s World War II era when there was a great housing shortage in the city and landlords were raising rents to extreme highs and, at least in some cases, throwing tenants out on the street with little notice. The rent-control laws were developed to protect tenants from unscrupulous landlords; the rent-controlled apartments that remain are a holdover from residents who have been living in the same apartment since before July 1, 1971. That means rent control applies to many older residents in New York City, but probably not to you.

If and when these apartments become available (usually because the tenant dies), they are renovated (many haven't been renovated for decades because of the low rent and lack of profit to the landlord), and rents are raised to fair market value. This often means an increase of many hundreds of dollars, and even thousands if the neighborhood has become very popular (like the Upper West Side, the Village, or Chelsea).

Family members often add themselves to rent-controlled leases so that they can take over the apartment if the opportunity should arise, although theoretically they're supposed to have lived in the apartment all along. If there is no family member to take over the apartment (a terrible tragedy for renters the city over—and every landlord's dream), rent-controlled apartments are converted to rent-stabilized apartments and the rent is raised to fair market value.

If, somehow, you should find yourself with the opportunity to latch on to one of these rare gems, call me first. But if you must have it for yourself, don't hesitate for a moment. If someone offers you a sublease on one of these apartments, don't wait for even one breath, or the opportunity will be lost. But realistically, you'll probably be like the rest of us. Aim to get a decent deal on a decent space and don't hold your breath waiting to win the renter's lottery.

GOVERNMENT RESOURCES FOR TENANTS

New York State Division of Housing and Community Renewal
dhcr.state.ny.us/ora/ora.htm
The Office of Rent Administration is responsible for regulating rents in approximately 1.2 million privately owned rental units statewide.

New York State Attorney General's Office
If you'd like information on tenants' rights, the attorney general publishes an extensive and extremely useful pamphlet at:
http://www.oag.state.ny.us/realestate/tenants_rights_guide.html

APARTMENT JARGON

You're probably familiar with the meaning of the terms "one-bedroom" and "two-bedroom" with reference to apartments; they're self-explanatory. The following are some other key terms you'll hear bandied about in reference to New York City apartments.

- Studio: A studio is an apartment that has a combined living and sleeping area. Generally it is one room with a small kitchen in a corner or in a little nook, and the rest of the space is used for living and sleeping (some people have a futon couch that they convert into a bed).

- Alcove Studio: An alcove studio is a modified version of a studio apartment. Off the studio is generally a "room" (the so-called alcove), which can be used for sleeping, but it will not have a proper door or doorway (otherwise it would be billed as a one-bedroom).
- Loft: A loft is a former commercial or industrial building that has been converted into apartments. Generally, these are large open spaces with high ceilings. They are usually found in Greenwich Village, SoHo, TriBeCa, Chelsea, Flatiron, lower Manhattan, and Brooklyn and often do not have the services of a doorman. Beware, though: The term "loft" now has a certain cachet and some unscrupulous brokers and landlords are advertising any large studio apartment as a "loft."

BUILDING JARGON

These are the most common terms used in describing New York City buildings:

- Walk-up: A building—often a brownstone or a townhouse—that has no elevator.
- Brownstone or Townhouse: Previously one-family homes with four or five stories, many brownstones and townhouses are now multiple-unit apartment buildings (with as many as ten studio or one-bedroom units). The units can be extremely small but also extremely charming, with original moldings from the time of construction (from the 1800s through the early 1900s). These buildings will not have a doorman and most likely no elevator.
- Prewar and Postwar: Buildings built before and after World War II (1940s through 1970s).

THINGS TO ASK AND CONSIDER WHILE LOOKING

Choosing an apartment is a very personal decision. Sometimes the decision will be an easy one based on only one thing: "Can I afford it?" Most New Yorkers spend one-fourth (or more) of their salary on rent each year. But even at the most basic level, there are still issues to consider and questions to ask when looking for a rental apartment.

First, figure out how much money you can afford to spend on your monthly rent. Figuring out an exact dollar amount will prevent you from wasting your time looking at apartments you can't afford—and you'll avoid the inevitable: feeling sorry for yourself when you see an apartment you love that doesn't fit within your budget.

Second, decide where you want to live and see if your allotted rent will realistically enable you to live in that neighborhood. For example, if you have $800 to spend and want to live alone, you'll be hard-pressed to find an apartment on the Upper West Side.

Third, what is the nearest public transportation? Most every New Yorker commutes to work on the subway, by bus, or on foot. Is it convenient to your office? This is a very important factor because when you calculate your commute, you have to account for the walking time back and forth to the bus or subway stop.

Fourth, is the apartment that you're looking at on the fourth floor of a brownstone? That means you have to walk up and down those stairs every

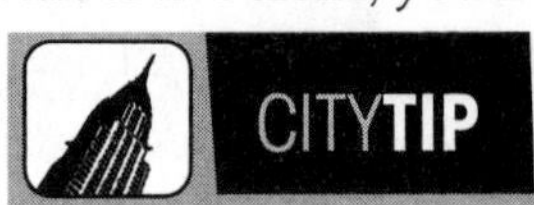

"If you hear of a good apartment building that has a long waiting list, and you're even so much as thinking about living in that building, you should get on the list no matter how long it is. The months and years pass by with unanticipated speed, you'll probably end up staying in New York longer than you planned (perhaps forever!), and good deals are worth the wait."

—Rachel Laiserin, technology project manager

day with your groceries, when the deliveryman comes with takeout food, to get the newspaper on Sunday morning, and to take out the garbage. Are you willing to accept the strain of the walk-up in exchange for a nicer apartment or better location than you otherwise could have afforded?

Fifth, how important is it to you to have a doorman in the building? Doorman buildings are safer, and the doorman can receive your packages and dry cleaning for you when you're at work or away on vacation.

Sixth, do you have children? If so, there are numerous factors to consider: the size of the apartment, the safety of the neighborhood, the nearby public and private schools, and the open spaces to run and play in, such as parks and playgrounds.

These are all issues that will come up when you're looking for your new apartment; you have to know what your top priorities are. I like to be close to Central Park so my son can choose from a selection of playgrounds and green spaces to run around in, and so I have a nice place to take our dog for walks. Many people who live near Central Park (with residential properties on all sides from 59th Street to 110th Street) wouldn't hear of living anywhere else. Others, who live downtown, couldn't care less whether they're near a park. To them, being near their child's school is most important. Or, for some, being close to the greenmarket, so they can buy fresh produce each week.

Following is a checklist of some important questions to ask yourself and your landlord when you're considering an apartment:

- What can I afford? Figure out a dollar amount.
- Is this the neighborhood in which I want to live?
- Do I want to live alone or with a roommate?
- Is there an elevator in the building? Is this important to me?
- Is there a doorman? Is this important to me?
- Am I allowed to have a pet? A cat? A dog?

- What schools are nearby? What public school district am I in? Are there any private schools nearby?
- Is the apartment big enough to have a roommate if I want one or later decide I need one?
- What is the nearest public transportation? Is it convenient for me?
- Are there any services available in the building?
- What are the nearby attractions? Is there a park?
- What is available in the neighborhood? Lots of restaurants? A grocery store? A bank?
- Is the neighborhood safe?
- Who lives in the neighborhood?
- "Is there anything I should know?" A good catch-all question. You never know what they'll say when you ask this one.

BEFORE YOU RENT: TAKE STEPS AND BE PREPARED

To rent an apartment in New York, there are many steps you'll have to take before you can actually sign the lease. It helps to be prepared, so that when the right apartment comes along, you'll be ready to sign on the spot.

Before you look, you'll need:

- A local bank account: You'll need to have a local bank account in order to get a certified check that will cover the cost of your rental. Landlords often won't accept out-of-state checks, or, for the first month and security deposit, personal checks either.
- A certified check: If you can't arrange to open a local account before you begin looking for an apartment, bring enough money in traveler's checks (to exchange at the bank for a certified check) to

cover the first month's rent and the security deposit, plus a little extra for incidentals (such as the cost of the bank check or broker's fee). You can also use one of the check-cashing kiosks located all over the city to get a money order, but they'll charge you a fee.

- A credit report: Your landlord will often require a credit report (which may cost you $25 to $50) before renting to you.
- Enough money for your deposit: To secure any apartment, you'll need first and last month's rent and a security deposit (usually equivalent to a month's rent).

Next is a checklist of necessary items and information that you must bring along when viewing apartments, for a landlord to even consider renting to you:

- Personal identification with photograph—a passport or driver's license should work (and preferably another piece of ID as well)
- A letter of employment, including your salary and start date
- A listing of all of your bank accounts and credit card numbers (list everything)
- A listing of personal and business references, including contact information
- A listing of previous landlords, including contact information
- Tax returns
- Pay stubs
- Any other sources of income with verification

ABOVE AND BEYOND THE RENT

Landlords in New York are a tough bunch, in part because local rental laws are skewed favorably to the renters. So, in order to protect themselves from a difficult tenant whom they won't be able to evict later, landlords want to check you out while they can, because it may be their last chance before you settle in for life. That's why the following seemingly unreasonable requirements are essential to most landlords (though some are stricter still and others slightly more flexible).

- You must earn, annually, forty to fifty times the amount of the monthly rent. That is to say, your rent will not be more than about a quarter of your salary (which is really more like a third to a half when you factor in taxes).
- If your salary does not make the cut, you will need a co-signer, or guarantor, to guarantee the lease. The best person to ask is a family member, preferably someone who lives in town or at least in the tristate area (New York, New Jersey, or Connecticut), owns property there, and has a large enough income to satisfy the landlord. Your guarantor will have to provide a lot of financial paperwork and documentation in order to satisfy your landlord, so prepare yourself, and them, psychologically before you begin the process.

TO HUNT ALONE OR WITH A BROKER?

Looking for a new apartment is an exciting process. It can also be overwhelming and frustrating. But, armed with the necessary information, finding your first apartment in New York can be a snap.

You must decide whether you want to look with a broker or on your own. Obviously there are pros and cons to both methods and you may decide one thing and, somewhere along the way, change to the other.

A broker can be a great asset because he or she can save you a lot of time (by showing you only apartments in your price range, only apartments that are known to be respectable and not already rented, and so on). The broker might also have exclusives—

apartments that no one else is showing. The broker will be able to tell you all about the neighborhood and the buildings within the area and help you find a good fit for your budget and lifestyle. They'll know the history of the buildings that you are viewing: Who is the landlord? Is the landlord responsible and reliable? Is there a lot of noise in the building? Street noise? Have there been problems here in the past?

A broker who finds you an apartment where you feel happy, safe, and satisfied is well worth the commission—but what about all of the other brokers?

One of the most important things to recognize about looking for a broker is that, if and when they find you your new residence, you must pay them a hefty commission of one month's rent—minimum (many require 10 to 15 percent of your first year's rent). Furthermore, the brokers who have these jobs (especially on the lower-priced rentals) tend to be from the bottom of the real estate barrel for one reason or another: Either they're new in the business or perhaps they're on the slippery side. So you need to know exactly what you're looking for and make sure you get it (but be realistic; you're not going to get a three-bedroom apartment on Fifth Avenue for $2,000 a month). Set forth clear specifications so the broker doesn't waste your time. Don't worry about hurting the broker's feelings, either—I assure you, the broker doesn't much care about yours. It never ceases to amaze me how many broker-related horror stories I hear that could have been prevented if my friends had cared more about themselves than about a broker's feelings.

Brokering is a high-volume business (especially with the lower-rent apartments). That means that your broker will have a limited amount of time to show you each apartment before having to run off to the next appointment. For the same reason, many brokers handle only one neighborhood (so

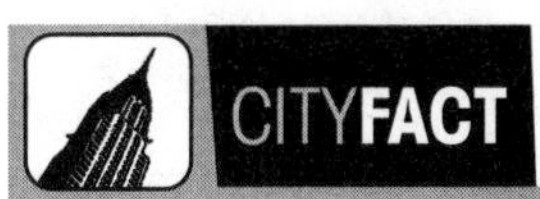

The New York Stock Exchange has an annual trading volume of $5.5 trillion.

they can shoot around from one building to another); if that neighborhood falls off your list, you might need to find another broker to work with who specializes in your neighborhood of choice.

Most important, do not let a broker push you into an apartment you don't want. Don't be afraid to speak up. If you don't like the person with whom you're working, ask for someone else. And do not take what your broker says as gospel. Some brokers may have hidden agendas, like getting a kickback from a landlord when placing a tenant into that landlord's building, or a bonus for renting a certain number of apartments in a particular building that year. The more informed you are, the better off and more protected you will be.

Which leads us to the next point: If you're willing to do the research and you are persistent (something you have to be *with or without* a broker), you can do exactly the same thing for yourself that the broker does, without having to give up a huge chunk of change. If you pound the pavement in your neighborhood of choice (look for "apartment[s] for rent" signs in windows, listings on craigslist.org, or listings in on-premises rental offices), you can view many of the same apartments that the brokers will show you. Many excellent apartment buildings are broker-free. So unless you read the paper or hear about the apartment via word of mouth (the grapevine is one of the best means of securing anything and everything in the City, and apartments are no exception), you'll never even see it with your broker. Furthermore, if your broker shows you an apartment that you read about in the paper and you decide to rent it, you still have to pay the commission—it doesn't matter that you could have found it on your own.

How you want to proceed will depend on how much time you have on your hands (if you already have a job, your time will be more limited) and how much time you have before you need to move. If you're living at home with your parents and commuting, you'll have more time to look than if you're sleeping on a friend's couch or in a hotel. Either way, looking at one apartment a week won't get you anywhere, nor will "just looking around" on a preliminary trip to the City a few months in advance. You have to make this your number one priority, and you can't rest until you've found your new home.

Pros of Using a Broker

A good broker will . . .

- Save you time
- Have exclusives on apartments and relationships with landlords
- Have more information than you could get on your own
- Know the neighborhoods better than you do
- Help you find a good apartment fit
- Know the history of the building (landlord, noise level, quality of building)

Cons of Using a Broker

Even if you find one of the above gems, a broker may . . .

- Require a minimum of one month's rent or up to 10 to 15 percent of one year's rent for the service of finding you an apartment
- Be at the bottom of the real estate food chain (read: inexperienced or scum of the earth), especially on lower-priced rentals
- Have a high-volume clientele that is often conversely related to quality of service
- Perhaps have a hidden agenda like getting kickbacks from a landlord or a bonus from a given apartment building
- Be a specialist in only one neighborhood
- Provide you with information that, with research, you could find on your own

ROOMMATES

TO SHARE OR NOT TO SHARE?

Some people are roommate people and some people aren't. Whether or not you have a successful roommate experience will depend on the personalities of you and your roommate and on the relationship you establish and develop over time. For some people the years they lived with a roommate were the best times of their lives, but for others, they were a nightmare they'd rather forget. Though you can't completely control the situation, there are certainly steps you can take to protect yourself and ensure a good match.

In New York, many recent college graduates, students of all ages (graduate, doctoral, art), newcomers to the City, and twenty- and thirty-something singles choose to live with roommates. Usually it's to save money, but plenty of people live with roommates because they feel safer, because they want to meet new people, because they want to live with friends, or because they can then afford a nicer apartment. What many people don't consider is whether or not they're cut out for the roommate lifestyle and how sharing an apartment will affect them.

The number one complaint of people with roommates is lack of privacy. Imagine coming home from a stressful day at the office and all you want to do is put your feet up, order takeout, and watch the news—but your Chatty Cathy roommate won't leave you alone. Your only option for privacy is to go out (who knows where) or to go to your room and close the door—if you have one.

The incompatible roommates—one of you is a night owl, the other a nine-to-fiver—is an age-old problem. The lack of flexibility that comes with having a roommate can ruin even the best of friendships. What if your roommate decides to move out on a moment's notice? Living with a roommate and wanting, or needing, a lifestyle change is often not as easy as breaking a lease with a landlord (most landlords don't mind when you break the lease and move out early, because that means that they can raise the rent). Usually, only one of you will have the lease—which means that that person holds all the power, responsibility, and rights. That's good if you want to stay in the apartment and ask your roomie to leave, but bad if your roommate skips out on the rent and you're stuck holding the bag.

For you roommate-seekers out there, take some steps to make life with your roommate pleasant and cooperative. Enter into the relationship as you would enter a marriage or a business partnership. In most cases, only one of the renters can be the leaseholder. Decide if you want to move in with someone who has all of the rights and all of the responsibility or whether you want to be the person holding the lease. There are a lot of benefits to being the leaseholder, but there are drawbacks too. The lease is in your name, so you're responsible for the full amount of the rent regardless of your roommate's contribution. Perhaps your roommate is chronically late with rent each month, or decides to move out on a moment's notice and doesn't have a replacement. Or, worse still, what if your roommate holds the lease and decides to move to Kansas and you're unable to renew the lease? What if your newfound love wants to move in? These are all common problems among roommates and the more steps you take to work things out in advance, the better off you'll be.

Pros of Living with a Roommate

- Save money—rent, utilities, phone, food
- Achieve economies of scale (a bigger and better apartment for the same amount of money each month)
- Live with a friend (or friends)
- Safety
- An instant new friend

Cons of Living with a Roommate

- Potential incompatibility
- Lack of flexibility
- Most landlords insist on having only one person's name on the lease, so one of you will have all of the responsibility, burden, and rights.
- A lack of privacy.

Deciding on a Roommate

- Sit down and have a heart-to-heart, get-to-know-you conversation with your potential roommate. The more you know about this person in advance, the more you will be able to anticipate and avoid conflict.
- Don't be afraid to pry. You're going to be roommates, so you'll learn all of each other's foibles sooner or later. Better you should know them sooner.
- Establish a clearly defined legal relationship. One person will hold the lease and therefore the responsibility to the apartment. Sometimes the leaseholder will pay more (you can take the bigger room to justify that)—but of course, you can always argue the opposite. You should also sit down with your roommate and set forth in writing what happens if your roommate decides to move out or is late with the rent or the bills.
- Establish a clearly defined, mutually respectful roommate relationship. After you define the legalities of the relationship, define the issues that will affect you both in the day-to-day.

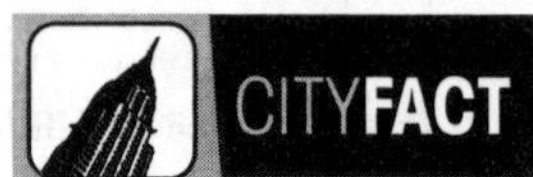

Not quite the system we have for garbage removal today: Until the 1840s, thousands of pigs roamed free on Wall Street, consuming refuse.

Issues to Discuss

- Do you want to split the groceries each week or do you each want to have your own shelves?
- Should you divide the phone bill each month or get separate lines? Do you even need a landline?
- How do you divide the utilities during the summer?
- What is the policy on using each other's belongings? Do you have to ask? What is okay to use without asking?
- If all the plates and dishes are yours, what happens when your roommate breaks something? If the DVD or CD player is yours, who replaces it if one day it doesn't work anymore? To whom does the replacement belong?
- What is the policy on houseguests, overnight guests, boyfriends and girlfriends?
- What is the policy on parties, music, and noise?
- On what day each month will the rent money be due, the bills paid, and the apartment cleaned?

All of these things may sound petty or even silly, but I spoke to people who have "broken up" over each and every one of these issues. So before you brush it off as irrelevant, think long and hard about what your priorities are and discuss them before the first box is moved in.

Helpful Hints

- Decide in advance whether you prefer to have a roommate of the same gender.
- The more roommates you have, the more the issues multiply.
- It helps to have a roommate of a similar age.

The golden rule of happy (and successful) roommates: If a problem arises, speak up! Do not let issues fester until they become much bigger than they have to be. If your roommate is doing something that is making you crazy (finishing the milk and not replacing it, taking your newspaper to the office, playing music at full volume), let your feelings be known right away.

FINDING A ROOMMATE

Perhaps the best tool at your disposal is your mouth. Open it wide and start talking, because it's likely that you'll mention it to someone's aunt who has a friend who has a son-in-law whose sister is looking for a roommate. And then you're sitting pretty. So talk it up and tell everyone you encounter that you're on the hunt.

Now, if you don't have success finding a roommate via word of mouth, there are a number of other options available. Just be wise about it—there are many scams out there and the roommate-matching business is not entirely free of shady characters. Here, I list only the most reliable and the favorites: only a handful of listings, but along with word of mouth and university referrals, they should be all you need. And remember, as with all other things, if it sounds too good to be true, chances are it is.

Craigslist
newyork.craigslist.org
An excellent resource for finding everything—roommates are no exception. You may have to wade through some undesirables to find the sincere offerings, but there are many gems to be had. If you already have an apartment, another solution is to conduct an open house. This is where you post a roommate-wanted ad and

invite potential roommates to see the apartment within a specific timeframe. Invite a friend to keep you company (and safe), and don't list your address for all to see—you can supply it upon request. This is a good way to meet a lot of potential tenants at once and greatly reduce your hunting time. Bear in mind that because people will be coming in and out you won't have time to conduct in-depth interviews—keep a list of the potential roomies you like so you can schedule follow-up interviews at another time.

Rainbow Roommates
124 West 60th Street
New York, NY 10023
(212) 757-2865
(212) 627-8612
rainbowroommates.com

RR services all five boroughs and the Greater New York Metro area. It is a service dedicated to finding roommates for gay, lesbian, bisexual, transgender, and gay-friendly people from around the world in affordable and comfortable housing.

Roommate Finders
Westover Building
253 W. 72nd St., Suite 1711
New York, NY 10023
(212) 362-0162
roommatefinders.com

Roommate Finders is the oldest in the business by far (they've been in business since 1979, nineteen years longer than any other roommate service in the City). When matching up prospective roommates, they take into account thirty-five

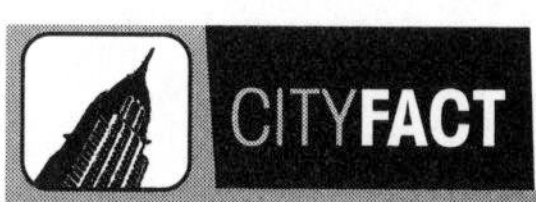

A 2007 economic analysis of the real estate market by the *New York Times* indicates that renting is often more economical than buying.

different factors, including personality, income, age, and lifestyle. They cover Manhattan from 95th Street down to Battery Park for a $300 flat fee.

OTHER PLACES TO LOOK

National Roommates
nationalroommates.com

Best utilized as a jumping-off point in your search for a roommate, National Roommates is a clearinghouse for roommate-finder organizations. Begin here and allow the links to lead you to other regional services, which are generally better.

The New York Times

Check especially online. See Resources in Chapter 7.

The Village Voice

Check especially online. See Resources in Chapter 7.

CHAPTER SIX

BUYING AN APARTMENT IN THE CITY OR A HOME IN THE SUBURBS

As discussed in detail in Chapter 5, I strongly advise newcomers to New York City, absent extraordinary circumstances, to rent before buying. But let's assume that you are ready to buy, for whatever reason. Maybe you lived in New York before and you're moving back, or perhaps you have a compelling tax reason that requires you to buy something now. Maybe you know you want to live in a specific neighborhood because you want your child to attend the public school there (just be sure to confirm the district boundaries before you buy). Or you could be a professional real estate investor who objects to renting on principle. It's always possible that you just stumble across a really good deal. Or you're stubborn and you won't take my advice? Fine, you won't hurt my feelings.

When purchasing, the universe of apartments is similar to what you'd examine in a prospective rental situation, so many of the same rules apply: You have to figure out where you want to live, what your budget will allow, and all your other preferences. So if you skipped over Chapter 5 on your first go-round, go back and read it now.

As a prospective apartment owner in New York, you are faced with the age-old question of "condo or co-op?" Physically, they're the same—you can't tell by standing in an apartment whether it's a condo or a co-op. But the buying processes are quite different.

When you buy a condominium, you're buying your unit outright. Either you buy your apartment from the previous owner, or, if it's a new building, you buy it from the investment/development group. Either way, you own the actual, physical apartment. You pay your mortgage to the bank, your taxes to the government, and your common charges (covering care for common areas like the lobby, hallways, laundry room and utilities, costs for insurance, maintenance, salaries for doormen) to the building. You are autonomous in your ownership so you can renovate your apartment as you see fit (though you will be responsible for any damage you do to the building in the process) and rent it out should you choose to do so. There is an elected condo board, but the board's control is limited to the common aspects of the building. The board traditionally does not have the right to restrict you from selling your apartment or subletting it if you so choose. By the same token, because there are no restrictions on who can buy in to the building, you may find that the demographics of your neighbors are regularly in flux.

Co-ops have traditionally been an altogether different matter. When you buy in to a co-op, you buy the right to live in your apartment by purchasing shares in a corporation. Each apartment has a share value, which is based on the size and desirability of the unit, assigned to it at the co-op's inception. The owners/leaseholders own the building together, and they decide (via the co-op board) who can buy in to the building, whether a member can undertake a major renovation, what work will be done to maintain and improve the building, and so forth. Co-ops are usually far more exclusive than condos, and owners reserve the right to keep it that way. Someone who buys in to a specific co-op building may be buying because he or she likes the outlook and policies of the other tenants. When people buy in to the building, they'll want to guard their right to keep those policies from changing. A family-oriented building might keep unattached singles out, and they are entitled to do so. Some co-ops are so exclusive that they demand that all apartments be purchased outright for cash—no mortgages of any kind are permitted.

Financially, co-op members are responsible for the building as a whole. Each member is responsible for monthly maintenance charges (which are based on the number of shares assigned to each unit). These payments go toward paying the building's expenses, which include property taxes, repairs, improvements, insurance, operating costs, and perhaps a mortgage or loan payments. This is not to say that people who own condos don't pay property taxes too; it's just the way the payments are divided—either you pay your taxes to the building, or you pay them directly to the government. In a condo the property is your own, the same as if you owned a house. Therefore, you pay the taxes directly to the government. In a co-op, the monthly maintenance charges include your taxes, which, based on the building as a whole, are paid to the government.

There is also more of an element of risk involved in buying in to a co-op, because if one of the members defaults on monthly maintenance fees, the other members are responsible for picking up the slack (another reason why co-op boards can be very strict when reviewing and assessing a potential buyer).

In either instance, co-op or condo, it is very important to consult with a seasoned real estate attorney, who will be able to decipher for you the ins and outs of the building's financial situation. Just as the board will be checking out all of your credentials, you check out theirs. If the building just had its roof replaced, you may be buying in to an extra $500,000 of debt (which will be divvied up among owners and added into your monthly service charges). Is the apartment worth it to you? Or could you find one that is equally as nice that doesn't have that extra debt attached? Of course, at any time a roof could go or an elevator could have to be replaced. You can't make your decision in fear of the future, but with the help of an expert, you can decide as wisely as facts permit at the time.

According to Irene Keating, director of relocation services at Douglas Elliman (one of the largest brokerages), New York City is unique in that co-op buildings constitute approximately 85 percent of all occupant-owned apartments, versus only 15 percent for condos; therefore your selection will be somewhat dictated by supply and demand. But don't get too bogged down in the formal definitions of co-ops and condos. Gone are the days when co-ops and condos were two completely different animals. The differences are disappearing, formally and informally, as buildings work to make the best financial arrangements possible. For example, where once condos used to be unable legally to take out loans on behalf of the building (for repairs and so on), now they can do so and finance the payments in the form of monthly common charges. And condos are now figuring out ways to guarantee some exclusivity and more control to their boards. Some apartments are now advertised as hybrid "cond-ops." The bottom line is, when assessing the costs and investment value of a co-op versus a condo, you have to look at each building as a separate entity.

Condo Basics

- You own your apartment outright.
- Everyone in the building owns the common areas together.
- Monthly maintenance fees tend to be low because each condo owner is responsible to pay only for a share of the common areas.
- You can renovate your apartment as you wish, as long as it does not affect the building.
- Condos are usually less restrictive than co-ops.
- Condos are usually less exclusive than co-ops.
- Condos usually have no one protecting the best interest of the building as a whole.
- You can sell your apartment to whomever you choose.
- Typically, you can sublet your apartment to whomever you want and for as long as you want.
- Condos usually require 15 to 20 percent of the cost of the apartment down.

Co-op Basics

- A co-op is a corporation. You own your apartment in the form of shares in the corporation (rather than the apartment itself). Your shares are based on the value of your apartment (based on the square footage and desirability).
- When you buy in to a co-op, you are buying exclusivity.
- Co-ops can be very restrictive, because the members are acting to protect the interests of the building.
- Co-op members have the right to deny you the sale of an apartment if they don't approve of the prospective buyer (as long as the refusal is not discriminatory in nature).

- Monthly co-op payments tend to be higher than those of condos (but payments include property taxes).
- You must seek board approval before planning any major renovations.
- There is greater financial risk in a co-op.
- Co-ops generally require 20 to 25 percent of the cost of the apartment down (sometimes more).

THE FINANCES

Work out the finances of what each apartment will cost, including

- Money down
- Monthly common charges or maintenance fees
- Monthly mortgage payment (and the percentage of the payment that represents interest)
- Property taxes
- Closing costs
- Costs of needed renovations or repairs
- Utility costs (e.g., are heat and cooking gas included as part of the common charges, or do you pay separately for them?)

Only after you have added up all of the numbers (having calculated mortgage-interest payments as tax deductions) and assessed all of the financial factors can you make an informed decision.

REALTORS AND RESOURCES

For listings of the Realtors who can help you find a home, see Chapter 7, "Realtors and Resources."

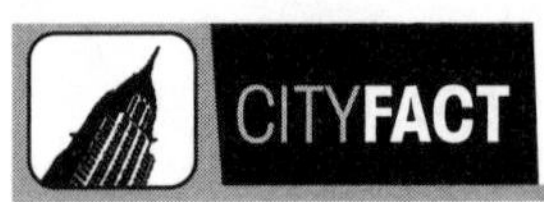

You'd think everybody would want to have celebrity neighbors, but movie stars, rock stars, and other household names are often rejected by co-op boards that want the building to remain exclusive, low-key, and unencumbered by the host of problems (reporters and photographers lingering about, for starters) that celebrities attract.

BUYING A HOUSE IN THE SUBURBS

Finally, if you choose to live in the suburbs, you will most likely want to purchase a house. Buying a house in the tristate area isn't really any different from buying a house anywhere else in America—it's just a little more expensive.

TO HUNT ALONE, OR WITH A REALTOR

Whereas many people in the City buy, sell, and rent apartments without working with a particular real estate broker, it is almost unheard-of for people in the tristate area to buy houses without brokers. Assuming that you are not familiar with the region and you'd like to find something fairly quickly, I recommend finding an area broker, to make your search as painless and efficient as possible.

As a specialist in the field, your broker should know the neighborhoods and the schools in each area and should be able to connect you with exactly what you're looking for. They'll also be happy to do it in a hurry, because the faster they sell you a house, the faster they make their commission. Furthermore, community real estate brokers are likely to take the time necessary to sell you what you want, because there is the greater likelihood of repeat and referral business, and building a solid clientele depends upon good service. This is very different from the rental business, because brokers who find rental units for tenants anticipate never hearing from or seeing those tenants again, so why should they care how you feel about them in the end?

To hunt alone (and educate yourself on the market), check the town's local paper (online too) for listings by regional real estate agencies and independent sellers. Mention to everyone you know that you're house-hunting (you never know what you will turn up) and check the Internet—this is likely the biggest financial and personal decision you'll make for some time and therefore merits a thorough search.

All of the big realty companies have branch offices throughout Long Island, New Jersey, and Connecticut, so if there is one company that you are partial to or that you have had good luck with in the past, check the phone book or the Internet. Chances are good that there will be a branch in the area in which you are looking to buy.

CHAPTER SEVEN

REALTORS AND RESOURCES

This chapter covers the resources you'll need to rent or buy in New York City and the surrounding areas:

- Internet resources: listings of the key websites you'll want to use to plan your housing search
- Real estate agents: the brokers who can help you rent or buy, in the city or suburbs
- Temporary housing: solutions for those who move first and rent or buy later

INTERNET RESOURCES

Every large real estate company has a website and many have extensive up-to-date apartment and house listings complete with photos and floor plans; most have a variety of practical information too. Even Craigslist posts by-seller real estate listings these days.

In addition to reading up on available apartments themselves, there are also some very important New York–centric information and entertainment sites you should not proceed without. Before you plunk down any money, do some reading and research on one or more of the following websites. You'll be a New York City housing insider in no time—and a real hit at your next cocktail party.

REAL ESTATE BLOGS AND NEWS SOURCES

Curbed
www.curbed.com
If you really want to keep your New York real estate knowledge on the cutting edge, read Curbed every day. Founded in 2004, Curbed is a blog, updated a dozen or more times a day, that has become one of the key sources of information about New York City real estate and neighborhoods. The most highly trafficked real estate blog on the Web, it contains everything from brass-tacks

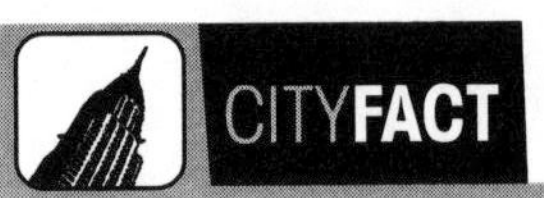

The New York City Landmarks Preservation Commission was created in 1965 as a result of the tremendous public outcry in the wake of the demolition of the magnificent old Penn Station. Now, more than three decades later, plans are finally under way to replace the undistinguished new Penn Station with a more dignified version similar to the grand railroad stations of old.

information about market prices and new developments to amusing stories about brokers, celebrity deals, and restaurants to constantly updated links to just about every other important real estate website.

Brownstoner
www.brownstoner.com
A well-written real estate blog focusing on Brooklyn.

Matrix
matrix.millersamuel.com
A blog written by Jonathan Miller of the appraisal firm Miller Samuel, focusing on the real estate economy.

The Real Estate
www.observer.com/therealestate/
A New York real estate blog from the staff of the *New York Observer* newspaper.

The Real Deal
www.therealdeal.net
The *Real Deal* is a print magazine (mostly distributed to people in the real estate business), and the website contains many of the articles from the magazine (for free), as well as video and up-to-the-minute news.

Triple Mint
www.triplemint.com
The Triple Mint blog tracks new developments in New York, and focuses on architecture.

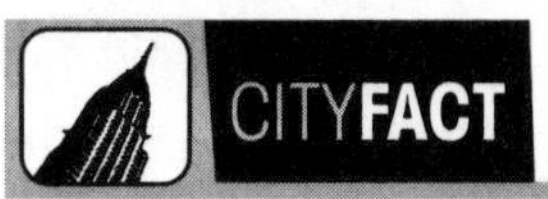

The New York City Marathon was first run in Central Park in 1970 by 127 runners who completed the 26.2-mile race by looping around and around the Park Drive in Central Park. In 2005, the marathon's thirty-fifth running, 36,856 people crossed the finish line after having run through all five of the City's boroughs, making it one of the most celebrated days in the City each year.

The Cooperator
cooperator.com
This is the website of the *Cooperator,* a monthly magazine focusing on co-ops and condos.

Habitat Magazine
habitatmag.com
Also a co-op and condo magazine, with a frequently updated website.

LISTINGS META-SEARCH

Streeteasy and Trulia
www.streeteasy.com and www.trulia.com
Streeteasy and Trulia are extremely powerful real estate research tools the likes of which used to be available only to industry insiders. You can, for example, search for a building and find all the apartments for sale in that building, as well as that building's sales history: how much apartments in the building have sold for over time, and whether prices are headed up or down.

OTHER LISTINGS META-SEARCH WEBSITES

Base4Space
base4space.com

CityCribs
citycribs.com

Natefind
www.natefind.com

PropertyRover
propertyrover.com

Real Property Research

ACRIS
nyc.gov/html/dof/html/jump/acris.shtml
ACRIS allows you to search public records about specific properties.

Property Shark
propertyshark.com
Searches across many types of records so you can gather intelligence on a property you're considering.

Zillow
www.zillow.com
Estimates the value of any property, and provides many other search tools.

NEWSPAPERS

The New York Times
nytimes.com
Some would claim that, in addition to word of mouth, this is the only tool you need to rent or buy an apartment in New York City—and they wouldn't be far off. Widely available all over the city and tristate area, the *Times* features apartment

On February 19, 2000, the Museum of Natural History opened its completely renovated planetarium in the new Rose Center for Earth and Space, which is the most expensive ($210 million) and technologically advanced planetarium in the world.

listings (and listings for houses outside of the City) in the Real Estate section of the Sunday paper ($3.50). Get a jump start on the competition by looking online before the paper comes out and by buying the paper on Saturday night.

The Village Voice
www.villagevoice.com
A free weekly publication that is widely available on many street corners (look for them in the brightly colored, usually red, newspaper boxes). The *Voice* is an especially good resource for downtown (Greenwich Village, East Village, SoHo, TriBeCa, and Chelsea) rentals and sales. It also includes listings for all five boroughs and northern New Jersey. New issues appear on Wednesdays. Also check online to get a jump start on the competition.

REALTORS

New York City is unlike most other places in that you can't always just go to one real estate agent and see every apartment that you want to see. Realtors in the City sign contracts with sellers to have "exclusives" on apartments. That means that if you want to see an apartment, you have to see it with the broker who has the exclusive. Or, you may be able to see the apartment with another broker who has an arrangement with the exclusive broker. This is what's known as a brokered split, and it's becoming more common, almost routine. If you buy, the two brokers split the commission. Still, real estate brokers will often push hard to have you see their exclusives and not other apartments. So select firms carefully on the basis of size, listings, specialty, or service, because to some extent that choice will determine what properties you see.

There are also buildings that, because they are so large, have in their orbits brokers who specialize in just that specific building or complex. If so, you'd do well to go through those building specialists. For example, there are brokers who specialize in sales and rentals in Battery Park City, whose population is larger than that of many small towns. The same would apply to Lincoln Towers on the Upper West Side, which is one of the largest condo communities in Manhattan. There are also co-op and condo buildings that don't use brokers, especially new buildings that might have their own salespeople, whom you must go through in order to buy in. That's why, when selecting your real estate broker, you must have a clear idea where you want to live, which will in turn help determine which firm (or building agent) you use. You may also use several brokers; however, the fewer brokers you deal with the easier it will be to organize your search.

Following is a list of the most noteworthy real estate companies in New York, divided into major firms and smaller or specialty firms (the specialists are subdivided by neighborhood).

For the majors, I have listed branch offices in every neighborhood and each company's website. Be sure to check the websites of each company for updated lists of branch offices (the opening or closing of a realty office is a common sight in the City), names of and contact information for brokers, practical and helpful information about preparing for your search, and of course for the extensive apartment listings.

For the smaller brokerages, I have listed websites only. Many of these brokerages don't have walk-in offices, and their websites function as virtual offices. Others are decentralized, and you might deal with different brokers in different home offices depending on which property interests you. You should always start with the website, then move on to phone contact and in-person meetings. There's no need to feel overwhelmed by the number of brokerages in New York City. You just have to be methodical in your research. Once you've focused on a neighborhood and narrowed your criteria you'll be surprised how few apartments are actually in your target range. At some point, you may transition from feeling overwhelmed to feeling that there aren't enough choices—really, it happens!

I hesitate to recommend one brokerage over another; each has strengths and weaknesses by building and neighborhood. But from the following list, if you happen to be in a given neighborhood and want to drop into a real estate office to talk to a broker, you can't go wrong by visiting Corcoran or Prudential Douglas Elliman—they are huge, diverse brokerages with excellent reputations. At the same time, don't overlook other brokerages, both large and small. In your New York City real estate search, as in much of life, there are no true shortcuts.

THE MAJOR BROKERAGES

BELLMARC REALTY
bellmarc.com

West Side
424 Columbus Avenue
(212) 874-0100

East Side
1015 Madison Avenue
(212) 517-9100

Midtown
681 Lexington Avenue
(212) 688-8530

Broadway
936 Broadway
(212) 239-0900

Downtown
16 East 12th Street
(212) 627-3000

BROWN HARRIS STEVENS
bhsusa.com

Residential Sales East Side
655 Madison Avenue, 3rd Floor
(212) 906-9200

Residential Sales Upper East Side
1121 Madison Avenue
(212) 317-7700

Residential Sales West Side
1926 Broadway, Mezzanine
(212) 588-5600

Residential Sales Village
2 Fifth Avenue
(212) 906-0549

Residential Sales TriBeCa
43 North Moore Street
(212) 452-4500

Residential Sales Brooklyn Heights
129 Montague Street
Brooklyn
(718) 875-1289

Residential Sales Park Slope
100 Seventh Avenue
Brooklyn
(718) 230-5500

CITI HABITATS
www.citi-habitats.com

Main Office, Union Square
250 Park Avenue South, 12th Floor
(212) 400-1300

Upper West Side
465 Columbus Avenue
(212) 957-4100

222 West 72nd Street
(212) 712-2722

Upper East Side
400 East 84th Street
(212) 794-1133

1456 First Avenue
(212) 774-3800

Midtown West
346 West 57th Street
(212) 489-7777

Midtown East/Murray Hill
937 Second Avenue
(212) 400-2400

Chelsea
155 Seventh Avenue
(212) 937-9677

Gramercy Park/Flatiron
32 East 22nd Street
(212) 260-9720

West Village
114 Perry Street
(212) 400-2500

East Village
37 Third Avenue
(212) 937-8500

Greenwich Village
214 Sullivan Street
(212) 253-2525

Financial District
100 John Street
(212) 619-1212

COLDWELL BANKER HUNT KENNEDY
cbhk.com

West Side
329 Columbus Avenue
(212) 877-1300

East Side
555 Madison Avenue
(212) 326-0300

Downtown
401 Avenue of the Americas
(212) 255-4000

Brooklyn
155 Seventh Avenue, Brooklyn
(718) 622-7600

CORCORAN
corcoran.com

Corcoran has become a New York City area real estate giant in the past decade, though the company has been around for more than thirty years. Between the writing of the first edition of this book and the researching of the book you hold in your hands,

Corcoran has gone from having one office to more than ten, and now claims to be the largest residential brokerage in the City.

12th Street
36 East 12th Street
(212) 500-7000

Carnegie Hill
1226 Madison Avenue
(212) 360-6160

Chelsea/Flatiron
636 Sixth Avenue
(212) 444-7800

East Side
660 Madison Avenue
(212) 355-3550

East Village
49 East 10th Street
(212) 253-0100

Gallery
2253 Broadway
(212) 721-7227

Harlem
2224 Frederick Douglass Blvd.
(212) 678-7200

SoHo
490 Broadway
(212) 941-2500

West Side
888 Seventh Avenue
(212) 721-4600

Brooklyn Heights
124 Montague Street, Brooklyn
(718) 852-9050

145 Montague Street, Brooklyn
(718) 237-1700

Fort Greene
65 Lafayette Avenue, Brooklyn
(718) 210-4000

Park Slope
125 Seventh Avenue, Brooklyn
(718) 499-3700

FENWICK KEATS GOODSTEIN REALTY
fenwick-keats.com
(888) FEN-WICK
Selling and renting properties throughout Manhattan

Main Office
401 West End Avenue
New York, NY 10024
(212) 787-0707

Flatiron
64 West 21st Street
(212) 444-3300

West Side
2244 Broadway
(212) 579-9300

East Side
211 East 46th Street
(212) 755-1500

Downtown
201 West 11th Street
(212) 352-8140

HALSTEAD PROPERTY, LLC
www.halstead.com

Relocation Office
770 Lexington Avenue
(212) 381-6521

East Side
1356 Third Avenue
(212) 734-0010

West Side
408 Columbus Avenue
(212) 769-3000

Greenwich Village
831 Broadway
(212) 253-9300

SoHo
451 West Broadway
(212) 475-4200

Midtown
770 Lexington Avenue
(212) 317-7800

Harlem
175 Lenox Avenue
(212) 381-2203

Brooklyn Heights
150 Montague Street
Brooklyn
(718) 613-2000

Cobble Hill
162 Court Street
Brooklyn
(718) 613-2020

Riverdale Office
3531 Johnson Avenue
Riverdale
(718) 878-1700

PRUDENTIAL DOUGLAS ELLIMAN
elliman.com
One of the largest residential brokerages, with branches all over the City

Relocating Office
(212) 891-7640

East Side
575 Madison Avenue
(212) 891-7000

980 Madison Avenue
(212) 650-4800

485 Madison Avenue
(212) 350-8500

West Side
1995 Broadway
(212) 362-9600

TriBeCa Gallery
90 Hudson Street
(212) 965-6000

Greenwich Village
51 East 10th Street
(212) 995-5357

137 Waverly Place
(212) 675-6980

Downtown
26 West 17th Street, 7th floor
(212) 727-6102

Harlem
2169 Frederick Douglass Boulevard
(212) 995-5357

Brooklyn Heights
156 Montague Street, Brooklyn
(718) 780-8100

Cobble Hill
189 Court Street, Brooklyn
(718) 522-2929

Williamsburg
299 Bedford Avenue, Brooklyn
(718) 486-4400

Bayside
209–18 Northern Boulevard
Bayside, Queens
(718) 631-8900

Flushing
39-09A Main Street, 2nd Floor
Flushing, Queens
(718) 888-0909

SOTHEBY'S INTERNATIONAL REALTY
www.sothebysrealty.com

East Side
38 East 61st Street
(212) 606-7660

Downtown
379 West Broadway
(212) 431-2440

STRIBLING
stribling.com

Uptown
924 Madison Avenue
(212) 570-2440

Downtown
340 West 23rd Street
(212) 243-4000

TriBeCa
246 West Broadway
(212) 941-8420

WARBURG REALTY
warburgrealty.com

Greenwich Village
65 West 13th Street
(212) 327-9600

TriBeCa
100 Hudson Street
(212) 380-2400

Harlem
2235 Frederick Douglass Boulevard
(646) 253-0300

SMALLER AND SPECIALIST BROKERAGES

Ardor NY
ardorny.com

Benjamin James
benjaminjames.com

City Connections Realty
cityconnectionsrealty.com

CitySites NY
citysitesny.com

DJK Residential
djkresidential.com

DwellingQuest
dwellingquest.com

Eychner Associates
eychner.com

GO Properties NY
gopropertiesny.com

HH Realty Group
www.hhrealtygroup.com

Klara Madlin
klaramadlin.com

Kurland Realty
kurlandrealty.com

Leslie J. Garfield & Co.
lesliegarfield.com

Mark David & Company
www.markdavidny.com

Massey Knakal Realty Services
masseyknakal.com

McIntosh Company
co-opsny.com

Metro Spire
metrospire.com

The Modlin Group
modlingroup.com

Nest Seekers International
nestseekers.com

NYC Living Realty
nyclivingrealty.com

Peter Ashe
peterashe.com

The Real Estate Group NY
www.tregny.com

Rose Associates
rosenyc.com

RP Miller & Associates
rpmillernyc.com

Shvo Group
shvogroup.com

Triumph Property Group
triumphproperty.com

Vickers Realty Ltd.
vickersrealtyltd.com

Winslow & Company LLC
www.findnycloft.com

NEIGHBORHOOD SPECIALIST BROKERAGES

MANHATTAN: DOWNTOWN

JMK Realty
jmkrealty.com

Meisel Real Estate
meiselrealestate.com

NY Living Solutions
nyls.net

MANHATTAN: LOWER EAST SIDE

Loho Realty
lohorealty.com

Misrahi Realty
misrahirealty.com

MANHATTAN: CHELSEA

DG Neary Realty Ltd.
dgneary.com

MANHATTAN: UPPER WEST SIDE

Marilyn Korn
marilynkornrealty.com

Wohlfarth & Associates
wohlfarth.com

MANHATTAN: UPPER EAST SIDE

Edward Lee Cave, Inc.
edwardleecave.com

Gumley Haft Kleier
ghkrealty.com

MANHATTAN: UPTOWN

Harlem Homes
harlemhomes.com

Stein-Perry
steinperry.com

Uptown Homes
(212) 862-7173
Bob Pollock is a Harlem specialist who doesn't maintain a website; however, he's well worth contacting if you're looking to live in the neighborhood.

Vertical City Realty
verticalcityrealty.com

Willie Kathryn Suggs
williesuggsharlem.com

BROOKLYN

Aguayo & Huebener
ahrlty.com

Apartments and Lofts
aptsandlofts.com

Betancourt & Associates
betancourtrealestate.com

Brooklyn Cornerstone
brooklyncornerstone.com

Brooklyn Properties
brooklynproperties.com

Coldwell Banker Labarca
labarcacoldwellbanker.com

The Developers Group
thedevelopersgroup.com

Fillmore Real Estate
fillmore.com

Harbor View
harborviewrealty.com

LoftNinja
ninjalistings.blogspot.com

Mary Kay Gallagher
marykayg.com

Real Renters
realrenters.com

Warren Lewis
warrenlewis.com

TEMPORARY HOUSING

Although temporary housing is a great option in many cities, it is a bit trickier to come by in New York. The options for mainstream accommodations (hotels, short-term-stay furnished apartments, extended-stay hotels, hostels) are generally either extremely overpriced or extremely dingy—or a combination of both. You will find that apartments in New York are rented at an alarming pace. If you are ready to rent and you have everything in order, it can take as little as a day, a week, or, for the very selective types, a month to find yourself a new home. Because of this, you should take steps to ensure that you don't have to shell out a bunch of cash (short-term fully equipped lease apartments start at the low, low price of $2,200 per month—if you're lucky—and easily range up to $12,150) or settle into a ratty hostel while you're looking. If you know someone in the City, find out if you can impose for a few nights while you get your bearings. For cramped New York apartment dwellers, allowing friends to stay over is a favor that lasts a lifetime, but ask anyway because they'd happily ask you too.

If you are being hired in advance by a corporation, try to get them to include temporary housing in your relocation package (or a housing allowance) while you look for something permanent. Many big law, accounting, and investment firms will offer this outright with no negotiation at all.

If you have no choice but to seek temporary housing, go for the less-mainstream options. They do tend to be a little more work to arrange but it will be well worth the effort, because the accommodations will be more pleasant, you'll save a bundle of cash, and you'll probably make some friends along the way. Some decent temporary-housing options include:

- College dorm rooms (only if it's summer)
- Subletting an apartment (from a friend, cousin, brother of a friend's cousin, or via Craigslist.org)
- YMCA/YMHA
- Unhosted apartments
- Women's/Men's residences
- Servicemen's and Servicewomen's residences

COLLEGE DORM ROOMS

Many of the universities and colleges in New York have little housing or no housing at all, even for their students, so the choices are limited.

New York University (NYU)
14A Washington Place
(212) 998-4621
nyu.edu/housing/summer

SUBLETTING

The best way to sublet is to know someone who is leaving the City for a while and wants to have someone in the apartment paying the rent. If this seems like a long shot because you don't know a single soul in town, try the next best option, newyork.craigslist.org. You can also try scouring the walls of the nearest college campus (see Chapter 12 for a lengthy listing), but the thing about student sublets is that many students prefer to rent to fellow students, people affiliated with their university, or people clever enough to find their posting. Many students in New York City live off campus because the City is their campus, and many students don't have the luxury of living in a campus dorm. So whether they're off for a semester abroad, taking a year off from school, or leaving for the summer, students have tons of apartments that are available on a short-term basis, and many of them post notices of availability at the entryways to university buildings. So read the walls and search the Internet. If on the off chance you still haven't turned anything up, you may find a few sublets advertised in the *Village Voice* and the Sunday *New York Times.*

YMCA/YMHA

De Hirsch Residence
92nd Street YMHA/YWHA (Young Men's/Women's Hebrew Association)
1395 Lexington Avenue
(212) 415-5650
www.92y.org

Short stays (30 to 45 days) are priced as follows:

- A large single room is $80 per day.
- A regular single room is $75 per day.
- A double room is $60 per person per day.
- A small double room is $50 per person per day.

For stays of 46 days or longer prices are monthly as follows:

- A large single room is $1,395 per month.
- A regular single is $1,295 per month.
- A double room* is $1,095 per person per month.
- A small double room* is $995 per person per month.

* Shared rooms are for residents who are 28 years of age and younger.

The accommodations are similar to college dorm rooms. They are fully furnished and have shared bathrooms and kitchens. In order to be eligible, you must apply for a room (you can't just show up, even if it's on a short-stay basis), which takes approximately one week to process, and you must be a full-time student, have a full-time job, or a combination of the two. It is advisable to file your paperwork for residence at least two months in advance in order to secure a room. There is also a fully equipped health club in the building (including a twenty-five-yard pool—a rarity in NYC), which you can use for an extra fee.

YMCA IN MANHATTAN
(917) 441-8800
ymcanyc.org

There is a main reservation center, open during business hours, for most of the listed YMCA branches. You can also call each Y directly or book online for all of the area YMCAs.

Vanderbilt YMCA
224 East 47th Street
(212) 756-9600

This is a coed facility. Rates are $83 for a single, $93 for a double (with bunk beds) per night and include the use of the health club and pool. Singles and doubles have shared baths.

West Side YMCA
5 West 63rd Street
(212) 875-4101
(212) 875-4206

Rooms are available to men and women at a rate of $89 per single and $99 per double (with bunk beds). There is an upgraded floor that has twelve private bathrooms at a rate of $99 per single and $105 per double, also with bunk beds. These rates include the use of the health club and pool.

Harlem YMCA
180 West 135th Street
(212) 281-4100

Rooms are available for men and women on separate floors with shared baths. One floor is coed. Single rooms with shared bath are $53 per night, doubles (with bunk beds) are $94 per night, student rates are $231 per week, and senior rates are $196 per week. Rooms include television, refrigerator, and closet.

YMCA IN BROOKLYN AND QUEENS

The following YMCAs in Brooklyn and Queens are also sources of clean, comfortable accommodations.

Greenpoint YMCA
99 Meserole Avenue
Brooklyn
(718) 389-3700

Rooms are $43–$60 per person per day, with shared bathrooms. This includes access to all facilities including gym, swimming pool, and fitness classes.

North Brooklyn/Twelve Towns YMCA
570 Jamaica Avenue
Brooklyn
(718) 277-1600

Single rooms at a rate of $40 per day or $280 per week. This includes access to all Y facilities, including the steam room.

Flushing YMCA
138-46 Northern Boulevard
Flushing, Queens
(718) 961-6880

Single rooms are $55 per night and $330 per week with a maximum stay of 28 days. Doubles (with either two twins or a large bed) are $75 per night, and triples (with one queen and one twin bed) are $85. All facilities are included.

Jamaica YMCA
89-25 Parsons Boulevard
Jamaica, Queens
(718) 658-7233
Single rooms are $53 per night and doubles are $70 (with bunk beds or a double). This includes use of facilities.

CORPORATE APARTMENTS

Empire State Properties
empirestateproperties.com
Leading specialist in providing short-term furnished relocation housing.

UNHOSTED APARTMENTS

Unhosted apartments are the ideal alternative to corporate apartment rentals. You stay in someone's apartment (they're not there), in a real building (as opposed to corporate glass and steel), in a real neighborhood, and you can settle in while you're looking for your permanent residence. I've listed only the oldest and most reputable companies, though many more have sprung up in recent years.

Abode
P.O. Box 20022
New York, NY 10021
(212) 472-2000
(800) 835-8880
abodenyc@aol.com
abodenyc.com

Apartments ranging from studios (starting at $145 per night) to three-bedroom/three-bath ($4,000 or more), all available on a nightly basis with a minimum of four nights. With stays of one month or longer, price adjustments can be negotiated.

Oxbridge Property Services
1623 Third Avenue, Suite 204
New York, NY 10128
(212) 348-8100
inquiry@oxbridgeny.com
oxbridgeny.com

Oxbridge offers apartment rentals on a daily, weekly, and monthly basis in a range of neighborhoods. Prices start at $115 per night.

Gamut Realty Group, Inc.
115 East 57th Street, 11th Floor
New York, NY 10022
(212) 879-4229
info@gamutnyc.com
gamutnyc.com

The majority of the fully furnished rental apartments start at around $2,000 per month, although there are also a few less-expensive exceptions.

WOMEN'S RESIDENCES

Most of the women's residences require a minimum stay of three months, so they may not be the ideal option, but they are safe, clean, and cheap, and most of them even include a few meals.

The Salvation Army/Markle Residence
123 West 13th Street (between Sixth and Seventh Avenues)
(212) 242-2400
themarkle.org

The Markle is run by the Salvation Army and is a safe bet (and a great deal) at $85 per night. Weekly rates start at $248 in a quad room, $330 per week in a small single, and $280 in a small double. Monthly rates are available too. The price includes two meals per day, sheets, and towels. Guests must apply for a room and there is usually a waiting list, so apply early. Rooms are open to women age 18 to 35 and guests must either be students or employed.

Parkside Evangeline Residence
18 Gramercy Park South
(212) 677-6200
Parkside is also run by the Salvation Army. There is a three-month minimum stay (though during slow periods, they will allow shorter stays). Most rooms are singles with private baths (there are a few doubles and a few singles with shared bath). The cost is $191 to $300 per week and $700 to $1000 per month for an excellent Downtown location, and that includes breakfast and dinner. Apply at least one month in advance.

St. Mary's
225 East 72nd Street
(212) 249-6850
Rooms are $50 per day, $150 to $200 per week with shared bath and a minimum three-month stay.

Webster Apartments
419 West 34th Street
(212) 967-9000
(800) 242-7909
websterapartments.org
Webster offers rooms at $232 to $245 per week, based on your salary and status (working students and interns). Accommodations are single rooms with shared baths. Two meals per day are

included. A nice change to the facility's policy is that "women who come to New York for business purposes can stay at Webster as visitors" for $75 per day, and that includes a full breakfast. For temporary residence, there is a three-day minimum. Apply in advance.

MEN'S RESIDENCES

Kolping House
165 East 88th Street
(212) 369-6647
residence@kolpingny.org
kolpingny.org

The Kolping House offers rooms to interns and students between the ages of 21 and 30. All rooms are singles with shared baths. Rates are $60 per day and $185 per week with a maximum stay of three months. Rates include one meal per day. Application is necessary and there is a $50 application fee. Letters of reference are also necessary.

SERVICEMEN'S AND SERVICEWOMEN'S RESIDENCES

The Navy Lodge
North Path Road
Staten Island, NY 10305
(718) 442-0413
(800) NAVY-INN
www.navy-lodge.com

The Navy Lodge is a hotel for military personnel; any active-duty serviceperson, retiree, reservist, or honorable discharge (with a military ID) can book a room at the hotel for $85 a night. These same people can also book a room for relatives at the same rate. Active-duty personnel can reserve sixty days in advance; all others can book thirty days in advance.

Soldiers', Sailors', Marines' & Airmen's Club (operated by the USO)
283 Lexington Avenue (between 36th and 37th Streets)
(212) 683-4353
www.ssmaclub.org

The Soldiers' and Sailors' Club is a tremendous bargain for military, former military, and service personnel (NYPD, NYFD, and EMS). The rates start at $25 per night for enlisted parties and go up to $120 for double occupancy in the "VIP suite." Guests of eligible personnel may also stay at these rates. Stays can range from one to twenty-one days. For individuals, rooms and baths are shared.

PART THREE
MOVING

CHAPTER EIGHT

PLANNING THE MOVE

Written for both the first-time mover and the relocating veteran, this chapter contains information and resources that will help you get ready for your big move to New York City. If money is foremost on your mind, you'll find a section on budgeting for the move and tips on how to save money throughout the process—as well as a budget-planning guide. If time is also precious, you'll find time-saving tips and even suggestions for how to get out of town in a hurry. You'll find help with preliminary decisions, the planning process, and packing, as well as tips and advice on uprooting and resettling your family (and your animal companions). A budget worksheet, a set of helpful checklists, and a task timeline complete the chapter.

PAYING FOR YOUR MOVE

Moving is one of those expenses that is easily forgotten about—until it's right upon you, and then the reality of just how much it's going to cost is often a shocker. How much your move will cost depends on a number of factors: whether your employer is helping with the expenses, how much stuff you have, and how far you are moving.

To get an idea of how much your move will cost, start calling around to different moving companies for estimates and make a list of these fees.

If you don't have the money saved, start saving as soon as possible. Also, remember other potential sources of money:

- Income from the sale of your car, furniture, or other belongings (hold a garage or yard sale).
- The cleaning and damage deposit on your current rental and any utility deposits. You probably won't be reimbursed until after your move, though, so don't plan on this for up-front expenses.
- Your employer, who may owe you a payout for vacation time not taken.
- Saved money from closed accounts. Settle up on cable, gym membership, and other local services one month in advance to save money for the move.

TAXES AND YOUR MOVE

Did you know that your move may affect your taxes? As you prepare to move, here are some things to consider:

- Next year's taxes. Some of your moving expenses may be

tax-deductible. Save your receipts and contact your accountant and the IRS for more information. Visit www.irs.gov or call the IRS at (800) 829-1040 for information and to obtain the publications and forms you need.

- State income tax. New York State collects income tax, so you'll want to figure that into your salary and overall cost-of-living calculations. Remember to find out how much, if any, of the current year's income will be taxable in your old state.
- Other income sources. You'll want to consider any other sources of income and whether your new state will tax you on this income. For example, if you are paying federal income tax on an IRA that you rolled over into a Roth IRA, you may also have to pay state income tax on your rollover IRA.
- After you move or when filing time draws near, consider collecting your receipts and visiting an accountant to help with the transition.

THE BUDGET MOVE (MONEY-SAVING TIPS)

Here you'll find some suggestions for saving money on your move.

Saving on Moving Supplies

- Get boxes in the cheapest way possible. Ask a friend or colleague who has recently moved to give or sell you their boxes. Ask your local grocery, liquor store, or department store for their empty boxes.
- Check online and in the classified ads; people sometimes sell or give away all their moving supplies for a flat rate, and it's a great way to recycle. Alternatively, post a message on websites like Craigslist asking for boxes and other moving supplies.
- Borrow supplies like packing-tape dispensers and box knives instead of buying them.

- Use your paper recyclables or linens for packing your breakables instead of buying new packing materials—good for the environment and your wallet.
- Get online and shop around for the best prices on packing tape and other supplies. Here again, Craigslist can be a real bonanza, as can eBay.
- Before you give away all of your old sheets, towels, and linens, use them for padding and protection for your move.

Saving on Labor

- If you use professional movers, consider an "I pack, you drive" arrangement, in which you pack your belongings into boxes in your home, and the moving company simply loads, moves, and unloads the boxes.
- Call around and compare estimates.
- If you move yourself, round up volunteers to help you load and clean on moving day. If you want to keep your friends long beyond moving day, reward them with moving-day snacks, meals (pizza or sandwiches tend to be best), and beverages. A small gift is nice too (you can't go wrong with gift cards—pick friends' favorite coffeeshops). You may also get called for payback to help them move someday.
- Save on child and pet care. Ask family or friends to watch your young children and pets on moving day.
- If you are renting your own U-Haul, look in newspapers, an Entertainment book, on the Web, or in an AAA guide for discounts.

Saving on Trip Expenses

Overnight the Night Before You Depart

- Where will you stay the night before you depart? A hotel or motel might be most comfortable and convenient, but you could save a little money if you stay the night with a friend or relative.

- Alternatively, if you have the gear, maybe you'd enjoy unrolling your sleeping bag and "roughing it" on your own floor the night before you leave town.

Overnight on the Road

- Look into hotel and motel discounts along your route. Hotel discount websites abound (www.hotels.com is a great place to start). Check in with your club memberships and credit cards.
- If your travel involves an overnight stay and you're game for camping, check into campgrounds and RV parks along your route. Be sure to ask whether a moving truck is allowed.

Note: It is important to mention that if you are packing a truck and driving it yourself, there is no tradeoff for the safety of you, your family, and your belongings. If you stay in a motel or hotel, be certain that the neighborhood is safe and the parking is secure. This is a time when it's worth it to spend a little extra money for the long-term payoff of the safety and security of your family and your worldly possessions. Before you load the first box, be sure the truck locks, and trade it in for another one if you have any doubts.

SCHEDULING YOUR MOVE

Try to allow yourself at least three months to plan and prepare. This long lead time is especially important if you plan to sell or buy a home or if you are moving during peak moving season (May through September). If you plan to move during peak season, it's vital to reserve two to three months in advance with a professional moving company or truck rental company. The earlier you reserve, the more likely you are to get the dates you want. This is especially important if you're timing your move with a job-start date or a house-closing date, or are moving yourself and want to load and move on a weekend when your volunteers are off work.

WHEN IS THE RIGHT TIME TO MOVE?

If your circumstances allow you to decide your move date, you'll want to make it as easy as possible on everyone who is moving:

- Children adjust better if they move between school terms (entering an established class in the middle of a school year can be very difficult).
- Older adults have special needs you'll want to consider.
- Pets fare best when temperatures aren't too extreme, hot or cold.

THE "GET OUT OF TOWN IN A HURRY" PLAN

First the bad news: Very little about the move process can be shortened. Now the good news: The choices you make might make it possible to move in less time. The three primary resources in a successful move are time, money, and planning. If you're short on one, be prepared to spend more of the others to get the job done.

Immediately check into the availability of a rental truck or professional moving service. Next, give your landlord notice or arrange for an agent to sell your home. (If you own your home, you may find it harder to leave town in a hurry.) If your employer is paying for your move, ask if it offers corporate-sponsored financing options that will let you buy a new home before you sell your old one. Then consider the following potentially timesaving choices:

- Move less stuff. Of all the moving tasks, packing and unpacking consume the most time. The less you have to deal

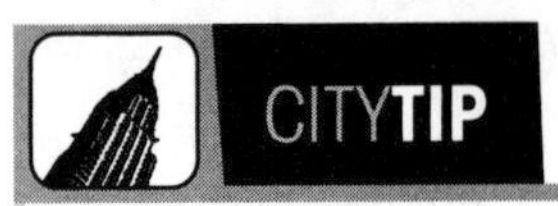

"Talk to everyone, because the person sitting next to you on that park bench could end up being your new best friend, your roommate, your employer, or even your spouse."

—Susan Barash, author

with, the quicker your move will go. If you have been thinking about tossing that old couch or buying a new dining room table—*now is the time.*

- Make a quick-move plan. Quickly scan through Chapters 8 and 9, highlighting helpful information. Use the checklists and the task timeline at the end of this chapter to help you.
- You can be out the door sooner if you hire a professional cleaning company to come and clean everything, top to bottom, including the carpets. Again, the time you save will cost you money—but it may well be worth the tradeoff.

PLANNING AND ORGANIZING

Start a move notebook. This could be as simple as a spiral-bound notepad or as elaborate as a categorized, tabbed binder. Either way, you'll find it invaluable when chaos hits. In your notebook, keep detailed notes, such as reminder lists, directions, and addresses, and tape your receipts. Of course, you'll want to keep *this* book with your notebook as well. Keep yourself organized and on target by using the moving task time lines at the end of this chapter. Assign yourself and family members "to-do-by" dates for each task on the checklist. To help yourself gauge what you've got to get done in the coming weeks, read through the Moving chapters so nothing catches you by surprise.

The section of the Moving Task Time Line that will help you the most at this point is "Decision Making: Weeks 12 to 9," which you'll find at the end of this chapter.

If you were wondering why all cabs in New York City are yellow, you're not alone. John Hertz, who established the Yellow Cab Company in 1907, read a study by the University of Chicago that specified that yellow was the easiest color to spot. The rest is history.

PRELIMINARY DECISIONS

Before you even begin to plan your move, there are a number of decisions you'll need to make regarding your current residence, how you will move (do it yourself or hire a professional), and your new area.

LEAVING YOUR CURRENT HOME (RENTAL PROPERTY)

Leaving a rental unit involves notifying your landlord and fulfilling your contractual obligations. This won't be a problem unless you have a lease agreement that lasts beyond your desired move date (and even then, your landlord might not mind an early departure, if given fair notice).

Your rights and options are dictated by state and local landlord/tenant laws and by your lease agreement. Exit fees can be expensive, depending on the terms of your lease. Here are some tips that may help you get out of a lease gracefully (and not add to your expenses).

- Know your rights. Laws governing landlord/tenant agreements and rights vary by state and municipality. Consult state and local law and call and obtain a pamphlet on renters' rights for your state and municipality.
- Review your lease agreement. There's no point in worrying until you know whether you have anything to worry about—and no use finding out too late that there were things you could have done.

CITYTIP

The name "the Big Apple" initially had nothing to do with the state's autumnal crop. It was picked up by a journalist, John Fitzgerald, in the 1920s when he overheard some stablehands in New Orleans refer to racetracks in New York City as "the Big Apple." Fitzgerald named his column "Around the Big Apple." The name had appeal and cachet and a decade later, jazz musicians came to refer to New York City, and especially Harlem, as the Big Apple, meaning the center of the jazz universe, because, as the lore goes, they would say "There are many apples on the trees of success, but when you pick New York City, you pick the big apple."

- Look for a way out. If you have to leave before your lease is up, ask your landlord to consider letting you out of your lease early or to allow you to find a replacement tenant to fulfill your lease term. If your move is due to a corporate relocation, your landlord or the property management company may be more willing to be flexible with exit fees—especially if you provide a letter from your employer. (And you may be able to get your employer to pick up the cost if you can't get the fees waived.)
- Adjust the timing. If you need to stay a month or two longer than your current lease allows and you don't want to sign for another six months or longer, ask your landlord for a month-to-month agreement lasting until your move date.

LEAVING YOUR CURRENT HOME (OWNED PROPERTY)

If you own your home, you'll either sell it or rent it out. If you sell, you'll either hire a real estate agent or sell it yourself. If you rent it out, you'll either serve as your own landlord or hire a property management agency to manage the property for you. Here are a few quick pros and cons to help you with the decisions you face.

Hiring a Selling Agent: Pros

- Your home gets exposure to a wide market, especially if the agent you choose participates in a multiple listing service.
- Homes listed with a real estate agent typically sell more quickly.
- Your agent will market your home (prepare and place ads and so on), and will also schedule and manage open houses and showings.
- Your agent will advise you and represent your interest in the business deal of selling, including offers, negotiation, and closing, guiding you through the stacks of paperwork.

Hiring a Selling Agent: Cons

- Hiring an agent requires signing a contract. If, for whatever reason, you want out, you may find it difficult to break the contract (it's wise to read carefully and sign only a short-term contract).
- You pay your agent a fee for the service, typically a percentage of the selling price.

Selling Your Home Yourself: Pros

- You don't pay an agent's fee.
- You retain more control over showings, open houses, walkthroughs, and so on.

Selling Your Home Yourself: Cons

- Selling a home takes time. You must arrange your own showings and schedule and conduct your own open houses. Considering everything that must happen during move preparation, you will probably be swamped already. Add home showings (which are arranged around the buyer's schedule, not yours) to the list, and you may find yourself looking for an agent to help you after all.
- You pay for marketing costs. The cost of flyers, newspaper ads, or listing your home on a "homes for sale by owner" website can really add up.
- Since you don't have a real estate agent to represent you in the sale, you may need to hire an attorney eventually.

RENTING OUT YOUR PROPERTY

If you prefer to rent out your home, you can turn it over to a property management agency or be the landlord yourself. The services an agency will perform depend on the agency and your agreement with them.

STRATEGIC FINANCIAL ISSUES RELATED TO RENTING OUT YOUR OLD HOME

If your property is located in a desirable neighborhood that is appreciating in value 3 percent or more annually, keeping it may in the long run defray or overcome the cost of management fees. If you rent out your property, it ceases being your primary residence. Find out from your accountant if this will affect your federal or state income taxes or local property taxes (some counties and municipalities give owner-occupied credits that reduce the tax burden). If there is an impact, you'll want to figure the difference into your decision of whether or not to sell and into the total you charge for rent.

DECIDING HOW TO MOVE: HIRING PROFESSIONALS OR MOVING YOURSELF

At first, you may be inclined to handle your own move to save money. But there are other factors to consider, and, depending on your situation, you may actually save money if you use professional services. Consider the range of service options some professional companies offer. The right combination could save you some of the headache but will still compete with the cost of a do-it-yourself move. For example, some professional moving companies offer a "you pack, we drive" arrangement, in which you pack boxes and the moving company exclusively loads, moves, and unloads your belongings. Call around and inquire about rates.

The section of the Moving Task Time Line that will help you the most at this point is "Decision Making: Weeks 12 to 9," which you'll find at the end of this chapter.

The Pros of Using Pros

- Time. You may not have the hours it will take to pack, move, and unpack, but professional movers do—that's their job.
- Materials. The moving company provides boxes and packing materials.*
- Packing. The movers pack all boxes (unless your contract states that you will pack).*
- Loading and Unloading. The movers load your belongings onto the moving van and unload your belongings at your destination.*
- Unpacking. The movers remove packed items from boxes and place items on flat surfaces.*
- Cleanup. The movers dispose of packing debris such as boxes, used tape, and padding.*
- Experience. The movers will know just what to do to transport your precious belongings in good condition.
- Safety. The movers do the lifting, which could save you a real injury.

Professional moving contracts typically include the services marked with an asterisk (*). Don't count on something unless you know for sure that the contract covers it, though—it's a good idea to ask your mover a lot of questions and to read the contract carefully.

The Cons of Using Pros

- Administrative chores. Using professionals requires you to do some up-front work: obtaining estimates, comparing

and negotiating prices and move dates, reviewing contracts, and comparing insurance options.
- Loss of control. The movers typically take charge of much of the packing and loading process, and you need to adapt to their schedule and procedures.

The Pros of a Self-Move
- Control. You pack, so you decide what items get packed together, how they get packed, and in which box they reside.
- Cost-cutting. You may save some money. But as you compare costs, be sure to factor in all self-move-related moving and travel costs. These include fuel, tolls, mileage charge on the rented truck, food, and lodging.

The Cons of a Self-Move
- Risk to your belongings. Because of inexperience with packing, loading, and padding heavy and unwieldy boxes and furniture, you may inadvertently damage your property.
- Risk to yourself and your friends. You or your volunteers may injure yourselves or someone else.
- Responsibility. Loading and moving day are hectic, and you're in charge. Make sure you have some idea about liability should someone get injured beyond bumps and scrapes.
- Reciprocal obligations. If you use volunteers, be prepared to return the favor.

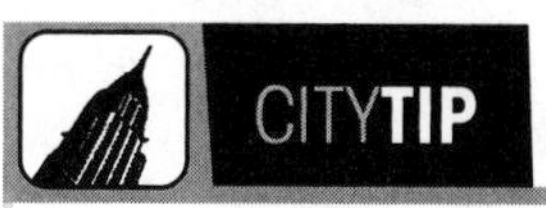

"As a New Yorker, there are certain things you should do at least once while you're living in the City, like go to the Halloween parade in Greenwich Village and to the Feast of San Gennaro in Little Italy."

—Carol Rossi,
Assistant District Attorney

OTHER THINGS TO KNOW ABOUT PROFESSIONAL MOVING SERVICES

Your moving company may or may not provide the following services, or may charge extra for them. Be sure to ask.

- Disassembling beds or other furniture
- Removing window-covering hardware (drapery rods, miniblinds) or other items from the walls or ceiling
- Disconnecting and installing appliances (dryer, washer, automatic ice maker)
- Disconnecting and installing outside fixtures such as a satellite dish, a hose reel, and so on
- Moving furniture or boxes from one room to another

MOVING INSURANCE IN A PROFESSIONAL MOVE

By U.S. law, the mover must cover your possessions at $0.60 per pound. This coverage is free. Consider taking out additional coverage, though, because under this minimal coverage, your three-pound antique Tiffany lamp worth thousands of dollars at auction fetches exactly $1.80 if the moving company breaks it.

Your homeowner's or renter's insurance provider may be willing to advise you on moving insurance options, and the moving company will offer you a number of insurance options. Be sure you understand each option: what it covers and what it costs you. Ask a lot of questions and read everything carefully. Hopefully, everything will come off without a hitch, but it's best to be prepared and well informed should something break or show up missing.

STORAGE

If you want your moving company to store some or all of your possessions temporarily, inquire about cost and the quality of their facilities:

- Are the facilities heated (or air-conditioned, depending on the time of year that matters to you)?
- Does the moving company own the storage facility or subcontract storage to someone else? If they subcontract, does your contract with the moving company extend to the storage facility company?

NEW YORK STORAGE COMPANIES

American Self-Storage
(212) 714-9300
americanselfstorage.com
Twelve locations in the five boroughs and New Jersey

Chelsea Mini-Storage
(212) 564-7735
chelsea-mini-storage.com
Chelsea Mini-Storage is the largest self-storage facility in the nation, with a million square feet of storage space under one roof.

Extra Space Storage
(800) 895-5921
www.extraspace.com
Locations throughout the five boroughs, New Jersey, Connecticut, and Long Island.

Keepers
(212) 674-2166
www.keepers-storage.com
Locations throughout the five boroughs, New Jersey, and Long Island

Manhattan Mini Storage
(212) STO-RAGE; (800) 786-7243
www.manhattanministorage.com

Tuck-It-Away
(212) 368-1717
tuckitaway.com
Self-storage and ministorage in New York and New Jersey

CHOOSING A MOVER

- Start by asking around. Chances are your friends, family, or colleagues will have a personal recommendation.
- Take their recommendations and list them in your notebook, each on a separate sheet. Call these companies to request a no-obligation, free written estimate—and take notes on your conversation.
- Find out if the company you're talking to offers the services you need. For example, if you want to ship your car along with your belongings, ask if this service is available.
- Do a little investigating. Ask the company to show you its operating license, and call the Better Business Bureau to ask about complaints and outstanding claims.
- Do online searches to see what customers are saying: were they satisfied?

GETTING AN ESTIMATE

You need to know what kind of estimate the moving company is giving you. The two most common are "nonbinding" and "binding." A nonbinding estimate (usually free, but potentially less accurate) is one in which the moving company charges you by the hour per worker per truck and quotes you an approximate figure to use in your planning. Depending on circumstances, your final cost could be significantly greater than what shows up in the estimate.

The second type is a binding estimate, which you typically pay for. In this type, the professional mover performs a detailed on-site inspection of your belongings and quotes a flat price based on the following:

- The amount of stuff you're moving, whether it is fragile or bulky, and how complicated it is to pack
- Final weight
- Services provided
- Total length of travel

Once you choose a mover, it's a good idea to have a representative visit your home, look at your belongings, and give you a written (binding) estimate. It may cost you money, but it helps prevent surprises when it comes time to pay the final bill.

You play a big role in making sure that the estimate you receive is accurate. Be sure you show the moving company representative everything you plan to move.

- Remember to take the representative through every closet, out to the garage, into the shed, down to the basement, up into the attic, and to your rented storage facility if you have one.
- Tell the representative about any item you don't plan to move (because you plan to get rid of it before you move). Then be sure to follow through and get rid of it, so there are no surprises on moving day.
- Point out any vehicles you want to ship along with your household goods, and ask your representative to include the cost in your estimate.

WHAT MIGHT INCREASE YOUR FINAL BILL

It is reasonable to expect that certain unforeseen circumstances can increase your final bill, including:

- You do the packing and it's incomplete or done improperly.
- Circumstances beyond your control increase the time and labor involved in your move. For example:

  - You're moving out of or into an apartment and movers don't have access to an elevator (perhaps it's broken).
  - Access at either location is restricted (for example, there is no truck parking at the nearest access point).
- You change your move destination after you receive your written estimate.
- You require delivery of your belongings to more than one destination.

RESEARCHING YOUR NEW AREA

The section of the Moving Task Time Line that will help you the most at this point is "Decision Making: Weeks 12 to 9," which you'll find at the end of this chapter. Other chapters of this book discuss the details of New York City.

Here are some additional move-related tips and resources.

General City Information

- Visit your local library and read up on New York City.
- Go online and read the *New York Times* (nytimes.com), *New York* magazine (nymag.com), *Time Out New York* (www.timeout.com/newyork), and the *Village Voice* (www.villagevoice.com).
- Have a friend or family member mail you a week's worth of newspapers or have a subscription delivered via postal mail.

JOBS, HOUSING, AND COST OF LIVING

Chapters 1 through 4 in this book address issues of housing and cost of living, including recent statistics. If you aren't relocating for a particular job, read up on the work scene in "Working in the City," Chapter 13, further along in this book.

CHOOSING SCHOOLS

Selecting schools is of the utmost importance to parents (who want their children to get the best possible educations and to be happy) and to the children who will be attending them. See "Local Schools and Colleges," Chapter 12, for extensive discussion of the school scene in New York City and the tristate area. Be sure to begin your school search as far in advance as possible (a year ahead is optimal—some parents start even earlier).

PLANNING AND TAKING AN APARTMENT-HUNTING TRIP

Preparing and planning a rough itinerary in advance will help you make the most of your apartment-hunting trip. Ideally, by this point, you will have narrowed your search to two or three neighborhoods or areas.

- Gather all documents and information that might be required for completing a rental application.
- Consider compiling all this information into a "rental résumé." Even though most landlords won't accept a rental résumé in lieu of an application, spending the time up front could be helpful in a market where rentals are scarce. Handing the landlord a rental résumé lets them know you're serious about finding the right place and are professional in how you conduct your affairs.
- Go prepared to put down a deposit. Typically, landlords require first and last

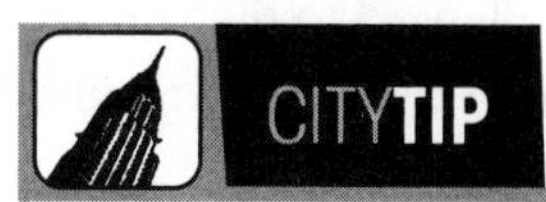

"Don't be afraid to go out on a limb or try something new—join the weekly folk dance party at the 92nd Street Y, or register for that acting class you're secretly dying to take (but are afraid to try). There's something wonderful about NYC, because you're completely anonymous, even when everyone is looking."

—Andrew Gordon, litigation attorney

month's rent and a security deposit (usually equal to a month's rent). Landlords often require a certified check for these payments, so you'll need a local bank account or enough traveler's checks to exchange for a certified check at a local bank.

- Get maps and plan for your travel. Will you go via taxi, subway, or rental car? The more time you put into your planning up front, the more time, money, and frustration you'll save in the long run.
- Take your Move Planning Notebook. List properties you want to visit, one per notebook page. Clip the classified ad or printout from the Internet and affix it to the page. Write notes about the property, pros and cons of the neighborhood, rent rate, deposit amount, and terms.

PLANNING

Now that you've made pre-move decisions, it's time to plan for the physical move. First, you'll need to organize your moving day. Next, you'll need to prepare to pack. These are the sections of the Moving Task Time Line that will help you the most at this point:

- "Organizing, Sorting, and Notifying: Weeks 9 to 8"
- "Finalizing Housing Arrangements and Establishing Yourself in Your New Community: Weeks 8 to 6"
- "Making and Confirming Transportation and Travel Plans: Week 6"
- "Uprooting: Weeks 5 to 4"
- "Making and Confirming Moving-Day Plans: Week 3"

You'll find the Moving Task Time Line at the end of this chapter.

PLANNING FOR MOVING DAY

The Professional Move:

- Confirm your move dates and finalize any final contract issues.
- Ask what form of payment movers will accept (check, money order, certified check, traveler's checks) and make necessary arrangements.

The Self-Move: Organizing Volunteers

- Ask friends and relatives to "volunteer" to help you load the truck on moving day.
- Set up shifts, and tactfully let your volunteers know that you are counting on them to arrive on time and stay through their "shift."
- A week or two before moving day, call everyone to remind them.
- Don't forget to provide drinks, snacks, and meals to keep your crew going.

PLANNING CARE FOR YOUR CHILDREN AND PETS

Moving day will be hectic for you and everyone in your family, and potentially dangerous for your young children. Make plans to keep younger children and pets occupied, whether that means taking them to someone else's house or having someone watch them on site—at a safe distance from all the activity.

PLANNING YOUR MOVING-DAY TRAVEL

Driving

- If you will be renting a truck, be prepared to put down a sizable deposit the day you pick up the truck. Some truck rental companies accept only a credit card for this deposit, so come prepared.

- If you belong to an automobile club such as AAA, contact them to obtain maps, suggested routes, alternate routes, rest-stop information, and a trip packet, if they provide this service.
- Visit an online map site such as www.mapquest.com, where you'll find not only personalized maps but also door-to-door driving directions and estimated travel times.
- Find out in advance where to return the rental truck.

Traveling by Air, Train, or Bus

- Make sure your cell phone is charged.
- Arrange for tickets and boarding passes.
- Speak with the airline or the train or bus company to make any special arrangements such as wheelchair accessibility and assistance, dietary restrictions, or special arrangements for children.
- Dress comfortably.
- If you will be traveling with young children, plan to dress them in bright, distinctive clothing so you can easily identify them in a crowded airport, train station, or bus terminal.

PREPARING TO PACK: WHAT TO DO WITH THE STUFF YOU HAVE

Moves are complicated, time-consuming, and exhausting. But the process has at least one benefit—it forces us to consider simplifying our lives by reducing the amount of our personal belongings. If you plan to keep it, you must also pack it, load it, move it, unload it, and unpack it. Here are some suggestions for sifting through your belongings as you prepare for packing.

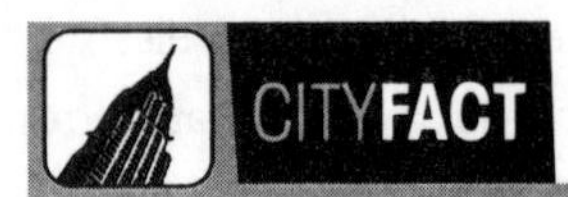

The Statue of Liberty is 305 feet tall from the base of her pedestal to the tip of her torch. She has a 35-foot waist, an eight-foot-long index finger, and she weighs 450,000 pounds.

- Start in one area of your home and mentally go through everything before moving to the next area.
- Ask yourself three questions about each item (sentimental value aside):
  - Have we used this in the last year?
  - Will we use it in the coming year? For example, if you're moving to a more temperate climate, you might not need all your wool socks and sweaters.
  - Is there a place for it in the new home? For instance, if your new home has a smaller living room, you might not have room for your big couch or need all your wall decorations.

If you answer no to any or all of these questions, you might want to consider selling the item, giving it away, or leaving it with a friend or family member.

PACKING

Here are some tips to help you with one of the most difficult stages of your move—packing.

- Follow a plan. Pack one room at a time. As you near completion of each room, leave one or two boxes open to accommodate items you'll be using up to the last minute and odds and ends that turn up as you progress throughout the house.
- On the outside of each box, describe the contents and room destination. Be as specific as you can, to make unpacking easier. If you are using a professional moving service but doing the packing yourself, you can also consider numbering boxes and creating a separate list of box contents and destinations.
- Put heavy items such as books in small boxes to make them easier to lift and carry.

- Don't put tape on furniture (to keep drawers closed, for example), because it may pull off finish when you remove it.
- As you pack, mark and set aside the items that should go in the truck last (see checklist at the end of this chapter). Mark and set aside your "necessary box" (for a list of items to include in this box, see the checklist at the end of this chapter).

PACKING FRAGILE ITEMS

- When packing breakables like expensive dishes and glasses, use boxes and padding made for these items or lots of linens from around your house. You may have to pay a little if you buy these boxes, but you're apt to save money in the long run because your dishes are more likely to arrive unbroken.
- Pad mirrors, pictures, and larger delicate pieces with sheets and blankets.
- Computers fare best if they are packed in their original boxes. If you don't have these, pack your hardware in a large, sturdy box and surround it with plenty of padding.
- Use plenty of padding around fragile items.
- Mark FRAGILE on the top and on all sides of boxes of breakables, so that no matter how a box is stacked, it's impossible to miss.

WHAT *NOT* TO PACK

- Don't pack hazardous, flammable, combustible, or explosive materials. If you have a gas grill and you're taking it with you, empty the tank. Any power tools, like mowers, that require gasoline should be emptied of all fuel. These materials are not safe in transit.
- Don't pack valuables such as jewelry, important financial and legal documents, and records for the moving van. Keep these with you in your car trunk or personal suitcase.

PACKING AND UNPACKING SAFELY WITH YOUNG CHILDREN

No matter how well you've childproofed your home, that lasts only until the moment you start packing. Here are some tips to keep your children safe.

- Items your children have seldom or never seen will pique their curiosity, presenting a potential hazard, so consider what you are packing or unpacking. If you stop packing or unpacking and leave the room even for a moment, take your kids with you and close the door—or put up a child gate.
- Keep box knives and other tools out of reach.
- As you disassemble or reassemble furniture, keep track of screws, bolts, nuts, and small parts. Bag them up, label them, and keep them out of reach.
- Beware of how and where you temporarily place furniture and other items (think twice before leaning mirrors against the wall). For the same reason, consider how high you stack boxes.
- On arriving at your destination, if you can't find someone to babysit, set aside a room in your home where your children can safely play. If things get desperate, set up the television and DVD player so kids can unwind (remember, moving is stressful for them, too) and tune out all of the racket going on around them.
- Walk through your new home with children and talk about any potential dangers such as a swimming pool or stairs, establishing your safety rules and boundaries in advance.
- If you have young children who are unaccustomed to having stairs in the home, place gates at access points. If you haven't unpacked the gates yet or don't have any, chairs at the bottom and top of the staircase to block access are a good substitute (make sure the chairs are secure—especially at the top of the staircase). If your child is walking and curious, walk up and down the stairs together a

few times holding the railing until they become accustomed to using the stairs.

HANDLE WITH SPECIAL CARE: UPROOTING AND SETTLING THE PEOPLE AND PETS IN YOUR LIFE

The most important advice you can hear is this: Involving children as much as possible will help transform this anxiety-causing, uncertain experience into an exciting adventure. Here are some suggestions for making the transition easier:

- Involve children early: Ask for their input on decisions and give them age-appropriate tasks such as packing their own belongings and assembling an activity bag to keep them busy while traveling.
- Don't make empty promises: Kids can hear the hollow ring when you say, "It'll be just like here. Just give it time," or "You can stay friends with your friends here." That's true, but you know it's not true in the same way, especially if you're moving far away.
- Deal with fear of the unknown: If possible, once you have purchased your new home, take children with you on an "exploratory trip." It may be more expensive and require extra effort in the short term, but it will ease the transition and help children get used to the idea of a home—they might even get excited about it in the process.
- Provide as much information as you can: If it's not possible to take children with you when you visit new neighborhoods, homes or apartments, and schools, take a camera or video camera. Your children will appreciate the pictures, and the preview will help them begin to adjust to the idea of a new home. You can also use a map to help them understand the new area and the route you will take to get there.

- Make time to talk with your children about the move. Especially listen for—and talk about—the anxieties your children feel. By doing so, you will help them through the move (your primary goal)—and you'll open up the pathways of communication at the same time. This is always important but is especially so now, when children are feeling uncertain and insecure about all the changes (most of which they likely have no control over).
- Share your own feelings with your children. Be sure to keep an overall positive outlook about the move, but don't be afraid to tell your children that you too feel sad about leaving your friends and your old home. Add that you're also excited about the new friends and adventures that surely await you all.
- Make it fun. Give older children a disposable camera and ask them to photograph your move. Once you arrive and are settled in, make time together to create the "moving" chapter of your family photo album. Encourage children to send photos to friends in your old hometown with letters describing the move and your new neighborhood.

HELPING FAMILY MEMBERS MAINTAIN FRIENDSHIPS

Moving doesn't have to end a friendship.

- Give each child a personal address book and have them write the e-mail address, phone number, and mailing address for each of their friends.
- Stay in touch. Establish an e-mail address for every family member (if they don't already have one) before you move, so they can give it out to friends. Many Web mail services are free and can be accessed from anywhere you can access the Internet. These include gmail.com, yahoo.com, and hotmail.com.
- Make (and follow through with) plans to visit your old hometown within the first year following your move. Visit friends and drive by your old home, through neighborhoods and past

landmarks. This reconnection with friends and fond memories will help your family recognize that it is possible to move and still keep up old friendships.

TRAVELING WITH YOUR PET

- Keep a picture of your pet on your person or in your wallet just in case you get separated from Fido or Fluffy during the move.
- Place identification tags on your pet's collar and pet carrier.
- Take your pet to the vet for an examination just before you move. Ask for advice on how you can help your pet through the move—what you can do before, during, and after the move to make the transition as smooth as possible.
- Find out if you will need any health certificates for your pet to comply with local regulations in your new home, and obtain them when you visit the vet.
- If your pet is prone to motion sickness or tends to become nervous in reaction to excitement, tell your vet, who may prescribe medication for your pet.
- Ask for your pet's health records so you can take them to your new vet.
- If your pet is unusual—say, a ferret or a snake or other reptile—there are specific laws in New York regarding the transportation and housing of such an animal. Contact the Department of Agriculture or a local veterinarian to find out.
- Cats: It's wise to keep your cat indoors, at least for the first two weeks until it recognizes its new surroundings as home. Because of traffic, litter, strays, and, yes, the occasional rodent, few New Yorkers ever let their cats outdoors.

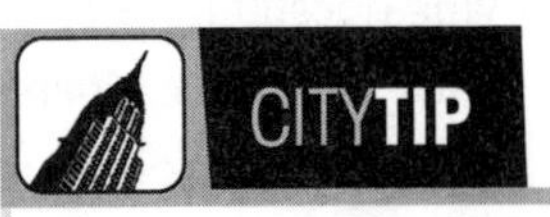

"Keep a running list of things you want to do in and around the City so that when you get that free evening or weekend, you don't have to spend your time figuring out what to do—you can just go ahead and do it."

—Renato Bardini, restaurant manager

• Dogs: If appropriate, walk your dog on a leash around your neighborhood to help it become familiar with the new surroundings and learn its way back home (though you'll never unleash your dog in New York City, except in fenced-in, designated dog runs).
• If your pet will travel by plane, check with your airline regarding fees and any specific rules and regulations regarding pet transport.
• Your pet will need to travel in an approved carrier (check with your airline regarding acceptable types and sizes).
• Your airline may require a signed certificate of health dated within a certain number of days of the flight. Only your vet can produce this document.

CHECKLISTS

Moving Supplies

Packing and Unpacking

___ Tape and tape dispenser. (The slightly more expensive gun-style dispenser is a worthwhile investment, because its one-handed operation means you don't need a second person to help tape boxes closed.)
___ Boxes. (It's often worth it to obtain specialty boxes for your dinnerware, china set, and glasses. Specialty wardrobe boxes that allow your hanging clothes to hang during transport are another big help. Otherwise, free boxes from grocery and liquor stores should do the trick.)
___ Padding such as bubble wrap.
___ Markers.
___ Scissors and/or a knife.
___ Large plastic bags.
___ Inventory list and clipboard.
___ Box knife with retractable blade. (Get one for each adult.)

Loading and Moving

__ Rope and bungee cords. (If nothing else, you'll need them to secure heavy items to the inside wall of the truck.)

__ Padding blankets. (If you use your own, they will likely get dirty during the move. Don't use your favorite bedspread and linens for the job. Padding is available for rent at most truck rental agencies if you need it.)

__ Hand truck or appliance dolly. (Most truck rental agencies have them available for rent.)

__ Padlock for the cargo door.

The "Necessary Box"

Eating

__ Food and beverages. (Pack enough durable foodstuffs for right before you depart, your travel, and the first day in your new home. Don't forget disposable utensils, plates, and cups.)

__ Instant coffee, tea bags, and so on.

__ Roll of paper towels and "wet wipes" (great for cleanups of unexpected messes).

__ Garbage bags.

Bathing

__ A towel for each person.

__ Soap, shampoo, toothpaste, and any other toiletries.

__ Toilet paper.

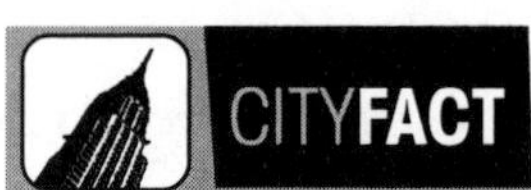

New York City has 578 miles of waterfront.

Health Items

__ First-aid kit including pain relievers.
__ Prescription medicines.

At Your Fingertips

__ List of contact information. (Make sure you can reach relatives, the moving company, the truck driver's cell phone, and so on.)
__ Small tool kit. (You need to be able to take apart and reassemble items that can't be moved whole.)
__ Reclosable plastic bags to hold small parts, screws, bolts.
__ Spare lightbulbs. (Some bulbs in your new home might be burned out or missing.)
__ Night-light and flashlight.

Overnight Bag

__ Enough clothes for the journey plus the first day or two in your new home.
__ Personal toiletries.
__ Cell phone charger.

Items for Kids

__ Activities for the trip.
__ Snacks (familiar favorites and special treats).
__ Favorite toys and anything else that will help children feel immediately at home.

Pet Checklist

__ Food.
__ A big bottle of the water your pet is used to drinking.

__ Dishes for food and water.
__ Leash, collar, and identification tags.
__ Favorite toy.
__ Medicines.
__ Bed or blanket.
__ Carrier.
__ Paper towels in case of accidents.
__ Plastic bags and a scooper.
__ Litter and litter box for your cat or rabbit.

Last Items on the Truck

Cleaning

__ Vacuum cleaner.
__ Cleaning supplies.

General

__ Necessary box.
__ Setup for kids' temporary playroom.
__ Other items you'll need the moment you arrive.

New Home Safety Checklist

General

__ Watch out for tripping hazards. They will be plentiful until you get everything unpacked and put away, so be careful, and keep a path clear at all times.

Heat, Fire, Electrical

__ Be sure nothing gets placed too close to heaters.
__ Test smoke, heat, and carbon monoxide detectors. Find out your fire department's recommendations

regarding how many of these devices you should have and where you should place them. If you need more, go buy them (remember to buy batteries) and install them.

___ Find the fuse or breaker box *before* you need to shut off or reset a circuit.

Water

___ Check the temperature setting on your water heater. For child safety and fuel conservation, experts recommend 120° Fahrenheit.

___ Locate the water shutoff valve in case of a plumbing problem.

Moving Task Time Line

Decision Making: Weeks 12 to 9

___ Consider your moving options (professional versus self-move) and get quotes.

___ If you are being relocated by your company, find out what your company covers and what you will be responsible for.

___ Set a move date.

___ Choose your moving company or truck rental agency and reserve the dates.

___ You should already be applying to local schools for young children.

If You Own Your Home

___ Decide whether you want to sell or rent it out.

___ If you decide to sell, choose a real estate agent and put your home on the market or look into, and begin planning for, selling it yourself

___ If you decide to rent out your home, decide whether

you want to hire a property management agency or manage the property yourself.

__ Perform (or hire contractors to perform) home repairs.

If You Currently Rent

__ Notify your landlord of your plans to vacate.

__ Check into cleaning obligations and options.

Tour Your New City or Town

__ Familiarize yourself with your new neighborhood by reading up.

__ Contact a real estate agent or property management agency to help you in your search for new lodgings.

__ Go on a school-hunting and house- or apartment-hunting trip to your new town or city.

__ If you will be moving during a peak travel period (summer and holiday times) make arrangements now. (If not, you'll see another reminder farther along in the time line.) If you will be flying, book early for cheaper fares.

Additional items:

____

____

____

____

____

____

Organizing, Sorting, and Notifying: Weeks 9 to 8

__ Obtain the post office's change-of-address kit by calling 1-800-ASK-USPS or visiting your local post office or moversguide.usps.com (where you'll find the form and helpful lists of questions and answers).

__ Complete and send the form.

__ List and notify people, businesses, and organizations who need to know about your move. You may not think of everyone at once, but keep a running list and add people as you remember them. As you notify them, check them off.

__ Start sorting through your belongings to decide what to keep. Make plans to rid yourself of what you don't want: Pick a date for a garage sale; call your favorite charity and set a date for them to come pick up donations; call your recycling company to find out what they will accept.

__ For moving insurance purposes, make an inventory of your possessions with their estimated replacement value.

__ If you have high-value items (such as antiques) that you expect to send with the moving company or ship separately, obtain an appraisal.

Additional items:

____

____

____

____

____

____

Finalizing Housing Arrangements and Establishing Yourself in Your New Community: Weeks 8 to 6

__ Home: Select your new home and arrange financing; establish a tentative closing date or finalize rental housing arrangements.

__ Insurance: Contact an agent regarding coverage on your new home and its contents as well as on your automobile.

__ Finances: Select a bank, open accounts, and obtain a safe deposit box.

__ New Home Layout: Sketch a floor plan of your new home and include room measurements. Determine how your present furniture, appliances, and decor will fit.

__ Mail: If you haven't found a new home, rent a post office box for mail forwarding.

__ Services: Find out the names and phone numbers of utility providers and what they require from you before they will start service (for example, a deposit, a local reference). Make a list of your providers and service start dates. Schedule service to start a few days before you arrive.

Additional items:

____

____

____

____

____

____

Making and Confirming Transportation and Travel Plans: Week 6

__ Schedule pickup and delivery dates with your mover.

__ Make arrangements with your professional car mover.

__ If you need storage, make the arrangements.

__ Confirm your departure date with your real estate agent or landlord.

__ Make your travel arrangements. If you will be flying, book early for cheaper fares.

__ Map your driving trip using an atlas or online mapping website, or ask your automobile club for assistance with route and accommodation information.

Additional items:

____

____

____

____

____

____

____

Uprooting: Weeks 5 to 4

__ Hold your garage sale, or donate items to charity.
__ Gather personal records from all health care providers, your veterinarian, lawyers, accountants, and schools.
__ Notify current utility providers of your disconnect dates and your forwarding address.

Additional items:

____

____

____

____

____

____

____

____

____

Making and Confirming Moving-Day Plans: Week 3

__ Make arrangements for child care and pets on moving day.

__ Call moving-day volunteers to confirm move date and their arrival time.

__ Obtain traveler's checks for trip expenses and cashier's or certified check for payment to mover.

__ Have your car serviced if you are driving a long distance.

Additional items:

____

____

____

____

____

____

Week 2

__ If you have a pet, take it to the vet for a checkup. For more pet-moving tips, see the section earlier in this chapter on moving with pets.

__ Arrange for the transportation of your pet.

__ If you are moving into or out of a high-rise building, contact the property manager and reserve the elevator for moving day.

__ Drain the oil and gas from all your power equipment and kerosene from portable heaters.

Additional items:

____
____
____
____
____
____

Moving Week

__ Defrost the freezer.
__ Give away any plants you can't take with you.
__ Pack your luggage and your necessary box for the trip (see the list provided in this chapter).
__ Get everything but the day-to-day essentials packed and ready to go.

Additional items:

____
____
____
____
____
____

Moving Day

__ Mark off parking space for the moving truck using cones or chairs.
__ See Chapter 9 for further to-do items.

CHAPTER NINE

MOVING DAY AND BEYOND

This chapter guides you through the next stage in your move: moving day, arriving, unpacking, and settling in. Here you'll find important travel tips for both the self-move and the professional move, information related to a professional car move, and pointers for your first days and weeks in your new home.

THE PROFESSIONAL MOVE

Early on moving day, reserve a large place for the moving truck to park. Mark off an area with cones or chairs. If you need to obtain parking permission from your apartment building's super or management, do so in advance.

GUIDE THE MOVERS

Before work starts, walk through your old residence with the movers and describe the loading order. Show them the items you plan to take yourself. (It's best if these are piled in one area and clearly marked, maybe even covered with a sheet or blanket until you're ready to pack them in your car.)

Remain on-site to answer the movers' questions and to provide special instructions.

BEFORE YOU DEPART

Before you hit the road, you will need to take care of some last-minute details:

- Walk through your home to make sure everything was loaded.
- Sign the bill of lading. But first, read it carefully and ask any questions. The bill of lading is a document the government requires movers to complete for the transportation of supplies, materials, and personal property. The mover is required to have a signed copy on hand, and you should keep your copy until the move is complete and any claims are settled.
- Follow the movers to the weigh station (if there is one). Your bill will be partly based on the weight of the property moved.

"When furnishing and decorating your apartment, carry a tape measure and floor plan with you at all times—you never know when you're going to stumble across that perfect end table you've been searching for. Measure not only your apartment but also the dimensions of all doorways, staircases, and elevators through which you'll have to transport your purchases. If possible, take these measurements before you even move in."

—Tim Shepard, design consultant

UNLOADING AND MOVING IN

Be sure to take care of these details once the movers arrive at your new home:

- Have your money ready. (Professional movers expect payment in full before your goods are unloaded.)
- Check for damage as items are unpacked and report it right away.
- Unless the company's policy prohibits gratuities, it is customary to tip each mover. Fifty dollars is a good amount; you may want to tip more or less based on the service you receive (especially if your move requires excessive stair climbing).

THE SELF-MOVE

The following tips should help you organize and guide your team of helpers, as well as make the moving day run more smoothly:

- The day before your move, create a task list. Besides the obvious (loading the truck), this list will include tasks such as disconnecting the washer and dryer (if you are taking them with you) and taking apart furniture that can't be moved whole.
- Plan to provide drinks and food for your volunteers. Make it easy on yourself and provide pizza (delivered or picked up by a volunteer), chilled sodas, and bottled water.
- On moving day, remember you are only one person. If you need to, appoint someone to help you with tying up loose ends like last-minute packing or cleaning out the refrigerator while you oversee the volunteers and answer questions (or vice versa—appoint someone who knows the details of your plan to oversee the volunteers while *you* tie up the loose ends).

- Be sure you have almost everything packed before your help arrives. Last-minute packing creates even more chaos and it's likely that hastily packed items will be damaged during loading or transit.
- If you end up with an even number of people, it's natural for people to work in pairs, because they can carry the items that require two people. If you have an odd number of people, the extra person can rotate in to provide for breaks or work on tasks you assign.
- Be sure to match a person's physical ability with the tasks you assign.
- Appoint the early shift to start on tasks like taking apart furniture (such as bed frames) that can't be moved whole.
- Before work starts, walk through the house with your volunteers and give an overview of your loading plan.
- Know your moving truck and how it should be packed for safe handling on the road (ask the truck rental company for directions).
- Load the truck according to the directions your truck rental agency gave you. Tie furniture items (especially tall ones) to the inside wall of the truck. Pack everything together as tightly as possible, because items will shift as you take to the road.

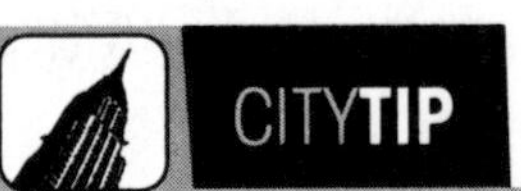

"Find the local thrift store, Salvation Army office, Goodwill Industries, or another charity that accepts clothing and furniture donations. With apartment space at a premium, when you buy new items you usually have to give away some of the old to make room. If you give to charity, you'll help the needy—and get a tax deduction to boot! Some good organizations: Cancer Care Thrift Shop (free pickups for some items), Memorial Sloan-Kettering Thrift Shop (free pickups for furniture), Stuyvesant Square Thrift Shop, Grand Street Settlement (free pickup), and City Opera Thrift Shop."

—Toby Kovacs,
client services manager

MOVING-DAY TRAVEL

ARRIVING BY PLANE

There are three major international airports that serve the New York metropolitan area. In New York City, they are LaGuardia Airport and JFK International Airport (both in Queens) and, in New Jersey, Newark Liberty International Airport (in Newark).

From each airport you'll have many transportation options to get into the City: taxi, bus, shuttle, car service, helicopter, ferry, and even a bus-subway combo. See Chapter 11 for specifics.

ARRIVING BY CAR

It could take you a decade and a Ph.D. to learn all of the different ways to drive into Manhattan and the other boroughs—these various routes are a frequent source of discussion and debate, particularly among suburban commuters. All you need to know, at the most basic level, is that I-95 from the north and south and I-80 from the west will all lead you to Manhattan. If you are a member of AAA, get a Triptik tailored to your exact itinerary; if not, use a map or get online and check out one of the following websites (or a few to cross-reference) for directions that are best suited to your travel plans.

Google Maps
maps.google.com

Mapquest
www.mapquest.com

Microsoft Maps
maps.live.com

Yahoo! Maps
maps.yahoo.com

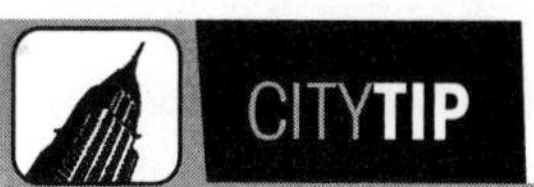

"Don't put anything in your apartment unless you absolutely love it. If you've lived in a house all your life, get ready to pare down to the bare essentials in preparation for apartment life. Most New York apartments offer limited closet space, no storage space, and little room for expansion. Better to have a few nice things than a lot of junk and clutter."

—Steve Mohr, antiques dealer

ARRIVING BY BUS

Long-distance buses (Greyhound, Trailways, Peter Pan, Vermont Transit, and others) arrive into the City at the Port Authority Bus Terminal, which is located between 40th and 42nd Streets and Eighth and Ninth Avenues.

ARRIVING BY TRAIN

Amtrak trains arrive at Penn Station (31st to 33rd Streets, between Seventh and Eighth Avenues).

SELF-MOVE

Driving a Truck

- A loaded moving truck handles far differently than the typical car. Allow extra space between you and the vehicle you are following. Drive more slowly and decelerate and brake sooner—there's a lot of weight sitting behind you.
- Realize that no one likes to follow a truck. Other drivers may make risky moves to get ahead of you, so watch out for people passing when it's not safe.
- Know your truck's height and look out for any low overhangs and tree branches. Especially be aware of the overhang at gas stations.
- Most accidents in large vehicles occur when backing up. Before you back up, get out, walk around, and check for obstacles—or better yet, have an adult family member or traveling companion direct you (ask them to

"In New York City, anything can be delivered—and often at any time of the day or night. A lot of newcomers don't realize this, because they come from towns where everyone has a car. So just remember that here you don't have to carry anything—not even your groceries."

—Nancy Kessler, attorney

stay in a safe spot while they direct you). Allow plenty of room to maneuver.

- Stop and rest frequently.
- At every stop, do a walk-around inspection of the truck. Check tires, lights, and the cargo door. (If you're towing a trailer, check trailer tires, door, hitch, and hitch security chain.) Ask your truck rental representative how often you should check the engine oil.
- At overnight stops, park in a well-lit area and be sure to lock the cargo door with a very secure lock.

If You're Flying or Traveling by Train or Bus

- Coordinate with the moving van driver so that you arrive at about the same time.
- Plan for the unexpected, such as delays, cancellations, or missed connections.
- Keep in touch with the truck driver (by cell phone, if possible), who may also experience delays for any number of reasons: mechanical problems, road construction, storms, or illness.
- Dress comfortably.
- If you are traveling with young children, dress them in bright, distinctive clothing so you can easily identify them in a crowded airport, train station, or bus terminal.

PROFESSIONAL MOVERS MAY NEED HELP, TOO

Make sure the movers have directions to your new home. Plan your travel so that you will be there to greet them and unlock. Have a backup plan in case one of you gets delayed. It is also a good idea to exchange cell phone numbers

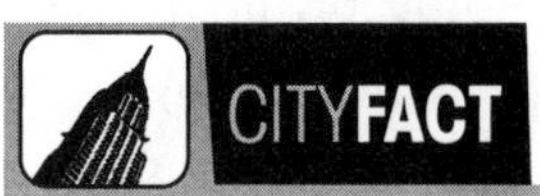

Macy's is the world's largest store, covering 2.1 million square feet and carrying over 500,000 different items. In 1862, Macy's established a new holiday tradition and standard with the introduction of the first ever in-store Santa Claus.

with the driver so you can stay in touch in case one of you is delayed.

TIPS FOR A PROFESSIONAL CAR MOVE

A professional car carrier company can ship your car. Alternatively, your moving company may be able to ship it in the van along with your household goods. Ask around and compare prices.

- Be sure that the gas tanks are *no more than one-quarter full.*
- It's not wise to pack personal belongings in your transported auto, because insurance typically won't cover those items.
- If your car is damaged in transport, report the damage to the driver or move manager and note it on the inventory sheet. If you don't, the damage won't be eligible for insurance coverage.

UNPACKING AND GETTING SETTLED

You made it. Welcome home! You're well on your way to getting settled and having life return to normal. As you unpack boxes, arrange the furniture, and hang the pictures, here are a few things to keep in mind:

- Approach unpacking realistically. It's not necessary (and probably not possible) to unpack and arrange everything on the first day.
- Find your cleaning supplies and do any necessary cleaning.
- Consider your family's basic needs (food, rest, bathing) and unpack accordingly:
    - Kitchen: Start with the basics; keep less frequently used items in boxes until you decide where you want everything to go.
    - Bedrooms: Unpack bedding and set up and make beds.

- Bathroom: Because this tends to be a small room with little space for boxes, unpack the basics early and find a place to store the remaining boxes until you have a chance to finish up.

MAINTAINING NORMALCY . . . STARTING FRESH

During the move and the days following, it's good to keep things feeling as normal as possible. But this can also be a fresh starting point: a time to establish (or reestablish) family rituals and traditions. Beyond the family, this is a time to meet and connect with new neighbors, schoolmates, and your religious or other community.

- Keep regular bedtimes and wake-up times (and naps for kids if appropriate).
- If you typically eat dinner together, continue to do this, despite the chaos.
- If you typically have a regular family time—an activity or outing—don't feel bad if you must skip it one week because of move-related chores, but restart this ritual as soon as you can. In fact, your family may appreciate this special time even more in the midst of the upheaval and change.

Rome wasn't built in a day, and neither are friendships. If your move means you have to start over, take heart: Persistence and work will pay off over time. Here are a few suggestions for making your first connections with people in your new area.

- Give family members who need it encouragement in making new friends.
- Get involved in activities your family enjoys and make time in

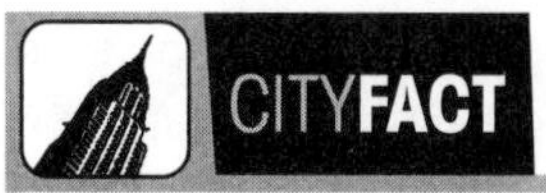

It doesn't quite roll off the tongue like "Broadway," but Broadway's original name was the Wiechquaekeck Trail.

your schedule for bonding with them, even though moving and resettling is a hectic and busy time.

- Meet and connect with your religious community.
- If you see them, introduce yourself to your new neighbors.

DISCOVERING YOUR COMMUNITY

Here are some suggestions for getting settled in your new surroundings:

- Be sure every family member gets a feel for the neighborhood and main streets; memorizes your new address; learns (or carries) new home, office, and cell phone numbers; and knows how to contact local emergency personnel.
- Go exploring on foot, bike, subway, bus, or by car (in the suburbs) and start learning your way around.
- Locate your local post office and police and fire stations, as well as hospitals and gas stations near your home.
- Scout your new neighborhood for grocery stores, pharmacies, dry cleaners, restaurants, and other points of interest.
- Register to vote.
- Visit the Department of Motor Vehicles to obtain your driver's license and register your vehicle (see below).
- If you haven't already done so, transfer insurance policies to an agent in your new community.

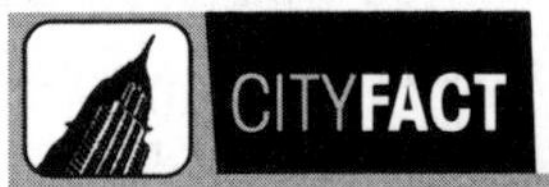

Established in 1858, Macy's has a long and impressive history in New York City. In 1866 Macy's was the first ever to promote a woman to an executive retail position as the store superintendent. During World War II, with supplies hard to come by, the Macy's Thanksgiving Day balloons were deflated and the rubber was donated to the war effort, providing 650 pounds to the cause. Today, the Macy's Fireworks Spectacular is the largest July 4th fireworks display in America.

VEHICLE REGISTRATION

If you're moving to New York with a car, you must have the following information to register your vehicle:

- Proof of ownership
- Completed vehicle registration/title application form
- New York State insurance card
- Proof of inspection
- Sales tax clearance (available at motor vehicle office)
- Identification with proof of name and birth date
- Odometer Disclosure Statement, if the car is less than ten years old
- Bill of sale
- Registration fee

To change your out-of-state license to a New York State license (and to avoid the written and practical tests), you must have a valid (or expired within the last twelve months) license from another state.

TAKING CARE OF THE FINANCIAL IMPLICATIONS OF YOUR MOVE

Now that you have arrived, you can take care of some of the financial and tax implications of your move. Here are some things to think about (it's also wise to consult an accountant):

- Some of your moving expenses may be tax-deductible. Prepare for tax filing by collecting receipts from your move. Also contact the Internal Revenue Service to obtain the publications and forms you need. Visit www.irs.gov or call (800) 829-3676 and ask about relocating.
- State income tax. In New York, you'll need to file a state income tax return.
- Other income sources may have tax implications. As you prepare to file, you'll want to consider any other sources of income and whether your new state will tax you on this income. For example, if you are paying federal

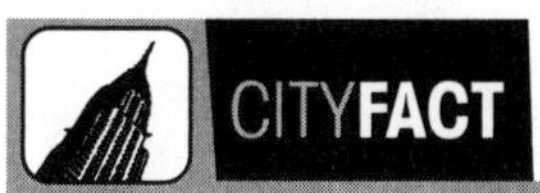

Babe Ruth hit the first-ever home run in Yankee Stadium in the first game he played there.

income tax on an IRA that you rolled over into a Roth IRA, you may also have to pay state income tax on your rollover IRA.

HOME AT LAST

Once the truck is unloaded, the boxes are unpacked, and the pictures are hung, and once you're sleeping in a bed—instead of on a mattress on the floor—you'll dream sweet dreams. As each day passes and you and your family begin to settle into your new home, the stress of your move will turn into a distant memory, you'll begin to discover the opportunities and possibilities of your new city, new job, new school—and your new home.

PART FOUR

GETTING TO KNOW NEW YORK

CHAPTER TEN

WHAT'S AROUND TOWN

Welcome to New York! This is what you've been waiting for. This is what makes all the headaches, heartaches, and hassles of living in the City worth it: the restaurants, museums, theater, music, dance, culture, education, activities, culture, glamour, and people. But wait—there's more! In New York City, not only is something always going on, but typically there are hundreds of different events and performances happening on any given day around all the five boroughs. Your problem will not be finding something to do, but deciding *which* thing to do. Should you go to the Second Avenue Street Fair or the Sixth Avenue Annex Antique Fair and Flea Markets? Should you eat at a Thai restaurant on the Upper West Side, Upper East Side, or in Queens? Go for a hike in Staten Island's Greenbelt, stroll through Central Park, check out Brooklyn's Prospect Park, or play chess in Washington Square Park?

You'll be faced with more choices than this each and every day you live in New York, and it's good to know what's out there so you can spend your time wisely. That means you'll need some tools to help you along. It used to be that to find out what was going on in New York you had to subscribe to several magazines and newspapers and make a ton of phone calls. Today, although the magazine and newspaper listings are still helpful, almost everything can be found online.

This chapter contains extensive listings of ongoing activities and events; however, what you see here is just the tip of the iceberg—and a rapidly melting iceberg at that. Things in New York change day to day, new venues open, old ones close, and major projects are undertaken and completed. So, in addition to listing entertainment options, I've also provided the resources, online and off, to help you get started figuring out what's going on and what to do.

RESOURCES

EVENT AND ACTIVITY LISTINGS

NYC & COMPANY

Formerly known as the New York Convention & Visitors Bureau, NYC & Company is New York City's official tourism marketing organization. You're going to be a New Yorker, not a tourist, but the NYC & Company website (nycvisit.com) is an amazing resource for visitors and locals alike. In addition

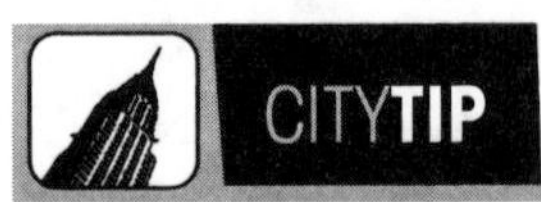

"Learn your way around New York City as soon as you can. Study the maps, find the best subway stations and bus routes near your home and office, and memorize which major streets run north, south, east, and west. Make this a priority, because it'll save you a whole lot of time."

—Johnny Moore, actor

to its comprehensive website, which lists almost every activity you can think of, NYC & Company also maintains five information kiosks around the city: one in Midtown Manhattan (810 Seventh Avenue near 53rd Street); one downtown (southern tip of City Hall Park); one in Chinatown (at the triangle where Canal, Walker, and Baxter Streets meet); one in Harlem (at the Apollo Theater, 253 West 125th Street); and one in the Financial District (at the Federal Hall National Memorial, 26 Wall Street). These are great places to find anything from a subway map to brochures on just about everything going on in the City.

NEW YORK MAGAZINE

The print version of *New York* magazine has always contained some of the best event and entertainment listings, and now that the listings are available online (nymag.com) it's an even more useful tool: searchable, up to date, and free. Everything from arts and events to restaurants and children's activities are well covered here.

TIME OUT NEW YORK

New York magazine's main competitor is *Time Out New York.* Luckily, you don't have to choose: you can use both! The *Time Out New York* (which many New Yorkers abbreviate TONY) website (www.timeout.com/newyork) has many of the same listings as *New York* magazine, but TONY has a reputation for being a little bit hipper and younger, and the listings reflect that. TONY also has a sister publication, *Time Out New York Kids,* which maintains a great website with kid-oriented listings at www.timeout.com/newyork/kids.

THE *NEW YORK TIMES*

The Sunday Arts & Leisure and Friday Weekend sections of the *Times* contain diverse listings, and are available online at nytimes.com.

WHERE NEW YORK

You may have seen *WHERE* magazine in your hotel room in one of many cities. *WHERE New York* is targeted at the traveler, but has become a heavily utilized resource for locals now that its listings are online at www.whereny.com.

IN NEW YORK

Not to be confused with *New York* magazine, *IN New York* maintains a strong listings website at in-newyorkmag.com.

Prized by New York hipsters, the following five websites are not to be missed: Flavorpill (flavorpill.net/newyork) is great for event listings and focuses on the avant-garde; Nonsense NYC (nonsensenyc.com) is an e-mail listserv that features weekly e-mails with information on the weirdest happenings around NYC each week; if you feel you haven't filled your hipster quotient with those two, try Not For Tourists (notfortourists.com)—or NFT—for more "edgy" activities around town. For all of you rockers, www.ohmyrockness.com and brooklynvegan.com are the two sites that young hipster rockers turn to, to be cutting-edge and the first in the know.

Other websites that contain listings of events and activities are CitySearch (newyork.citysearch.com) and the online versions of the *Village Voice* (villagevoice.com), *New York Post* (nypost.com), *New York Daily News* (nydailynews.com), and *New York Press* (nypress.com).

MAPS

New Yorkers always look like they know where they're going, but these days it's entirely possible that before they set out on their determined marches they used Google Maps (maps.google.com), Microsoft Maps (maps.live.com), or Mapquest (www.mapquest.com).

Type in the address of your destination, or even just its name, and you'll get a zoom-able map of your destination with everything from the nearby subway stations to the direction that traffic on each surrounding street runs. Print it out, fold it up, put it in your pocket, and you'll never get lost. (If you're really cutting-edge, you can get GPS maps on your PDA or cell phone, but if you're that far ahead of the curve you don't need me to tell you.) One of the great features of Microsoft Maps and Google Maps is the aerial view. Almost every block in Manhattan and nearby has been painstakingly photographed from all four compass angles. So you can not only get a map, but also see what your destination really looks like. (This is a great tool for apartment-hunting.)

THE PERFORMING ARTS

THEATER

New York's theater scene is so diverse and extensive (and often expensive), it can be overwhelming. But a few tools can help you manage the information, zero in on what you want to see, and help you secure the tickets—often at a discount.

What's playing?

All of the online resources at the beginning of this chapter—the *New York Times, New York* magazine, *Time Out New York,* etc.—contain the listings of most Broadway, Off-Broadway, and Off-Off-Broadway shows. In addition, there are several theater-specific resources worth knowing about.

For a listing of Broadway shows, www.broadway.com is a great tool, and

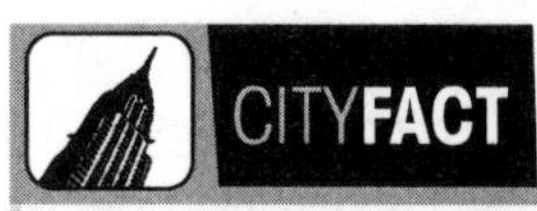

The City is home to 42 farmers' markets (known locally as greenmarkets) in 31 locations throughout the five boroughs, and they are administered by the Council on the Environment of New York City (www.cenyc.org). The greenmarket farmers serve 250,000 customers weekly and donate approximately 500,000 pounds of food to City Harvest and other hunger relief organizations annually. Best known is the Union Square Greenmarket (open year-round Monday, Wednesday, Friday, and Saturday). Despite its urban image, New York State is a major agricultural producer, ranking third in dairy production and second in apples, grapes, cabbage, and maple syrup.

for Off-Broadway shows check www.offbroadwayonline.com. Telecharge (telecharge.com) is a central location for buying tickets for many New York shows. The Mayor's Office of Film, Theatre and Broadcasting (nyc.gov/html/film/html/theatre/theatre_home.shtml) has useful information such as the seating plans of the major theaters.

Useful for when you're out and about and don't have access to the Internet is the Broadway Line (888-BROADWAY), a service of the League of American Theatres and Producers. Using the interactive phone menus, you can search for Broadway shows by title or by genre, and then purchase tickets directly over the phone. There's also a website at livebroadway.com.

TKTS, with booths near Times Square (47th Street between Broadway and Seventh Avenue, but temporarily at West 46th Street, in the Marriott Marquis, while the 47th Street location is being renovated) and in the South Street Seaport (199 Water Street), is a service of the Theatre Development Fund (212-221-0885, tdf.org). You can get same-day tickets to Broadway, Off-Broadway, and many other performances at half price. The South Street Seaport TKTS booth is the less crowded of the two, but expect long lines at both. You have to be flexible if you use TKTS, because they're only selling unsold tickets. Don't expect to get in to the most popular shows (though you never know), but do expect to find a great bargain.

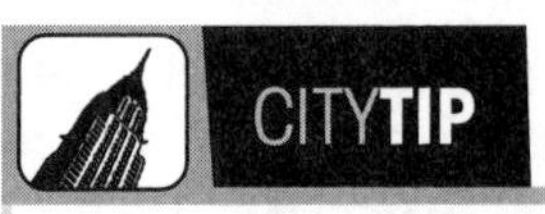

"Despite rising admission prices, some of the best museums in New York offer free or 'pay-what-you-wish' admission on one night each week. Plus, watch for the 'Museum Mile' celebration each summer, where all the Fifth Avenue museums open their doors for free."

—Maria Tucci, accountant

If you qualify, you can also join the Theatre Development Fund (TDF). The same organization that brings you TKTS, TDF allows students, teachers, union members, retirees, civil service employees, staff members at nonprofit organizations, performing arts professionals, and members of the armed forces and clergy to join and receive mailings about discount tickets.

Of course, you can also just show up at any theater's box office. You'll pay full price, but you won't incur Telecharge or other service fees. And sometimes the box office has "rush tickets," which are seats that are, for various reasons (returns, unsold house seats, etc.) made available only shortly before curtain time. Sometimes if you just wait before the show, and you're only one or two people, you can get the best seats in the house for a show that was sold out.

Some people use ticket brokers, which I don't recommend, because with a little planning you should be able to see any show without paying a huge markup. But if you absolutely must have tickets, and if money is no object, a licensed ticket broker is a viable option. If you must, try Full Access (www.fullaccessent.com) or Keith Prowse (www.keithprowse.com).

DANCE

In addition to the general listings mentioned earlier, the following are major dance companies:

Alvin Ailey American Dance Theater
The Joan Weill Center for Dance
405 West 55th Street (at Ninth Avenue)
(212) 405-9020
alvinailey.org

American Ballet Theatre
Contact information:
890 Broadway
New York, NY 10003
(212) 477-3030
www.abt.org
(The theater is located at Lincoln Center.)

Dance Theatre of Harlem
466 West 152nd Street
(212) 690-2800
dancetheatreofharlem.com

New York City Ballet
Lincoln Center
(212) 870-5660
www.nycballet.com

MUSIC

The following are major music venues. For other musical performance listings, use the general listings above.

Alice Tully Hall
1941 Broadway
(212) 875-5000
lincolncenter.org
Mostly classical music

Avery Fisher Hall
10 Lincoln Center Plaza
(212) 875-5030
lincolncenter.org
Mostly classical music

Brooklyn Academy of Music
30 Lafayette Avenue
Brooklyn, NY 11217
(718) 636-4111
bam.org
Dance, film, music, theater, and opera seven days a week

Carnegie Hall
156 West 57th Street (between Broadway and Seventh Avenue)
(212) 247-7800
www.carnegiehall.com
Classical, jazz, and more

92nd Street Y
1395 Lexington Avenue
New York, NY 10128
(212) 415-5607
www.92y.org
Lectures and interviews, readings by award-winning authors. Dance performances and concerts including classical, cabaret, jazz, and popular music

Town Hall
123 West 43rd Street
(212) 997-1003
the-townhall-nyc.org
Lectures, films, and music at affordable prices

THE VISUAL AND STUDIO ARTS

The following are major museums. In addition, the city has many art galleries and smaller exhibitions. The general listings above will get you to those, and also keep you up to date on what each museum is doing. Note also that almost every museum has free admission on at least one evening a week (though some museums are free all the time or have "suggested donation" amounts).

American Museum of Natural History
79th Street and Central Park West
(212) 769-5100
amnh.org
This, in my opinion, is the greatest museum in the world. I am a paying member (there are wonderful benefits to membership—

you never have to wait in line to get your tickets, and you get free or discounted admission to all special exhibits and shows and discounts in the shops and museum cafés), even though admission is by "suggested donation."

Asia Society Gallery
775 Park Avenue
(212) 288-6400
asiasociety.org
America's leading institution dedicated to educating Americans about Asia.

Children's Museum of Manhattan (CMOM)
212 West 83rd Street
(212) 721-1234
cmom.org
Educational and interactive exhibits targeted at kids.

China Institute Gallery
125 East 65th Street
(212) 744-8181
chinainstitute.org
Exhibitions of Chinese art and culture from the China Institute in America.

The Cloisters
Fort Tryon Park
(212) 923-3700
www.metmuseum.org
The Cloisters is the branch of the Metropolitan Museum devoted to

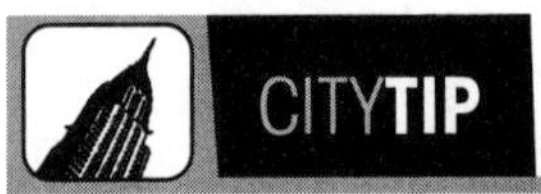

"A savvy New Yorker is an off-season traveler in her own town. The top attractions, restaurants, and stores in New York are often brutally crowded—so don't go when they're busy. The same restaurant that was packed on Saturday night may be nearly empty at lunchtime on Tuesday. Even the most popular stores tend to be empty first thing in the morning, when they've just opened. Learn what everybody else is doing, and then don't follow the herd."

—Emily Fries,
healthcare consultant

the art and architecture of medieval Europe. It's located on four acres overlooking the Hudson River in northern Manhattan's Fort Tryon Park, in a building that incorporates elements from five medieval French cloisters.

Cooper-Hewitt, National Design Museum
2 East 91st Street
(212) 860-6898
cooperhewitt.org

Specializing in decorative arts, the Cooper-Hewitt is housed in a building (the Carnegie Mansion) that is as magnificent as the art.

El Museo del Barrio
1230 Fifth Avenue (at 105th Street)
(212) 831-7272
elmuseo.org

New York City's only Latino museum, this cultural center for Spanish Harlem is dedicated to Puerto Rican, Caribbean, and Latin American art.

The Frick Collection
1 East 70th Street
(212) 288-0700
frick.org

A fabulous, manageable art museum—my favorite is the Impressionist collection.

Guggenheim Museum
1071 Fifth Avenue
(212) 360-3500
guggenheim.org

Modern art is on display in this famous Frank Lloyd Wright building.

The International Center of Photography (ICP)
1133 Avenue of the Americas (at 43rd Street)
(212) 857-0000
icp.org

A museum devoted to photography and photojournalism.

Intrepid Sea, Air & Space Museum
Pier 86 (46th Street and 12th Avenue)
(212) 245-0072
www.intrepidmuseum.org

Open in fall 2008 after an extensive restoration.

The Jewish Museum
1109 Fifth Avenue (entrance on 92nd Street)
(212) 860-1888
jewishmuseum.org

Permanent collection exhibitions of 4,000 years of Jewish art and culture, with rotating exhibitions ranging from photography to the lives of consequential personalities like Sigmund Freud to graphic artists and their artwork (comic books). The museum also features wonderful programs for children and families.

The Metropolitan Museum of Art
1000 Fifth Avenue (from 81st to 84th Streets)
(212) 535-7710
metmuseum.org

Art treasures, ancient and modern, from around the world. Simply walk in and pick a gallery—you can't go wrong, whatever you choose.

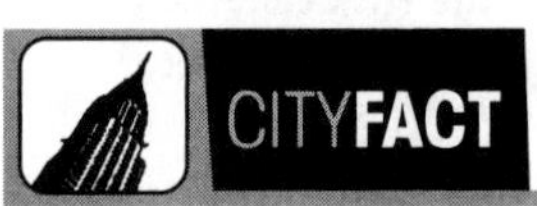

The New York City public bus system consists of 300 routes and carries 600 million people a year (by far the most in the nation) on 4,200 buses. By tradition New York's bus and subway fares have always been identical, but they strayed apart for two years (between 1948 and 1950), when the bus fare was seven cents and the subway fare was ten.

Morgan Library & Museum
25 Madison Avenue
(212) 685-0008
morganlibrary.org

Newly renovated and expanded, the Morgan Library is one of the more manageable and interesting museums.

The Mount Vernon Hotel Museum
421 East 61st Street
(212) 838-6878
mvhm.org

Formerly known as the Abigail Adams Smith Museum, this eighteenth-century coach house was once the home of Abigail Adams, daughter of the second president, John Adams.

Museum for African Art
www.africanart.org

This wonderful museum is in the process of moving to a brand-new building at 1280 Fifth Avenue (at 110th Street), so check its website for progress.

Museum of Arts & Design
40 West 53rd Street
(212) 956-6047
madmuseum.org

Formerly the American Craft Museum, the Museum of Arts & Design (MAD) is the country's premier institution dedicated to the collection and exhibition of contemporary objects created in clay, glass, wood, metal, and fiber. It's getting a much-deserved new building on Columbus Circle in fall 2008.

Museum of American Folk Art
45 West 53rd Street
(212) 265-1040
folkartmuseum.org
Featuring eighteenth- and nineteenth-century paintings, quilts, sculptures, and the work of contemporary self-taught artists.

Museum of Jewish Heritage
18 First Place
Battery Park City
(212) 509-6130
mjhnyc.org
A living memorial to the Holocaust.

Museum of Modern Art
11 West 53rd Street
(212) 708-9480
moma.org
Newly renovated and expanded, MoMA now even has several excellent restaurants.

Museum of the City of New York
1220 Fifth Avenue (at 103rd Street)
(212) 534-1672
mcny.org
Local-history museum including exhibitions of items from the original Dutch settlement, toys, and theatrical memorabilia.

Museum of the Moving Image
36-01 35th Avenue
Astoria, Queens
(718) 784-0077
movingimage.us
Formerly the American Museum of the Moving Image, this institution houses all sorts of film-related artifacts, holds screenings

of interesting films, and offers educational programs to students, teachers, and the general public.

National Museum of the American Indian
U.S. Customs House
1 Bowling Green (near Battery Park)
(212) 668-6624
www.nmai.si.edu
Dedicated to the preservation, study, and exhibition of American Indian life, languages, literature, history, and arts.

New-York Historical Society
170 Central Park West
(212) 873-3400
www.nyhistory.org
Yes, it's spelled with a hyphen. A wonderful American-history museum.

Nicholas Roerich Museum
319 West 107th Street
(212) 864-7752
roerich.org
Dedicated to the work of Nicholas Roerich, a Russian-born artist.

The Paley Center for Media, formerly the Museum of Television and Radio
25 West 52nd Street
(212) 621-6800
mtr.org
Dedicated to preserving television and radio programs.

South Street Seaport Museum
Pier 17
Fulton and South Streets
(212) 669-9424
southstseaport.org
Exhibitions on the history of the port of New York.

Theodore Roosevelt Birthplace
28 East 20th Street
(212) 260-1616
www.nps.gov/thrb
One of the City's most unusual museums, this National Park Service historic site honors the life of President Theodore Roosevelt.

Whitney Museum of American Art
945 Madison Avenue
(212) 570-3676
whitney.org
Exhibitions focusing on American art and culture.

OUTDOORS IN NEW YORK

In the late 1990s, when *Outside* magazine chose New York as one of the top ten cities in the world for outdoors enthusiasts, there were more than a few raised eyebrows. But why? As *Outside* put it, "New Yorkers approach sport with the same in-your-face moxie they bring to every other pursuit." And, in addition to having a parks system unparalleled for its diversity, New York lies at the crossroads of some of the most beautiful regions in America: the Hudson Valley, the Jersey shore, the Connecticut shore, the Catskills, the Poconos, and Long Island. In addition to all that was previously listed, there are numerous other ways to take advantage of New York outside: in-line skating in any of the parks (free clinics in Central Park on weekends);

running along the streets, rivers, or parks (once again, Central Park tops the list with the six-mile park-drive loop and the 1.6-mile dirt reservoir track); riding your bike up the West Side along the Hudson River and over the George Washington Bridge . . . you name it, you've got it—just walk (or run, or skate, or bike) out your door.

PARKS

The best place to start if you're trying to get information on a particular City park is to visit the Department of Parks & Recreation online (nycgovparks.org). The park system has more than 28,000 acres of land and includes 854 playgrounds, 700 playing fields, 500 tennis courts, thirty-three outdoor swimming pools, ten indoor swimming pools, thirty-three recreation and senior centers, fifteen miles of beaches, thirteen golf courses, six ice rinks, four major stadiums, and four zoos.

City of New York Parks and Recreation
The Arsenal, Central Park
830 Fifth Avenue
(212) 360-8111
Twenty-four-hour hotline: (800) 201-PARK
nycgovparks.org

Battery Park

Utilized primarily by downtown residents and weekend strollers, Battery Park is an especially lively destination in the summer and is almost twenty-three acres in size, covering from New York Harbor to Battery Place and Pier A to State Street.

Bryant Park

On Sixth Avenue from West 40th to West 42nd Streets, Bryant Park is a favorite destination for workweek picnic lunches, summer music, and outdoor movies.

Central Park

Bordered by Central Park South (59th Street), Fifth Avenue, Central Park West, and 110th Street, this is the gem of the city. Central Park is an 843-acre park with a zoo, skating rinks, swimming pool, playgrounds, ball fields, theater, running track (1.6 miles around the reservoir), and lots more. It is the refuge for New Yorkers year-round.

City Hall Park

Bordered by Broadway, Park Row, and Chambers Streets, City Hall Park is at the foot of the Brooklyn Bridge and affords great views of the bridge, courthouses, and City Hall.

Fort Tryon Park

Running from Riverside Drive to Broadway and West 192nd Street to Dyckman Park, Fort Tryon Park in northern Manhattan is almost sixty-seven acres and includes the Anne Loftus Playground (Broadway and Riverside Drive), the Bennett Rest sitting area (West 191 Street and Bennett Avenue), and the Jacob Javits Playground (Margaret Corbin Circle).

The Greenbelt

Located in central Staten Island, the Greenbelt is a flagship park of the City (like Central Park, Riverside, Fort Tryon, and Prospect Parks—and a handful of others) and comprises almost 3,000 acres of forest, wetlands, lakes, ponds, and streams. Not only can you hike, explore, and chill out here, you can also play golf at La Tourette and play tennis or a game of softball at Willowbrook.

Prospect Park

Located between Prospect Park West, Flatbush, Parkside, and Ocean Avenues, Prospect Park is Brooklyn's crown jewel and measures in at about 526 acres.

Riverside Park

Located on the Hudson River from 72nd Street up to 158th Street, Riverside Park is about 297 acres and is utilized by residents from all of the boroughs.

Union Square Park

Between Broadway and Fourth Avenue (Fourth Avenue is the continuation of Park Avenue South) from East 14th to East 17th Streets, Union Square Park is most notable for its greenmarket on Mondays, Wednesdays, Fridays, and Saturdays, and for its very popular dog run.

Van Cortlandt Park

Located in the Bronx (between Broadway, Jerome Avenue, City Line, and Van Cortlandt Park South), Van Cortlandt Park is a whopping 1,146 acres in size and includes multiple playgrounds, a mansion, a golf course, and plenty of room to run, roam, and play.

"Take advantage of New York's public libraries. There are so many of them to choose from (over 1,000) and some, like the branch on 42nd Street and Fifth Avenue, are among the biggest and best in the world. It's also a good place to escape."

—Fatima Elmjid, Flushing, Queens (via Casablanca, Morocco), ice cream scooper

Washington Square Park

Bordered by Fifth Avenue, Waverly Place, MacDougal Street, and West 4th Street, Washington Square Park has long been a favorite hangout of teenagers, punk rockers, chess players, jugglers, NYU students, and dog owners (on account of the dog run). The striking entry arch will remind visitors of the Arc de Triomphe in Paris, which it's modeled after.

ZOOS

The Bronx Zoo
Bronx River Parkway and Fordham Road
(718) 367-1010
wcs.org

Worth the trip at any time of year, this is the nation's largest urban zoo and has long been a favorite destination of children and adults alike. Wednesdays are free.

Central Park Zoo
Fifth Avenue (at 64th Street)
(212) 861-6030
wcs.org

New York Aquarium
West 8th Street and Surf Avenue
Brooklyn
(718) 265-FISH
wcs.org

Prospect Park Zoo
450 Flatbush Avenue
Prospect Park, Brooklyn
(718) 399-7339
wcs.org

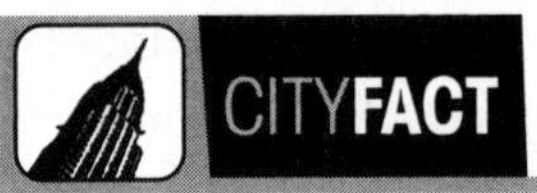

The Brooklyn Bridge opened on May 24, 1883, and was for many years the world's longest suspension bridge. It was the brainchild of John Augustus Roebling, who died during its construction, and was completed by his son, Washington Roebling. A week after its opening, a dozen pedestrians were trampled to death in a stampede when somebody shouted (falsely) that the bridge was collapsing. A year later, P. T. Barnum crossed the bridge with a herd of twenty-one circus elephants to demonstrate its architectural soundness.

Staten Island Zoo
Clarence T. Barrett Park
614 Broadway (at Colonial Court)
Staten Island
(718) 442-3100
statenislandzoo.org

This zoo has a noteworthy snake collection and a children's zoo as well.

GARDENS

Brooklyn Botanic Garden
1000 Washington Avenue
Brooklyn
(718) 622-4433
bbg.org

The New York Botanical Garden
200th Street and Kazimiroff Boulevard
The Bronx
(718) 817-8700
nybg.org

Queens Botanical Garden
43–50 Main Street
Flushing, Queens
(718) 886-3800
queensbotanical.org

Free

Staten Island Botanical Garden
Snug Harbor Cultural Center
1000 Richmond Terrace
Staten Island
(718) 273-8200
sibg.org

Free

Conservancy Garden
Central Park between 104th and 105th Streets, near Fifth Avenue
A beautiful, free, and underutilized Manhattan garden.

ICE SKATING

There are many outdoor rinks within the City. Wollman (between 62nd and 63rd, enter at 65th) and Lasker (at 106th, most easily accessible from 110th Street) rinks in Central Park rank high with locals. But a special favorite of New Yorkers and tourists alike is ice skating at Rockefeller Center ("Rock Center" to locals).

Rockefeller Center
Fifth Avenue (between 49th and 50th Streets)
(212) 332-7654
rapatina.com/iceRink
Skate rentals available

RUNNING

New York Road Runners Club (NYRRC)
9 East 89th Street
(212) 860-4455
www.nyrrc.org
NYRRC is a great place for meeting other people, getting matched up with running partners for safe running, and expanding your running horizons. Offering free group runs, among other things, from the kiosk in Central Park (at Fifth Avenue and 90th Street, Engineers' Gate) at 6:30 A.M. and P.M. on weekdays and at 10 A.M. on weekends, the NYRRC is a cornerstone in many New Yorkers' lives.

FITNESS CLUBS

While it's certainly possible to exercise outdoors for free most of the year, many New Yorkers choose the convenience, versatility, and camaraderie of health-and-fitness clubs. Often your choice of fitness club will be easy: You'll join the one nearest your home, or nearest your office. It's also possible that your employer has arranged a discount with a nearby fitness club, so be sure to check your benefits package. But remember, as with group life and disability insurance, the deals your employer arranges aren't always the best deals—you may do better (and find a place more to your liking) if you shop around. Your health insurer may also provide a partial reimbursement. If you need special facilities, like tennis courts or a full-size swimming pool, your choices are more limited, and you may have to travel a bit to a club that's right for you.

Some of the city's major fitness club chains are Bally (ballyfitness .com), Crunch (crunch.com), David Barton (davidbartongym.com), Dolphin (dolphinfitnessclubs.com), Equinox (equinoxfitness.com), New York Health & Racquet Club (nyhrc.com), and New York Sports Clubs (www.mysportsclubs.com).

There are also YMCA/YWCA locations throughout the five boroughs (www.ymca.net), as well as the 92nd Street YMHA/YWHA (a Jewish alternative to the YMCA, www.92y.org). These tend to be good choices for swimmers, as they have some of the larger pools in town. Also noteworthy for its great pool is Asphalt Green (asphaltgreen.org).

Be sure to educate yourself before you sign a health/fitness club contract. Fitness clubs sometimes employ high-pressure sales tactics, because they're always eager to get new members. And remember that fitness clubs in New

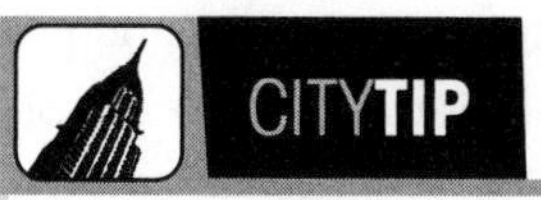

"Many theaters sell standing-room-only tickets, which means exactly that: You get to see the show for much, much less money—but you have to stand in the back of the theater. After the first intermission, though, at all but the hottest, newest, most popular shows, you should be able to find a place to sit where someone else decided to leave or didn't show up in the first place."

—Karen Marcus, account manager

York are regulated by the New York Health Club Services Act. The act states that (1) no fitness club contract can exceed $3,600 per year (excluding tennis and racquetball facilities); (2) no fitness club contract can be for a term longer than 36 months; and (3) all fitness club contracts are cancelable within three days of the signing of the contract, and at any time for any of the following reasons: if the fitness club ceases to offer the services stated in the contract; if the consumer moves 25 miles from any fitness club operated by the seller; and if, upon a doctor's order, the consumer cannot receive the services as stated in the contract for a period in excess of six months. Such notices must appear on all fitness club contracts. The fitness club must provide refunds within fifteen days of such cancellation.

AMATEUR SPORTS LEAGUES

There are many different ways to join sports leagues in and around the City. The easiest and most typical way is through your job. Many large corporations and professional associations sponsor team sports each season. For example, the Lawyers Basketball League is taken very seriously by participants and followers alike, so much so that league games and standings are reported daily in the *New York Law Journal.* To join your company's team (whatever the sport), look for a sign-up sheet, generally circulated or posted in a prominent place or e-mailed around so that everyone has the opportunity to get involved. If you don't see a sign-up sheet, ask around or call the human resources department.

If it should turn out that your company doesn't participate in the corporate leagues, you have a few choices: You can volunteer to start your company's first team yourself, or, if that's

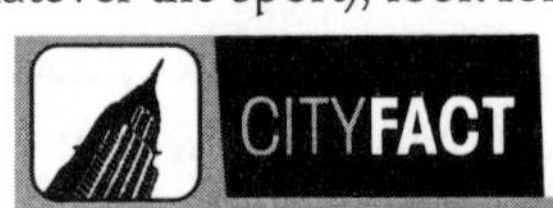

The City has more than 18,000 restaurants, representing nearly every one of the world's cuisines. The largest is the Bryant Park Cafe and Grill, which seats 1,420 people, followed by Tavern on the Green, which seats 800. Chinatown's largest restaurant, Jing Fong, is the size of a professional football field.

too ambitious, you can instead join a league through a professional association with which you are already affiliated (or wish to join). See Chapter 13 for a list of professional associations. If none of these options suits you, you can walk by a few of the City's many ball fields, watch for a while, then ask team players how to get involved.

For people living outside of the City, there are also neighborhood leagues. Ask your real estate broker when you're house-hunting. Ask at the neighborhood schools, check the local papers and the freebie papers in the grocery store, and, again, ask around at the playing fields, because the people who hang out there are likely to have the most information.

PROFESSIONAL SPORTS

The major professional sports teams in the New York area are:

Major League Baseball

New York Mets, National League East
Shea Stadium (soon to be at their new stadium, Citi Field, as of opening day 2009), Queens
newyork.mets.mlb.com

New York Yankees, American League East
Yankee Stadium (moving to the new Yankee Stadium nearby, in 2009), Bronx
newyork.yankees.mlb.com

National Football League

New York Giants, National Football Conference East
Giants Stadium at the Meadowlands Sports Complex, East Rutherford, New Jersey
giants.com

New York Jets, American Football Conference East
Giants Stadium at the Meadowlands Sports Complex, East Rutherford, New Jersey
www.newyorkjets.com

National Basketball Association

New York Knicks, Atlantic Division, Eastern Conference
Madison Square Garden, Manhattan
www.nba.com/knicks

New Jersey Nets, Atlantic Division, Eastern Conference
Continental Airlines Arena at the Meadowlands Sports Complex, East Rutherford, New Jersey
www.nba.com/nets

Women's National Basketball Association

New York Liberty
Madison Square Garden, Manhattan
www.wnba.com/liberty

National Hockey League

New Jersey Devils, Atlantic Division, Eastern Conference
Prudential Center, Newark, New Jersey
devils.nhl.com

New York Islanders, Atlantic Division, Eastern Conference
Nassau Veterans Memorial Coliseum, Uniondale, New York
islanders.nhl.com

New York Rangers, Atlantic Division, Eastern Conference
Madison Square Garden, Manhattan
newyorkrangers.com

Major League Soccer

New York Red Bulls
redbull.newyork.mlsnet.com

Tennis

The U.S. Open tennis tournament is played at the USTA Billie Jean King National Tennis Center in Queens (www.usopen.org).

DINING OUT IN THE BIG APPLE

Some towns have high school football; New York has restaurants. To say that New Yorkers are passionate about restaurants is a major understatement—when it comes to dining out, we're possessed, obsessed, and discerning. We eat enough to support more than 18,000 establishments, ranging from Gray's Papaya (where two frankfurters and a tropical fruit drink cost $2.75) to Per Se (where a nine-course chef's tasting menu can be had for $250 per person, plus tax and service). And that's not to mention the thousands of street vendors and gourmet (and not-so-gourmet) markets that function as takeout food sources for busy residents.

Back in the day, if you wanted to stay on top of what was going on in the restaurant universe, your research pretty much started and finished with the weekly *New York Times* Dining In, Dining Out section, which in and of itself is larger than many small-town newspapers. You might also have taken a look at *New York* magazine's food coverage. Today, the *New York Times, Time Out New York,* the *Village Voice,* and the other major periodicals remain important sources for New York restaurant information, but the center of gravity has shifted toward the Internet.

Online, you'll find restaurant blogs, discussion websites, searchable databases, and of course the websites of the newspapers and magazines, most of which post all their restaurant information online for free. The following are a few of the best places to look online for restaurant information.

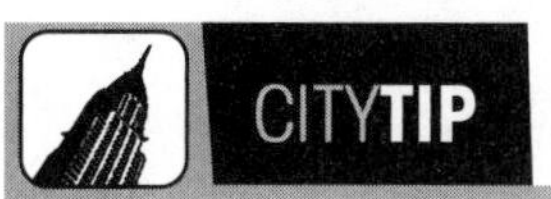

"Make time for adventures—why bother living here if you're not going to explore? For a virtual trip to an exotic foreign land, instead of getting on an airplane, grab the 7 train to Little India in Jackson Heights or Chinatown in Flushing. The sights, sounds, and smells will be like a trip to the East—but you'll still be back in time to sleep in your own bed."

—Diane Burrowes, marketing director

BLOGS

Eater (eater.com): This is the restaurant equivalent of the Curbed real estate blog (it's published by the same people). It's updated several times a day with the latest restaurant openings, closings, gossip and news tidbits. It's highly addictive.

Grub Street (nymag.com/daily/food/): From *New York* magazine food staff, this blog competes directly with Eater and also updates throughout the day. Sometimes a food story breaks first on Grub Street, other times on Eater. The die-hard foodies read both.

Diner's Journal (dinersjournal.blogs.nytimes.com): The *New York Times* dining section staff contributes to this blog, which is updated every day or so, often with full-length essays that aren't available in the *New York Times* print edition. It's the place where the *Times* restaurant reviewers and food writers speak more casually about their work, and where a lot of the juiciest information tidbits are hidden.

DISCUSSION

The eGullet Society (eGullet.org) runs an international discussion website with thousands of members and well over a million posts. The New York area is particularly active. If you want to see what the in-the-know gourmets are saying about a restaurant, or you want to ask a question, this is the place. You need to join to be able to post (membership is free), but anybody can read.

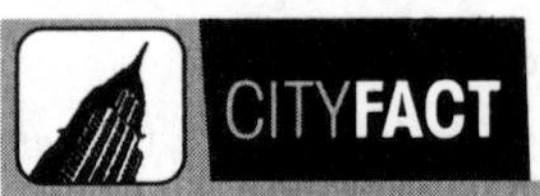

The Greenbelt, at 2,500 acres, is the pride of Staten Island. More than three times the size of Central Park, this incredible nature preserve offers, among other things, well-marked hiking trails and regularly scheduled talks, walks, and programs.

Chowhound (www.chowhound.com) is another large food website with vibrant online discussion. The focus is more on the cheap-eats end of the spectrum, though everything is covered.

SEARCHABLE DATABASES

CitySearch (newyork.citysearch.com) is a great place to look for names and addresses of restaurants. You can search by neighborhood, cuisine type, and various other features.

MenuPages (menupages.com) has menus from more than 6,000 New York restaurants in a searchable database. Great for planning your evening. You can even search for your favorite dish and pull up all the restaurants in a neighborhood that serve it.

NEWSPAPER AND MAGAZINE FOOD COVERAGE ONLINE

The *New York Times* Dining section (nytimes.com/pages/dining) is updated every Wednesday (late Tuesday night, actually) and has the most extensive coverage of the New York dining scene. You can also search through the old restaurant reviews back to 1991.

***New York* magazine (nymag.com)** expends a lot of effort on dining coverage, and contains many high-quality stories each week.

***The New York Sun* (nysun.com)** is a relatively new New York newspaper that now has more than 100,000 readers. Many of its food stories are available online for free, though others are available only to paid subscribers.

Not For Tourists (notfortourists.com) is a hipster guidebook series as well as a website with great up-to-the-minute intel. The NFT angle is that this is a guide for locals in their own city—as well as commuters, and visitors who are determined not to be tourists.

The Village Voice **(villagevoice.com),** ***New York Post*** **(nypost.com),** ***New York Daily News*** **(www.nydailynews.com),** ***New York Press*** **(nypress.com)**, and ***Crain's New York Business*** **(www.crainsnewyork.com)** all also maintain websites and offer interesting food content.

ONLINE RESERVATIONS

Many New York restaurants now accept reservations online, through the **OpenTable (OpenTable.com)** system. It's a free service, and it can save you hours on the phone—and money (frequent users earn bonuses and coupons). Particularly nice is the feature that allows you to search for every available table at a given time. So, for example, if you have to take a group of four people out at 9 P.M. next Saturday night, OpenTable will tell you every available table at every restaurant in its system within a certain range of 9 P.M. A few key restaurants are not on the system, but more and more are being added every month. If all of the tables are booked, it's still worthwhile to give a call—most restaurants have a waiting list for last-minute cancellations and they always keep a few tables to themselves. Polite persistence has been known to pay off.

ESSENTIAL RESTAURANTS

New York has famous restaurants that everyone has heard of, such as the Rainbow Room and the Russian Tea Room. But you won't see many real New Yorkers at those places, unless they're entertaining clients or family from out of town. Likewise, remember that the very popular *Zagat Survey* is, to a lot of New Yorkers, really just a handy address book—serious diners tend not to rely on a public opinion poll for their dining advice. Instead, a truly food-obsessed New Yorker might read reviews and websites from reputable print and online sources (preferably several of them, including those listed previously), talk to friends, and interrogate the management before settling on a place for dinner.

The following are just a few of the most important restaurants in New York, plus my favorites in several essential categories. Most of these are "destination" restaurants, meaning you have to plan to go to them because you don't live or work nearby. But dining is often a neighborhood affair, so when it comes to finding the best places within walking distance of your home or office, you'll want to use the search resources above. Good luck—it's a wonderful adventure!

The $ signs indicate the price of food only, at dinnertime (most restaurants have lunch and off-hours specials—a great opportunity for budget-conscious diners). Expect tax, tip (16.5 percent is standard in New York—just double the tax—or more in a very exclusive restaurant), and drinks to add considerably to your bill.

$ = cheap; less than $10 per person
$$ = moderate; $10 to $35 per person
$$$ = expensive; $35 to $70 per person
$$$$ = luxury; $70 and up per person

NEW YORK'S TOP RESTAURANTS

The following are generally considered to be the top restaurants in the City. They're all very expensive, though they often have less pricey lunch options:

Jean Georges $$$$
One Central Park West (at Columbus Circle)
(212) 299-3900
jean-georges.com
The flagship restaurant of legendary French chef and restaurateur Jean-Georges Vongerichten

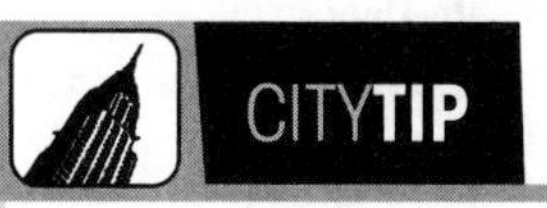

"There are all sorts of free events all over the City throughout the year, but the best time to take advantage of free events is during the summer. In Central Park, for example, there are concerts (rock, country, classical, and even opera), fireworks displays, and dramatic productions. For some events, like the Shakespeare in the Park performances, you'll have to line up to get tickets, but for others, like the concerts, you just show up."

—Karen Poznansky, television producer

Le Bernardin $$$$
155 West 51st Street (between Sixth and Seventh Avenues)
(212) 489-1515
le-bernardin.com
The reigning champion of French seafood restaurants in America.

Masa $$$$
10 Columbus Circle (at 60th Street)
4th Floor
(212) 823-9800
masanyc.com
Incredibly expensive Japanese restaurant in the Time Warner Center.

Per Se $$$$
10 Columbus Circle (at 60th Street)
4th Floor
(212) 823-9335
perseny.com
The New York restaurant of Thomas Keller, the famed chef of the French Laundry in Yountville, California. In the Time Warner Center.

Best Pizza

Patsy's $$
2287 First Avenue (between 117th and 118th Streets)
(212) 534-9783
This is the only Patsy's location that serves truly outstanding pizza—the others are not managed by the family. It's in a touch-and-go neighborhood, so plan your travel during daytime or with a group.

Sally's Apizza $$
237 Wooster Street
New Haven, CT
(203) 624-5271

Real New Yorkers aren't afraid to admit it when the best of something is outside the City. We know, for example, that California has great Mexican food, and we don't. And we know that the best pizza in America can be found not in New York City, but rather in nearby New Haven, Connecticut. This is a great night out for die-hard pizza lovers. If you're going to make the trip, call in advance (try between 3:00 and 5:00) to be sure they're not on vacation—and you can try for a reservation, too. Open for dinner only. Closed on Mondays. Expect a wait, especially on Thursday through Sunday (unless you were able to secure one of those hard-to-get reservations).

Best Moderately Priced Chinese

New Green Bo $–$$
66 Bayard Street
(212) 625-2359

Excellent, authentic Shanghai cuisine. Really stands out against the competition.

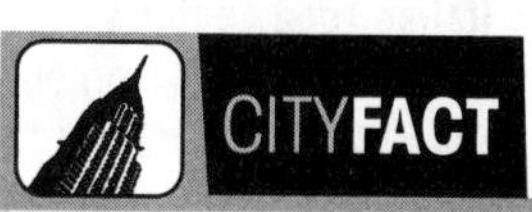

Snug Harbor, opened in 1833 on Staten Island as a home to retired sailors, now functions as a cultural center for the community. Sitting on 83 acres of land (some of it waterfront), and protected by the New York City Landmark Preservation Commission, Snug Harbor offers classes, year-round concerts, readings, and dance and stage performances.

Best Steakhouse

Peter Luger $$$
178 Broadway (just over the Williamsburg Bridge)
Williamsburg, Brooklyn
(718) 387-7400

Without question, the best in New York. Well worth the trip to Brooklyn.

Sparks $$$
210 East 46th Street (between Second and Third Avenues)
(212) 687-4855

An eminently respectable alternative for those who just won't leave Manhattan. World-class wine list.

Best Korean

Woo Chon $$
8 West 36th Street (between Fifth and Sixth Avenues)
(212) 695-0676

Twenty-four-hour Korean restaurant with tabletop barbecue.

Best Jewish Deli

Katz's Deli $–$$
205 Houston Street (near Ludlow Street)
(212) 254-2246

The site of the classic scene in *When Harry Met Sally.*

Best Italian Deli

Italian Food Center $
186 Grand Street (corner of Mulberry)
(212) 925-2954

Old-world Italian sandwiches in the heart of Little Italy.

Best Burger

Shake Shack $
shakeshacknyc.com

In Madison Square Park near Madison Avenue and 23rd Street. Open spring, summer, and fall only. Expect a wait.

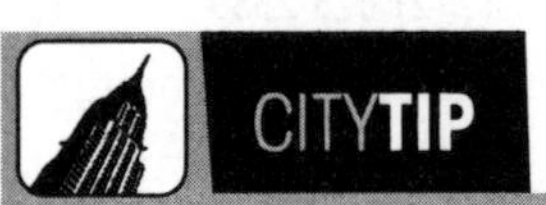

"Being part of a studio audience while a TV show is being taped is a real blast—and it's free! You can plan in advance and send in a postcard requesting tickets for a specific date, or, if spontaneity is more your speed, you can line up for stand-by seats. *Late Show with David Letterman* tops my list."

—Pablo Vasquez,
building superintendent

Burger Joint at Le Parker Meridien Hotel $
118 West 57th Street (between Sixth and Seventh Avenues)
(212) 708-7414

Hidden away off the lobby of LPM, this lively burger joint serves juicy, no-frills burgers wrapped in wax paper. It has counter service only, and there's often a wait for tables.

Best Hot Dog

Gray's Papaya $
2090 Broadway (corner of 72nd Street)

Papaya King $
179 East 86th Street (corner of Third Avenue)

These competing establishments (Mr. Gray used to work at Papaya King) both serve great frankfurters. New Yorkers drink papaya juice with them—try it, you'll love it.

Best Diner

Junior's $$
386 Flatbush Avenue (corner of DeKalb Avenue)
Brooklyn
(718) 852-5257

The definitive Brooklyn diner, with orange vinyl banquettes and some of the world's best cheesecake.

Best Dive

Chat 'n' Chew $$
10 East 16th Street (between Fifth Avenue and Union Square West)
(212) 243-1616

You can't help but love the BLTs and pink-frosted chocolate cake at this contemporary take on the greasy spoon.

Best Pasta

Becco $$
355 West 46th Street (between Eighth and Ninth Avenues)
(212) 397-7597

Three varieties of amazing homemade pasta daily, with little damage to your wallet.

Best Soul Food

Charles' Southern-Style Kitchen $
2841 Frederick Douglass Boulevard
(between 151st and 152nd Streets)
(212) 926-4313

The genuine article. Charles started by selling his food out of a truck. Now he's a neighborhood legend. The fried chicken is highly recommended.

Best Moderately Priced Thai

Sea Thai $$
75 Second Avenue (between 4th and 5th Streets)
(212) 228-5505

This popular Thai restaurant was featured in the television series *Sex and the City* and in the movie *Garden State*. It features club music and fits the hipster bill. The owners also operate a small local chain of Spice restaurants and another branch of Sea Thai in Williamsburg.

Sripraphai Thai Restaurant $$
6413 39th Ave
Woodside, Queens
(718) 899-9599

Great homestyle Thai food with friendly and enthusiastic service.

Best Brazilian Rodizio

Churrascaria Plataforma $$
316 West 49th Street (between Eighth and Ninth Avenues)
(212) 245-0505

All-you-can-eat roasted meat feast.

Best Late Night

Blue Ribbon $$
97 Sullivan Street (between Prince and Spring Streets)
(212) 274-0404

Outstanding fried chicken.

Best All-Night

Yaffa Cafe $
97 St. Marks Place (between First Avenue and Avenue A)
(212) 674-9302

Eclectic menu with great salads served twenty-four hours a day, seven days a week. A fun hangout with attitude.

Best McDonald's

McDonald's $
160 Broadway (between Cortlandt Street and Liberty Street)
(212) 385-2063

They're all the same, right? Wrong! This flagship McDonald's has live music on a grand piano, a doorman in topcoat and tails, hostesses, marble tables, a digital stock ticker, a gift shop, flowers, and a dessert menu (including cappuccino and espresso).

The Bronx Zoo and Wildlife Conservation Society Park is the largest metropolitan zoo in the United States. It contains 4,000 animals (with more than 500 species) living in natural habitats. At the City's four zoos (Bronx, Central Park, Queens, and Prospect Park) and one aquarium, there are a total of 17,875 animals and 1,210 species.

A YEAR IN NEW YORK

It would be impossible to list everything that happens in New York City in a single day, no less an entire year. Even a list of only major events would be quite long: The official NYC & Company website (nycvisit.com) lists 3,339 of them for the year 2007—and that's just one source! However, if you want to look at all the events listed for a given time period, or break it down by category, nycvisit.com is a good starting point.

The calendar of events below highlights just a few of the year's big events—the ones by which New Yorkers keep time.

Calendar of Events

JANUARY

Kick off the year with the New Year's Eve Midnight Run at 12:01 A.M. on January 1 in Central Park. Hosted by the New York Road Runners Club (212-860-4455, nyrrc.org)

The New York National Boat Show (lasting ten days), the first and longest-running boating event of its kind, at the Javits Center, exhibits the latest in boats, related equipment, and seaworthy toys (212-216-2000, www.nyboatshow.com).

Join in the Three Kings' Day community celebration and parade at El Museo del Barrio (212-831-7272, elmuseo.org).

Leading dealers in the field of so-called visionary art—also sometimes called naive art or art of the self-taught—exhibit their wares at the Outsider Art Fair, at the Puck Building in SoHo (212-777-5218).

FEBRUARY

Chinese New Year celebrations, which are spread over the course of two weeks, include lots of noisy fireworks, banquets, and the paper-dragon dance that winds through Chinatown (212-484-1222).

During the Westminster Kennel Club Dog Show, as many as 3,000 dogs strut their stuff at the annual event at Madison Square Garden (800-455-3647, westminsterkennelclub.org). It is the second-longest-running animal event in the country (after the Kentucky Derby).

The Annual Empire State Building Run-Up is an invitational event in which 150 runners run, push, scramble, and wheeze up the 1,576 stairs to the 86th-floor observation deck (esbnyc.com).

The Empire State Building is the site of the Valentine's Day marriage marathon, when couples marry on the observation deck (212-736-3100, esbnyc.com).

MARCH

St. Patrick's Day Parade: One of the longest-running (and recently most controversial) events in NYC, the parade starts at 11:30 A.M. at 44th Street, goes up Fifth Avenue, and turns onto 86th Street for the finish.

The International Asian Art Fair, where dealers from around the world show articles from the Middle East, Southeast Asia, and the Far East. Part of Asia Week in New York (212-642-8572, www.haughton.com/asian).

LATE MARCH–EARLY APRIL

The Ringling Bros. and Barnum & Bailey Circus arrives in New York each spring and, upon its arrival, the animals are walked (around midnight) from Penn Station to Madison Square Garden, where the circus takes place (ringling.com).

The Triple Pier Expo (Piers 88, 90, and 92) is a big antiques event, but, if you miss it in the spring, there's a showing in November as well (212-255-0020, stellashows.com).

The Macy's Flower Show takes place each year in Rockefeller Center the week before Easter (www.macys.com).

The Easter Parade goes up Fifth Avenue, ending at St. Patrick's Cathedral, at 51st and Fifth.

APRIL

Antiquarian Book Fair at the Seventh Regiment Armory (featuring first editions, rare volumes, manuscripts, autographs, letters, atlases, drawings, prints, and maps, with prices ranging from low double digits well into five digits and beyond).

The Major League Baseball season kicks off (running through September—or

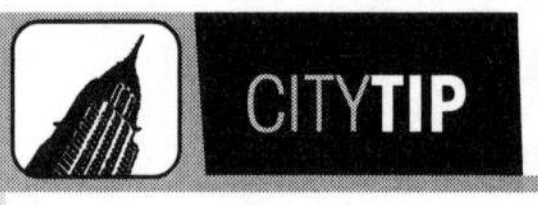

"New York is expensive, but it's also the discount and bargain capital of the world. Be sure to seek out discount dining plans (like the Transmedia card) and theater tickets (through the official Theatre Development Fund half-price ticket booths). And if you see something that's too expensive, ask when it will go on sale—or try to negotiate. Real New Yorkers never pay retail!"

—Jane Smith, paralegal

October, if we're lucky). New York Yankees in the Bronx (718-293-6000, newyork.yankees.mlb.com) and the New York Mets at Shea Stadium, in Queens (718-507-8499, newyork.mets.mlb.com).

MAY

Cherry Blossom Festival at the Brooklyn Botanic Garden (718-622-4433,bbg.org).

Bike New York: The Great Five Boro Bike Tour. A forty-two-mile ride that begins in Battery Park and ends with a ride across the Verrazano-Narrows Bridge (212-932-0778).

The International Fine Art Fair. Renaissance to twentieth-century art. Park Avenue Armory.

Congregation Shearith Israel (the Spanish and Portuguese Synagogue, the oldest congregation in America) sponsors a Sephardic Fair (212-873-0300).

Tap Dance Extravaganza; events are held around Manhattan (718-597-4613).

Memorial Day Weekend (and Following Three Weekends)

Washington Square Outdoor Art Exhibit, an arts-and-crafts fair with hundreds of exhibitors in and around the park (212-982-6255).

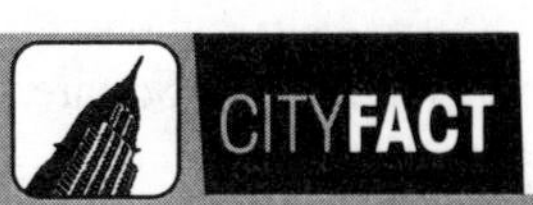

The Edgar Allan Poe Cottage in the Bronx is where, from 1846 to 1849, the poet and his wife resided while he was writing. The cottage is open for tours, and among the items on display are period furniture and changing exhibitions.

JUNE

The Belmont Stakes at Long Island's Belmont Park Racetrack (718-641-4700, www.nyra.com).

Lesbian and Gay Pride Week features the world's biggest annual gay pride parade, a film festival, and countless other events.

National Puerto Rican Day Parade up Fifth Avenue (www.national puerto ricandayparade.org).

JVC Jazz Festival New York is a huge event featuring jazz greats and unknowns all around town (festivalproductions.net).

The Mermaid Parade is the country's largest art parade and an original creation (www.coneyisland.com/mermaid.shtml).

The Affordable Art Fair is an art fair for art lovers of all budgets (aafnyc.com).

LATE JUNE–EARLY JULY

The Washington Square Music Festival features free outdoor concerts on Tuesday evenings with classical, jazz, and big-band sounds (212-431-1088).

JUNE–AUGUST

Midsummer Night Swing, a fabulous outdoor dance event at Lincoln Center's Josie Robertson Plaza. Open dance and nightly lessons (212-875-5766, lincolncenter.org).

HBO/Bryant Park Summer Film Festival. Monday-night movies in Bryant Park are happening—and a real scene, so if you spend more time watching the people than the movies, you don't have to worry, it's all free (bryantpark.org).

Central Park SummerStage features free events on weekday evenings and blues, Latin, pop, African, country, dance performances, opera, and readings on weekends (212-360-2777, www.summerstage.org).

Shakespeare in the Park (212-539-8500; 212-539-8750 seasonal phone at the Delacorte, publictheater.org), sponsored by the Joseph Papp Public Theater at Central Park's Delacorte Theater, tackles the Bard and other classics, often with a star performer or two from the big or small screen.

The New York Philharmonic gives free concerts around the City in area parks (212-875-5656, nyphil.org).

Celebrate Brooklyn features pop, jazz, rock, classical, klezmer, African, Latin, and Caribbean music and theatrical performances, at the band shell in Prospect Park in Brooklyn (718-855-7882, briconline.org/celebrate). And it's all free.

EARLY JULY-MID-AUGUST

The Museum of Modern Art presents classical music, performed by students of the Juilliard School, in the Summergarden on Friday and Saturday evenings (212-708-9400, moma.org/calendar).

JULY

Independence Day

The Fourth of July festival's downtown festivities include live entertainment, arts and crafts, and a parade from Bowling Green to City Hall.

South Street Seaport July Fourth festival

The East River July Fourth Fireworks are the best you're likely to see—ever! Vantage points are best from 14th to 41st Streets along the FDR Drive (which is closed to cars for the event) and the Brooklyn Heights Promenade.

Lincoln Center Festival features classical and contemporary music concerts, dance, stage works, and non-Western arts.

AUGUST

Lincoln Center Out of Doors (212-875-5108, lincolncenter.org) is a series of music, dance, and family-oriented events lasting almost the entire month.

Harlem Week is the world's largest African American and Hispanic festival. Events include concerts, gospel performances, the Black Film Festival, and the Taste of Harlem Food Festival (212-862-7200, harlemweek.harlemdiscover.com).

CITYTIP

"Take advantage of all the free events and performances in New York City. There are many, many offerings, especially in the summer: the New York Philharmonic, Metropolitan Opera, and Shakespeare performances in Central Park, free outdoor movies in Bryant Park, lunchtime concerts at the Winter Garden at the World Financial Center. And, come November, don't forget to cheer the 38,000 runners in the NYC Marathon!"

—Aaron Laiserin, Web designer

The Mostly Mozart festival at Lincoln Center includes free afternoon concerts and evening concerts for a fee (212-875-5103, lincoln center.org).

The Brooklyn County Fair—just like in the country.

LATE AUGUST–EARLY SEPTEMBER

U.S. Open tennis tournament held at the USTA Billie Jean King National Tennis Center in Queens (800-524-8440, www.usopen.org).

SEPTEMBER

Labor Day Weekend

The West Indian American Day Parade is New York's largest parade (held in Brooklyn) and only one of the many events that this festival features. Festivities begin Friday night with salsa, reggae, and calypso music at the Brooklyn Museum and end Monday afternoon with a huge parade. Floats, costumed dancers, stilt walkers—nothing is missing. And don't forget about the West Indian food and music (212-484-1222).

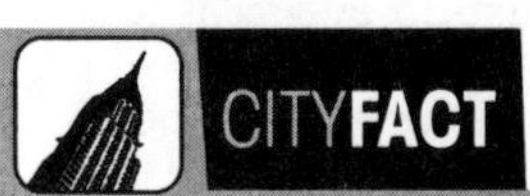

The original Shea Stadium, in Queens, has been home to the New York Mets since April 17, 1964. It is also famous for the legendary Beatles concert that was held on August 23, 1966, and the visit of Pope John Paul II, which occurred on October 3, 1979. The new stadium, Citi Field, is scheduled for completion in time for opening day 2009.

Mid-September

The Feast of San Gennaro is held on Mulberry Street, in honor of the patron saint of Naples. This fabulously colorful event is a great scene in New York's Little Italy.

Broadway on Broadway. A free two-hour outdoor concert held in Times Square by cast members of Broadway shows.

New York Is Book Country. Along Fifth Avenue, between 48th and 57th Streets, publishers set up shop so you can see their upcoming wares, meet authors, play games, and sometimes even get free stuff (212-207-7242).

LATE SEPTEMBER–EARLY OCTOBER

The New York Film Festival is the city's most prestigious annual film event (212-875-5610, filmlinc.com/nyff/nyff.html).

OCTOBER

The International Fine Art and Antique Dealers Show. One of the world's finest shows (212-642-8572, www.haughton.com).

Greenwich Village Halloween parade. A must-do event, at least once (914-758-5519).

OCTOBER–APRIL

New York Rangers hockey at home at Madison Square Garden (newyorkrangers.com).

New York Knicks basketball at home at Madison Square Garden (www.nba.com/knicks).

"Get to know the wonders of New York by renting some of the most important movies about the City: *Breakfast at Tiffany's, Midnight Cowboy, When Harry Met Sally, A Thousand Clowns, The Apartment, Barefoot in the Park, King Kong, Metropolitan, On the Town, The Freshman,* plus *Annie Hall* and anything else by Woody Allen."

—Irving Metzman, actor

NOVEMBER

The New York City Marathon is a citywide event for runners and spectators alike. Participants run through all five boroughs before finishing up in Central Park.

The Veteran's Day Parade heads down Fifth Avenue to the United War Veterans Council of New York County.

The Fall Antiques Show is held at the Seventh Regiment Armory (212-777-5218, armory.wordpress.com).

Thanksgiving Day

The Macy's Thanksgiving Day Parade is a favorite New York event (as is the "balloon stroll" the night before, where City folk gather to watch the balloons being inflated). Gigantic balloons coast down Central Park West, starting at 77th Street and finishing up at Macy's at Herald Square.

NOVEMBER–JANUARY

The Radio City Christmas Spectacular features the fabulous Rockettes at home at Radio City Music Hall (212-247-4777, radiocity.com).

Thanksgiving Weekend through New Year's: Christmas Windows Are a New York City Tradition. The Best Decorations Are Traditionally Seen At:

Saks Fifth Avenue (611 Fifth Avenue at 49th Street)
Lord & Taylor (424 Fifth Avenue at 38th Street)
Bloomingdale's (Lexington Avenue at 59th Street)

FAO Schwarz (767 Fifth Avenue at 58th Street)
Barneys (660 Madison Avenue between 60th and 61st Streets)
Macy's (Broadway at 34th Street)

It's best to start at 58th Street and stroll down Fifth Avenue until you hit Saks (stopping at Rockefeller Center and St. Patrick's Cathedral), stroll up the other side of Fifth to 57th, and then walk over to Madison to see Barneys' windows and the other shops along Madison Avenue (like the Polo store at 72nd Street). Macy's requires a special detour farther downtown.

DECEMBER

Handel's *Messiah* is performed at the Cathedral Church of St. John the Divine on Amsterdam Avenue (at 112th Street, 212-316-7540, stjohndivine.org). Call for details.

Midnight Mass on Christmas Eve is held at the Cathedral Church of St. John the Divine with music for choir, brass, and organ, a sermon, and candle lighting. The service usually begins at 10:30 P.M. (Call for details, 212-316-7540, stjohndivine.org).

Midnight Mass on Christmas Eve is celebrated at St. Patrick's Cathedral on Fifth Avenue and 50th Street (212-753-2261, saint patrickscathedral.org).

The Giant Chanukah Menorah is lit at Grand Army Plaza (Fifth Avenue and 59th Street).

The Rockefeller Center Christmas tree, one of the tallest in the country, annually makes headlines when it is first lit—the event draws thousands of spectators each year.

New Year's Eve

The ball drops in Times Square.
Fireworks
And at least one hundred other events

AWAY FOR THE WEEKEND

New Yorkers travel far and wide for their weekend escapes. Some favorite destinations, like the Hamptons, the Jersey shore, and most of the Hudson Valley, are less than 100 miles away. But others are more far-flung, like the Vermont ski resorts of Mount Snow, Bromley, and Stratton. All of the following out-of-town destinations are accessible by public transit, so don't fret if you don't have wheels—most New Yorkers don't own cars, yet still manage to live both in and out of the City.

One of the greatest places in the world to spend weekends, holidays, and vacation times is New York City itself. Don't get caught up in the get-out-of-town mentality common to so many young professionals. One of the reasons you're moving to New York is, presumably, to take advantage of all this town has to offer.

Often, instead of going out of town, my family will "take a vacation" at home. We plan a solid weekend of activities, including arts performances, trips to one of the City's zoos, museum visits, restaurant meals, and even some touristy things we wouldn't ordinarily do. This is a particularly effective strategy on Memorial Day, July Fourth, and Labor Day weekends, when Manhattan is deserted by locals, and reservations and tickets are easy to come by.

LONG ISLAND

Long Island is not only home to many of the most desirable New York suburbs, it's also a fabulous weekend and vacation destination all year round. With vineyards on the North Fork and the Hamptons on the South Fork, there is plenty to amuse the beachgoer, the nature lover, the socialite, and the antisocial alike. From Manhattan, you can get to the East End of Long Island on the Long Island Expressway, or catch one of the many buses running from the City. This can be far more relaxing than driving—especially in heavy traffic—and the bus drivers know all the shortcuts and often get you there quicker than if you were driving yourself. Train service also runs between Penn Station and points east on Long Island. And some Long Island destinations, like Jones Beach, are only a few miles past the city limits.

JONES BEACH

With enough parking for close to 25,000 cars, calling Jones Beach a popular destination would be an understatement, and it's easy to see why: Jones Beach is easily accessible to the City, and has six miles of beach and ocean. Despite the weekend crowds, the sand is clean, and it's a refreshing change and getaway from summer in the City. There are also dozens of concerts at the Jones Beach Boardwalk Bandshell all summer long (visit jonesbeach.com for details and listings).

Via public transportation from Manhattan, catch the LIRR out of Penn Station to Freeport and connect with buses (the N88) to Jones Beach (for schedules and fare information: (718) 217-5477 or mta.info). From Queens, catch the LIRR en route from Manhattan at Jamaica or Woodside and connect with the same buses in Freeport.

If you're driving from Westchester, Manhattan, the Bronx, Brooklyn, or Queens, take the Long Island Expressway east or Grand

Central Parkway east to Northern State Parkway east to Wantagh State Parkway south to Jones Beach State Park. Or take the Belt Southern State Parkway east to Wantagh State Parkway south to Jones Beach. If you're driving from eastern Long Island take the Northern State Parkway west or Southern State Parkway west to Wantagh State Parkway south to Jones Beach State Park.

THE HAMPTONS

Far more exclusive than any other beach community in the area (based on cost alone), the Hamptons, on the South Fork of Long Island, are the hot summer spot for Manhattan yuppies and West Coast movie moguls alike. Hitting the beach, shopping in town, and simply soaking up the glitz are all part of a day in the life of the Hamptons summer scene. You can also have a look at the East Hampton Historical Society (101 Main Street, 631-324-6850), the Parrish Art Museum (25 Job's Lane, 516-283-2118) in Southampton, or the Sag Harbor Whaling Museum (200 Main Street, 516-725-0770)—or grab a few holes at the Montauk Downs golf course. East Hampton is the heart of the Hamptons scene and worth a visit if you enjoy envying the lifestyles of the rich and famous. (Check out this website for additional cultural attractions: fordyce.org/long_island/history/East_Hampton.) It also has some excellent restaurants, shopping, and nightspots. For further information contact the Southampton Chamber of Commerce (76 Main Street, 631-283-0402, southamptonchamber.com), the East Hampton Chamber of Commerce (79A Main Street, 631-324-0362, www.easthamptonchamber.com), and the Montauk Chamber of Commerce (742 Montauk Highway, 631-668-2428, www.montaukchamber.com).

Via public transportation from Manhattan, head for the LIRR for trains out of Penn Station (718-217-LIRR, mta.info/lirr). Or if you prefer the bus, the Hampton Jitney (212-362-8400 or 631-283-

4600, hamptonjitney.com) is a comfortable coach with frequent service. The Hampton Luxury Liner is the more expensive competitor (631-537-5800, hamptonluxuryliner.com), and is marketing itself as the "first-class alternative" to the Jitney. Both make pickups around the City.

If you've got wheels, take the LIE to exit 70, go right for three miles to Sunrise Highway east (also known as Route 27). Follow 27 to Southampton and beyond—it's the only route to the end of the island.

SHELTER ISLAND

Sheltered between the North and South Forks of eastern Long Island, this haven is ideal for those seeking refuge from the City, the Hamptons, and the see-and-be-seen scene prevalent in so many other summer resort areas. On the docket are bike riding, fishing, golf, tennis, hiking, sunbathing, reading, or just plain relaxing. Most summer residents rent for the entire summer or own their houses, so the comings and goings aren't as pronounced as elsewhere. There's a selection of hotels, mostly B&B accommodations, which are pleasant and fit in perfectly with the spirit and atmosphere of the island. For more information contact the Shelter Island Chamber of Commerce (631-749-0399). Via public transportation from Manhattan, take the LIRR to Greenport.

By car from Manhattan, take the Midtown Tunnel to I-495, LIE to exit 73 (Riverhead). Turn right onto Route 58 (Old Country Road) east to the traffic circle (about two miles). Continue heading east on 58 for approximately two more miles (until 58 turns into Route 25). Continue until you reach Greenport and see the Shelter Island Ferry sign. Turn off Front Street (Route 25) and onto Fifth Street headed south. Take a left onto Wiggins Street (Route 114) to the ferry landing.

FIRE ISLAND

One of the most interesting beach communities in America, with a heavy gay population, Fire Island offers wide and beautiful beaches and quaint, diverse, walkable towns (cars are forbidden on most of the island)—and it's only an hour from the City. A narrow barrier island, with the Atlantic Ocean on one side and the Great South Bay on the other, Fire Island is a summer playground as well as a nature lover's paradise. Ocean-washed beaches, dunes, and maritime forests round out the thirty-two-mile-long Fire Island National Seashore, which contains natural features such as the Otis Pike Wilderness Area (the only national wilderness in New York) and the Sunken Forest (a 300-year-old holly forest).

Ferries to the various Fire Island communities (operated by Fire Island Ferries, Inc., 631-665-3600, fireislandferries.com) depart from the town of Bay Shore, on the South Shore of Long Island. Frequent LIRR trains to Bay Shore, plus a cheap, shared cab ride to the ferry, provide the simplest means of getting to Fire Island. It's also possible to drive (about an hour from Midtown Manhattan) and park at the ferry terminals.

THE HUDSON VALLEY

Just north of New York City, the Hudson Valley is rife with charming towns. The area is especially beautiful (and popular) in the autumn months, when many New Yorkers journey north to see the leaves change hue. If you're up for a scenic drive (as opposed to heading for a particular destination), take Route 9 along the eastern side of the river; if you're on a schedule, take the Taconic State Parkway. Trains run up the Valley from Grand Central Station, or you can take a boat tour of the Hudson River. The Hudson Valley is also a favorite destination of devoted cyclists.

Harriman State Park, to the west of the Hudson River, is a great place for hiking or a summer swim in one of the park's three lakes. Bear Mountain State Park is popular with nature lovers from all around, with hiking trails, swimming, fishing, cross-country skiing, sledding, and ice skating. The park's Trailside Museum and Wildlife Center has exhibitions on the area and acts as a refuge for rescued animals. And the Shawgunks are an area favorite for City rock climbers (check out gunks.com for the inside scoop).

North of Bear Mountain is the United States Military Academy at West Point (where Grant, MacArthur, and Eisenhower did their training). The campus is made up of red brick and graystone Gothic and Federal buildings.

Via public transportation, take the Short Line bus for service to Bear Mountain and West Point (800-631-8405, www.coachusa.com/shortline). For information on Hudson River cruises, try Hudson Highlands Cruises (845-534-SAIL or 7245, commanderboat.com) or Rip Van Winkle Cruises (845-340-4700, hudsonrivercruises.com). Another option for those without wheels is to sign up for a tour, especially during the fall foliage season. One of the best is through the 92nd Street Y (212-996-1100, www.92y.org), but the buses fill up early, so plan ahead.

With wheels: Drive across the George Washington Bridge to the Palisades Parkway to Bear Mountain. Pick up Route 9W north to Highland Falls and West Point.

For information, contact the Palisades Interstate Park Commission (845-786-2701, njpalisades.org/pipc.htm).

THE JERSEY SHORE

If your only knowledge of New Jersey comes from the movies, where the much-maligned state is portrayed as New York's garbage dump, you'll be completely floored by the majestic New Jersey coastline. More than 125 miles long, the Jersey shore runs from Sandy Hook in the north to Cape May in the south. By far the most touristed area of

New Jersey, the shore's commerce centers around the beaches and, of course, the casinos of Atlantic City (which account for most of the 178 million annual tourists). The New Jersey Transit North Jersey Coast train service provides frequent train service, from May through Labor Day, to beaches from Long Branch to Bay Head. Trains run from Penn Station, Hoboken, and Newark. By car, take the Lincoln Tunnel or the George Washington Bridge out of the city to the Garden State Parkway, which goes to all major Jersey shore destinations.

BELMAR, SPRING LAKE, AND BAY HEAD

Belmar's long-standing reputation as a party town has eroded over the past few years, and it's now far less wild than it used to be—the bars now close at midnight and the police are cracking down on loud parties and public drinking. Yet it's still got a young, vibrant, beach-party scene. Belmar is very popular with those who want to let off a little steam without traveling too far from the City, and with fishing aficionados.

Spring Lake, traditionally called the Irish Riviera because of its heavy population of Irish Catholic vacationers, offers beautiful Victorian inns, B&Bs, and hotels. It is probably the most expensive and exclusive town on the Jersey shore.

Bay Head is the last stop on the North Jersey coastline. Known as a quiet, peaceful hamlet, Bay Head offers public access to the beach, although there's no boardwalk. Instead, the beach is lined with Cape Cod homes. Swimming conditions are excellent.

ATLANTIC CITY

Since 1977, when casinos (and gambling) came to town, Atlantic City has become one of the most popular tourist destinations in the country. Though there's little beyond gambling and boxing (there is a boardwalk, but it's a bit seedy, even by traditional boardwalk standards), if you're into gaming, it's a fun place to visit. Avoid the town and head right for your casino hotel of choice (Trump, Caesars, whichever). It's best to make an overnight trip of it if you're coming from the City, though die-hard gamblers utilize the many bus companies (like Academy) that have departure points from all over the City, and will do the whirlwind bus-gamble-buffet-gamble-buffet-gamble-bus round-trip in a day. You can also score some great off-season and midweek hotel deals and turn your trip to Atlantic City into a real extravaganza. On a personal note, one of my great life casino moments was when I was at Merv Griffin's Beverly Hills Buffet at the Resorts International casino, and I saw none other than Merv Griffin—with Eva Gabor on his arm. Just try to beat that action!

THE POCONOS

Formerly identified with tacky honeymoon resorts, the Poconos have undergone a renaissance of late and are now dotted with tasteful, secluded country inns and offer incredible scenery and a variety of outdoor activities.

Towns include East Stroudsburg (and the famous Inn at Meadowbrook), Canadensis (the Overlook Inn and the Frogtown Inn), and South Sterling (the Sterling Inn). Shopping centers on Route 390 between Cresco and Mountainhome, with crafts, country stores, Portuguese linens, and antiques. Three classic old Poconos resorts are the Inn at Pocono Manor (3,000 acres of grounds), Buck Hill (6,000 acres), and Skytop Lodge (newly renovated with 5,500 unspoiled acres).

Contact Pocono Mountains Visitors Bureau (800-POCONOS, www.800poconos.com) for further information.

By car, take the GWB to I-80W to Pennsylvania exit 52; then follow Route 447N toward Canadensis.

THE CATSKILLS

Lying north of the City and west of the Hudson River, New York's Catskill Mountains are associated the world over with great comedy and entertainment. Milton Berle, Danny Kaye, Jackie Mason, Eddie Fisher, Neil Sedaka, Buddy Hackett, Red Buttons, Alan King, Joan Rivers, Woody Allen, Mel Brooks, Jerry Lewis, Freddie Roman, and Sid Caesar all got their starts at the "Borscht Belt" resorts of the Catskills. People still come in droves to the famed resort hotels of the region, such as Kutsher's, the Raleigh, and the Villa Roma, but the Catskills now also boast a more epicurean side, with country inns and bed-and-breakfast retreats popping up all over the beautiful landscape. Nature lovers will find plenty to do around the high peaks of the majestic Catskill mountaintops, in the crystal clear mountain lakes, or on the rapids of the Delaware River.

Automobile access to the Catskill region is via Route 17, also known as the Quickway. The Quickway begins at Harriman, exit 16 off the New York State Thruway (I-87). The Quickway heads west toward Lake Erie and intersects several north–south highways: I-81 at Binghamton; Route 15 at Painted Post; and I-84 at Middletown.

Short Line Buses (800-631-8405, www.coachusa.com/shortline) run often from the Port Authority Bus Terminal.

VERMONT

Primarily a winter ski destination for New Yorkers (most aren't willing to travel this far for outdoor activities at other times of the year, because we have equally great attractions much closer by), southern Vermont ski resorts are the closest thing to big mountain skiing that the East Coast has to offer. In 1999, *SKI* magazine picked Bromley as one of the top twelve family ski resorts in the country. By car, take the Taconic State Parkway all the way north to the border, then follow directions for the individual resorts. There is some bus service and limited train service available, but it's slow and intermittent.

THE CONNECTICUT SHORE

Just minutes beyond New Haven, you'll discover the charming coastal towns of Connecticut. Starting with Stony Creek, Guilford, and Madison, these towns dot the shoreline eastward to the border with Rhode Island. This is New England at its best: old saltbox homes, 300-year-old churches, quaint town greens (planned during colonial times as the center of every town—a meeting place for people and grazing spot for animals), and village stores. Antiquing here is serious business—you're likely to find plenty of antique furnishings to accompany all those Colonial homes. Most of the people living here are year-round residents, so you're less likely to find the shifting population common to beach towns during summer months—here, you're likely to see the same people in town, at the neighborhood grocer, or at the ice cream parlor as you would at the movie theater and the beach.

Farther east along the shoreline, in towns like Niantic, Old Lyme, and Mystic, there is a dramatic population change during the summer months, with tourists traveling the coast and stopping at many of the towns for a real taste of coastal Connecticut and New England. B&Bs line the coast, and many are the quintessence of a B&B: a Victorian home with antique furnishings, home-baked scones for breakfast, and perhaps even a refreshing glass of iced tea on arrival.

By car, take I-95 past New Haven. Follow I-95, watching for signs to each and all of the towns you wish to visit. For a more scenic route, beyond Branford, exit at the first town of interest and, after visiting the town, continue along on Route 1 instead of the interstate.

It's very difficult to access the Connecticut shore via public transportation. You can get as far as New Haven on the Metro North trains out of Grand Central, and then it's possible to rent a car or catch a cab. But, realistically, to visit this region, you're better off with a car.

CHAPTER ELEVEN

FINDING THE ESSENTIALS

One of the most disorienting things about moving to a new town is the disruption of your daily routine. You need a new pharmacist, new doctors, a new place of worship, and new ways to get around. New York is doubly confusing, though, because New Yorkers do everything differently from the rest of the country. Most of us don't have cars, we shop in tiny urban stores, and we're used to having every conceivable service at our beck and call twenty-four hours a day. In this chapter you'll learn about the essential services New Yorkers rely upon.

HOW TO FIND THE BEST OF ANYTHING

This chapter, and the previous one, contain many general listings; however, the Internet holds the key to the esoteric and niche services you may be looking for. Whether it's a dry cleaner or an exterminator, custom upholstery or ecofriendly building supplies, you can find it in *New York* magazine's Best of New York database: http://nymag.com/bestofny

PUBLIC TRANSPORTATION

BUSES AND SUBWAYS

You'll be hard pressed to find better, more convenient, or more cost-effective public transportation anywhere in the world. Just about everything—buses and subways—runs twenty-four hours a day, seven days a week. The per-ride fare, whether you go one stop on the bus or subway, or ride from one end of the Bronx to the other end of Queens, is currently $2 (the interborough express buses are $5). Transfers between buses are free (have exact change and ask the driver for a transfer), and the bus-to-subway transfers are free, too, if you have a MetroCard. The Staten Island Ferry, departing from the southernmost tip of Manhattan and running to Staten Island, is free of charge. All five boroughs have extensive bus and subway routes, though the subway lines in Manhattan—which connect with the Bronx, Queens, and Brooklyn—don't connect with Staten Island. The most direct way to get to Staten Island from Manhattan via public transit is on the ferry.

Bus numbers, routes, and schedules are posted on poles at all bus stops. Each borough has its own bus map, available on the Metropolitan Transit Authority's website, mta.info. You can also get printed maps on board many of the buses, and at NYC Visit kiosks. Often, though, for bus service in Manhattan, it's easiest to just ask around, study the "poles" where the routes are posted, and learn which buses are best for you. For the most part, you'll probably use only a few different routes, perhaps a crosstown and a downtown (many buses follow straightforward routes along the Manhattan grid up or down the north–south avenues and crosstown on the east–west streets). Subways are generally faster and more efficient, except when traffic is light or you have a long way to walk to reach the subway. To cut your travel time during commuter hours, you can try a Limited Stops bus (they have fluorescent "Limited" signs on the dashboards, or they say "Limited" on their digital displays). These buses make stops approximately every ten blocks at major intersections and crosstown connections. They are the bus equivalent of an express train or subway.

Every subway station and every individual subway car contains a full-size map detailing the entire 714 miles of routes. Subway maps are easy to obtain; just ask for a free map at the token booth (we still call them token booths even though they don't sell tokens anymore), and, if they're out, ask at the next one, or look on mta.info. If you're having difficulty figuring out your route or stop, just ask someone. Most New Yorkers are friendly and are more than happy to help if they can. You can also ask for help at the token booth.

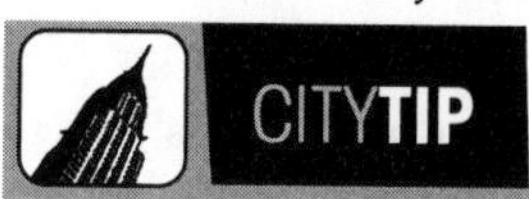

"Finding the right doctor for yourself and your family takes time and effort, so do it when you're healthy. As soon as you move to New York, schedule a physical exam. That way, if you have medical problems in the future, you'll already have a relationship with a physician and you won't get stuck being treated by a stranger—or in an emergency room."

—Penny Shaw, physical therapist

Payment

As mentioned above, the fare for a subway or local bus ride is $2. The fare for an express bus ride is $5 (express buses are interborough coaches; they are not the Limited Stops buses—those cost $2 like any regular bus). Up to three children

44 inches tall and under can ride for free on subways and local buses when accompanied by a fare-paying adult. Infants (under two years of age) ride express buses free if the child sits on the lap of the accompanying adult.

Although it's still possible to deposit exact change (coins only, no pennies) when boarding a bus, the predominant method of payment for public transportation in New York City is now the MetroCard. To ride the subway, you must have a MetroCard. Tokens are obsolete—you can now buy them only at souvenir shops.

MetroCards are easy to acquire: You can get them in any subway station from a teller at what used to be the token booth, from an automated machine that accepts credit and debit cards as well as cash, from many convenience stores and newsstands, or by mail. There are several types of MetroCards; however, if you are a frequent rider of public transportation, you'll save money by buying a minimum of five rides up front or "unlimited ride" cards, rather than paying per ride.

The Pay-Per-Ride MetroCard, also known as just the "Regular" MetroCard, allows you to put any amount of money on your card and to have $2 per ride deducted. However, you also get a 20 percent bonus if you put $10 or more on the card. The MetroCard allows you to transfer for free from bus to bus, or from bus to subway, or subway to bus (subway transfers don't require leaving the station, so there's no card to swipe) so long as you're making one continuous trip (two hours). If you pay with exact change for your ride, you can transfer only from bus to bus, not bus to subway.

The MetroCard EasyPay Xpress card is just like a regular MetroCard, except it's tied to your credit card or bank account for automatic replenishment. So, once you have one, you never have to go to a machine to refill it again.

The Unlimited Ride MetroCard is ideal for people who commute to work every day by public transportation. The current cost of a monthly (30 days) unlimited-ride card is $76. If you ride to and from work five days a week, at $2 a ride that would be $80. So you start with a $4 savings, and then all your weekend and non-work-related rides are essentially free. Unlimited cards are insured against loss when purchased at a vending machine with a credit or debit card.

There are also some other MetroCard permutations available, like the 1-Day Fun Pass for $7, the 7-Day Unlimited Ride MetroCard for $24, the 7-Day Express Bus Plus MetroCard for $41, and the JFK-AirTrain 10-Trip MetroCard for $25.

Reduced-fare MetroCards are available for seniors and disabled riders. Visit mta.info for information and applications.

TAXIS AND CAR SERVICE

Taxis are widely available around Manhattan south of 96th Street (they're harder to come by north of 96th Street on the East Side, and north of 118th Street—Columbia University—on the West Side). All you have to do is stick out your hand and hail one. How do you tell if a taxi is available for a pickup? If the light on the roof is illuminated, the cab is available. If it's dark, the cab is full. If the "off duty" sign is illuminated, it's not available for service.

Outside of Manhattan it's a bit trickier, but the general rule is that on the major thoroughfares in Queens and Brooklyn you can usually hail a cab. Otherwise, north of 96th Street in Manhattan, and around Queens, Brooklyn, and the Bronx, there are other certified taxi services besides the Yellow Cabs for transportation, and you can usually hail one that is circling about.

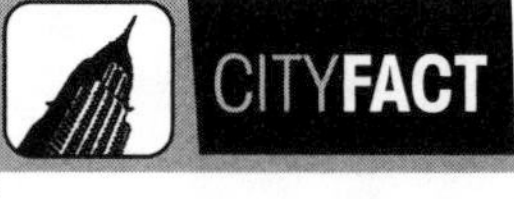

Established in 1881, New York's Department of Sanitation is the world's largest, collecting and transporting over 12,000 tons (24,000,000 pounds) of residential and institutional garbage and recycling a day. New York's businesses, whose garbage is collected by private companies, generate another 13,000 tons.

Taxi fares are regulated, and drivers stick to the meter (rates are posted on the doors and inside every cab). At present, the fare is $2.50 upon entry and 40 cents for each additional "unit." A unit is either one-fifth of a mile when the taxicab is traveling at six miles an hour or more, or 60 seconds when not in motion or traveling at less than 6 miles per hour. There is a night surcharge of 50 cents from 8:00 P.M. until 6:00 A.M., and a peak-hour weekday surcharge of $1 Monday through Friday from 4:00 P.M. to 8:00 P.M. It is customary to tip about 20 percent of the fare. You'll also be expected to pay for any tolls if you take any bridges or tunnels that have tolls. If for some reason the driver doesn't start the meter, you should ask him to do so after he begins to drive (this is *extremely* uncommon), unless you're on a flat rate from one of the airports (see Airport Transportation).

Car service is a comfortable way to travel around the city and to the airports (see below for listing and details). Rates are either by the trip, as with the airports, or by the hour. By the hour in Manhattan, usually with a two-hour minimum, prices start at $35 per hour for a sedan (through Carmel Car and Limousine Service; see car service listings below).

Outside of Manhattan, car services are becoming more and more heavily utilized, as there often aren't enough taxis to go around. It is important to get the rate up front. If you like a particular driver or car service, ask if they do pickups (most do) and get a card. If you haven't yet bonded with a particular driver, information for different car services is often posted in building lobbies.

AIRPORT TRANSPORTATION

Taken together, New York City's three major airports—John F. Kennedy International Airport (JFK), Fiorello LaGuardia Airport (LGA), and Newark Liberty International Airport (EWR)—handle more flights than those of any other city. Yet airport transportation remains complicated. On a clear, sunny day during the off hours, you may be able to hop in a taxi or car service and be whisked into Midtown Manhattan in a half hour or less. But come rush hour, or the slightest sign of bad weather, things start to fall apart.

There have been some improvements since the first edition of this book, most notably the new AirTrain service. The AirTrain monorails, at JFK and Newark, pick passengers up at the terminals and connect to nearby municipal public transportation. But this can be a slow process. At JFK, for example, AirTrain takes passengers to the terminus of the A, J, and E subway lines, and it can take another 60 to 75 minutes from there to get to Manhattan. With waiting and transfers, one has to allow more than two hours for the trip. Unfortunately, New York's airports still don't have the one transportation option so many people want: a train that stops at the terminals and then whisks passengers to stations in the major Manhattan neighborhoods. As a result, you must always first take either a bus or subway to transfer to the airport transportation. A word to the wise: unless you're a bodybuilder, you will not want to attempt these maneuvers with heavy luggage.

The following are the ways to get into the City from the three major area airports. There are also two smaller commercial airports close by (as well as many private ones): Westchester Airport (HPN) in White Plains, and MacArthur Airport (ISP) in Islip, Long Island. For information on the smaller airports, see their websites: whiteplainsairport.com and macarthurairport.com.

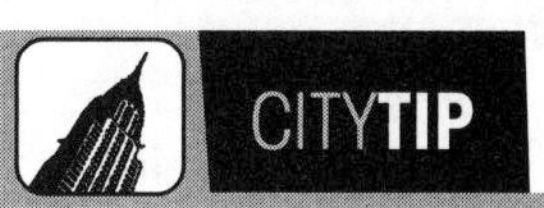

"When you move into a new neighborhood, spend a couple of hours with a pad and pen systematically exploring every street and avenue within reasonable proximity of your home. Walk into all the shops and restaurants, even if they don't immediately strike your fancy. You're certain to find some unusual things on the side streets that you wouldn't have otherwise discovered on your daily walk to the bus or subway, like a small specialty bookstore or an interesting bar or a favorite butcher."

—Andrew Shafran, garment industry executive

JOHN F. KENNEDY INTERNATIONAL AIRPORT

Jamaica, Queens, New York
(718) 244-4444
panynj.gov

JFK is New York's largest airport, and one of the largest in the world, serving more than 110 international airlines. JFK is 15 miles from Midtown Manhattan.

Taxi

$45 flat fee (nonmetered) plus bridge and tunnel tolls and gratuity; 30 to 60 minutes to Midtown Manhattan. It winds up being about $60 in the end. If you want to share a taxi, ask the dispatcher if he can match you up with someone else, or ask someone in the taxi line if they'd like to share a ride—you'll split tolls and share the fare.

AirTrain
panynj.gov/airtrain

$5.00 (children under 5 free) plus a separate fare for the connecting subway or bus; 60 to 90 minutes to Midtown Manhattan. AirTrain's light rail makes a 1.8-mile loop to the nine airline terminals. It takes eight minutes to complete the loop. There's also a 3.3-mile extension with stops at airport car rental facilities and the long-term parking lot, which terminates at the Howard Beach subway station for the A subway line. A trip from JFK to Jamaica or Howard Beach will average about 12 minutes. It then takes 60 to 75 minutes for the A subway to get to Midtown Manhattan. There's also an AirTrain stop at the Jamaica station where you can transfer to the Long Island Rail Road trains, the E, J, and Z subway lines, and several dozen bus lines.

Public Bus

You can also get from JFK to the Howard Beach A subway station by public bus. The bus fare is $2, but it's essentially free because you get a free transfer to or from the subway. AirTrain is much more convenient, though, and well worth the extra $5.

Shuttle Buses

Gray Line/Express Shuttle USA
www.coachusa.com/newyorksightseeing
(212) 315-3006 or (800) 451-0455

$13 to $19 one-way to Midtown Manhattan; 45 to 60 minutes. The bus stops at major hotels between 23rd and 63rd Streets. Waiting time at the airport for the shuttle: approximately 20 minutes. From Midtown: Hourly pickup service available from major hotels between 23rd and 63rd Streets in Manhattan. From the airport, find the Gray Line desk to arrange transportation; from Manhattan make reservations 24 hours in advance by phone or Internet.

New York Airport Service
nyairportservice.com
(718) 875-8200 or (800) 872-4577

$10 to $13 to Midtown; $17 to $23 to hotels; 45 to 60 minutes. Stops at hotels between 33rd and 57th Streets. New York Airport Service bus stops are located outside the baggage claim area at every terminal. Shuttles run 2 to 3 times an hour and stop at Grand Central Terminal (you can transfer from Grand Central to various hotels for an additional fee), Penn Station, and Port Authority Bus Station. From Manhattan, make reservations 24 hours in advance by phone or Internet.

SuperShuttle
supershuttle.com
(212) 209-7000 or (800) 258-3826

$15 to $20 one-way fare; 45 to 60 minutes to Midtown. Supershuttle is a shared-ride van service, which picks up from and drops off at your home, office, or hotel. At the airport, go to the Ground Transportation desk and use the SuperShuttle courtesy phone. From Manhattan, make reservations 24 hours in advance by phone or Internet.

Please also see Car Services, page 343.

FIORELLO LAGUARDIA AIRPORT (LGA)

Jackson Heights, Queens, New York
panynj.gov
(718) 533-3400

LaGuardia is New York's second-largest airport. It's much, much smaller than JFK, and handles mostly domestic flights (with a few to Canada and the Caribbean). It's also the closest, most convenient airport to Midtown or Uptown Manhattan. From the Upper East Side, on a good day, it's easy to get to LaGuardia in fifteen minutes. A lot of New Yorkers use LaGuardia whenever possible, and are even willing to pay a little more for flights or work their schedules around LaGuardia availability.

Taxi

The metered fare is likely to run $20 to $30 depending on point of origin and traffic, plus bridge and tunnel tolls and gratuity (figure another $10). If you want to share a taxi, ask the dispatcher if he can match you

LaGuardia Airport currently sits on a plot of land that, before the airport opened in 1939, housed the Gala Amusement Park. At the time that it opened, the airport was named North Beach Airport. It was renamed LaGuardia (for the mayor) shortly thereafter.

up with someone else, or ask someone in line—you'll split tolls and share the fare.

Public Bus

$2 (free transfer from subway). There are two subway/bus combinations you can use to get to LaGuardia Airport. The MTA's M60 bus stops at all LaGuardia terminals (MTA bus stops are marked "M60 to Manhattan"), starting at 5 A.M. and continuing through 1 A.M. the next day. The bus takes only about fifteen minutes from the airport to Manhattan, where it makes stops along 125th Street. After departing the airport, the M60 stops in Queens near the Astoria Boulevard station of the N and W subways, which serve Midtown and Downtown Manhattan. In Manhattan, the bus stops at Lexington Avenue (connections to the 4, 5, and 6 subway lines to Grand Central Terminal in Midtown), St. Nicholas Avenue (A, B, C, and D subway lines) and then turns and terminates at Broadway and 106th Street (connections to the 1, 2, and 3 subway lines).

Also, the Q33 bus will take you to the 74th Street/Jackson Avenue subway station, where you can connect with several subway lines: the E, F, R, V, G, and 7.

Triboro Coach also operates a twenty-four-hour bus service between LaGuardia and two subway connections in Queens. Look for the stops in front of each terminal marked "Q-33" and "Q-48." The Q-33 goes to the Roosevelt Avenue subway station (E and F subway lines), and the Q-48 goes to the 74th Street (Queens) station (7 subway line).

Shuttle Buses

The same companies that serve JFK also serve LaGuardia, at the same rates. See the JFK entries above for more details.

Please also see Car Services, page 343.

NEWARK LIBERTY INTERNATIONAL AIRPORT (EWR)

Newark, New Jersey
panynj.gov
(973) 961-6000

Newark Airport, while not quite as big as JFK, is still a massive airport serving 47 airlines, 36 of which are international. It's only 16 miles from Manhattan as the crow flies, but the tunnel connections tend to be slow (you have to cross the Hudson River to New Jersey), so it can easily take 60 minutes from Midtown.

Taxi

Expect the metered fare to be between $50 and $60. There's also a $5 surcharge for trips into New York during rush hour and on weekends, and a $15 surcharge to take a taxi from New York to Newark. Then there are the tolls and gratuity. It can easily cost $80 and take an hour or more. If you want to share a taxi, ask the dispatcher if he can match you up with someone else, or ask someone in line—you'll split tolls and share the fare.

AirTrain

panynj.gov/airtrainnewark

$5.50 (plus the cost of your ticket on NJ Transit or Amtrak to Penn Station in New York City). At Newark, the AirTrain connects from the terminals to a Rail Link station, where you can catch NJ Transit or Amtrak trains for rail travel to your final destination.

Shuttle Buses

Gray Line buses and SuperShuttle vans serve Newark, with rates and arrangements similar to their JFK and LaGuardia services. See JFK above for details. In addition, the following two companies serve Newark:

Gotham Limousine
gothamlimo.com
(888) 227-7997
$90 plus tolls and gratuity; 40 to 50 minutes to Midtown Manhattan. Provides on-demand limo service from the airport; go to the Ground Transportation desk upon arrival.

Olympia Airport Express
olympiabus.com
(212) 964-6233 or (908) 354-3330 or (800) 451-0455
$11 to $16; 40 to 50 minutes to Midtown. Frequent shuttle service (every 15 to 20 minutes) between Newark Airport and locations in Manhattan: Grand Central Terminal, Penn Station, Port Authority Bus Terminal, and Midtown hotels.

CAR SERVICES

There are dozens of car service companies in the city, and using one is a great way to get yourself a little peace of mind. The fare is predetermined (most companies charge $25 to LaGuardia, $40 to JFK, and $50 to Newark, plus tolls and tip, for a regular sedan—but be sure to ask!), so you don't have to worry about meters, directions, or hailing a cab. Call a day or more in advance for a reservation (though on occasion I've called only a few hours in advance, which works out some of the time), and a car will pick you up at home or meet you at the terminal. Note: If you're calling for an airport pickup and you have a lot of stuff, you can request to have your driver meet you near the luggage area—but usually you just meet outside so the driver doesn't have to park.

"Take advantage of the city during bad weather. When most people are running for cover, you can waltz into almost any restaurant in town (they get tons of cancellations when it snows), have the museums all to yourself, and get last-minute tickets to a sold-out show."

—Emerson DaSilveira, waiter

The following are a few of the City's many car services:

American Classic Limousines
1888nyclimo.com
(212) 979-0500 or (888) NYC-LIMO

BLS Limousine Service
blslimo.com
(800) 843-5752

Carmel Car and Limousine Service
www.carmellimo.com
(212) 666-6666

Gotham Limousine
gothamlimo.com
(888) 446-5466

Tel-Aviv Car and Limousine Service
telavivlimo.com
(800) 222-9888

HELICOPTER SERVICE

For those for whom money is no object, US Helicopter Service (flyush.com) provides helicopter transportation to the airports starting at $169 each way.

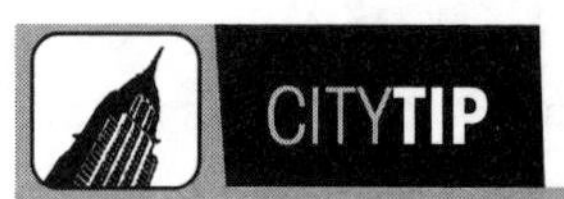

"When selecting a gym, visit a few that are near to work or home, because different gyms attract different clientele. What might work for the aerobics queen next door might not work for you."

—Norman Stewart, lifeguard

MEDICAL EMERGENCIES

A medical emergency is perhaps the most terrifying occurrence for a newcomer to any city, and most people have no idea what to do in an emergency beyond a vague notion that they should dial 911. But a call to 911 is just the beginning of effective management of a health emergency, and smart New Yorkers have to be aware of some information that's unique to this city.

I spoke to Dr. Stephan Lynn, director emeritus of the emergency department at St. Luke's–Roosevelt Hospital (one of the best in the City), and he offered the following advice that may save your life:

- As soon as you move to New York, learn the name and address of the best hospital within a reasonable distance of your home. When you are picked up by an ambulance, demand to be taken to that hospital. You have the right to be taken to any hospital you request as long as it is within ten minutes' drive and provided the ambulance staff does not believe your condition is critical (if you're critical, your request will be overruled and you'll be taken to the closest available hospital).
- When deciding whether to call for an ambulance, try to determine whether moving the patient will present a hazard. If there is any uncertainty, go ahead and call. But if the person can be moved without damage, the fastest way to get somebody to an emergency room may be in a taxi.
- When you speak to the ambulance operator, give as much specific information as you can. Be sure to indicate your cross streets (not just your numerical address), your apartment number and floor, and any special instructions for locating and entering your building. Give your phone number and make sure the line stays open in case the operator needs to reach you again.

- Contact your personal physician after you've summoned an ambulance. Your physician should be able to streamline the hospital admission and treatment processes.
- Don't be surprised if additional vehicles, such as police cars, arrive at the scene.
- In most cases, an ambulance will allow one person to accompany the patient in transit, but this is not always the case. If you need to travel separately, be sure to get the exact name and address of the hospital where the patient is being taken (many of the hospitals in New York have similar-sounding names).
- When you call 911 and report a medical emergency, an ambulance will be dispatched to your location. An ambulance is not free—you or your insurance will have to pay for it—but in a life-threatening emergency you shouldn't hesitate to call.

Emergency Phone Numbers

General Emergencies: 911
General Information: 311 (for any city agency or service other than 911, your call will be transferred to the relevant office)
Police Headquarters: 212-374-5000
Crime Victims Line: 800-771-7755
Rape/Battered Persons Crisis Center Hotline: 800-621-4673
Sex Crimes Unit: 212-267-7273
Samaritans of New York Suicide Hotline: 212-673-3000
Emergency Children's Services: 212-966-8000
Poison Control Center: 212-764-7667
Dental Emergencies: 212-573-9502
Doctors on Call: 212-737-2333
LIFENET Hotline for People Experiencing a Mental Health Crisis: 1-800-LIFENET

HOSPITALS AND EMERGENCY ROOMS

New York has some of the world's finest hospitals, and virtually all of them (save for the specialty centers) have twenty-four-hour emergency rooms. While the City's hospitals are excellent, they are also large and can be intimidating. Julie and Paul Lerner, authors of the *Lerner Survey of Health Care in New York,* advise you to be a "defensive patient." In particular, make certain all hospital staff members who touch you have washed their hands, and double-check all medications to be certain you've been given the correct prescription.

For the most part, if you require surgery or other hospital services, you won't choose your hospital—you'll just go to the hospital with which your physician or surgeon is affiliated. For specialized care and emergency room purposes, however, you should be aware of the most important New York hospitals and their areas of expertise. The specialties included following some of these listings are meant to highlight a hospital's strongest practice areas, but each hospital has many areas of competence that are not listed here. In the end, you'll want to choose a hospital in consultation with a qualified doctor.

Important Hospitals in Manhattan

Beth Israel Medical Center
16th Street and First Avenue
New York, NY 10003
(212) 420-2881
wehealnewyork.org
Specialties: cardiology, orthopedics

Columbia University Medical Center, NewYork-Presbyterian Hospital
161 Fort Washington Avenue
New York, NY
(212) 305-2500
nyp.org
Specialties: neurology, psychiatry, pediatrics, urology, cardiology, orthopedics, gastroenterology

Hospital for Joint Diseases
301 East 17th Street
New York, NY 10003
(212) 260-1203
med.nyu.edu/hjd/
Specialties: orthopedics, rheumatology

Hospital for Special Surgery
535 East 70th Street
New York, NY 10021
(212) 606-1930
hss.edu
Specialties: orthopedics, rheumatology

Lenox Hill Hospital
100 East 77th Street
New York, NY 10021
(212) 434-2000
lenoxhillhospital.org
Specialties: cardiology, obstetrics, orthopedics

Memorial Sloan-Kettering Cancer Center
1275 York Avenue
New York, NY 10021
(212) 639-2000
www.mskcc.org
Specialties: cancer treatment (by most accounts, the best in the country), gynecology, urology

Mount Sinai Hospital
1 Gustave L. Levy Place (99th Street)
New York, NY 10029
(212) 241-6500
www.mountsinai.org

One of the best overall hospitals in America. Specialties: geriatrics; gastroenterology; ear, nose, and throat; psychiatry; neurology; cardiology; obstetrics; urology

New York Downtown Hospital
170 William Street
New York, NY 10038
(212) 312-5000
downtownhospital.org

Specialties: cardiology

New York Eye and Ear Infirmary
310 East 14th Street
New York, NY 10003
(212) 979-4000
nyee.edu

Specialties: ophthalmology

New York Weill Cornell Medical Center, NewYork-Presbyterian Hospital (commonly known as New York Hospital)
525 East 68th Street
New York, NY 10021
(212) 746-5454
nyp.org

Specialties: psychiatry, neurology, urology, gynecology, gastroenterology, rheumatology

NYU Hospitals Center, Rusk Institute of Rehabilitation Medicine
400 East 34th Street
New York, NY 10016
(212) 273-7300
www.med.nyu.edu/rusk
Specialties: Rehabilitation

NYU Hospitals Center, Tisch Hospital
550 First Avenue
New York, NY 10016
(212) 263-7300
www.med.nyu.edu/about/overview/tisch.html
Specialties: Rehabilitation, rheumatology, orthopedics, cardiology

St. Luke's–Roosevelt Hospital Center, Roosevelt Hospital Division
1000 Tenth Avenue
New York, NY 10019
(212) 523-4000
wehealnewyork.org

St. Luke's–Roosevelt Hospital Center, St. Luke's Hospital Division
1111 Amsterdam Avenue
New York, NY 10025
(212) 523-4000
wehealnewyork.org

Important Metro-Area Hospitals Outside Manhattan

Brooklyn Hospital Center
(718) 250-8000
tbh.org

Caledonian Campus
100 Parkside Avenue
Brooklyn, NY 11226

Downtown Campus
121 DeKalb Avenue
Brooklyn, NY 11201

Long Island Jewish Medical Center
270-05 76th Avenue
New Hyde Park, NY 11040
(718) 470-7000
www.northshorelij.com
Specialties: geriatrics, cardiology

Maimonides Medical Center
4802 10th Avenue
Brooklyn, NY 11219
(718) 283-8533
maimonidesmed.org
Specialties: cardiology

Montefiore Medical Center
111 East 210th Street
Bronx, NY 10467
(718) 920-4321
www.montefiore.org
Specialties: geriatrics, rheumatology, cardiology

North Shore University Hospital
300 Community Drive
Manhasset, NY 11030
(516) 562-0100
www.northshorelij.com

Staten Island University Hospital
siuh.edu

North Site
475 Seaview Avenue
Staten Island, NY 10305
(718) 226-9000

South Site
375 Seguine Avenue
Staten Island, NY 10309
(718) 226-2000

Westchester Medical Center
Valhalla Campus
95 Grasslands Road
Valhalla, NY 10595
(914) 493-7000
wcmc.com

HHC Hospitals

In addition to the hospitals mentioned previously (and many others), the New York City Health and Hospitals Corporation (HHC) operates eleven public hospitals that contain one-third of the City's hospital beds. At these hospitals, everybody, whether insured or not, has the right to medical care based on a sliding scale of fees. For more information about HHC hospitals, contact:

New York City Health and Hospitals Corporation
125 Worth Street, Room 510
New York, NY 10013
(212) 788-3339
nyc.gov/html/hhc/html/home/home.shtml

FINDING A PHYSICIAN

In many cases your choice of physician will be limited by your medical insurance; however, when you do have a choice, two resources can help you select the best physicians.

New York magazine publishes an annual report on the City's best doctors, and the information is indexed in a special area of the *New York* magazine website: nymag.com/bestdoctors/.

In addition, Castle Connolly Medical Ltd., which is a healthcare research and information company that publishes several guides to top doctors—including one just about New York—maintains a searchable online database of its painstaking expert research on its website, castleconnolly.com

If you're uninsured, and can't afford to pay for private medical care, one option is the New York City Free Clinic. Run by NYU, one of the best medical schools, the Free Clinic provides comprehensive medical services to the uninsured and disenfranchised.

New York Free Clinic
16 East 16th Street
New York, NY 10003
(212) 206-5200
www.med.nyu.edu/nycfreeclinic

For uninsured New Yorkers who have limited budgets for insurance but want to be insured, the Healthy NY program provides several low-cost (by New York standards) insurance options for the self-employed and employees of small businesses.

Healthy NY Insurance Program
1-866-HEALTHY NY
ins.state.ny.us/website2/hny/english/hny.htm

There's also an organization called the Freelancers Union, which offers several low-cost insurance options for freelancers and the self-employed.

Freelancers Union
45 Main Street
Suite 710
Brooklyn, NY 11201
Telephone: (718) 532-1515
www.freelancersunion.org

PHARMACIES

Twenty-four-hour pharmacies are a necessity of life in the City that never sleeps. The chains CVS (www.cvs.com), Rite Aid (www.riteaid.com), and Duane Reade (duanereade.com) each have several area stores that offer this service.

WORSHIP

Whatever your religious beliefs, an astounding number of options await you in New York. Choosing a place of worship is a very personal (and sometimes political) decision, but the following tips from noted religion scholar Professor Richard I. Sugarman can help get you started:

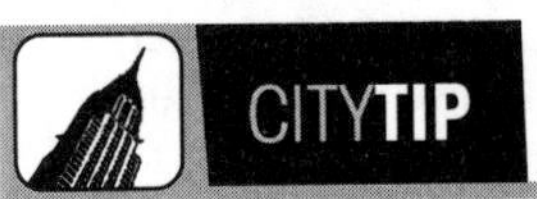

"Open bank accounts in New York City at the earliest possible time. Many landlords and other important service providers won't accept out-of-state checks, or they'll make you wait ten days for an out-of-state check to clear. Having a local bank account can save you a lot of headaches."

—Kenneth Matthews, landlord

- If you're already observant, discuss your move to New York with your current clergyperson. Using this approach, you may be able to get in touch with like-minded clergy here in New York.
- Visit several places of worship before deciding on one. Talk to members of the congregation and make sure you feel comfortable with the group's beliefs.
- The best listing of places of worship and times of services can be found in the first (National) section of each Saturday's *New York Times.*
- If you have a strong affiliation with a specific branch of a particular religion (for example, Lutheran Church of America or Reform Judaism), use the New York Yellow Pages to contact the headquarters of that group. This is the surest way to get a list of all the appropriate places of worship for you.
- Many people are prone to forget their religious observances when they move to a new community, especially if that community is a huge, anonymous-seeming city like New York. But your religion can be a great source of strength and comfort during this difficult transitional period, and participation in organized religion is a great way to meet local people who share your values. A relationship with a specific religious organization also gives you access to familiar clergy during emergencies, and can help you access school, child care, counseling, and community information.
- Remember, you're more likely to go to services if you choose a place of worship in your neighborhood.

THE MAIL

POST OFFICES

There are 183 United States Post Office locations in New York City. Most are open at least from 9 A.M. to 5 P.M. on weekdays and from 9 A.M. to 1:00 P.M. on Saturdays, and are closed on Sundays and national holidays. Some of the larger post offices have longer hours, and the General Post Office (zip code 10001), located at 33rd Street and Eighth Avenue, is open twenty-four hours a day, seven days a week. See www.usps.gov for information about post offices in a given zip code.

POST OFFICE BOXES

There is often a waiting list for post office boxes at the U.S. Post Offices, so many New Yorkers have turned to private vendors. There are twenty Mail Boxes Etc. franchises in and around New York, which tend to offer longer hours (many are open on Sunday) and better availability of private boxes than the post office. See mbe.com for specific neighborhood locations.

PACKAGES AND EXPRESS SHIPPING

FedEx has offices throughout New York (800-Go-FedEx or 800-463-3339, fedex.com) as do UPS (800-PICK-UPS or 800-742-5877, www.ups.com) and DHL (800-CALL-DHL or 800-225-5345, www.dhl.com).

PART FIVE

SCHOOLS, JOBS, AND VOLUNTEERING

CHAPTER TWELVE

LOCAL SCHOOLS AND COLLEGES

If you move to the average American suburb, your choice of school is simple: You'll most likely register your child at the local public school. Larger suburbs might have a few schools, one of which may be the best, which in turn may influence your choice of where to buy a home in the area.

But picking the right school for your child from among the more than 1,300 schools in New York City (and thousands more in the metro area) can be a daunting and overwhelming task. Just tackling the categories of schools—public and private, single-sex and coeducational, religious and secular, English language, bilingual, and ESL—can give you a headache. To make matters worse, in the area of education, New York City lives up to its reputation as a city of contrasts: Under the huge umbrella of its schools are some of the best *and* worst in the nation.

This chapter will arm you with the tools you need to begin the process of finding the best school for your child. In addition to listing contact information for each of the public school regions and districts in the City, there's also a list of what are generally considered to be the most noteworthy private schools, plus lists of private-education consultants and organizations that can aid you in decoding the system.

Choosing a college is a little easier: There are merely hundreds, not thousands, of colleges in New York. The second part of this chapter lists higher-education resources in several relevant categories.

NEW YORK CITY'S PUBLIC SCHOOLS

The New York City public school system is the largest in the country, with 10 school regions subdivided into 32 school districts, 1,200 public schools, and 75,000 teachers serving more than 1 million students. It's a massive bureaucracy, and due to the decentralized nature of the system (with the current trend being toward even more control at the individual school, district, and regional level, creating huge variations in policies, outlook, and philosophy), it can take dozens of surreal phone calls to learn the smallest tidbit of information and months of research to figure out whether your child is best off in your neighborhood school or in one of the alternative, charter, empowerment, or gifted-and-talented schools. But if you start your research early, at least one full year in advance, and follow the advice in this chapter—I spoke to dozens of education experts and made my own fair share of surreal phone calls to obtain the information following—your child can receive an excellent and free education within the City's multicultural and multilingual (Spanish, Arabic, Urdu, Korean, Chinese, Hindi, Hebrew, and Russian are spoken) public school system.

To make matters even more confusing, the City's public education system is in transition. When the first edition of this book was published, the Board of Education was the governing body for public schools. Now, the Board of Education no longer exists, and schools have been reorganized by the Department of Education. There have been many policy changes as well, and whole categories of schools have been created, while others have been renamed.

In most cases, before you can do anything else, you'll need to ascertain which school region and district your residence is in, so that you can contact the appropriate offices and begin the enrollment process. The Department of Education maintains an area on its website that allows you to enter any address and pull up the information about school options that apply to that address:

Department of Education Maps
maps.nycboe.net

You can also walk into the nearest school in your neighborhood and inquire yourself, though the Internet system is a very reliable place to start your investigation and you don't have to walk out your door.

In general, the Department of Education website is the place to start all your investigations. The Department of Education seems to have designed itself to avoid contact with the public as much as possible; however, the website is quite comprehensive:

Department of Education Website
schools.nyc.gov

In most of America, your child will attend the school in the district in which you live. The New York suburbs work the same way—in New Jersey, Westchester, Long Island, and Connecticut, where you decide to live ultimately determines if and where your child goes to public school, which is why residences in certain suburban school districts are more desirable and therefore more expensive than others. But in the five boroughs of New York City, it's a different world. There can be dozens of public schools in each region district, and there are many citywide schools, for which your child must be tested and admitted, sprinkled throughout the boroughs. Thus, though you may decide to live in Cobble Hill in Brooklyn, your child may commute to Hunter College Elementary School in Manhattan every day.

On the elementary and middle school levels, students are generally registered for the school within their district during the spring preceding the September they will begin school (and indeed, at the elementary school level most children do attend the school for which they are zoned). But the specialized schools (see following), for which your child must apply (and often be tested), begin the admissions process well in advance.

For kindergartners, preregistration is normally held in the beginning of May for the following academic year. And although kindergarten isn't mandatory in New York City schools, in order to be enrolled in a kindergarten class your child must be five years old by December 31 of the year for which you are requesting enrollment.

As for the nitty-gritty of registering your child, one parent (or guardian) must go to the designated school in your zone with proof of address (a copy of your lease or utility bill is sufficient); proof of immunization; either a birth certificate, baptismal certificate, or passport; and, of course, the child. For children entering kindergarten, proof of the countless (and painful) immunizations that your child has received is required; ask in your child's school or call the Board of Education for the excruciating details.

This straightforward registration process is only the beginning, and applies only if you are sending your child to a school for which your residence is zoned. There are, however, districts within every region, and some regions are "unzoned," which allows you to choose from among the many schools within the entire region rather than being limited to the school within your district. So if you would like to pursue public schools that are located outside of your district, you should begin the process of learning about the schools, educating yourself, and obtaining the necessary variances a full year ahead of the school year for which you are registering your child.

Children within the district have first priority for entrance, children within the region but outside of the district come second, and children outside of the region entirely are given third priority. Only children within the district absolutely must be accommodated by that school (assuming it is not a specialized school for which all children must be tested and where admission is based on performance). All others are accepted on a space-available basis.

For high school admission, there is yet another, entirely different, set of rules and standards. High schools within the City accept students from throughout the entire City, and the more restrictive rules that apply to elementary and middle schools do not apply to the high schools. In addition, there are so many specialized and alternative schools spread throughout each of the five boroughs that many students test to gain admission to their school of choice. Students

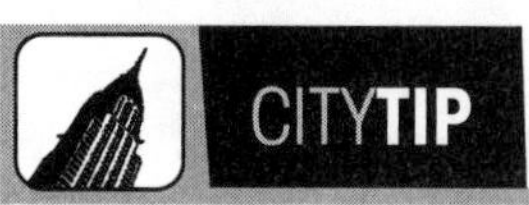

"A private school may be of the highest quality and the best reputation, but if it isn't a good match for your child, or doesn't mesh with your personal outlook and philosophy, then look elsewhere. A great school that's a bad match equals a bad school for your child's needs."

—Elayne Landis, educational consultant

take the Specialized High Schools Admissions Test in eighth grade in the hope of gaining admission to one of their preferred (top twelve choices) schools. So not only might your child be coming from a different region and district, but possibly even from an entirely different borough from the one where the school is located.

You may have gathered that the process of getting your child into a public school other than the one for which your residence is zoned is slightly more complicated than finding a taxi in the rain during rush hour in Midtown. But take heart: Thousands of parents each year take the initiative to secure the best educations for their children (a parent with a child especially gifted in music, for instance, may be in a perfectly desirable school zone but opt instead to jump through hoops in order to get the child into the Clinton School for Writers and Artists). If they can do it, so can you.

Schools that make it a policy to accept students from different regions and districts go by many names: charter, empowerment, alternative, specialized, and gifted-and-talented, to name a few. There is a healthy and continual evolution of the school programs that are offered, so check with the Department of Education online for the latest.

Glossary of Terms

Specialized: The city no longer uses the term "magnet school"; however, the old magnet schools still exist. The magnet designation was based on the concept of schools that attract students from other places, like a magnet. In many cities the term is used to describe schools that are for especially gifted children. In New York, such schools fall under the heading "specialized."

Charter schools: At the time of the research for this book, there were fifty charter schools in New York City and there has been the designation for an additional fifty charter schools. Charter schools are usually smaller and the school is given the autonomy away from the larger bureaucracy to set policies and practices.

Empowerment schools: This means that the principal and the school community have asked for a very high level of autonomy and in return have to be accountable for the outcome: performance of pupils, testing, attendance, and other concrete measures.

Gifted-and-talented: G&T programs are for children who are especially gifted or talented in a specific area: intellectually, artistically, or physically. These special programs within a school require a testing process for admission.

Alternative schools: The term "alternative school" is applicable to the high school level. A specific set of high schools are part of the alternative grouping, which is run by a separate superintendent, and offers a range of programs from one school to the next.

USEFUL CONTACTS

As mentioned before, with the prevalence of the Internet and the restructuring of the Board of Education, now called the Department of Education (DOE), it is very difficult to find a human to speak to regarding general school information.

If you can navigate the website of the DOE (schools.nyc.gov), however, you're probably better off. Here, not only do you get the information immediately (as opposed to having to mail in for it), but it will also save you the inevitable frustration of having to call around until you find the *right* person with whom you need to speak. So while I'd like to be able to provide you with a "handy" list of telephone numbers, I'm afraid in our Internet-oriented world, such a thing no longer exists. Type away and consider yourself lucky!

High School Directories
http://schools.nyc.gov/Offices/StudentEnroll/HSAdmissions/schprocess/default.htm

This page of the DOE website is your key to the City's high schools. Any number of helpful directories can be found here, including the Directory of Public High Schools, which is comprehensive and informative.

Assessment and Accountability
52 Chambers Street
New York, NY 10007
(212) 374-3990
http://schools.nyc.gov/daa/

This website provides information on testing, test results, and "accountability reports." Call the office for human contact and hard copies.

Parent Coordinators

Every school will now have the staff position of the "Parent Coordinator." The Parent Coordinator will have a direct telephone line so that parents do not have to navigate the busy general switchboard of their child's school. The Parent Coordinator is meant to be parents' first stop when looking for information about their child's school, the school system in general, and for issues or concerns that relate directly to the school. Parents are advised to stop by their child's school to introduce themselves to the Parent Coordinator.

District Family Advocates

Each school district has a Family Advocate, who can help relocating families navigate the system. The following are the phone numbers for the District Family Advocates in all the New York City school districts:

Manhattan Overall	***917-339-1700***
DISTRICT 1	212-602-9768
DISTRICT 2	212-356-3789
DISTRICT 3	212-678-5857
DISTRICT 4	212-828-3512
DISTRICT 5	212-769-7500
DISTRICT 6	917-521-3783
Bronx Overall	***718-828-2440***
DISTRICT 7	718-742-6500
DISTRICT 8	718-828-2653
DISTRICT 9	718-842-0138/7853
DISTRICT 10	718-741-5835
DISTRICT 11	718-519-2620/68
DISTRICT 12	718-328-2310 x4092
Brooklyn Overall	***718-935-3858/4242/4256***
DISTRICT 13	718-636-3234
DISTRICT 14	718-302-7689
DISTRICT 15	718-935-4263
DISTRICT 16	718-574-2824
DISTRICT 17	718-221-4372
DISTRICT 18	718-566-6005
DISTRICT 19	718-240-2700 x2
DISTRICT 20	718-759-3915
DISTRICT 21	718-714-2501/2500
DISTRICT 22	718-968-6116
DISTRICT 23	718-574-1100 x366
Queens Overall	***718-391-8300***
DISTRICT 24	718-592-3364
DISTRICT 25	718-281-7625
DISTRICT 26	718-631-6841
DISTRICT 27	718-642-5796
DISTRICT 28	718-557-2618
DISTRICT 29	718-341-8280 x1120
DISTRICT 30	718-391-8261
Staten Island	
DISTRICT 31	718-420-5627

Special Education Services
DISTRICT 75 (212) 802-1685

Alternative Schools
DISTRICT 79 (718) 557-2677

NYC Department of Education Site Map
schools.nyc.gov/SiteMap
If you are having trouble finding what you're looking for on the Department of Education website, go to the site map. If the information you are looking for is available on this site, you should be able to find it through this page.

Resources for Parents of Children with Special Needs
Special Education District 75
Bonnie Brown, Superintendent
Citywide Programs
400 First Avenue
New York, NY 10010
(212) 802-1500
schools.nycenet.edu/d75/district/default.htm
District 75 "provides citywide educational, vocational, and behavior support programs" at more than 350 schools in the five boroughs and Syosset, New York.

The New York Institute for Special Education
nyise.org
NYISE is "a private, nonprofit, nonsectarian educational facility which provides quality programs for children who are blind or visually disabled, emotionally and learning disabled, and preschoolers who are developmentally delayed."

Office of Vocational and Educational Services for Individuals with Disabilities (VESID)
www.vesid.nysed.gov

VESID provides a number of services including Early Childhood Direction Centers (which provide information for parents of children ages zero to five with physical, mental, or emotional disabilities) and a Special Education Policy Unit (which develops policy to help facilitate education and services for children with special needs). VESID works to ensure that children with special needs receive the education to which they are entitled.

Quality Services for the Autism Community
qsac.com
QSAC is a nonprofit organization that provides services for people with autism or pervasive developmental disorder (PDD) throughout New York City and Long Island.

Resources for Children with Special Needs, Inc.
116 East 16th Street, 5th Floor
New York, NY 10003
(212) 677-4650
resourcesnyc.org
An independent not-for-profit organization, RCSN can help with information and referrals, case management, advocacy, parent training, and support and information services.

School Regions and Districts

Region 1 (Districts 9, 10)
1 Fordham Plaza, Bronx, NY 10458
(718) 741-7090

District 9 Office
250 East 164th Street
Bronx, NY 10456
(646) 522-7535

District 10 Office
1 Fordham Plaza
Bronx, NY 10458
(718) 741-7090

Region 2 (Districts 8, 11, 12)
1230 Zerega Avenue
Bronx, NY 10462
(718) 828-2440

District 8 Office
1230 Zerega Avenue
Bronx, NY 10462
(718) 828-2440

District 11 Office
1250 Arnow Avenue
Bronx, NY 10469
(718) 519-2620

District 12 Office
1434 Longfellow Avenue, Room 409
Bronx, NY 10459
(718) 328-2310 x158

Region 3 (Districts 25, 26, 28, 29)
30-48 Linden Place
Queens, NY 11354
(718) 281-7575
90-27 Sutphin Boulevard
Queens, NY 11435
(718) 557-2600

District 25 Office
30-48 Linden Place
Queens, NY 11354
(718) 281-7625

District 26 Office
61-15 Oceania Street
Queens, NY 11364
(718) 631-6841

District 28 Office
90-27 Sutphin Boulevard
Queens, NY 11435
(718) 557-2805

District 29 Office
233-15 Merrick Boulevard
Queens, NY 11413
(718) 341-8280 x1120

Region 4 (Districts 24, 30, 32)
28-11 Queens Plaza North
Queens, NY 11101
(718) 391-8300

District 24 Office
98-50 50th Avenue
Queens, NY 11368
(718) 592-3364

District 30 Office
28-11 Queens Plaza North
Queens, NY 11101
(718) 391-8300

District 32 Office
797 Bushwick Avenue
Brooklyn, NY 11221
(718) 574-1100 x366

Region 5 (Districts 19, 23, 27)
82-01 Rockaway Boulevard
Queens, NY 11416
(718) 642-5800
1665 St. Marks Avenue
Brooklyn, NY 11233
(718) 922-4960

District 19 Office
557 Pennsylvania Avenue
Brooklyn, NY 11207
(718) 240-2700 x2

District 23 Office
1665 St. Marks Avenue
Brooklyn, NY 11233
(718) 922-4960

District 27 Office
82-01 Rockaway Boulevard
Queens, NY 11416
(718) 642-5800

Region 6 (Districts 17, 18, 22)
5619 Flatlands Avenue
Brooklyn, NY 11234
(718) 968-6100

District 17 Office
1224 Park Place, Room 246
Brooklyn, NY 11213
(718) 221-4372

District 18 Office
1106 East 95th Street
Brooklyn, NY 11236
(718) 566-6008

District 22 Office
5619 Flatlands Avenue
Brooklyn, NY 11234
(718) 968-6116

Region 7 (Districts 20, 21, 31)
715 Ocean Terrace
Staten Island, NY 10301
(718) 556-8350
415 89th Street
Brooklyn, NY 11209
(718) 759-4900

District 20 Office
415 89th Street
Brooklyn, NY 11209
(718) 759-4844

District 21 Office
521 West Avenue
Brooklyn, NY 11224
(718) 714-2501

District 31 Office
715 Ocean Terrace
Staten Island, NY 10301
(718) 420-5632

Region 8 (Districts 13, 14, 15, 16)
131 Livingston Street
Brooklyn, NY 11201
(718) 935-3900

District 13 Office
355 Park Place
Brooklyn, NY 11238
(718) 636-3234

District 14 Office
215 Heyward Street, Room 233B
Brooklyn, NY 11206
(718) 302-7600

District 15 Office
131 Livingston Street
Brooklyn, NY 11201
(718) 935-3900

District 16 Office
1010 Lafayette Avenue
Brooklyn, NY 11221
(718) 574-2800

Region 9 (Districts 1, 2, 4, 7)
333 Seventh Avenue
New York, NY 10001
(212) 356-7500

District 1 Office
220 Henry Street, Room 101
New York, NY 10002
(212) 587-4046

District 2 Office
333 Seventh Avenue
New York, NY 10001
(212) 356-7500

District 4 Office
319 East 117th Street, Room 402
New York, NY 10035
(212) 828-3590

District 7 Office
501 Courtland Avenue, Room 102
Bronx, NY 10451
(718) 742-6500

Region 10 (Districts 3, 5, 6)
4360 Broadway
New York, NY 10033
(917) 521-3700

District 3 Office
154 West 93rd Street, Room 122
New York, NY 10025
(212) 678-5857

District 5 Office
425 West 123rd Street, Room 205
New York, NY 10027
(212) 769-7500

District 6 Office
4360 Broadway
New York, NY 10033
(917) 521-3700

District 75 (Special Education)
400 First Avenue
New York, NY 10010
(212) 802-1685

District 79 (Alternative Schools)
90-27 Sutphin Boulevard, Room 213
Queens, NY 11435
(718) 557-2762

TOP PUBLIC HIGH SCHOOLS

There are now nine public high schools known as Specialized High Schools, for which the Specialized High Schools Admissions Test (SHSAT) is required (with the exception of Fiorello H. La Guardia High School of Music & Art and Performing Arts, which requires auditions and a review of academic records). These schools, all of which are specialized, are commonly regarded as the most competitive public high schools in New York City. Among them, some would say that the following outrank even the most selective of private and independent schools around the country:

Bronx High School of Science ("Bronx Science")
75 West 205th Street
Bronx, NY 10468
(718) 817-7700
bxscience.edu

Brooklyn Technical High School ("Brooklyn Tech")
29 Fort Greene Place (South Elliott Place at DeKalb Avenue)
Brooklyn, NY 11217
(718) 804-6400
www.bths.edu

Fiorello H. LaGuardia High School of Music & Art and Performing Arts ("Music & Art")
100 Amsterdam Avenue
New York, NY 10023
(212) 496-0700
laguardiahs.org

Stuyvesant High School
345 Chambers Street
New York, NY 10282
(212) 312-4800
www.stuy.edu

Other Useful Contacts

The Center for Educational Innovation–Public Education Association
28 West 44th Street, Suite 300
New York, NY 10036
(212) 302-8800
www.cei-pea.org

The CEI-PEA (PEA since 1895) is a public advocacy group that works to improve the public school system and to ensure that every child gets a good education. Everyone who works for the organization came out of the City's public schools and many were superintendents or principals in New York City or in other states. Part of the philosophy of the CEI-PEA is that the school is the center of change. Based on that belief, the organization is working with the City to give the schools more autonomy and more responsibility for the students' results (whether that means test scores, or attendance, or both). The CEI-PEA currently works in conjunction with 160 schools in New York City.

A *CEI-PEA Alert,* published four times a year, covers topics of interest to parents, educators, and the general public (recent topics include the new reorganization of the public school system, testing in schools, and addressing the Campaign for Fiscal Equity case). You may request a copy by calling and getting on the CEI-PEA's mailing list. The PEA also runs a very useful hotline (same number as listed) to answer parent queries about the public school system, ranging from "How can I get my child into a gifted program?" to "What is the best school in my district?"

Early Childhood Resource & Information Center
Division of the New York Public Library
66 Leroy Street (off Seventh Avenue South)
New York, NY 10014
(212) 929-0815
nypl.org/branch/local/man/ecc.cfm
Located on the second floor of the Hudson Park Branch Library, the Early Childhood Resource & Information Center (ECRIC) is a public library center dedicated to serving the needs of children ages birth to six and their families, teachers, and early-childhood

professionals. There is a family room with toys, books, educational tools, slides, climbing toys, and other stimuli to initiate learning through play.

92nd Street Y
1395 Lexington Avenue
New York, NY 10128
(212) 996-1100
www.92y.org

The 92nd Street Y offers a popular workshop multiple times each year called "Planning Your Child's Early School Years" which addresses the questions of parents with children of nursery-school age. The workshop is for parents of children eighteen months and older and helps them learn the ins and outs of navigating the web of choices. Issues addressed include what age children can begin preschool, what options are available, and how to choose the best nursery school for your child.

Helpful Websites about NYC Public Schools

Insideschools.org
www.insideschools.org

A project of Advocates for Children of New York and overseen by Clara Hemphill, this website is an excellent resource for parents trying to navigate the public school system.

New York City Department of Education
schools.nyc.gov

The New York City Department of Education website contains information and extensive links to other helpful sites.

New Visions for Public Schools
newvisions.org
An organization dedicated to getting the most out of New York City public schools.

Gotham Gazette
gothamgazette.com
"New York City news and policy"

Helpful Reference Guides

City Baby: The Ultimate Guide for New York City Parents from Pregnancy Through Preschool, 3rd ed., Kelly Ashton and Pamela Weinberg

The Manhattan Directory of Private Nursery Schools, Victoria Goldman and Marcy Braun

The Manhattan Family Guide to Private Schools and Selective Public Schools, 5th ed., Victoria Goldman

New York City's Best Public Elementary Schools: A Parent's Guide, Clara Hemphill and Pamela Wheaton

New York City's Best Public High Schools: A Parent's Guide, Clara Hemphill

New York City's Best Public Middle Schools, 2nd ed., Clara Hemphill with Pamela Wheaton, Deborah Apsel, Marcia Biederman, and Jacqueline Wayans

New York Independent Schools Directory, Hendin and Schulman, eds. Published by ISAAGNY and available at the Corner Bookstore (93rd Street and Madison Avenue) and from the Parents League of New York (see following for details).

INDEPENDENT AND PRIVATE SCHOOLS

There are well over one hundred private schools in and around New York City, ranging from religious to college-preparatory in nature.

If you decide to pursue a private education for your child, you will likely hear the term "independent school" tossed around. An independent school is a private, nonprofit organization that has membership in the Independent Schools Admissions Association of Greater New York (ISAAGNY). All participating ISAAGNY schools have agreed to accept the test administered by the Educational Records Bureau (ERB), which your child will have to take in order to gain admission to any of the independent schools.

Private schools are also privately owned and run, but unlike the independent schools, the schools must answer to someone other than a board of trustees (such as a religious official, if the private school has a religious affiliation and receives monies as a result).

The example of "questionable" literature illustrates the difference: If a teacher at the Trinity School (which is an independent school) puts a "questionable" title, such as *The Catcher in the Rye,* on the curriculum and the Episcopal Church decides that it does not approve, it is still ultimately the school's rather than the Church's decision how to proceed, because the school is an independent, self-governed entity. If, however, Trinity had been organized as a private school, with specific church affiliation and funding, that decision would be made by the Church.

When narrowing the scope of independent and private schools, there are a number of important issues to consider. Cost is clearly one factor. When the specifics of New York area tuition (often in the neighborhood of $30,000 per student per year) are discussed, drop-jawed mothers and fainting fathers are common occurrences. But if it's any consolation, private school tuition is expensive wherever you live (though admittedly, big cities like New York are at the high end of the spectrum). Private schools in and around other cities, like Hopkins School in New Haven, Connecticut (tuition fees are within $1,000 of the New York City area independent schools), and the Hawken School in the suburbs of Cleveland, have high tuition costs too (on a scaled grade-level basis, not including transportation, kindergarten costs more than $14,000 per year to almost $20,000 per year for a high school senior), if not quite as high as New York City and area schools. If cost is an issue, ask about scholarships and financial aid.

If you are in need of financial assistance, researching the options within the parochial school set is a good bet. Religiously affiliated schools, if they have the means available, are often the most accommodating of families in need of financial assistance. At these schools, your child will spend part of the day learning about religious subject matter and may be taught by nuns, priests, rabbis, or ministers. Do your research on this school (as with all others) to determine whether you are satisfied with all aspects of the education.

Other considerations are proximity to your home (Horace Mann, for instance, is in Riverdale, as are the Fieldston and Riverdale Country schools), grade span (pre-K or K–6, pre-K or K–8 or K–9, pre-K or K–12), school philosophy and outlook, the number of children per class and overall size of the school, religious affiliation, and whether you want your child to attend a single-sex or coeducational program. Obviously there are other factors to consider and, as you sift, you may find that your child would be best served by a small religious school, an all-girls program, or a neighborhood public school (where perhaps your child can be a big fish in a small pond and really shine).

An important and noteworthy shift on the New York City private- and independent-school landscape is the recent addition of such schools *downtown.* Historically, the Upper East Side—and Uptown in general—has been the center of gravity for these schools. Families with school-age children were not as much the norm downtown. But in recent years, the City culture has shifted and a lot of people starting families want to live downtown. As a result, independent schools such as Claremont have opened downtown, and the other schools "south of the border" (59th Street, in this particular case) have become more desirable. It is hard to specify exactly how big a shift this is, but suffice to say, the addition of independent and private schools downtown is a historic change for New York City.

Important Private Schools

The Allen-Stevenson School
132 East 78th Street
New York, NY 10075-0381
(212) 288-6710
allen-stevenson.org
All boys, K–9

The Brearley School
610 East 83rd Street
New York, NY 10028
(212) 744-8582
www.brearley.org
All girls, K–12

The Cathedral School of St. John the Divine
1047 Amsterdam Avenue
New York, NY 10025
(212) 316-7500
cathedralnyc.org
Coeducational, K–8

Claremont Preparatory School
41 Broad Street
New York, NY 10004
(212) 232-0266
claremontprep.org
Coeducational, Pre-K–8

Collegiate School
260 West 78th Street
New York, NY 10024
(212) 812-8500
www.collegiateschool.org
All boys, K–12

Columbia Grammar and Preparatory School
5 West 93rd Street
New York, NY 10025
(212) 749-6200
cgps.org
Coeducational, Pre-K–12

The Dalton School
dalton.org

First Program Admissions Office
53 East 91st Street
New York, NY 10128
(212) 423-5463
(for grades K–3)

Middle and High School Admissions Office
108 East 89th Street
New York, NY 10128
(212) 423-5262
Coeducational, K–12

The Dwight School
291 Central Park West
New York, NY 10024
(212) 724-7524 (admissions office)
www.dwight.edu
Coeducational, K–12

Dwight-Englewood School
315 East Palisade Avenue
Englewood, NJ 07631
(201) 569-9500
www.d-e.org
Coeducational, Preschool–12

Ethical Culture Fieldston School

Ethical Culture
33 Central Park West
New York, NY 10023-6001
(212) 712-8451
ecfs.org
Coeducational, Pre-K–5

Fieldston
4400 Fieldston Road
Bronx, NY 10471
ecfs.org

Fieldston Lower School
(718) 329-7313
Coeducational, Pre-K–5

Fieldston Middle School
(718) 329-7306
Coeducational, 6–8

Fieldston Upper School
(718) 329-7306
Coeducational, 9–12

Hackley School
293 Benedict Avenue
Tarrytown, NY 10591
(914) 631-0128
www.hackleyschool.org
Coeducational, K–12 day and boarding

Horace Mann School (upper and lower schools)
231 West 246th Street
Riverdale, NY 10471
(718) 432-4000
www.horacemann.org
Coeducational, N–12

The Nightingale-Bamford School
20 East 92nd Street
New York, NY 10128
(212) 289-5020
nightingale.org
All girls, K–12

Poly Prep Country Day School

Middle and Upper School
9216 Seventh Avenue
Brooklyn, NY 11228
(718) 836-9800
www.polyprep.org
Coeducational, 5–12

Lower School
50 Prospect Park West
Brooklyn, NY 11215
(718) 768-1103
Coeducational, N–4

The Riverdale Country School
5250 Fieldston Road
Riverdale, NY 10471
riverdale.edu

Upper School
Hill Campus
(718) 549-8810
Coeducational, 6–12

Lower School
River Campus
249th Street and Hudson River
(718) 549-7780
Coeducational, Pre-K–5

Rye Country Day School
Cedar Street
Rye, NY 10580
(914) 967-1417
www.ryecountryday.org
Coeducational, Pre-K–12

St. Bernard's School
4 East 98th Street
New York, NY 10029
(212) 289-2878
stbernards.org
All boys, K–9

The Spence School
22 East 91st Street
New York, NY 10128
(212) 289-5940
spenceschool.org
All girls, K–12

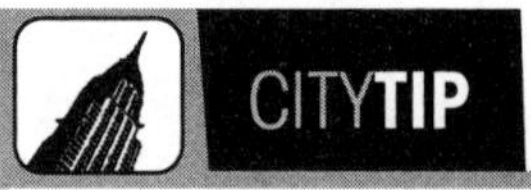

"New York City is full of excellent public schools, some of which rank among the top schools in America. To make public school work for your child, though, you need to do your homework. Start planning far, far in advance—at least a full year ahead of time—especially if you want your child to attend a public school other than the one for which your residence is zoned."

—Jessica Wolff, public school parent and former director of program outreach at the Public Education Association

The Town School
540 East 76th Street
New York, NY 10021
(212) 288-4383
www.thetownschool.org
Coeducational, N–8

Trevor Day School

Nursery and Kindergarten
11 East 89th Street
New York, NY 10128
(212) 426-3300
tds.org

Grades 1–5
4 East 90th Street
New York, NY 10128
(212) 426-3350

Grades 6–12
1 West 88th Street
New York, NY 10024
(212) 426-3360
Coeducational, N–12

Trinity School
139 West 91st Street
New York, NY 10024
(212) 873-1650
trinityschoolnyc.org
Coeducational, K–12

Places of worship such as synagogues and churches are good sources of additional information on nursery school and pre-K programs, and many offer their own excellent programs. If you work in the medical field, some of the more forward-thinking organizations (especially hospitals) offer early childhood education centers. Universities often have nursery programs, too, especially those that offer degrees in early childhood education. (In both instances, preference is usually given to employees and affiliated faculty and doctors.) Also check in at your neighborhood YMCA/YWCA. Many offer early childhood programs, as does the 92nd Street Y (the famous YMHA/YWHA on the Upper East Side of Manhattan).

Resources for Independent and Private Schools

American School Directory
www.asd.com

Extensive Internet directory of more than 105,000 schools, K–12, public and private, throughout the United States

Board of Jewish Education of Greater New York
520 Eighth Avenue, 15th Floor
New York, NY 10018
(646) 472-5300
www.bjeny.org/bjeny.asp

Among other things, provides services and support to 176,000 children through the more than 700 Jewish day, congregational, and nursery schools in New York.

Superintendent of Catholic Schools
1011 First Avenue
New York, NY 10022
(212) 371-1000 x2848

The Catholic Center will provide you with a list of Catholic schools within a specified region.

The VincentCurtis Educational Register
224 Clarendon Street
Boston, MA 02116
(617) 536-0100
theeducationalregister.com

The oldest *free* guide to K–12 private independent schools, summer schools, and summer camps.

The Handbook of Private Schools
Porter Sargent Publishers
11 Beacon Street, Suite 1400
Boston, MA 02108
(617) 523-1670
info@portersargent.com
portersargent.com

Detailed listings (including tuition fees, faculty and college placement records, and curriculum) of 1,600 private elementary and secondary boarding and day schools in the United States. Published since 1914.

Independent Educational Consultants Association
3251 Old Lee Highway, Suite 510
Fairfax, Virginia 22030-1504
(703) 591-4850
iecaonline.com

Free of charge, IECA can help families seeking professional advice (in, among other things, day and boarding school admission, learning disabilities, and at-risk teens) find a consultant that meets their needs.

Independent Schools Admissions Association of Greater New York (ISAAGNY)
www.isaagny.org

ISAAGNY is an organization of admissions directors and heads of school working to make school transitions easier for children and their families.

International Boys' Schools Coalition
www.theibsc.org
IBSC offers listings of hundreds of boys' schools, and staff provide personalized assistance.

Islamic Foundation of North America
islamicedfoundation.com
Up-to-date listings of local Islamic schools.

Jesuit Secondary Education Association
www.jsea.org
Information and links to Jesuit schools around the country

The Learning Disabilities Association of New York City Telephone Referral Service
(212) 645-6730
ldanyc.org
Information and referral agency with over 4,000 listings in the resource database. Resources include everything from where and how to get evaluations, tutoring, therapy, and legal rights to summer camps, school programs, advocacy, and lecture services. Resource listings for every type of learning disability. Parental support available.

National Association of Independent Schools (NAIS)
1620 L Street NW, Suite 1100
Washington, DC 20036
(202) 973-9700
nais.org
An important organization to be aware of, NAIS represents approximately 1,300 independent schools and associations in the United States. Of the 1,500 independent schools in the United States, more than 1,000 are members of NAIS.

The National Center for Learning Disabilities
381 Park Avenue South, Suite 1401
New York, NY 10016
(212) 545-7510
ncld.org
Extensive information about specific learning disabilities and related disorders, with local and national resources.

National Coalition of Girls' Schools
57 Main Street
Concord, MA 01742
(978) 287-4485
ncgs.org
Free directory of girls' schools in the United States; a list of useful publications and resources for parents and girls.

Network of Sacred Heart Schools
700 North Third Street
St. Charles, MO 63301
(636) 724-7003
www.sofie.org
An association of Sacred Heart schools across the United States. For information, call the school directly (a complete listing is on the website) or the general number above.

The New York Branch of the International Dyslexia Association
71 West 23rd Street, Suite 1527
New York, NY 10010
(212) 691-1930
nybida.org
NYBIDA offers referrals, training, information, and support to families and professionals.

New York State Association of Independent Schools (NYSAIS)
12 Jay Street
Schenectady, NY 12305
(518) 346-5662
www.nysais.org

Founded in 1947, NYSAIS is an association of more than 180 nursery, elementary, and secondary schools. Information and advice for parents is readily available on their website, as well as a directory of schools, resources for parents of special-needs kids and "diverse background" families too.

The Parents League of New York
115 East 82nd Street
New York, NY 10028
(212) 737-7385
parentsleague.org

An excellent source for learning all about the private, non-parochial, and special schools in the New York area. The Parents League of New York has been helping parents navigate the private-school system of the City and surrounding areas since 1913. For an annual membership of $185, or $285 for three years (it goes up about ten dollars every year), members receive copies of five different books published independently by the Parents League (*Parents League Guide to NY, Summer in New York, Parents League Review, Toddler Book,* and *Parents League News*). Included in the membership fee is an educational counseling session (one hour with a counselor and follow-up on the phone, or on an as-needed basis over the telephone) to further aid parents in suitably placing their children. For parents embarking upon the nursery school application and selection process, included in the membership fee (after paying your annual membership at the Parents League, you will never pay additional fees for services) is an early childhood workshop, which is offered multiple times a week during the school year. Groups are small (a maximum of ten parents) and the PL representative advises parents on what to do, when to do it, what to look for in a school, how to decide what school is a good match for your family, and so forth. A handy reference book listing all reputable nursery schools (all of which have been researched by the PL) and divided according to neighborhood is given to each participant. A one-hour advising session for summer camp placements (and other summer programs like summer abroad and summer school) is also available on an annual basis.

In addition to the educational resources, the Parents League keeps extensive, annually updated files on babysitters, tutors, birthday parties, summer programs, and parenting resources (advice, articles, referrals). Programs and workshops covering a wide range of topics ("Applying to Independent Schools" is always the biggest draw and is offered in a number of different locations) are also offered with membership. The Parents League also welcomes volunteers. See Chapter 14 for further volunteer information.

Peterson's Private Secondary Schools
www.petersons.com
Originally known for the *Annual Guide to Independent Secondary Schools,* Peterson's now offers extensive resources not only for finding the right school for your child (grades K–12) but also information and tips on how to pay for the school.

Private Independent Schools
Bunting & Lyon, Inc.
238 North Main Street
Wallingford, CT 06492
(203) 269-3333
buntingandlyon.com
A comprehensive directory of private schools.

Resources for Children with Special Needs, Inc.
116 East 16th Street, 5th Floor
New York, NY 10003
(212) 677-4650
resourcesnyc.org

An independent not-for-profit organization that can help with information and referrals, case management, advocacy, parent training, and support and information services.

EDUCATIONAL CONSULTANTS

Given the incredible range of school options in New York, it's no surprise that a cottage industry has arisen in the area of education consulting. Because they charge a fee, however, educational consultants are used primarily by parents looking to place their children into private schools. The following list includes only a selection of very reputable consultants, all of whom charge a fee to the family rather than to the school into which the child is placed (unlike a headhunter—something you want to avoid), and all of whom are members of IECA (the Independent Educational Consultants Association). There is a range of fees for educational consultants, but you should expect to pay in the neighborhood of $500 to $700 for a single consultation and $5,500 to $8,000 for full placements (this means consulting on what schools are appropriate for your child, help with applications and interviews, and follow-up through acceptance and the year following) through high school age. Expect to pay significantly more for college and graduate level consultations and placements.

It is important to note that unless you have extenuating circumstances, navigating and tackling the education process in New York City is something that you can surely accomplish on your own and with the help of organizations such as the Parents League.

Virginia Bush
444 East 86th Street
New York, NY 10028
(212) 772-3244
Consultations and soup-to-nuts consultancy for families with children going into grades two through twelve, and onward to college.

Howard Greene & Associates
39A East 72nd Street
New York, NY 10021
(212) 737-8866
howardgreeneassociates.com
Advisory service offering counseling to families, working with them to find the "best fit" school for each child. HGA advises on independent schools (for high schools—day school and boarding), camps, college, graduate school, and professional school. Offices in New York City; Westport, Connecticut; and Princeton, New Jersey.

Frank Leana
171 East 84th Street
Apartment 14D
New York, NY 10028
(212) 288-0399
frankleana.com
Advising on secondary school (private day school and boarding), college, graduate, and professional school levels.

Carol Gill, M.A.
Carol Gill Associates
369 Ashford Avenue
Dobbs Ferry, NY 10522
(212) 242-8541
(914) 693-8200
collegesplus.com
Counseling students and families in New York City and the tri-state area on all levels of education from elementary school through the graduate level.

COLLEGES AND UNIVERSITIES

The number of options for higher education in New York is, as you've by now come to expect, fairly mind-boggling. The City alone has twenty-three of its own public institutions, and that doesn't include all of the private universities and colleges, the adult education programs, and the institutions that offer the non-credit-bound student a selection of courses just for the sake of learning. The lists that follow should help you get started on your path to discovery.

CITY COLLEGES AND UNIVERSITIES

There are twenty-three City Universities and Colleges of New York (CUNY, 1-800-CUNY-YES, cuny.edu; eleven senior colleges; six community colleges; one technical college; a graduate school; a law school; and a medical school, which are all located within the five boroughs of New York City), many of which are highly reputable. In the "old days," especially following the big waves of immigration to the United States, ambitious people seeking a university education but lacking the necessary funds for a private university pursued degrees at the city-subsidized schools, which were hotbeds of debate, discovery, and intellectual pursuits.

Baruch College
1 Bernard Baruch Way
New York, NY 10010
(646) 312-1000
www.baruch.cuny.edu

Borough of Manhattan Community College
199 Chambers Street
New York, NY 10007
(212) 220-8000
www.bmcc.cuny.edu

Bronx Community College
West 181st Street and University Avenue
Bronx, NY 10453
(718) 289-5100
www.bcc.cuny.edu

Brooklyn College
2900 Bedford Avenue (at Avenue H)
Brooklyn, NY 11210
(718) 951-5000
www.brooklyn.cuny.edu

City College
138th Street (at Convent Avenue)
New York, NY 10031
(212) 650-7000
www1.ccny.cuny.edu

City University of New York Baccalaureate Program
The Graduate Center
365 Fifth Ave, Suite 6412
New York, NY 10016
(212) 817-8220
web.gc.cuny.edu/cunyba

City University of New York Graduate School of Journalism
(646) 758-7800
journalism.cuny.edu/journalism

City University of New York Online Baccalaureate
(212) 652-CUNY
www1.cuny.edu/online

City University of New York School of Law
65-21 Main Street
Flushing, New York 11367
(718) 340-4200
www.law.cuny.edu

City University of New York School of Professional Studies
365 Fifth Avenue
New York, NY 10016
(212) 817-7255
sps.cuny.edu

College of Staten Island
2800 Victory Boulevard
Staten Island, NY 10314
(718) 982-2000
www.csi.cuny.edu

The Graduate Center
The City University of New York
365 Fifth Avenue
New York, NY 10016
(212) 817-7000
www.gc.cuny.edu

Hostos Community College
500 Grand Concourse
Bronx, NY 10451
(718) 518-4444
www.hostos.cuny.edu

Hunter College
695 Park Avenue
New York, NY 10021
(212) 772-4000
hunter.cuny.edu

John Jay College of Criminal Justice
899 Tenth Avenue
New York, NY 10019
(212) 237-8000
jjay.cuny.edu

Kingsborough Community College
2001 Oriental Boulevard
Brooklyn, NY 11235
(718) COLLEGE
kingsborough.edu

LaGuardia Community College
31-10 Thomson Avenue
Long Island City, NY 11101
(718) 482-7200
www.lagcc.cuny.edu

Lehman College
250 Bedford Park Boulevard West
Bronx, NY 10468
(718) 960-8000
www.lehman.edu/lehman

Macaulay Honors College
365 Fifth Avenue, Suite 3313
New York, New York 10016-4309
(212) 817-1811
macaulay.cuny.edu

Medgar Evers College
1650 Bedford Avenue
Brooklyn, NY 11225
(718) 270-6024
mec.cuny.edu

New York City College of Technology
300 Jay Street
Brooklyn, NY 11201
(718) 260-5500
www.citytech.cuny.edu

Queens College
65-30 Kissena Boulevard
Flushing, NY 11367
(718) 997-5000
www.qc.cuny.edu

Queensborough Community College
222-05 56th Avenue
Bayside, NY 11354
(718) 631-6262
www.qcc.cuny.edu

The Sophie Davis School of Biomedical Education
160 Convent Avenue (at 138th Street)
Room H-107
New York, NY 10031
(212) 650-5275
med.cuny.edu

York College
94-20 Guy R. Brewer Boulevard
Jamaica, NY 11451
(718) 262-2000
york.cuny.edu

PRIVATE COLLEGES AND UNIVERSITIES

Adelphi University
South Avenue
Garden City, NY 11530
(516) 877-3052; (800) ADELPHI
www.adelphi.edu

Audrey Cohen College
75 Varick Street
New York, NY 10013
(212) 343-1234; (800) 33-THINK
metropolitan.edu

Barnard College
3009 Broadway
New York, NY 10027
(212) 854-5262
barnard.edu

Columbia University
2960 Broadway (at 116th Street)
New York, NY 10027
(212) 854-1754; (212) 854-5609 (career services)
www.columbia.edu

Concordia College
171 White Plains Road
Bronxville, NY 10708
(914) 337-9300
concordia-ny.edu

Cooper Union
30 Cooper Square
New York, NY 10003
(212) 353-4120
www.cooper.edu

Eugene Lang College
65 West 11th Street
New York, NY 10011
(212) 229-5665
newschool.edu/lang

Five Towns College
305 North Service Road
Dix Hills, NY 11746
(516) 424-7000
fivetowns.edu

Fordham University
441 East Fordham Road
Thebaud Hall
Bronx, NY 10458
(800) FORDHAM
www.fordham.edu

Hofstra University
Bernon Hall
Hempstead, NY 11549
(516) 463-6700
www.hofstra.edu

Iona College
715 North Avenue
New Rochelle, NY 10801
(914) 633-2502
iona.edu

Juilliard School
60 Lincoln Center Plaza
New York, NY 10023
(212) 799-5000
juilliard.edu

Long Island University, Brooklyn
University Plaza
Brooklyn, NY 11201
(800) 548-7526
www.brooklyn.liu.edu

Long Island University, C. W. Post
720 Northern Boulevard
Brookville, NY 11548
(516) 299-2900
www.cwpost.liu.edu/cwis/cwp

Long Island University, Southampton
239 Montauk Highway
Southampton, NY 11968
(800) 548-7526
www.southampton.liu.edu/academic/cont_studies

Manhattan College
Manhattan College Parkway
Riverdale, NY 10471
(718) 862-7200
manhattan.edu

Manhattan School of Music
120 Claremont Avenue
New York, NY 10027
(212) 749-2802
www.msmnyc.edu

New School University
66 West 12th Street
New York, NY 10011
(212) 229-5600
newschool.edu

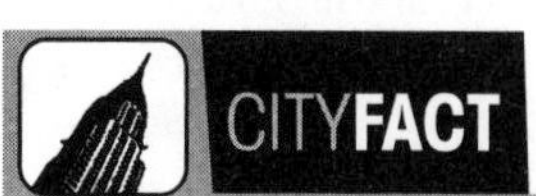

The New York City public schools consistently turn out the most Intel Science Talent Search (called the Westinghouse awards until 1998) semifinalists in the region.

New York University
22 Washington Square North
New York, NY 10011
(212) 998-4500
www.nyu.edu

Pace University
1 Pace Plaza
New York, NY 10038
(212) 346-1323
pace.edu

Parsons The New School of Design
66 Fifth Avenue
New York, NY 10011
(212) 229-8910; (800) 252-0852
parsons.edu

Polytechnic University, Brooklyn
6 MetroTech Center
Brooklyn, NY 11201
(718) 260-3100
www.poly.edu

Pratt Institute
200 Willoughby Avenue
Brooklyn, NY 11205
(718) 636-3670
www.pratt.edu

Sarah Lawrence College
One Mead Way
Bronxville, NY 10708
(914) 395-2510
www.slc.edu

School of Visual Arts
209 East 23rd Street
New York, NY 10010
(212) 592-2100
schoolofvisualarts.edu

State University of New York (SUNY)
(800) 342-3811
www.suny.edu
There are sixty-four SUNY campuses located throughout the state. SUNY is the largest university system in the country.

Weill Cornell Medical College
1300 York Avenue
New York, NY 10021
(212) 746-1036
med.cornell.edu

ADULT EDUCATION

Many of the colleges and universities mentioned offer continuing education classes that can be taken as night courses toward a degree. But for those looking to simply expand their horizons, there are a few New York classics that should not go unnoticed.

Gotham Writers' Workshop
1841 Broadway, Suite 809
New York, NY 10023
(212) WRITERS
www.writingclasses.com
This organization offers ten-week and one-day courses for adults (and eight-week courses for teens) on all aspects of writing, from adult and children's books to sitcom, poetry, playwriting, and memoir.

The Learning Annex
16 East 53rd Street, 4th Floor
New York, NY 10022
(212) 371-0280
www.learningannex.com

Offering courses ranging from CPR training and Zen Meditation & Everyday Life to How to Break into Stand-Up Comedy and Country-Western Line Dancing.

The New School for Drama
New School University
66 West 12th Street, Room 616
New York, NY 10011
(212) 229-5859
newschool.edu/drama/

New School for Social Research
New School University
66 West 12th Street
New York, NY 10011
(212) 229-5859
newschool.edu

92nd Street Y
1395 Lexington Avenue
New York, NY 10128
(212) 996-1100
www.92y.org

A broad range of courses from painting and photography to modern dance and financial planning.

CHAPTER THIRTEEN
WORKING IN THE CITY

New York City is the economic capital of the world, and there are more Fortune 1000 companies headquartered in New York than anyplace else. Combined with the businesses that service them, these megacorporations are the City's most significant employers, responsible for a third of New York's economy.

While it may seem to you that 9-11 was a long time ago, it is still very fresh in the minds of New Yorkers. Don't forget, thousands of the City's—and the world's—biggest and most important companies had offices in the World Trade Center buildings and nearby. It took a long time for the companies and staff to recover from the tragedy—and to relocate. Thankfully, though the wound is slow to heal, the workforce, along with everything else in the city, has bounced back quickly and admirably. In the years following 9-11, the people have proved resilient and the City is thriving now, just as before. The construction industry is booming, real estate prices are through the roof, and the cottage industries of security and counter-terrorism have sprung up, providing jobs (and safety) where there weren't any before.

New York is the national center of the arts, banking, publishing, finance, accounting, advertising, fashion, and law. It is home to the United Nations, and many major overseas corporations choose New York as their base of U.S. operations. New York is also one of the world's top tourism destinations, and its hospitality industry is a major—and growing—employer. Other significant industries include wholesale and retail, construction, real estate, healthcare, education, law enforcement, security, recruiting, graphic design, and nonprofit organizations. In addition, a substantial percentage of the workforce devotes itself just to making the City function, which translates into hundreds of thousands of jobs in public administration, transportation, and related services.

And that's only a partial list. Talk to ten different New Yorkers and they'll have ten (or more) different jobs, half of which you've probably never even considered or knew existed. The number of job descriptions in New York is infinite, limited only by your imagination. As with many things in New York (not just the job market), if you can't find it here, it probably doesn't exist (though a professional surfer might be better off in Hawaii than in Long Island).

Many dreamers come to New York and live off their savings (or work as temps, part-timers, or seasonal employees) while waiting for a break in the arts or in entrepreneurial ventures. Others, seeking an escape from the nine-to-five lifestyle, have carved out niches that could only exist in such a large city (you can make a nice living walking dogs or delivering doughnuts in New York—if you have enough clients). Unconventional employment arrangements are the norm in this most unconventional of cities.

For example, I have one friend who worked the night shift as a typist at a law firm to put herself through social-work school. That's right, in the City that never sleeps, the major law firms—and many other businesses—have twenty-four-hour secretarial pools. A more daring friend, trying to survive while starting his Internet business, supplemented his income by participating in medical studies at Columbia University, each of which put an extra $500 or more in his pocket (today, he spends that much on dinner anytime he wants). And another friend, an assistant chef suffering from burnout after five years at a three-star restaurant, took a job working at one of the farmstands at the Union Square Greenmarket, which enabled him to be outside all day and act as the "Dear Abby" of the greenmarket, advising people on how best to use the herbs they just bought to spice up their cooking. One day, he sold some carrots to a rich investor—and now he's the head chef at his own restaurant. As E. B. White writes, "No one should come to New York to live unless he is willing to be lucky. . . . In New York, the chances are endless."

BASIC ECONOMIC STATISTICS

New York is a city of extremes, with precious few statistically average residents. It's the richest and the poorest city in the country, with a huge immigrant population (more than half of New York's residents were born overseas) and a large, unofficial cash economy. Facts and figures can only tell us so much. New York is about opportunity and dreams, for which there are no statistics. And remember, you only need one job—although many New Yorkers have two or three!

COST OF LIVING

In most of the professions, New York salaries are the highest in the nation. Correspondingly, it is often said that New York has the highest cost of living of any American city—and this can be true if you don't adapt to the local way of life. Still, the three major items in the federal cost-of-living calculation are mortgage payments, property taxes, and the cost of maintaining two automobiles (these three items constitute more than a third of the cost-of-living picture). Many New Yorkers, however, rent their homes and live happily without cars (the City's walkability, combined with excellent public transportation, makes them unnecessary). Just switching from two cars to two MetroCards can free up nearly $14,000 for other purposes.

Many people perceive New York as expensive because it presents so many opportunities to spend money. And while it is true that the rent is very high, if you adhere to a strict household budget and avoid impulse buying, you can live very well on a moderate income. The rewards of living in New York are infinite, and cannot be measured in square feet or traffic flow. So, while New York consistently ranks low in the *Places Rated Almanac* and other national surveys of livability, it still remains the destination of choice for anybody with a dream.

JOB PROSPECTS

The New York and federal labor departments maintain extensive statistics on employment by region and sector. If you want to find out which areas of employment are growing and shrinking, salary averages for different types of jobs, or general workforce statistics, check these resources online:

U.S. Department of Labor
Bureau of Labor Statistics
www.bls.gov

New York State Department of Labor
labor.state.ny.us

EMPLOYMENT RESOURCES

The employment options in New York are virtually endless, and you might find yourself overwhelmed by the selection. Take steps to narrow the field and focus on the industries that interest you most. Use websites and placement agencies that specialize in your field. Talk to people at professional organizations—they might be able to help you with your search or direct you to someone who can. Casually tell everyone you meet that you're hunting for a job. It's amazing how many people find jobs that way.

The listings that follow are meant to be suggestions and aids to help you tackle your job search with ease, but this list is only a starting point. Some of these resources, especially the websites, will lead you to many others. And don't forget about the handy and free Yellow Pages. Last I checked, there were 25 pages (1,347 listings) of "Employment Agencies" in the New York City area alone.

RECRUITING CENTERS AND PERSONNEL AGENCIES

There are hundreds of recruiting centers, personnel agencies, and executive-search firms in the City. These companies all perform essentially the same service: They match qualified employees with appropriate employers—and they get a handsome commission from the employer for the service.

Tips for Selecting a Recruiting Center or Personnel Agency

1. Never pay a fee. Reputable agencies make their money exclusively through commissions paid by employers. If an agency asks you for money, find another one. There are plenty of fish in the sea, and you don't want to work with a company that can't even cover its own costs (or is trying to rip you off).
2. Find out how long the agency has been around. It's a dog-eat-dog world out there and, generally speaking, if the agency isn't a good one, it won't last long enough to make its mark.
3. Check an agency's website before you call. If you do a little homework, you might learn something you especially like about a particular agency—or something you don't. And you'll know from the website whether or not the agency even makes placements within your industry of choice. Ask about the number of placements the agency makes each year. Obviously, the higher the number, the more successful the agency.
4. Don't be afraid to ask a lot of questions. If for some reason you don't like the agency you've found, try another—there are plenty to choose from, and it's important to find a comfortable fit.

TEMPORARY JOB PLACEMENT AGENCIES

Temp agencies are an ideal starting point for those who are unsure about their future career paths, need some cash in a hurry, or want to ease their way into the New York workforce. I have many friends, in various stages of life—just out of college, in between jobs, pursuing new careers, recently relocated to the City—who have taken advantage of the lifestyle that temp work affords. And the universal opinion is that temp work is a great way to get a taste of a job without being committed.

Questions for Temp Agencies

1. Does the agency offer benefits? Many agencies, in response to the growing demand for temps, are now offering health benefits, 401(k) plans, bonuses, vacation time, and training in order to attract and keep a dependable and trustworthy stable of people in their employ. But be sure to read the fine print and ask lots of questions—many of these plans have strings attached or require substantial contributions from you.
2. Do the agency's temps get permanent jobs? Temporary placements sometimes lead to full-time positions, and it can only be a good sign if an agency has a strong track record of its temps being hired permanently.
3. Who are the agency's clients? An agency is only as good as the companies that use its temps.
4. How long will the initial appointment take? You may need to set aside half a day or more to register with a temp agency. You'll fill out many forms and possibly take some tests before you meet with a counselor.

Some of the agencies listed make not only temporary placements but also permanent ones. Be sure to call first—virtually all of the agencies require appointments.

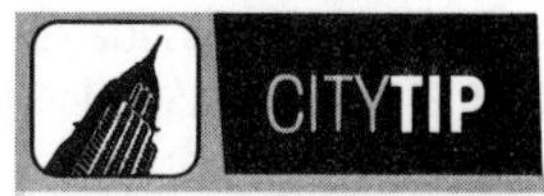

"Keep something to read or do—a book, a magazine, some homework—with you at all times. I live in Queens, so I spend extra time commuting to my job every day. The train may get delayed, but if I have reading material or a little chore to do, I don't mind the wait because I'm using my time productively."

—Tafima Awwad, City University student

Adam Personnel, Inc.
11 East 44th Street
New York, NY 10017
(212) 557-9150
adampersonnel.com

Specializing in office work with permanent and temporary placement in all industries including accounting, auditing, banking, fashion, law, and nonprofit.

Atrium
420 Lexington Avenue, Suite 1410
New York, NY 10170
(212) 292-0550
atriumstaff.com

Specializing in temporary, "temp to perm" (temporary placements that turn into permanent positions), and full-time job placements mostly in administration and office work. Also offers benefits (medical benefits, 401k plan, paid vacations, with restrictions) to registered staff.

Bon Temps/BT Associates
80 Broad Street, 5th Floor PMB #31
New York, NY 10004
(212) 732-3921
bontempsny.com

Since 1977, specializing in temporary placement of support staff with law firms and Fortune 500 companies in the following capacities: legal secretaries, word processors, paralegals, proofreaders, receptionists, and clerical support.

"Take a vacation at home. While most New Yorkers are fleeing the city on summer weekends and holidays, smart city slickers stay at home and take advantage of all the town has to offer while the hordes are competing for beach space in the Hamptons."

—Mazi Schonfeld, art dealer

Career Blazers Personnel Service
590 Fifth Avenue, 6th Floor
New York, NY 10036
(212) 719-3232
careerblazers.com

Job placement for office support staff in temporary and permanent positions

Core Staffing Services, Inc.
295 Madison Avenue, Suite 715
New York, NY 10017
(212) 557-6252
employcore.com

Covering the whole range of employment opportunities for temporary, temp-perm, and permanent job placements in the New York Metro area in a variety of industries. Founded in 1988

Diversity Services Group
295 Madison Avenue, 16th Floor
New York, NY 10017
(212) 685-9338
diversity-services.com

Full-service "from soup to nuts" staffing and consulting firm covering the wide spectrum of industries in New York for temporary and permanent placements

E. E. Brooke, Inc.
(212) 687-8400

Open since 1923, E. E. Brooke, Inc. specializes in making placements for full-time positions in corporate travel and other jobs related to the travel industry, including hotel management and secretarial positions.

The Forum Group
260 Madison Avenue, Suite 200
New York, NY 10016
(212) 687-4050
forumpersonnel.com

Making placements for temporary, permanent, and contract staffing in accounting, finance, and taxation; advertising, communications, market research, and marketing; information technology; office support and administration; human resources; and the medical and healthcare fields. Established 1974

Headway Corporate Resources
317 Madison Avenue
New York, NY 10017
www.headwaycorp.com

Headway specializes in job placements in administration, financial services, legal, personnel, secretarial, life sciences, and publishing. Clients with whom Headway makes placements include NYU, JPMorgan Chase, Bank of New York, and First America Corporation. Established 1974

Lloyd Staffing
58 West 40th Street, 14th Floor
New York, NY 10018
(212) 354-8787
www.lloydstaffing.com

Established in 1971, Lloyd Staffing does make placements for direct hire but specializes in temporary and contingent staffing. Look to Lloyd for placements in bilingual/global services, accounting and finance, administration, architecture, engineering, construction, nursing and healthcare, computing and technology jobs, legal, and any number of other professions.

Madison Avenue Temporary Service for Communications
271 Madison Avenue, Suite 1103
New York, NY 10016
(212) 922-9040
matsforcommunications.com

Daily, weekly, and long-term temporary assignments in advertising, publishing, public relations, and support and secretarial staff in Fortune 500 companies, broadcasting, Internet, and new media

Merlin Staffing
261 Madison, 27th Floor
New York, NY 10016
(212) 983-3533

Office support staff, primarily reception, word processing, bookkeeping, and secretarial

The Peak Organization
25 West 31st Street, Penthouse
New York, NY 10001
(212) 947-6600
peakorg.com

Temporary and direct-hire placements in numerous fields including banking and capital markets, legal support, litigation support, office support, accounting, and advertising and communications. Established in 1970

The Premier Group
275 Madison Avenue, Suite 1618
New York, NY 10016
(212) 986-6800
thepremiergroup.com

With offices in Manhattan, Westchester, New Jersey, and Connecticut, the Premier Group covers all the bases with placements in temporary,

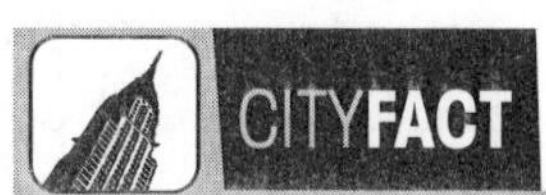

In 1698, the population of New York City was 4,937. Today, that many people work in an average-size Midtown office building.

temp-perm, and permanent staffing. TPG specializes in office support staff within the business, financial, legal, and medical industries.

RAS Temporary Services, Inc.
6 East 39th Street, Suite 501
New York, NY 10016
(212) 686-0123
rastemp.com
Placements in administration, legal support, clerical, and office support staff

Staffmark
10 East 40th Street, 20th Floor
New York, NY 10016
(212) 271-3900
staffmark.com
Temporary placements in office support staff including administration, clerical, and reception. The company also has an executive search branch, which makes permanent placements.

Taylor Grey Recruitment Consultants
369 Lexington Avenue, 4th Floor
New York, NY 10017
(212) 687-8100
taylorgrey.com
Offices in New York and Stamford, Connecticut. TGRC makes temporary and full-time job placements in high-end administrative and professional support staff. Established in 1991, TGRC is female-owned and -operated but caters to women and men alike.

The TemPositions Group of Companies
420 Lexington Avenue, 21st Floor
New York, NY 10170
(212) 490-7400
www.tempositions.com

With offices in Manhattan, Long Island, Westchester, and Connecticut, TemPositions covers the whole spectrum of the job market. Offering temporary, temp-hire, and direct-hire placements for secretarial, clerical, and related positions; a full range of information-technology jobs from the help desk all the way up to the programmers; writers, copy editors, and designers; human resources professionals; accounting personnel; legal support staff; hospitality and corporate food service; substitute teachers; and healthcare professionals in nursing, social work, and child care.

Tiger Information Systems
120 Broadway, 28th Floor
New York, NY 10271
(212) 412-0660
tigerinfo.com

This full-service placement agency does full assessments of potential clients and offers everything from training to part-time and full-time placements in a number of fields including (but not limited to) information technology, desktop publishing, graphic design, the written word, illustration, Web design, investment banking, and legal. The company was established in 1982, when word processing was in its infancy, to meet the needs of employers looking for well-trained and creative staff members.

The Tuttle Agency
295 Madison Avenue
New York, NY 10017
(212) 499-0759
tuttleagency.com

The Tuttle Agency is a full-service firm that makes temporary and direct-hire placements in administrative, legal, healthcare, financial, hospitality, fashion, sales, and other professions with Fortune 500 companies and others.

Vanguard Temporaries, Inc.
633 Third Avenue
New York, NY 10017
(212) 682-6400
temporarypersonnel.com
Making temporary and permanent placements in accounting and finance, administration and office services, and graphics positions, Vanguard Temporaries has offices in Manhattan, Westchester (White Plains), and Connecticut (Darien).

Winston Resources, LLC
122 East 42nd Street, Suite 320
New York, NY 10169
(212) 557-5000
winstonresources.com
With four professional divisions, Winston Resources covers a wide range of placements in personnel, office support staff, medical, advertising, human resources, legal, and banking positions. Different divisions offer different services, including temporary and permanent placements. Branch offices in New Jersey and New York.

EXECUTIVE RECRUITERS

Executive recruiters generally make placements for people who have been in an industry a minimum of two years—but this is not a hard-and-fast rule. Recruiters sometimes make placements for people who are new to an industry if they see a good match. Remember, it never hurts to ask!

Tips for Dealing with Executive Recruiters

1. Ask for references. How many people a year does the recruiter place in your field and at what salaries? How well established is the recruiter? Are the recruiter's clients happy, and do they stay at their jobs?

2. Does the recruiter demand an exclusive arrangement? If you're required to commit to just one recruiter, what do you get in exchange for that commitment? Ideally, a recruiter who demands an exclusive should guarantee you time, effort, and industry contacts above and beyond what any other recruiter can offer.
3. Don't be pressured into signing anything. If you're asked to sign an agreement, be sure you take the time to read and fully understand its provisions. A good, ethical recruiter will give you the time you need to make an intelligent decision.

Advice Personnel, Inc.
230 Park Avenue
New York, NY 10169
(212) 682-4400
adviceny.com

Founded in 1984, Advice Personnel is a boutique firm making placements for "the best talent" in the New York Metro area.

The Alfus Group
353 Lexington Avenue
New York, NY 10016
(212) 599-1000
thealfusgroup.com

Specializing in executive placements in the hospitality industry.

Bert Davis Executive Search, Inc.
425 Madison Avenue
New York, NY 10017
(212) 838-4000
bertdavis.com

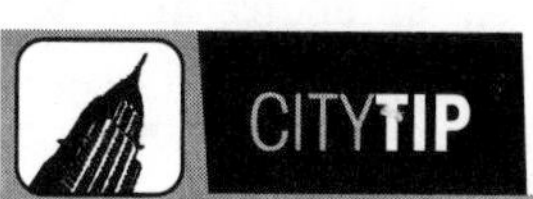

"Don't be afraid to try something new just because you think you might not like it. Even if the Japanese sculpture garden doesn't exactly sound like your cup of tea, you'll never know for sure until you give it a whirl—and the story value alone could be worth the price of admission."

—Donelle Davis, actress

Founded in 1977, BDESI specializes in placing senior management in the publishing, information services, and electronic-media fields.

Bornholdt, Shivas and Friends
33 Concord Road
Port Washington, NY 11050
(516) 767-1849
bsandf.com
Corporate clients include Bristol-Myers Squibb, Clairol, Coca-Cola Foods, Ernst & Young, Pfizer Inc., Sony Corporation—and the list goes on.

Spring Associates, Inc.
10 East 23rd Street
New York, NY 10010
(212) 473-0013
springassociates.com
Established in 1980, Spring Associates makes placements in public affairs, consumer marketing, investor relations, corporate communications, marketing communications, speechwriting, employee communications, financial communications, media relations, medical/healthcare, and high tech (dot-com, e-commerce, e-retail), among others.

JOB FAIRS

Job fairs, where dozens (and sometimes hundreds) of employers get together under one roof, are one of the most efficient ways to learn about a wide variety of jobs and to streamline the application and interview processes.

In addition to the selection of job fair resources listed, check these sources for the latest information:

Newspapers: Scour the local papers (including the free ones like *New York Press* and the *Village Voice*) for information on upcoming career-related events. For example, the *New York Times* sponsors Systems Information Technology (SIT) career fairs on a semiannual to quarterly basis. Check the Help Wanted sections for listings of upcoming job fairs sponsored by corporations (to maximize recruiting at their company career drives) and search firms.

And don't forget to check your favorite websites for job fair listings—many of them have calendars of job fairs weeks or months in advance.

Hotels and Convention Centers: Stay on top of the goings-on at area hotels and convention centers (such as the Javits Center, 212-216-2000—call for a brochure of upcoming events or go online at javitscenter.com). These are the largest spaces available in the City and are regularly used for job fairs and recruiting. Many fairs are also held just over the river in New Jersey (because space is cheaper and more plentiful). Check out the schedules for the job fairs listed with the organizations mentioned to get an idea of where fairs are held, and call the hotels and convention centers periodically to stay informed.

Online: See the Internet section following. Many of the websites listed include calendars of events (which often include listings of job fairs) and calendars of national career fairs. Search around; though they may be a bit tricky to find, most of the websites do include regional job and career fair information, and this is likely to be your best source of up-to-date information on job fairs that are coming to town.

Diversity Expo
diversityexpo.com
A New York City–based career fair geared toward the hiring of a culturally diverse pool of individuals with a college degree or a minimum of two years' full-time work experience. A lot of big-name companies and heavy hitters are in attendance looking for staff.

Fashion Career Expo
(212) 655-4504
fashioncareerexpo.com
This is the career fair of New York City's Fashion Week. Needless to say, if you're interested in a job in the fashion industry, this is a good place to start.

National Association of Colleges and Employers (NACE)
www.jobweb.com
Search for job fairs by location, date, and keyword. Hundreds of career fairs are listed here by date and location.

PSI Diversity Recruiting
NAACP Diversity Job Fair
psijobfair.com
PSI lists diversity job fairs around the country. PSI is the only organization with a diversity job fair that has the NAACP as the primary sponsor.

TechExpo Career Fairs
(212) 655-4505
techexpousa.com
Job fairs specializing in the technology industry. Security clearance is required to attend some of the fairs.

UNIVERSITY JOBS AND JOB PLACEMENT

Many universities and colleges have Career Services centers or Career Development offices where alumni (and sometimes referrals from other universities) can get free access to career counseling, job listings (job banks), and the multitudes of reference materials for which university career offices are famous. If you are neither an alumnus of the school nor a referral, sometimes you can still gain access to the resources. Some private universities charge a fee for this service, but many of the public universities don't. Plus, here's a secret born of the computer age: Many universities (even the ones that charge a fee for walk-in career services) have their career resources online for free.

You should also consider working for a university or college as administrative staff in one of the offices or departments. Check in regularly at each university's employment office, because jobs go quickly. If you are seeking a faculty position at a local university, contact that discipline's department directly, but be advised: The market is extremely competitive.

For a complete listing of New York area universities and colleges, see Chapter 12, "Local Schools and Colleges."

INTERNET RESOURCES

The Internet is an invaluable tool for finding jobs, and you don't have to be in New York to use it. As Jim Brown of the New York Department of Labor explains, "We always advise people to start their job search before they relocate." And the Department of Labor's website, Workforce New York (labor.state.ny.us/workforcenypartners/WFNYP_index.shtm), is a great place to start. In addition to one of the most extensive job banks on the Internet, it also has information specific to civil service openings, exams and applications, as well as a monthly calendar of job fairs and recruitment opportunities divided by region throughout New York.

There are also dozens of websites with huge job banks that are designed specifically to help you find your dream job, be it as a teacher, a pastry chef, or the manager of a hotel. Navigating these websites can take some getting used to, and it will take some time to figure out which site is best suited to you, but it's an excellent way to stay on top of things.

Academic Position Network
www1.umn.edu/ohr/teachlearn/tutorials/jobsearch/resources.html
APN posts jobs in higher education including faculty, professorships, staff, administrative positions, graduate fellowships, assistant fellowships, and postdoctoral positions. Search by availability in field of interest, position, country, and state.

Best Jobs USA
bestjobsusa.com
BJ USA features a job bank search, résumé services, listings of job fairs, career links, healthcare careers, relocation guide, salary survey, trade shows, best places to live and work, Best Jobs University, recruiting services, HR publications; and the list goes on.

Career Builder
careerbuilder.com
A full-service website with a job bank searchable by location, description, and keyword; offers advice on interviewing, résumés, and salary negotiations, and a host of other helpful insights.

Career Magazine
careermag.com
CM features a job bank, advice, résumé board, and articles pertinent to every aspect of work and your job search.

CareerPath.com
careerpath.com

Career Path features the Help Wanted sections (which offer approximately 150,000 job listings) from newspapers in six U.S. cities (including New York).

Career Resource Center
careers.org

A very comprehensive website with thousands of links, CRC claims to be "the most complete and extensive index of career-related websites."

Craigslist
newyork.craigslist.org

A great place to search for all things—and jobs are no exception.

Federal Jobs Digest
www.jobsfed.com

If working for the federal government is your dream, FJD is a good place to start your search. With opportunities in postal, clerical, management, legal, law enforcement, secretarial, engineering, science, computers, medical, math, accounting, auditing, and a host of other fields, FJD lists more than 2,500 available jobs around the country.

Government Jobs
nyc.gov

A helpful and extensive website about New York City, including a job bank of NYC government jobs.

Hoover's Online
hoovers.com
Hoover's details the best and the brightest with a "top 2,500 employers" listing. Also an excellent resource for links: Hoover's lists more than 4,000 company websites to which you can connect with the click of your mouse.

LawJobs.com
lawjobs.com
Includes posts of current openings, a roster of the 250 largest law firms in the country, salary survey, links, Q&A, and a law-employment library.

Monster.com
www.monster.com
Listing more than 400,000 jobs, Monster.com also provides numerous resources, from company profiles and career advice to résumé posting and a personal career account.

MonsterTrak
jobtrak.com
More than 300 university career counseling centers across the country act in partnership with MonsterTrak to place college students and recent college graduates in appealing jobs. MonsterTrak's database lists more than 500 new jobs daily from employers specifically seeking these college candidates.

New York Government Jobs
www.fedworld.gov/jobs/jobsearch.html
National listing of government jobs

USAJobs
www.usajobs.gov
The U.S. Government's official website, provided by the United States Office of Personnel Management. Offerings include listing of current job openings, openings that give preference to veterans, and online application.

In addition to the sites listed here, each of the Internet search engines (Yahoo!, Excite, and others) has job postings and resources, and many corporations have job banks and bulletin boards on their own websites.

SOCIAL SERVICE AGENCIES

Social service agencies, an excellent job-hunting resource in practical fields, offer career placement and sometimes career counseling. Because these organizations are nonprofit, they may charge you a nominal fee (the placement agencies do not, because they receive a finder's fee or bonus from the hiring company on placing a candidate), but many of them counsel free of charge—and also offer wonderful volunteer opportunities if you want to give a little back.

Federation Employment and Guidance Service (FEGS) Health and Human Services System
315 Hudson Street
New York, NY 10013
(212) 366-8400
fegs.org
Established in 1934 by the Federation of Jewish Philanthropies of New York, FEGS works to help disadvantaged people (whether that means physically or mentally disadvantaged, or a new immigrant), young people, older adults, and others with career planning, employment, skills training, advocacy, information, and referral services.

Goodwill Industries of Greater New York and Northern New Jersey
4-21 27th Avenue
Astoria, NY 11102
718 728-5400
www.goodwillny.org
Job placement and training for people with disabilities and other special needs in New York and northern New Jersey.

New York Urban League
204 West 136th Street
New York, NY 10030
(212) 926-8000
nyul.org
Assistance with job placement and career counseling.

New York Women's Employment Center
Women's Center for Education and Career Advancement
11 Broadway, Suite 457
New York, NY 10004
(212) 964-8934
wceca.org
Workshops, career counseling and "coaching," résumé assistance, training referrals, job placements, and an entrepreneurial program—all offered to women only, free of charge.

Selfhelp Community Services Inc.
520 Eighth Avenue
New York, NY 10018
(212) 971-7600
selfhelp.net
A remarkable organization, established in 1936 by a small group of refugees fleeing Nazi persecution, Selfhelp Community Services offers a three-week training program for home health aides and places trainees into jobs following completion. The training and placement service is offered free of charge. STRIVE classes.

PROFESSIONAL ORGANIZATIONS

Professional organizations are often excellent reference points for newcomers to New York because many organizations have branch chapters in other cities. Members from near and far who move to New York can have an immediate support network on arrival and, more often than not, even have access to the organization's resources before they move, thereby making for an easier and smoother transition. Those who are not yet members of a professional organization within their field may want to consider joining one (or many). These organizations are not only excellent networking arenas, but many also offer job-hunting resources (job banks, reference material, advice), educational seminars, lectures, luncheons, information centers, and a great place to make some new friends. And for those who are not yet set on a career path, many professional organizations also offer career fairs and conferences to educate and direct those just entering the field (primarily recent college graduates).

Advertising Club of New York
235 Park Avenue South, 6th Floor
New York, NY 10003
(212) 533-8080
theadvertisingclub.org

Advertising Women of New York
153 East 57th Street
New York, NY 10022
(212) 593-1950
www.awny.org

AWNY is an organization of women (primarily executives) involved in all aspects of the advertising industry—advertising, media, marketing, promotion, PR, and research. AWNY sponsors an annual career conference for both professionals and students, offers scholarships and public service programs, hosts seminars and luncheons (no ladies' lunching here—this is power lunching), and keeps a job bank.

American Association of Advertising Agencies
405 Lexington Avenue
New York, NY 10174
(212) 682-2500
aaaa.org
This association of advertising agencies gathers statistics, conducts surveys, and operates a research library (which is a storehouse of information on the advertising industry).

American Association of Exporters and Importers
11 West 42nd Street
New York, NY 10036
(212) 944-2230
aaei.org

American Institute of Aeronautics and Astronautics
85 John Street
New York, NY 10038
(212) 349-1120
aiaa.org

American Institute of Architects
200 Lexington Avenue, Suite 600
New York, NY 10016
(212) 683-0023
aiany.org

American Institute of Certified Public Accountants
1211 Avenue of the Americas
New York, NY 10036
(212) 596-6200
aicpa.org

American Institute of Chemical Engineers
3 Park Avenue
New York, NY 10016
(212) 591-7338
www.aiche.org

American Institute of Graphic Arts
545 West 45th Street
New York, NY 10036
(212) 246-7060
aigany.org

American Insurance Association
85 John Street
New York, NY 10038
(212) 669-0400
web@iso.com
www.aiadc.org

American Marketing Association
60 East 42nd Street, Suite 1765
New York, NY 10165
(212) 687-3280
nyama.org
Offers a mentoring program run by the career advisory board, online job listings, and seminars on marketing-related issues, including how to get a job and selling yourself through your résumé.

American Society of Composers, Authors and Publishers (ASCAP)
1 Lincoln Plaza
New York, NY 10023
(212) 595-3050
www.ascap.com

American Society of Interior Designers (ASID)
200 Lexington Avenue
New York, NY 10016
(877) ASK-ASID (877-275-2743)
Primarily a networking organization; the local chapters offer placement services and a job bank.

American Society of Magazine Editors
919 Third Avenue
New York, NY 10022
(212) 872-3700
magazine.org/editorial
Must be a senior editor to be a member. Hosts approximately twenty-four networking luncheons and guest speaker seminars per year.

American Society of Mechanical Engineers
345 East 47th Street
New York, NY 10017
(212) 591-7000
www.asme.org
Offers employment counseling and bimonthly regional job postings. ASME also offers seminars and conferences.

American Society of Travel Agents
18 West Marie Street
Hicksville, NY 11801
(516) 822-4602
www.asta.org

Asian Women in Business
1 West 34th Street, Suite 1202
New York, NY 10001
(212) 868-1368
awib.org

Association of Real Estate Women
15 West 72nd Street, Suite 31G
New York, NY 10023
(212) 787-7124
arew.org

Provides information on real estate trends and issues. Membership is open to men and women.

Cosmetic Executive Women
217 East 85th Street, Suite 214
New York, NY 10028
(212) 759-3283
cew.org

A not-for-profit organization open to women in the beauty industry. A minimum of two years' experience in a given field is required to join, though sponsorships, referrals, and mentoring are available to young women interested in pursuing a career in the industry.

Environmental Action Coalition
625 Broadway, 9th Floor
New York, NY 10012
(212) 677-1601

Job listings, internships, and volunteer opportunities.

Institute of Electrical and Electronics Engineers
345 East 47th Street
New York, NY 10017
(212) 705-7900
ieee.org

Large membership, with 50,000 student members.

League of Professional Theatre Women, New York
300 East 56th Street
New York, NY 10022
(212) 583-0177
theatrewomen.org

Members can fall within any area of theater production, including production staff, playwrights, administrators, lawyers, and critics. Must be sponsored by two members.

National Association of Black Social Workers
1969 Madison Avenue
New York, NY 10035
(212) 348-0035
nabsw.org

National Association of Social Workers, New York Chapter
15 Park Row, 20th Floor
New York, NY 10038
(212) 577-5000
naswnys.org

Mentoring, job listings, and employment seminars.

National League for Nursing
350 Hudson Street
New York, NY 10014
(212) 989-9393
nln.org

New York County Lawyers' Association
14 Vesey Street
New York, NY 10007
(212) 267-6646
nycla.org

More than 9,000 attorneys belong to the NYCLA. Benefits include a Legal Referral Service (referring more than 40,000 cases a year), forums, lectures and special events, Courtlink, financial services,

Lexis-Nexis access, continuing-legal-education courses, and an extensive legal library housing more than 200,000 volumes.

New York State Bar Association
One Elk Street
Albany, NY 12207
(518) 463-3200
www.nysba.org

With more than 64,000 members (all lawyers), representing every corner of the state, the NYSBA is the oldest and largest voluntary state bar association in the country. Be sure to check out the LawMatch Career Services link on the NYSBA website. It will lead you to a host of other helpful sites and possibly help you find your dream job.

New York Women in Communications
355 Lexington Avenue, 17th Floor
New York, NY 10016
(212) 679-0870
nywici.org

Sponsors mentoring programs and career counseling.

New York Women's Bar Association
234 Fifth Avenue, Suite 403
New York, NY 10016
(212) 889-7873
nywba.org

Public Relations Society of America
33 Irving Place, 3rd Floor
New York, NY 10003
(212) 995-2230
prsa.org

Job referral services, a research center, and development programs.

Women's Sports Foundation
Eisenhower Park
East Meadow, NY 11554
(516) 542-4700
www.womenssportsfoundation.org
Sponsors an internship program, offers training grants, and maintains a large information bank on women's sports and fitness.

Young Menswear Association
1328 Broadway
New York, NY 10001
(212) 594-6422
the-yma.com
This association is open to young individuals wishing to enter the industry. YMA offers scholarships and helps with job placement (résumé bank).

CHAPTER FOURTEEN

VOLUNTEER AND COMMUNITY INVOLVEMENT

When people first move to New York City, they're usually so busy and so overwhelmed that the last thing they want to think about is volunteering their time to help others. Big mistake!

Volunteering in New York City is not only a great opportunity to do good in the community, it's also one of the best ways to meet like-minded people and make new friends. And making friends is what makes life in the big city livable. I know people who have found jobs, lifelong friends, apartments, and even spouses through the incredible social network of New York's volunteer organizations. So find a couple of extra hours in your week to help the community—you'll be doing everybody, including yourself, a big favor.

In addition to the organizations listed, the following are ways to unearth some of the best philanthropic prospects:

- An excellent jumping-off point for volunteer opportunities in New York is VolunteerNYC.org (www.volunteernyc.org/volunteer). Last I checked, there were 680 organizations listed with 978 volunteer opportunities available.
- Contact your block, neighborhood, or community association. Most residential areas of New York City have several active, overlapping, local organizations that do everything from running soup kitchens to planting trees.
- Stop by your church, synagogue, mosque, or temple. Religious organizations are some of the foremost providers of charitable services in the New York City area. If you are unaffiliated, stop by a neighborhood religious organization of your choice. Most don't require membership or affiliation—volunteers are welcome regardless of religious beliefs and practice.
- Check with your college or graduate school alumni association. Most major institutions of higher learning have thriving New York–area alumni chapters, which often host annual or semiannual volunteer projects.
- Inquire with any professional or political organizations to which you belong. Most have long-standing relationships with reputable charities.
- Ask at your office about employee volunteer days and weekend or evening projects organized by your employer.
- Call the local chapters of major national philanthropic organizations, like the American Lung Association. All

"Find a place where you enjoy hanging out—a restaurant, bar, coffeeshop—and become a regular there. Surprisingly, even in this huge town, it's not difficult to become a regular after only a few visits—and it's nice to have a place where you can comfortably hang out alone, or impress your friends when you share your haunt."

—Mary Lesser, artist

the big players on the national charity scene have New York chapters, and most welcome volunteers.

- Visit Master Planner Online (www.kinteramasterplanner.com) for a comprehensive listing of thousands of major benefits, openings, and special events for the upcoming year. Many of these events are tied to organizations that need volunteers.
- As with all things in New York City, talk to everybody. You never know—your next-door neighbor could be the world's number one authority on charitable organizations. And there's no substitute for a firsthand account when you're trying to learn which group is best for you to join.

Volunteer Opportunities

826NYC
372 Fifth Avenue
Brooklyn, NY 11215
(718) 499-9884
826nyc.org

826NYC is a wonderful tutoring program dedicated to encouraging and assisting children ages 6 through 18 (and their teachers) with writing skills. Volunteers are especially needed during school hours, though if you can't volunteer during school-time hours, 826NYC is happy to have your time whenever you're able to offer it. In addition to tutors, 826NYC can use volunteers with skills in IT, writing, copyediting, or design.

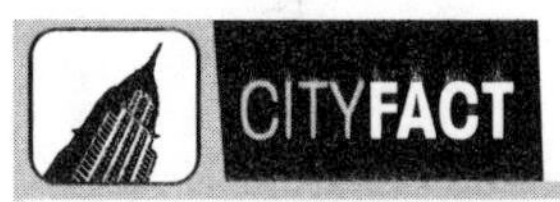

Built in 1904, the St. Regis Hotel (on 55th Street between Fifth and Madison Avenues) was designed and built with the intention of replacing, in elegance and distinction, the Waldorf-Astoria Hotel. Today, it still ranks as one of New York's most expensive and distinguished hotels. Recent guests have included Michael Jordan and Elton John.

Bronx Zoo
Friends of the Zoo
The Wildlife Conservation Society
2300 Southern Boulevard
Bronx, NY 10460
(718) 220-5142
wcs.org

Volunteering at the Bronx Zoo is a highly desirable endeavor, but it isn't for everyone. You can't just walk in and volunteer for an hour a month. Volunteering requires an extended commitment (two years or more) and a devoted personality. But if you do decide to take the plunge, the rewards are tremendous. Volunteers (or docents) do everything from giving zoo tours, to delivering mini-talks and acting as "exhibit interpreters." To become a Friend of the Zoo, candidates need to complete an application form, pass an interview, and participate in a six-month training program. To volunteer at the other city zoos, check out the wcs.org website for additional details (click: Volunteer).

Central Park Conservancy
14 East 60th Street
New York, NY 10022
(212) 310-6600
www.centralparknyc.org

To volunteer call (212) 360-2751 or e-mail to volunteer@centralparknyc.org. Volunteer opportunities abound at the CPC, and the hundreds of volunteers who participate are proof enough. You can get your hands dirty as a Horticulture and Maintenance volunteer, or meet visitors from around the

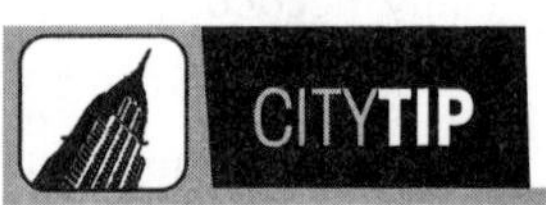

"Even though New Yorkers can be abrasive, we don't mean any harm by the sarcasm and directness. It's just our way. You'll get used to it."

—Hank Vergona, artist

world as a Conservancy Greeter or a Conservancy Guide. A little too "woodsy" for your taste? Volunteers can participate in Special Events and fundraising too. This organization is perfect for those who love the outdoors. Volunteers can contribute a few hours a week or more.

City Harvest
(917) 351-8700
cityharvest.org

City Harvest aims to feed the City's hungry and goes a long way toward doing so by collecting food daily from restaurants, cafeterias, farmers' markets, and a few individuals. CH collects 57,000 pounds of food per day and distributes it to emergency food programs operated by 500 CH-approved agencies throughout New York City. To get involved, CH encourages people to sponsor canned food drives, Thanksgiving turkey drives, or baby food and infant formula drives (runs from Mother's Day through Father's Day each year) from their home or office. Other volunteer opportunities range from being an office assistant to "green market rescue." Volunteers also participate in the cooking and nutrition education classes that take place at some of the 500 agencies with which City Harvest works. More than 1,000 volunteers participate.

Craigslist
newyork.craigslist.org

If you're looking for something in New York, chances are good you'll find it on Craigslist—and volunteer opportunities are no exception.

Located on West 70th Street, Congregation Shearith Israel is the oldest Jewish congregation in the country. The congregation was established in 1654.

Green Guerillas
greenguerillas.org

Manhattan Office:
214 West 29th Street, 5th Floor
(212) 402-1121

Brooklyn Office:
677 Lafayette Avenue (between Marcy and Tompkins)
(718) 906-1000

In 1973, Liz Christy, a Lower East Side artist, collected friends and neighbors to clean out a vacant lot on the corner of Bowery and Houston Streets. Calling themselves the Green Guerillas, they created a vibrant community garden and established the modern community gardening movement. Each year, hundreds of Green Guerillas volunteer thousands of hours in community gardens citywide. "Workdays are festivals of planting, weeding, watering, and mulching."

The International Center in New York
50 West 23rd Street, 7th Floor
New York, NY 10010
(212) 255-9555
intlcenter.org
volunteer@intlcenter.org

The Center works toward helping newcomers to the country adjust with ease by teaching English conversation skills and American culture to newcomers to the United States. There are a number of different areas in which volunteers can get involved—the Center needs writing tutors, professional mentors, workshop instructors, professional con-

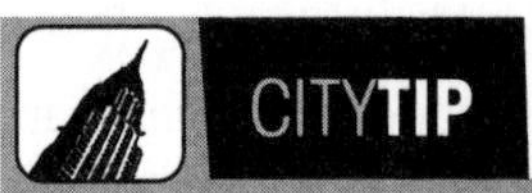

"I grew up in rural California, where we took space and peace and quiet for granted. But in New York, with so many people packed into such a small area, you have to make time to find private places. They're out there—parks, museums, atriums, gardens, libraries, grand old hotel lobbies, and out-of-the-way cafés—so discover a few favorite places for yourself and visit them often. That's how I stay sane."

—Sarah Bleasdale, opera singer

sultants, and administrative, fundraising, and marketing assistants. To volunteer you must submit a completed application form and interview with a staff member.

New York Aquarium
Coordinator of Volunteers
West 8th Street and Surf Avenue
Brooklyn, NY 11224
(718) 265-3450
nyadocent@wcs.org
wcs.org

Interested parties are required to apply, interview, and attend training sessions in order to become aquarium volunteers (docents). Therefore, the Aquarium is recommended only for highly committed individuals. Volunteers might assist in hands-on exhibits, showing visitors how to handle animals in the Rocky Coast Touch-It-Tank and the Ray Pool, teach visitors about marine habitats and animals, answer questions, give directions, or assist the Education Staff.

New York Cares
214 West 29th Street, 5th Floor
New York, NY 10001
(212) 228-5000
nycares@nycares.org
nycares.org

New York Cares is ideal for the newcomer to New York, because the organization specifically coordinates volunteer projects to fit in with busy lifestyles, and makes an effort to keep the activities social at the same time. Projects are scheduled on weekdays and weekend

Mayor Fiorello H. La Guardia was the first mayor to move into residence at Gracie Mansion (at the East River at 88th Street), which, during his third term in office, became the official mayoral residence.

mornings, afternoons, and evenings, and a volunteer can give a few hours per week or a few hours per year. There is no intensive training or screening process, and volunteers can participate on a short- or long-term basis. All projects are team-based, so you get to bond as a team and meet new people. You can also arrange to volunteer with or as a group, if you are in an alumni association, a work group, a club, or a religious group.

Partnership for Parks
The Arsenal
Central Park
(212) 360-1310
partnershipsforparks.org

This is an initiative of the City Parks Foundation and the City of New York Parks & Recreation. Anyone can volunteer with Partnership for Parks, be it for a onetime clean-up project or on a more regular basis as a tutor or a coach. Volunteers work in parks all over New York City doing everything from leaf cleaning in the fall to handing out leaflets and maps on New Year's Eve.

CITYTIP

"New York is so big, it can be a lonely place, especially for new people. But if you find a group of people with similar interests to your own, you've found an instant community—and New York has an organization for everything. If you're in a profession, join a professional association. If you're a ballplayer, get involved in a league. Or just volunteer for a charity you admire."

—Kevin Hayden, civil engineer

Police Athletic League
34½ East 12th Street
New York, NY 10003
(800) PAL-4KIDS
(800) 725-4543
palnyc.org

"Founded in 1914, the mission of the Police Athletic League is to help develop and protect New York City children during their critical development years using education, recreation, socialization and arts and sciences to inspire them to lead meaningful and productive lives"—from the Police Athletic League website.

The Police Athletic League is the largest youth agency in New York City, serving 65,000 youngsters each year with a wide range of educational and recreational programs. PAL is always looking for volunteers in a sports-related capacity (coaches and part-time teachers for track, baseball, softball, flag football, and golf) as well as for crafts and personal hobbies. For those more interested in the classroom and less in the ball field, there are volunteer opportunities for after-school and evening-time tutors in homework assistance, résumé building, test prep, high school and college applications, and more. Volunteers are welcome and needed in all five boroughs.

Project Happy
425 East 25th Street
(212) 772-4613 (project director)

Project Happy deserves special mention because it is a remarkable sports and recreation program for disabled children and adults ages 6 through 30. Run by the program director, Penny Shaw, it operates almost entirely with the help of volunteers. Founded by Shaw at Hunter College more than a quarter of a century ago in conjunction with a wheelchair-bound colleague, the program continues to thrive and operates on Saturdays during the school year.

"New Yorkers move fast, and they don't usually smile at one another on the streets. But beneath those gruff exteriors lie the nicest people in the world. Don't be afraid to ask for directions, or advice, from that New Yorker on line ahead of you. Every New Yorker has an opinion about everything—and you may even make a new friend!"

—Robert Woods, bookseller

Recording for the Blind & Dyslexic
545 Fifth Avenue
New York, NY 10017
(212) 557-5720
www.rfbd.org

Recording for the Blind & Dyslexic is in need of dedicated volunteers to participate as "general readers" (reading books on any and all subjects for children and adults) and readers with professional knowledge in any number of different fields including science, math, history, accounting, finance, and more. RFBD requires only a minimum of two hours a week to share on an ongoing basis. Volunteers will be involved with all aspects of recording.

INDEX